Adding English

A Guide to Teaching in Multilingual Classrooms

Elizabeth Coelho

Pippin Publishing

Edited by Dyanne Rivers
Typeset by Jay Tee Graphics Ltd.
Cartoons by Pat Cupples
Indexed by Kathy O'Handley
Printed and bound in Canada by AGMV Marquis Imprimeur Inc.

First printed October, 2003; reprinted February, 2004; reprinted June, 2004; reprinted September, 2005; revised and reprinted September, 2007.

We acknowledge the assistance of the OMDC Book Fund, an initiative of the Ontario Media Development Corporation.

National Library of Canada Cataloguing in Publication

Coelho, Elizabeth, 1946–
    Adding English : a guide to teaching in multilingual classrooms /
Elizabeth Coelho ; Dyanne Rivers, editor ; Pat Cupples, illustrator ; Kathy O'Handley, indexer.

Includes bibliographical references and index.
ISBN 0-88751-095-7

1. English language—Study and teaching as a second language.
2. Linguistic minorities—Education. 3. Multicultural education.
I. Rivers, Dyanne II. Title.

LC3715.C636 2003   428'.0071   C2003-904455-6

10 9 8 7 6 5

To my father, Geoffrey Summers (1920–2003),
who first taught me about social justice
and the power of education to transform the world.

Acknowledgements

This book could not have been written without the generous support and contributions of friends and colleagues. Many of the activities are based on the classroom practice of the many colleagues with whom I have worked over the years, and many of the photographs that enliven the book were taken by colleagues. As well, colleagues and mentors read and commented on various drafts, saving me from ghastly mistakes and pointing me in new directions when necessary. Any errors that remain are entirely my own.

I would like express specific thanks to the staff, parents, and students of the following schools, for allowing photographs taken in their schools and classrooms between 1997 and 2003 to be used in this book.

CD Farquharson Junior Public School, Toronto District School Board
Cedar Drive Junior Public School, Toronto District School Board
Country Hills Public School, Waterloo Region District School Board
Cummer Valley Middle School, Toronto District School Board
Maryvale Public School, Toronto District School Board
Pineway Public School, Toronto District School Board
R.J. Lang Elementary and Middle School, Toronto District School Board
Rockford Public School, Toronto District School Board
Scarborough Village Alternative Public School, Toronto District School Board
Sir Sandford Fleming Secondary School, Toronto District School Board
Summer Language Program, Toronto District School Board
West Hill Public School, Toronto District School Board
Western Technical-Commercial School, Toronto District School Board

I would also like to express my thanks to the colleagues who contributed many of the photographs.

Maaike Buma, Waterloo Region District School Board
Carol Gordon, Toronto District School Board
Bev Horton, Toronto District School Board
Kathy Lazarovits, Toronto District School Board
Al Weinberg, Toronto District School Board

The following experts commented on various drafts of the manuscript and gave valuable advice.

Jim Cummins, Ontario Institute for Studies in Education, University of Toronto
Marjatta Holt, English Language Program, University of Toronto
Suzanne Holunga, The Language Centre, Toronto
Veronica Lam, Toronto District School Board
Irene McKay, George Brown Community College, Toronto
Stephanie Paulauskas, The Language Centre, Toronto
Hetty Roessingh, University of Calgary
Jura Seskus, English Language Program, University of Toronto

And as always, thanks to the students, teachers, and student teachers with whom I have worked over the last three decades and whose experiences, ideas, and questions are included in this book in various ways.

Contents

Introduction

Whether you are teaching an English-as-a-second-language class or integrating English language learners into a mainstream K–12 classroom program, this book offers information and advice to help you support students who are learning English at the same time as they are learning curriculum content.

In writing *Adding English*, one of my motivations was to help develop basic principles and outline exemplary practices that can ensure that English language learners have access to equitable educational opportunities. Throughout the English-speaking world, there are wide variations in the kind and amount of training that teachers receive for working in linguistically and culturally diverse classrooms. This book is intended to provide student teachers, new teachers, and seasoned educators with the knowledge and skills required to teach effectively in the multilingual classrooms that are increasingly the norm in communities in Canada, the United States, the United Kingdom, Australia, and New Zealand.

The title, *Adding English*, is a reminder that the teacher's task is to *add* English to students' existing language repertoires. We should encourage English language learners to maintain and continue to develop their own languages, because the ability to speak more than one language is an asset to the individual, the community, and the nation. Learning English as a second language is — or should be — a process of enrichment rather than of remediation or replacement.

Terms

I have used *ESL* to refer to the English-as-a-second-language programs that are commonly available to English language learners. In many school districts, as well as in educational policy documents and curriculum guidelines, and in many other books on this topic, students who are learning English are called "English-as-a-second-language students" or

"ESL students." It is important to note, however, that English is, in fact, a third or fourth language for many of these students.

In addition, the term *ESL student* implies that the learner is receiving English language instruction from a specialist language teacher, whereas this is frequently not the case. Many students who are new to English when they arrive in an English-language school never receive ESL support. Others who receive ESL instruction for the first year or two and who continue to need support for language learning are no longer receiving any support from an ESL teacher.

I have chosen to use the term *English language learners* to describe students who are in the process of learning English, whether or not they are receiving support through a designated ESL program. This choice is consistent with the recent work of some of the leading scholars in the field of bilingual and second language education, such as Jim Cummins of the Ontario Institute for Studies in Education of the University of Toronto. Though I have kept technical language to a minimum, all teachers need a certain basic vocabulary to understand the process of second language acquisition and plan instruction for English language learners. Key terms and concepts are highlighted throughout the book.

Organization

The 13 chapters of *Adding English* are organized into four sections.

I A Welcoming Environment

The two chapters in this section are intended to help you and your colleagues provide an inclusive and welcoming environment for newcomers and for students of various linguistic and cultural backgrounds, whether they are native-born children enrolling in Kindergarten or newcomers from a country on the other side of the world.

II How English Works

This section is about the English language: the least you need to know in order to understand why students use the language they way they do. Intended for teachers with little previous knowledge of linguistics or grammar, this section summarizes basic terms and concepts relating to the English sound and grammar systems and discusses the origin and structure of English words, the writing system, and how language is used in various real-life contexts, including the school. This information will help you act as a language model and informant for English language learners.

III The Language Learning Environment

This section discusses what is involved in language learning and how teachers can support the process. It outlines the advantages and disadvantages of different ways of organizing second language instruction and explains how you can organize your classroom to support second language learners. The section concludes by suggesting activities for students who are just beginning to learn English.

IV Language Learning across the Curriculum

This section is about supporting English language learners in all classrooms. You will learn how to provide the scaffolding necessary to support comprehension, promote language production, and enhance the academic performance of English language learners, as well as native speakers of English. You will also find suggestions for approaching assessment, evaluation, and reporting.

How to Use This Book

The material is organized in a sequence that provides background knowledge about English language learners, the English language, and the language learning process before describing classroom strategies and learning activities that demonstrate how this knowledge can be applied. Please approach the book in any way that makes sense to you, however. Throughout the book, you will find chapter references to key concepts that are introduced elsewhere in the book. A glossary defines key terms and concepts, and an index enables you to find key topics quickly.

I have chosen not to write this book in a formal academic style. Because I preferred not to interrupt the flow of the text by embedding names and dates, for example, I have not identified references in the usual academic style. Each chapter, however, concludes with a section titled "To Learn More …" This includes sources and suggests additional readings and resources, including books, articles, and Web sites, that can be used to explore topics in more depth.

I | A Welcoming Environment

A welcoming and inclusive multicultural school is one in which students and parents of all linguistic and cultural backgrounds feel welcome, valued, and included. The chapters in this section are intended to help you and your colleagues establish a welcoming, inclusive environment for all students, whether they are native-born children enrolling in Kindergarten or newcomers from a country on the other side of the world.

The first chapter, "English Language Learners from Far and Near," provides background information about English language learners: where they come from and what their needs are as they adjust to a new cultural and educational environment. It also describes how to help newcomers get off to a good start in their new school and how to establish a positive and trusting relationship with parents.

The second chapter, "Creating an Inclusive Classroom," describes strategies and approaches that can help you create a classroom that values linguistic and cultural diversity and promotes respect and understanding among all students.

1 English Language Learners from Far and Near

Students who are adjusting to a new cultural and educational environment have particular needs. This chapter discusses these needs and how schools can provide a warm welcome that helps English language learners get off to a good start.

Where Do English Language Learners Come From?

Every year, hundreds of thousands of people immigrate to new countries. The push factors that motivate people to emigrate are much the same as those that have always driven people to pull up stakes and move to new countries. These factors include war or civil conflict, political or religious oppression and other human rights abuses, poor social and economic conditions, and lack of educational or career opportunities.

In choosing a new country, emigrants are influenced by pull factors. These include the scale of a country's immigration program; its record as a place of safety, tolerance, and peace; the availability of educational and career opportunities; and its reputation for promoting social, political, and religious freedom.

New Immigrants

Some English language learners in your classroom may have arrived as immigrants last week, last year, or several years ago. Though most newcomers plan to stay, some arrive as international — or visa — students who intend to return to their homeland after completing their education. Others arrive as refugees who may have fled their homeland in traumatic circumstances. Some may have been separated from their family or have witnessed the death of family members.

Native-Born Children

Others who are learning **English as a second language** may be native-born children who speak a first language other than English and encounter English for the first time only when they enter school. Most of these children are the sons and daughters of immigrants who speak a language other than English at home. In North America, Australia, and New Zealand, however, some live in Aboriginal communities that predate the arrival of Europeans. Others, such as Mennonites and Amish,

Some children who were born in North America begin learning English when they start school.

The English language learners in this classroom come from countries around the world and speak many languages.

live in communities that have preserved their cultural and religious traditions, including their language. Although children from these communities may not be new immigrants, they are still entering a new linguistic and cultural environment when they arrive at school.

The impact of immigration on schools has been profound. In Canada, for example, the cities of Toronto, Ontario, and Vancouver, British Columbia, attract large numbers of immigrants. About 50 percent of the students in these cities' schools speak a first language other than English. In Toronto, 17,500 newcomers from more than 175 countries enrolled in publicly funded elementary and secondary schools in 2001. Though diversity on this scale is unparalleled in the world, statistics from other areas show that linguistic diversity is a feature of many urban schools.

Students from French-Speaking Communities

Some countries have more than one official language. In Canada, for example, both English and French are official languages. Students from French-speaking communities, however, may live in areas where there is no French-language school. As a result, these students, too, may be new to English when they start school. In addition, new immigrants to Canada may settle first in Quebec, and their children may begin school in French before moving to an English-speaking area and enrolling in an English-language school. These children may have been in Canada for several years or they may be Canadian born. Although they are not newcomers, they still need support in learning English.

Students from English-Speaking Communities

Some students who also need support in learning English are from English-speaking communities. Though they may come from countries or communities where English is both the official language and the language of instruction, the variety of English they have learned is so different from standard English, or so-called school English, that they may have difficulty communicating with their teachers.

Understanding the Needs of English Language Learners

Most English language learners need a program of language instruction, as well as support in adjusting to a new cultural environment and school system. At the same time, they need to be involved in an academic program that enables them to continue their education in other subjects.

Language Instruction

Students arrive with varying levels of English proficiency and may need different kinds of English-as-a-second-language support. Chapter 10 includes an overview of models for providing ESL support.

Most beginning language learners need intensive support to acquire English. They may be intimidated at first, especially if the grammar system and script of their own language are entirely unrelated to

English. These learners need a tremendous amount of visual and contextual support, as well as a safe learning environment in which they can make the mistakes that are a necessary part of language learning. They also need help from peers and, if possible, access to their own language to clarify ideas and instructions. At the same time, they need to be integrated into mainstream classrooms and activities for part of the school day, so that they can interact with English-speaking peers and become socially integrated into the life of the school.

Other students may be at one of several stages of developing proficiency in English. Some students, especially adolescents, may have been exposed to **English as a foreign language** in their home country. These students may have studied English for an hour or two a week, or in some cases, they may have attended schools where English was the language of instruction. Students who studied English before immigrating to an English-speaking country are often shocked to find that their level of proficiency is not advanced enough for them to study effectively in English. In this, they are no different from most English-speaking students who have studied a language such as French in an English-language school. These students would not be ready to receive all their instruction, complete all assignments, or write tests and examinations in French.

Depending on their level of proficiency in English, English language learners need varying levels of ESL support. They also need to be integrated into mainstream classes for some subjects. In these classes, they need encouragement and support to participate in classroom activities and continue learning English at the same time. Chapter 12 outlines strategies for integrating language and content instruction.

No matter what stage language learners have reached on the path to English proficiency, it is important to remember that most have already developed age-appropriate levels of proficiency in at least one language and that students who have received some schooling in their own country may be highly literate in their own language. The task of the school is to help these students add English to their repertoire of language(s), enabling them to learn effectively in an environment in which English is the language of instruction. At the same time, it is important to do everything possible to support the students' continued development in their first languages, at least until English catches up. Chapters 2 and 10 suggest strategies for capitalizing on students' knowledge of their first language.

Adjustment Period

For many English language learners and their families, the period of adjustment and acculturation to a new land and a new school system is painful. Even native-born children find a new school environment intimidating at first. Those who have come to their new school from other countries may also be coping with feelings of loneliness, homesickness, and displacement. Even when a family has been planning the move for months or years, the reality of life in a new country is often a shock for adults and children alike.

Most newcomers pass through four stages of adjustment after arriving in a new country.

- *Stage 1* — Arrival and first impressions: During the first few days and weeks in a new country, immigrants may experience feelings of adventure, optimism, and even euphoria. During this time, they may celebrate their good fortune in embarking on a new phase of life or in escaping a desperate situation in their home country. At the same time, they may also be anxious about their new situation. Some students may choose to observe, rather than participate in, classroom situations as they try to figure out what is going on.

Adapting to a new climate presents a challenge to many newcomers.

- *Stage 2* — Culture shock: As newcomers begin to identify intimidating, distasteful, or strange aspects of their new environment, they may experience feelings of discomfort, dislocation, and alienation. Students' emotions may fluctuate between feelings of curiosity, adventure, and optimism, and feelings of sadness, loss, and despair. Anxiety and frustration, as well as communication difficulties, may make learning to live in a new culture seem like an unachievable goal. Some may feel that the majority culture threatens their sense of identity and completeness and seek support by bonding exclusively with members of their own ethnic group.

  During this stage, individual members of a community or family may react differently. Some may feel a sense of loss so intense that they are overwhelmed by pessimism and withdraw or act out their unhappiness in other ways. Teachers must be alert to the signs and prepared to give students special consideration and support at this time. Other students, meanwhile, may be more optimistic, expecting things to get better.

- *Stage 3* — Recovery and optimism: Immigrants and refugees are often extraordinarily resilient, and recovery from culture shock brings a renewed sense of optimism and autonomy. The stresses they have experienced and overcome may have helped them develop coping skills that will stand them in good stead throughout their lives. Although they may still feel pressure, students begin to develop confidence in their ability to overcome difficulties, including those associated with learning the new language. They are able to communicate adequately for most day-to-day purposes and begin to feel that they are making progress at school. Some may begin to form friendships with students outside their own cultural or linguistic group.

- *Stage 4* — Acculturation: After a period that may last a year or two, or even many years, most newcomers resolve internal conflicts by re-creating their identities. They may choose to integrate, adopting some of the values and practices of the new culture while maintaining aspects of their original culture. Many children adopt different cultural styles depending on the context. Children who can move comfortably between languages and cultures have learned to value their heritage and to be flexible in their interactions with others of various cultural backgrounds. Integration may also involve developing **bilingual** competence.

  In contrast, individuals who feel that their own cultural heritage has little value in the wider society may choose to assimilate into the mainstream and discard their original culture and language. Though assimilation was once the purpose of most educational programs for immigrants and minorities, it is no longer the stated goal of education in many countries.

Individual students — even members of the same family — may pass through these stages of adjustment at different rates or even skip a stage entirely. The stages are not always clearly delineated. They sometimes overlap, so that an individual may appear to have reached a particular stage of acculturation in one area while remaining at an earlier stage in another. Children who enter welcoming and supportive classrooms, for example, may become comfortable and confident at school long before they are comfortable interacting with strangers or in less familiar contexts in the wider society. Some immigrants report feelings of great optimism and seem to experience little or no difficulty during the transition period, while others experience great pain and frustration and sometimes become stuck in the second stage.

For refugees, school may seem like a safe haven after months or years of displacement and confusion. At the same time, they may be dealing with feelings of displacement, grief, and loss that may make it difficult at first for them to do well at school.

It is important not to forget the needs of visa students, most of whom are living away from home for the first time and may also be doing their own cooking, shopping, banking, cleaning, and other daily chores. In addition, they may be coping with loneliness and homesickness.

Schools play a very important role in supporting newcomers through this adjustment period and helping them integrate into the mainstream without sacrificing important aspects of their culture and identity. Ways of welcoming newcomers are discussed later in this chapter, and Chapter 2 includes suggestions for creating an inclusive classroom that honors students' linguistic and cultural backgrounds.

Program Adaptation

Students who arrive from other countries need to continue their education at the same time as they learn English. To help them do this, the mainstream curriculum, which is designed for proficient English speakers, must be adapted to enable second language learners to participate. In linguistically and culturally demanding subjects such as social studies and language arts, major adaptations may be required. Even in mathematics, which may appear to be less linguistically demanding, skills such as problem solving and communication may require a level of English proficiency that newcomers do not yet possess. Chapter 13 provides specific guidance on adapting the mainstream program for language learners.

Some newcomers may have experienced significant disruption in their education or come from countries where their access to education was limited for socioeconomic reasons. As a result, these students may not have developed the age-appropriate literacy skills or academic background in their own language. Because they have not had the opportunity to acquire the skills and knowledge possessed by other students their age, these educationally disadvantaged students would have difficulty relating to the age-appropriate curriculum even if it were offered in their own language. As a result, they need an intensive program of language and literacy instruction, as well as academic upgrading, to help them learn English and catch up to their age peers.

This poster welcomes students in many languages.

Questions for the Initial Interview

Which language or languages did your child first learn in the home?

What language do you now use in your home?

What is the child's dominant language (the language in which the child is now most proficient)?

How many years has the student been in school?

What was the language of instruction?

Have there been any interruptions in schooling?

Was the child in school every day?

How large were the classes?

Has the student developed any literacy skills in the first language? If so, at what age did the child begin to read?

What special aptitudes or interests has the child shown at school?

Has the student experienced learning difficulties or received any specialized education?

What is the nature of the child's experience with English, if any, in the home country or since arrival?

Are educational records available? (If so, have them translated and evaluated by a bilingual educator who is familiar with the education system in the student's home country.)

Welcoming Newcomers to the School

From their first day, students and their parents will form an impression of the new school and how well they are likely to fit into it. Because first impressions are important, schools must provide a warm welcome to students and families whose first language is not English. Whether a school receives one newcomer a year or more than a hundred, it is essential to prepare effective welcoming procedures for reception and orientation, initial assessment and placement, monitoring and counseling, and fostering parental involvement.

Reception and Orientation

A welcoming school plans for the arrival of newcomers, whether they are arriving from a neighboring city or halfway around the world. The procedures suggested in this section not only help ensure a smooth transition for the students and the receiving teachers, but also reassure parents about what lies ahead for their children.

FIRST CONTACT

Many factors help create a welcoming first impression.

- Create welcome signs in the languages of the community and display them prominently around the school. Ask parents and students to help make the signs.
- Organize special intake and orientation days for students and parents of various language backgrounds.
- Make sure that all members of the school's support staff are trained to receive new students in a welcoming manner and know the routines to follow. The first contact with the school is usually at the front desk, and it is essential that this contact be reassuring. Unprepared staff members may unintentionally communicate the message that the school is not ready to receive these students or their parents. Provide a script for staff to use, as well as a list of contact people who can help in various languages.
- Designate a reception team. As well as ESL staff, an elementary school team might include a school administrator, and a high school team might include a guidance counselor.

THE RECEPTION INTERVIEW

As soon as a new family arrives, welcome them and find a suitable space to conduct a private interview.

- Unless the student and parents are fluent in English, ask an interpreter to help. If no bilingual teachers are on staff, use a professional interpreter, if possible. Many school jurisdictions hire professionally trained multilingual staff. It is also possible to use community volunteers, as long as training is provided and confidentiality guidelines are established and observed. To ensure confidentiality and maintain appropriate social relationships, it is best not to ask another parent or student to interpret.
- Complete the registration form yourself, asking questions to elicit the necessary information. It is best not to ask the parents to fill in the form, as they may be intimidated by the design of the form and may be unable to read English well enough to understand what is required. An interview format helps set parents and student at

ease and enables you to ask additional questions about the student's language background, educational background, immigration history, and so on.

- To elicit accurate information, explain the intent of the questions. It is not uncommon, for example, for parents to report greater use or knowledge of English than is the case, especially if they believe that the school values English more highly than other languages. Instead of asking, "Do you speak English?" or "What language do you speak?" you can say, "The students in our school speak many languages. We are proud of this. We can also give special help to students who are learning English. What languages do you speak?"
- Allow plenty of time for the interview. It takes more than twice as long to communicate through an interpreter because both words and entire concepts, such as *field trip*, *home form*, *brown-bag lunch*, and *credit course*, must be translated and explained.
- Start a reception dossier on each newcomer and add to it as the student settles in over the next few weeks.

INFORMATION FOR PARENTS

To help parents feel comfortable and confident about their child's start in the new school, provide them with basic information about school routines. Don't overload the family with new information during this first encounter, however. Welcoming procedures are intended to establish a relationship so that orientation can continue during the weeks and months ahead.

- Create a one-page information sheet or small brochure that parents can take home. It should include information about the school day; the principal's name; the school phone number; the names and phone numbers of other contacts at the school; the dates of holidays, professional development days, and parent-teacher interviews; what to do if the student is absent; and so on. Make this available in the languages of the school and include specific information, such as the names of the student's classroom or home form teacher and the ESL teacher, and the name and phone number of a community contact person or organization.

Student Ambassadors

Train student ambassadors to help welcome and orient new students. Discuss how a recent arrival might feel during the first few days of school, encouraging ambassadors who have themselves been new students to draw on their experiences.

Ambassadors can explain classroom routines, ensure that the new student knows key locations in the school, describe school services, and sit beside the newcomer for the first couple of weeks to explain what is going on and to offer help when needed. Don't expect the ambassador to become the newcomer's buddy, however. The ambassador's responsibilities should be specific and finite; friendship may result, but it is not the purpose of the program. In middle and secondary schools, an ambassador may

- explain how to read the timetable
- escort the new student to classes for the first full cycle
- help the student to find a locker and demonstrate how to use the lock
- help the newcomer get a bus pass
- accompany the newcomer to the cafeteria for the first few days
- introduce the new student to extracurricular activities

This student ambassador is helping a newcomer find his way around the school.

- Give the new student a starter kit of materials. These may include pens and pencils, colored markers, a ruler, an eraser, and a notebook or binder. A picture dictionary also makes an excellent welcoming gift.
- Provide information about the availability of **heritage language programs**. These programs, which are intended to help children maintain and continue to develop proficiency in their first language, are sometimes called international language programs. Encourage parents to continue to use their first language at home. Explain that proficiency in the first language is important for continued cognitive growth and supports the acquisition of English. Using the first language also helps unite the family by maintaining effective communication at home during the adjustment period and is an important source of cultural pride and individual self-esteem. Chapter 8 includes more information on the importance of students' first languages.
- Provide information about resettlement services in the neighborhood and encourage the parents to join language classes for adults. Many school districts offer ESL programs for adults. Governments may also provide resettlement services and language training programs, often through community agencies.
- Introduce the newcomer to a student ambassador from her or his homeroom or ESL class. Ask the ambassador to escort the student and the family on a brief school tour, including a visit to the student's classroom or homeroom and the ESL room. Meeting another of the same background is encouraging for newcomers, especially if the ambassador has successfully passed through the adjustment period and is comfortable in the school. If an ambassador of the same background is not available, the help of a sympathetic English-speaking peer is also appreciated.

Ambassadors should reflect the ethnic and cultural makeup of the school, though some newcomers may be more comfortable with an ambassador of the same sex. Ensure that many students have an opportunity to play this leadership role.

Recognize the important role played by ambassadors by giving them a button or certificate or displaying their names and photographs in a prominent place in the school.

Initial Assessment and Placement

Whether students entering a new school are native-born children starting Kindergarten or newcomers who have already begun their education in other countries, their needs must be assessed accurately. Some special guidelines apply, however, when assessing and placing students whose first language is not English.

When English language learners arrive at the school, start an **assessment portfolio** to document their progress. Include a record of the initial interview and the assessment information you gather. During the year, work with other teachers to add samples of work, observation checklists and forms, and information collected through conferences and journal responses. This will help you track students' progress and identify special needs or strengths.

The portfolio may be maintained by the ESL teacher or a counselor with special responsibility for monitoring the progress of English language learners. It can be shared with parents during parent-teacher interviews and with students during student-teacher conferences. Some students may wish to maintain their portfolio electronically, as part of a personal Web site.

INITIAL ASSESSMENT AND PLACEMENT IN ELEMENTARY SCHOOLS

Elementary English language learners should be placed in classes with their age peers. At one time, some schools and school jurisdictions placed beginning language learners a year or two behind their age peers on the assumption that they would learn English more quickly if they didn't face the challenges of learning new skills and knowledge at the same time. This practice may negatively affect students' self-esteem, however, and offers no advantage in helping students learn English or catch up to their peers academically. In addition, research shows that a second language is acquired more efficiently when learners want and need to know the information that is being conveyed. Involvement in an age-appropriate curriculum rather than a curriculum designed for younger children is much more likely to be stimulating and engaging.

Language learners may be withdrawn from the mainstream classroom for ESL support for part of the school day, or the ESL teacher may work with the classroom teacher to develop an appropriate program for the newcomer. Exceptionally shy or timid students may benefit from staying in the ESL classroom for the first few days.

Language learners may be withdrawn from the mainstream classroom for part of the school day.

Over a period of several weeks, both the ESL and classroom teachers can assess the student's linguistic and educational needs in a low-stress environment. This initial assessment information is extremely important for tracking the child's progress in the months and years ahead. Though assessment procedures may vary according to the age of the child, it is not usually appropriate to use formal tests because most are developed for use with native speakers of English. Formal tests may also intimidate newcomers, who are already dealing with the stress of immersion in an unfamiliar linguistic and cultural environment. Instead, informal assessment strategies can be used.

Informal Language Assessment Strategies

A variety of informal strategies — based on observation, individual interviews, and carefully structured reading and writing tasks — can help you gather information about a child's level of education and knowledge of English.

- Ask children who have already received some schooling in their first language to produce a writing sample in this language. Even if you can't read it, this sample can provide useful information: Can the child write in the first language? Does the letter or character formation appear to be appropriately developed? How long does the child take to produce the piece? Does the child check and edit the piece? How simple or complex does it appear?
- To assess competence in simple day-to-day social interaction in English, engage the child in conversation. Begin with questions such as, "What is your name?" If the student can respond with appropriate information (though not necessarily with correct grammar or pronunciation), continue with a simple interview.
- Use pictures and concrete objects (e.g., pictures of numbers and upper- and lower-case letters, color samples, shapes, and various real objects, such as those found in the classroom) to assess the student's vocabulary. Ask the student to name the letters or numbers in English or point to a specific item when you name it.

- Use simple props and instructions to assess the child's ability to follow simple oral instructions in English (e.g., "Give me the blue ball," "Put the ball in the box," "Show me the smallest one," or "Open the book at page 4").
- To assess listening comprehension, read a simple picture book aloud while the child looks at the illustrations. Then ask questions based on factual comprehension and, if the child is able to respond, ask questions designed to encourage her to offer personal responses and opinions and to make inferences.
- To assess reading comprehension, supply several picture books, both fiction and non-fiction, and ask the child to choose one. Talk about the book and read a page or two aloud before asking him to continue reading silently. Then ask questions about the story. Do not ask the child to read aloud. Children who stumble over pronunciation may be able to understand if they read silently, whereas fluent oral readers may actually understand little of what they read.
- Collect a writing sample in English by asking the child to write a response to the story or by offering a choice of photos or magazine pictures to stimulate writing. Ensure that the pictures include people and situations representing a variety of ethnic, cultural, and geographic contexts.

Pictures like these can be used to stimulate writing in English.

- Observe how the child uses language in the classroom. How does the child establish social relationships; follow oral directions and classroom routines; use the first language; interact with peers in English; engage in partner, small group, whole class, and individual activities; retain key vocabulary from one day or week to the next; and use strategies to gain meaning or communicate in English (e.g., ask questions, use first language resources, and initiate interaction)?

FIRST LANGUAGE ASSESSMENT

In elementary schools, most language learners adjust relatively smoothly and begin to communicate in English very quickly. As time goes by, they begin to participate more actively in both mainstream and ESL classroom activities. Some newcomers may, however, have trouble adjusting or learning English. In these cases, an in-depth assessment of the student's language and mathematics skills conducted in the first or **dominant language** is advisable. This assessment, which must be conducted by a bilingual educator who is familiar with the school system in both the student's home country and new country, provides a much clearer picture of the student's educational background than an assessment conducted in English only and helps determine what additional assessment or support is required.

A first language assessment is also essential when teachers observe learning difficulties that seem to be more severe than those experienced in the normal process of second language acquisition. Students from countries where education has not been consistently available may have significant gaps in their educational background. Other students — about the same percentage as in the general population — may have a learning disability or other unidentified exceptional need.

Because many students stop developing in their first language once they are immersed in an English-language school environment, the first language assessment should be conducted as soon as possible. Even a year later, a child struggling in English may not be able to do much better in her first language unless she has received the support and instruction necessary to continue developing in that language.

A first language assessment can provide the following information:

- Detailed and accurate information on the student's educational background, oral language development and literacy skills in the first language, and conceptual development in mathematics.
- Other relevant information (e.g., cultural adjustment, family issues, and medical, social, or emotional needs).
- Whether additional assessment is required.
- Whether linguistic and cultural adaptations are appropriate when other assessments (e.g., psycho-educational assessment and speech and language assessment) are called for.
- Recommendations for placement and program support

INITIAL ASSESSMENT AND PLACEMENT IN SECONDARY SCHOOLS

To determine the appropriate placement for adolescents, an assessment should be conducted before the student is placed in classes, streams, levels, and subjects. Ideally, this initial assessment would be conducted by staff who are both knowledgeable about the education system in the student's country of origin and trained in second language assessment techniques. The assessment may include several components and involve several staff members. As a result, it may take more than a day to coordinate all the procedures. In some school districts, newcomer reception centers provide assessment and orientation services; in others, this work is completed by in-school staff.

The procedures should include an assessment of educational background, an assessment of skills in mathematics, and an assessment of the student's proficiency in speaking, reading, and writing English. Gather this information in an assessment portfolio and make a provisional placement.

For adolescents, an initial assessment is essential before a provisional placement is decided.

Adolescents need not be placed with their age peers in all courses. Some may be placed ahead of their age peers in some courses (e.g., if their math skills are advanced) and with younger students in others (e.g., at a beginning level in French or computer studies if they have never studied these subjects).

Educational Background Assessment

During the initial interview, find out as much as possible about the student's previous education. If the student has brought education-related documents, have them assessed by an educator who is familiar with the education system that issued them. Many students do not bring documents, however, often because they left their home country under conditions of extreme urgency or danger. Ask these students detailed questions about their previous education. Do not confine your questions to the subjects taught in your own school system; many students have studied subjects such as philosophy, religion, and citizenship, which may not be included in your jurisdiction's curriculum. Show students textbooks containing charts, graphs, diagrams, maps, and other visual material and ask them to identify items that seem familiar. Some students may bring textbooks or notebooks used in their previous schools.

As suggested on page 25, some students may need a more detailed educational assessment conducted in their first language. A first language assessment can be especially informative when there have been gaps in a student's education or when school personnel are unfamiliar with the education system in the country or countries where a student was previously educated. Arrange this assessment as soon as possible so that the student can be placed in an appropriate program and given the necessary support.

Mathematics Assessment

Begin by showing a student math textbooks at various levels and asking him to point out concepts that seem familiar. Because the order in which math concepts are taught varies from country to country, encourage students to skip topics that seem unfamiliar and look ahead for others that are familiar. Some students may be able to show you the textbooks they used in their former schools.

Prepare two tests that begin with simple computation problems drawn from the elementary curriculum and move on to more difficult problems drawn from the secondary school curriculum. The tests should be nearly identical, with only the numbers changed. To reduce anxiety and allow the student time to review, give him one test to take home for practice. The next day, administer the second test. Encourage him to skip problems he cannot do and look ahead for familiar items.

English Language Assessment: Oral Proficiency

During the initial interview, find out whether the student has been exposed to English. If the student studied English before immigrating, find out for how many years and for how many hours a week. Some students may, for example, have received some English language training in refugee camps.

If students have had no exposure to English, they are beginning learners of English, and no further assessment is necessary. If the student has some knowledge of English, however, assess his oral proficiency by conducting an informal interview in English. The chart

Assessing Mathematical Skills and Knowledge Fairly

- Avoid problems that require students to use a calculator. Many come from countries where mental computation is emphasized and calculators are not allowed.
- Do not expect students to use the algorithms taught in your local curriculum. Methods of carrying out procedures such as regrouping (borrowing and carrying) and long division often vary from country to country.
- Do not expect students to show every step in solving a problem. Many have been taught to do as much mental computation as possible.
- Use metric measures unless the student is from a country that uses another system (e.g., imperial measure is still used in English-speaking Caribbean countries).
- Avoid culturally based problems such as those associated with sports, fruit and vegetables, and geographical knowledge.
- Provide the test in the student's own language if possible. These tests must be translated by someone who is not only proficient in both languages but also familiar with mathematical terms and the mathematics curriculum.

Oral Assessment Interview Questions

1. What is your name?
2. How old are you?
3. Where were you born?
4. On what date were you born?
5. What language do you speak at home?
6. What is your address?
7. How many years did you go to school in your country?

Proceed to the next questions only if the student was able to answer questions 1 to 7. Questions 8 to 15 are intended to elicit longer answers that will help you assess students' use of grammatical features such as plurals, subject-verb agreement, and verb tenses. Sometimes you may need to use additional prompts such as, "Can you tell me more about that?" or "Begin your answer like this …"

8. How did you get here today? Begin your answer like this: "I …"
9. Why did you (your family) come to Canada?
10. Tell me about your last school. How was it different from this one? Did you like it? Why? What subjects did you like?
11. Finish these descriptions: A good teacher is someone who … A good student is someone who …
12. What are you going to do when you leave here today?
13. What are your hopes and wishes for the future?
14. Where do you think you will be five years from now?
15. What do you think you will be doing five years from now?

on this page provides questions that help assess how well the student understands oral English. Do not expect the student to answer questions 1 to 7 in complete sentences: this would be unnatural. A one-word answer that makes sense indicates comprehension. Chapter 13 includes some sample descriptors of oral language performance that can be used to assess a student's responses and assist in placement.

English Language Assessment: Reading Comprehension

When students have formally studied English, assess their reading comprehension to find out how well they are likely to be able to deal with the language of instruction. Keep in mind, however, that reading assessments administered in English provide only an indication of students' reading performance *in English*. They do not measure students' level of comprehension *in reading*, which may be much higher than their performance in English suggests. A student who reads at a Grade 3 level in English, for example, may be able to read at a much higher level in Korean. For this reason, be very cautious about interpreting this assessment.

Oral reading tests also present problems because students who are reading aloud in a second language may concentrate more on pronunciation than on comprehension and may derive little or no meaning from what they read. It is not unusual for students to read aloud fluently while remaining unable to answer comprehension questions. Conversely, they may falter while reading aloud a passage that they are able to comprehend when they read silently.

Standardized tests may also present problems because they are developed for use with native speakers of English who are familiar with the mainstream culture. As an alternative to formal or standardized tests, use informal assessment procedures, such as graded reading and cloze passages. These focus on comprehension and are much less intimidating to students than formal tests.

Graded reading passages and follow-up comprehension questions provide useful information about specific reading skills such as understanding the main idea, finding details, following sequence, relating cause and effect, and making inferences. Some reading inventories include reading passages at various levels and comprehension questions of various types. The content of these inventories, however, often assumes cultural knowledge that many newcomers are unlikely to possess.

You may prefer to select passages from **graded readers** that have been developed specifically for English language learners. These are often graded using labels such as "beginner" and "low-intermediate" or according to students' vocabulary level: 500 words, 1000 words, and so on.

You can also select your own passages and grade them yourself. Some word processing programs, such as Microsoft Word, include a feature that measures the reading level of passages. Then you can develop clearly worded comprehension questions. You might ask the questions orally or design questions that require simple true-or-false answers. Show students how to answer the questions.

When you interpret the results, remember that the readability rating was normed using native speakers of English. Many English language learners possess much more background knowledge and a much higher literacy level than they are able to demonstrate in English.

Graded reading passages are useful when it is important to know how an English language learner's performance compares with that of native speakers. A 17-year-old who reads in English at a Grade 5 level, for example, is likely to experience difficulty in a Grade 12 social science course.

Cloze passages are reading selections from which certain words have been omitted. The term *cloze* derives from *closure* and refers to the ability to infer whole images or patterns from incomplete information. Readers who can fill in the missing words, or meaningful alternatives, demonstrate an important comprehension strategy: the ability to use context to figure out meaning.

Originally devised as a way of matching text and readers, cloze tests are also useful in assessing an individual student's comprehension of a text. Chapters 12 and 13 include suggested uses for the cloze procedure. To create a cloze test, choose several short graded reading passages of various levels of difficulty about subjects that are likely to be familiar to the reader. Students from Africa or the Caribbean, for example, are unlikely to have much knowledge of winter and winter sports. Add a title and short introduction to provide a context for each passage.

Construct the cloze passages by leaving the first and last sentences intact and deleting every seventh or ninth word from the other sentences (every seventh word is more challenging). Some of the deleted words will be **content words** (nouns, verbs, etc.) and some will be **function words** (prepositions, articles, conjunctions, etc.). Leave a blank where words were deleted.

Start with a passage that you think the student will be able to read. If you are unsure, begin with the easiest. Tell the student to fill in each blank with a word that makes sense. If she can't think of the word in English, encourage her to supply a word in her first language. If she is able to understand the meaning of the passage, she will insert words that make sense in the context.

In scoring the test, accept all meaningful words. Do not expect students to fill in the exact words used in the original piece. A response that is grammatically incorrect but semantically correct (i.e., correct in meaning) indicates that the student understands the passage. If you are not sure why a student inserted a particular word or phrase, ask.
Scoring is approximate, depending on whether you deleted every seventh or ninth word, and the extent to which the content is within the learner's previous experience. Here is a guide.

- If at least 75 percent of a student's responses are appropriate, he or she is able to independently read and draw meaning from text at that level.
- If between 60 and 75 percent of a student's responses are appropriate, she or he is able to read at that level only with instructional support.
- If less than 60 percent of a student's responses are appropriate, he or she is at the frustration level and is unable to comprehend text at that level.

Eventually you may decide to develop your own standards by testing your test on readers whose levels are already known.

English Language Assessment: Writing

If a student was able to participate in the reading assessment, the next step is to collect a writing sample. Ask students whose proficiency in

English is limited to respond to a picture by listing what they see. Others may construct a more detailed description or write a story. If students are more advanced, collect samples of different kinds of writing (e.g., a piece of personal writing, a narrative, a letter, a descriptive piece, and an expository piece).

To create an English writing sample, students may describe what they see in a picture like this or use the picture as inspiration for writing a more detailed story.

Writing Assessment Topics

Give students a choice of topics. Those who have studied English as a foreign language in their home country or who have already participated in an ESL program in another school may be able to respond to one of the following topics:

- Write a letter to a friend in your own country. Tell your friend about your first days in your new country.
- Write a letter to introduce yourself to your new teachers.
- Describe your favorite teacher in your former school.
- Describe a holiday that you celebrate in your country.
- Do you think boys and girls should go to separate schools? Why?

Provide **bilingual dictionaries** for students to use. The purpose of this assessment is to find out how they handle a writing task, using all the resources available. If a student asks you for a word, say and write it so that the student can copy it and continue writing. You might, however, ask him to identify the words he looked up or that you gave him.

Take a **holistic approach** to assessing these writing samples. Consider the writer's purpose, and the relevance of the information and how it is organized before turning your attention to word choice and surface features such as sentence structure, spelling, and punctuation.

It is also helpful to collect a writing sample in the student's first language. Even if you have no immediate access to bilingual support, a writing sample can provide the kind of information outlined earlier in this chapter.

PROVISIONAL PLACEMENT

Newcomers must be placed in programs that offer them the best chance of achieving success and satisfying their aspirations. As a result, their initial placement should be provisional or tentative. Decisions about a student's placement affect her or his entire school experience. Unfortunately, newcomers are sometimes placed in classrooms where the only likely outcome is failure, either because the students are inadequately prepared for the subject or because the teacher is inadequately prepared for the students. To minimize errors of this kind, review the initial placement in a couple of weeks and at regular intervals afterwards.

Most secondary school students need to be placed in an ESL class and, perhaps, one or two content courses designed specifically to meet the needs of English language learners. If courses like this are not available, a planned program of support should be offered through resource or itinerant teachers, volunteers, and trained peer tutors.

Beginning learners of English benefit from being placed in at least one mainstream subject where they can interact with English-speaking peers. Most can participate successfully in the mainstream mathematics program, for example, as well as in subjects such as physical education, family studies, art, and music.

Keep in mind that some students need much more support than others. Those whose education has been interrupted and whose first-language literacy is limited benefit from being placed in one classroom with a trained ESL teacher for at least half the school day. This enables them to concentrate on basic literacy, numeracy, and academic skills.

Monitoring and Counseling

Once students are placed in a program designed to meet their needs, it is important to monitor their progress and offer continuing support. All students feel more secure if someone in the school understands their needs, and this is especially true of newcomers. Institute procedures for tracking students' progress throughout the year and from year to year. This monitoring should continue through the period of linguistic and cultural adjustment, which lasts at least five years.

- Designate a team responsible for gathering and reviewing information about students' performance.
- Reach out to students. In schools with a guidance counselor, the counselor might visit ESL classes to explain the role of the guidance department. Most newcomers have no experience of guidance programs. They need information about the services that are available and reassurances about the confidentiality of the counseling relationship.
- Organize information sessions about the education system for newcomers in grades 7 and up. Explain how the system is organized, the courses necessary for graduation, and the programs that will prepare them to enter either the workforce or a post-secondary institution.
- Organize peer-support programs for newcomers and parent networks to support their families. Group sessions for specific linguistic and cultural groups can be very helpful if a particular group faces difficult issues.
- Coordinate support for students who are experiencing academic or personal difficulties. Educational psychologists, bilingual educators, and community agencies may be able to help.
- Organize a mentoring program that pairs newcomers with students who have adjusted successfully to the new cultural and educational environment and can serve as role models. Mentors should be at least a year older, of the same sex, and if possible, of the same ethnocultural background.

ASSESSING SPECIAL NEEDS

Like their English-speaking counterparts, some English language learners have special learning needs. They may have a learning disability or a behavioral disorder, or they may be talented or intellectually gifted. It is important, however, to be extremely cautious in making this judgment. When recommending or interpreting the results of a psychological assessment, it is essential to take into account the fact that the student may be unfamiliar with some of the cultural knowledge and experiences that are taken for granted when these assessments are created. As a result, the findings may not be accurate.

This does not mean that English language learners with special needs cannot be identified, even if they are very recent arrivals. Some special needs may become evident during the initial reception interview, especially if these needs have been identified in the home country or relate to a physical disability such as a hearing impairment. Some students may have special educational needs that have not previously been identified, however, especially if they are from countries where special education services do not exist or are very limited.

It is important to identify students with special needs as soon as possible so that they can receive additional support. Teachers may identify these needs by observing the student's learning rate and strategies and assessing the student's growth in English. Before making a referral for further assessment — by an educational psychologist, for example — begin with a first language assessment, as described earlier.

It is also important to consider all the factors that may be affecting a student's learning (e.g., access to previous schooling, quality of schooling, previous exposure to English, emotional factors related to the circumstances of immigration, and the amount and nature of the ESL support provided). This helps you distinguish between academic difficulties that are a result of limited schooling and problems that may indicate a learning disability.

A first language assessment helps determine whether a student's behavior can be attributed to the normal process of adjusting to the new culture and language or to deeper psychological problems, for example, is the newly arrived child who remains silent for several weeks simply experiencing the silent period that is a normal part of second language acquisition for many children? See Chapter 8 for more information on the silent period and other aspects of the second language acquisition process.

Involving a bilingual educator in additional assessments such as psychological tests is a good idea. The tests can then be conducted in the first language and **culturally biased** items can be identified and eliminated or interpreted with caution. Make sure that parents are informed of and involved in the process.

Parental Involvement

A supportive relationship between home and school helps immigrant students adjust successfully to their new environment. To foster this supportive relationship with their multilingual, multiracial, multicultural communities, schools must welcome the presence and participation of all students, their parents or guardians, and the wider community.

- Communicate effectively with the parents of all students. Some parents may have difficulty understanding written communication in English, such as school handbooks, report cards, newsletters, and information about field trips. Even if the parents understand English, these communications often assume that they also understand the school system. Important documents should be translated into the languages of the students in the school.

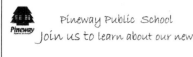

Pineway Public School
Join us to learn about our new

Pineway Child Care Learning Centre
Before and After School Care
Extra Curricular Activities
Nutritious Hot Lunches

Wednesday, January 22, 2003
5:30 p.m.
Room 209 (beside the Parking Lot Door)

(over)

Pineway小學
誠邀閣下參觀新人事管理

Pineway托兒教育中心

課前及課後托兒服務
課餘活動
營養豐富熱午餐

開放時間: 二○○三年一月二十二日(星期三)
下午五時三十分
地點: Pineway小學二○九室(停車場門口側)

Translating important announcements into the languages spoken by parents fosters a supportive relationship between the school and the community.

- Encourage parents to help their children continue to develop in their first language. See Chapter 8 for more information on the importance of students' first languages.
- Support heritage languages. Visit a heritage or international language class in your school or a neighboring school. You will gain insights into the kind of learning experiences that are familiar to many English language learners, and the teacher and students will appreciate your interest and support. Some secondary schools offer credit courses in heritage languages, such as Punjabi and Korean, that are spoken in the community.
- Make parent-teacher meetings and interviews more accessible to immigrant families. Meetings that parents can attend on the way home from work may be convenient. Instead of scheduling evening meetings, some schools have tried setting them up on Saturdays or Sundays. Some schools hold meetings outside the school, in apartment recreation rooms or community centers. Personal telephone calls in the home language, usually in the evenings, are an effective way of communicating with parents and inviting them to meetings. Explain the purpose of the meeting and make it clear that parental involvement is a crucial factor in students' success.
- Hold meetings with specific groups of parents, using interpreters and community workers to communicate with the parents in their home language. It may also be helpful to organize meetings to discuss specific topics, such as parenting in a new culture. Invite representatives of community groups to act as resources at these meetings. In parent-teacher interviews and meetings, avoid or explain jargon such as *achievement chart*, *rotary schedule*, and *mandatory credits*.
- Promote bilingualism and **biculturalism** as goals for students. Children must adopt behavior appropriate to the home and the school, and they may find it less stressful if their parents approve of the behavior and learning styles adopted at school. Parents are much more likely to approve if they feel that the school supports the home culture and is not encouraging their children to become completely assimilated.
- Explain some of the cultural and philosophical foundations of schools and classrooms in your country. Activities that some parents and students may regard as frivolous (e.g., field trips, projects, and group work) may make more sense if teachers explain their pedagogical underpinnings and help parents and students understand the rationale for a student-centered, activity-oriented approach. It is also helpful if parents and students understand that individual expression is highly valued in many Western cultures.

  At the same time, the school must be willing to incorporate some of the values of the communities it serves. Schools might, for example, designate a room where Muslim students can say Friday prayers. Material dealing with sexuality and personal relationships might also be studied in single-sex groupings.
- Be specific about expectations for behavior, such as completing homework, arriving on time, being prepared for class, and so on. Make sure that the school code of conduct is worded in simple and concrete terms, with specific examples that all students and parents can relate to. Examples might be shown visually, using drawings and cartoons by the students in the school. The code of conduct could also be displayed in the languages of the school.

- Promote positive intercultural relations. Ensure that all students and parents are aware of your school jurisdiction's policy on racial and ethnocultural harassment, and that all staff members know the steps to follow when they become aware of harassment.
- Provide multilingual materials in the school library and organize a home-reading program in the primary grades with books in the languages of the community.
- Involve parents in finding and creating resources in their languages. Groups of parents can create signs and notices, produce bilingual picture books for younger children, and read or tell stories in their own language. Involvement like this enhances the status of parents and of the languages spoken in the community. It also helps draw parents into a mutually supportive relationship with the school.
- Acknowledge the significance of the special days and holidays observed by the students attending the school.
- Ensure that classroom and hallway displays depict people from many cultures in many settings.
- Encourage community groups to use the school for cultural events, organizational meetings, and religious observances. Community use of the school fosters a sense of belonging and ownership, and parents who have attended cultural events in the building are more likely to feel at ease visiting the school for matters to do with their children's education.

To Learn More …

Books and Articles

Anisef, P. and Kilbride, K.M. eds. *Managing Two Worlds: The experiences and concerns of immigrant youth in Ontario.* Toronto: Canadian Scholars' Press Inc., 2003.

Useful background reading for educators working with immigrant youth.

Artiles, J., and A. Ortiz, eds. *English Language Learners with Special Education Needs: Identification, Assessment, and Instruction.* Washington, D.C.: Center for Applied Linguistics and Delta Systems, 2002.

Advice on identifying, placing, and teaching English language learners with special needs.

Asgedom, Mawi. *Of Beetles and Angels: A Boy's Remarkable Journey from a Refugee Camp to Harvard.* Chicago: Little, Brown, 2002.

This book is inspirational. Mawi Asgedom fled civil war in Ethiopia and survived a Sudanese refugee camp for three years. After being resettled in The United States at age seven, Mawi overcame poverty, racism, language barriers and personal tragedy to graduate from Harvard University. Ideal for reading aloud to students. Additional information and resources are available from the website: <www.mawispeaks.com>.

British Columbia Teachers' Federation. *A description of current issues and best practices for ESL learners: five case studies.* Vancouver, B.C.: BC Teachers' Federation, 2003.

Reports from five different schools or districts on strategies for identifying and supporting English language learners with additional needs. www.bctf.bc.ca/TeachingtoDiversity

Churchill, S., and I. Kaprielian-Churchill. *The Pulse of the World: Refugees in Our Schools.* Toronto, Ont.: OISE Press (now University of Toronto Press), 1994.

Describes refugees' experiences and how educators can help them make a successful transition to a new society.

Cloud, N. "Special Education Needs of Second Language Students." *Educating Second Language Children: The Whole Child, the Whole Curriculum, the Whole Community.* F. Genesee, ed. New York: Cambridge University Press, 1994.

Detailed advice on identifying and supporting English language learners who also have special needs.

Coelho, E. *Teaching and Learning in Multicultural Schools: An Integrated Approach.* Clevedon, England: Multilingual Matters, 1998.

Provides more detailed information on various topics discussed in this chapter, such as linguistic and cultural diversity, immigration policy, and the immigrant experience.

Ferguson, C. *Reaching Out to Diverse Populations: What Can Schools Do to Foster Family-School Connections?* A Strategy Brief of the National Center for Family and Community Connections with Schools. September 2005.

Available online at <www.sedl.org/connections>. This article gives practical research-based advice on parental involvement in a linguistically and culturally diverse community.

Fowler, J., and Hooper, H., 1998. ESL Learners With Special Needs In British Columbia: Identification, Assessment and Programming, British Columbia Ministry of Education, Skills and Training.

Deals with the often difficult distinction between the normal process of second language acquisition and possible indicators of a learning disability or other exceptionality, and provides guidelines for assessment and programming. www.bctf.bc.ca/TeachingtoDiversity

Lucas, T. *Into, through and beyond Secondary School: Critical Transitions for Immigrant Youths.* Washington, D.C., and McHenry, Ill: Center for Applied Linguistics and Delta Systems, 1997.

Examines the transitions made by immigrant youth adjusting to a new linguistic and cultural environment, a new personal identity, and a new school structure. Recommends ways to serve these students more effectively.

Multilingual Resources for Children Project. *Building Bridges: Multilingual Resources for Children.* Clevedon, U.K.: Multilingual Matters, 1995.

Many interesting ideas for bringing community languages into the school.

O'Malley, J.M., and L.V. Pierce. *Authentic Assessment for English Language Learners.* Reading, Mass.: Addison Wesley (now Pearson Education), 1996.

How to develop and use assessment methods for various purposes, including initial placement. Includes reproducible checklists and rubrics that can be adapted as needed.

Opoku-Dapaah, E. *Somali Refugees in Toronto: a Profile.* North York, Ontario: York Lanes Press, 1995.

This study examines the social, cultural, and linguistic backgrounds of Somalis in Canada, as well as their interaction with service organizations and mainstream society. Includes recommendations for government agencies, education, and social services.

Porter, J. *New Canadian Voices.* Toronto, Ont.: Wall and Emerson, 1991.

Collection of student writing about the immigrant experience can be used with students to stimulate talking and writing or with teachers to raise awareness of the experiences and needs of immigrant and refugee students.

Rutter, J. *Refugee Children in the Classroom.* Stoke-on-Trent, England: Trentham Books, 1994.

Provides background information on refugees in Britain, and makes practical suggestions for welcoming and supporting refugee children in schools.

Yau, M. *Refugee Students in Toronto Schools: An Exploratory Study.* Toronto, Ont.: Toronto Board of Education (now Toronto District School Board), 1995.

Provides background information on refugee students from various regions, examines how schools have responded to their needs, and recommends courses of action for educators.

Videos and Software

B.C. Institute against Family Violence. *Life in the Family: A New-comer's Guide to Parenting Issues in Canada.* B.C. Institute against Family Violence, 2002.

Developed for adult ESL classes, video and curriculum package provides information and resources that address issues faced by immigrant families as they adjust to new perspectives and laws relating to parenting and discipline. Could be used as a discussion starter in parent-teacher meetings. Available at <www.bcifv.org/esl.html>.

Jamaican Canadian Association. *FRESHIES – The Experiences of Caribbean Newcomer Youth.* Jamaican Canadian Association, 2000.

This 30-minute video is about the experiences of 15 new-comer youth from the English-speaking Caribbean. They discuss reuniting with their parents and their experiences at school. www.jcassoc.com

Settlement Workers in Schools. *New Moves: An Orientation Video for Newcomer Students.* Citizenship and Immigration Canada (Ontario Region), 2005.

20-minute video features interviews with several students who talk about their experiences as newcomers and offer advice to help other newcomer students to adapt successfully to their new school environment. Available in various languages. Users' guide is also available. Additional video and print resources on various topics of interest to newcomer families and the professionals who work with them are available at www.settlement.org/edguide

Talk to Your Child in your First Language (Primary Language Literacy Project). n.d. Ottawa-Carleton District School Board and First Words Preschool Speech and Language Program.

Manual, video, and parent booklets in several languages encourage parents to use their first language to help young children develop strong language skills.. For information on how to order the materials: First Words / Infant Hearing Program, Pinecrest Queensway Health & Community Services, 1365 Richmond Road, 2nd Floor, Ottawa, Ontario K2B 6R7. Phone: 688-3979

Toronto District School Board. *You Have Language: Foundation for Sucess.* (2007)

Video for parents, available in several languages, showing parents and caregivers engaged in home language activities that prepare children for success in learning English later on. www.tdsb.on.ca/educators

Welcome Booklet CD Rom. (nd) London, U.K: Mantra Lingua

This software creates a personalized booklet of the school in 19 languages. Designed for schools in the UK, the program is an ingenious example of how to use software to provide orientation materials and other important communications in community languages. For more information: <http://www.mantralingua.com>

Websites and Online Resources

British Columbia Ministry of Education. *English as a Second Language Learners: A Guide for ESL Specialists.* Victoria, B.C.: British Columbia Ministry of Education Special Programs Branch, 1999. <www.publications.gov.bc.ca>.

Includes guidelines for reception and orientation as well as sample assessment materials.

Cultural Profiles Project. <www.settlement.org/cp>.

Site includes online profiles of about 100 home countries of immigrants. Profiles are also available in hard copy. Suitable for student projects and as background for teachers.

Centre of Excellence for Research on Immigration and Settlement. <ceris.metropolis.net>.

Up-to-date research and a monthly electronic bulletin on the impact of immigration and the integration of immigrants into Canadian society.

International Children's Institute. <www.icichildren.org>.

Based in Montreal, Quebec, and Toronto, Ontario, this organization supports the development of programs and services for children who are experiencing stress related to displacement, war, and immigration. Training workshops and materials are available for educators.

Médecins sans Frontières (Doctors without Borders). <www.msf.org>.

Provides information about refugee situations around the world. Links provide access to MSF websites in various countries.

Settlement.org. <www.settlement.org>.

Resources and background information for newcomers to Canada and the teachers, settlement workers, and others who work with newcomers.

United Nations High Commissioner for Refugees. <www.unhcr.ch>.

Provides current news on refugee issues, as well as country-specific information about refugees.

2 Creating an Inclusive Classroom

In multicultural schools, it is important to prepare all students — not just newcomers and not just those who are learning English — to participate in a culturally diverse society.

The most effective preparation takes place in classrooms where students of all backgrounds feel valued as members of the school community, learn to respect one another and explore linguistic and cultural differences in a positive way, and welcome newcomers, whether they have arrived from another school in the same community or another country — and whether they speak English or are beginning learners of the language.

Use strategies such as the following to create an inclusive learning environment:

- Welcomes and introductions
- Class photographs
- Questionnaires and language surveys
- Roots and routes
- Inclusive displays
- Peer tutors and partners
- Support for the efforts of language learners
- A multilingual classroom environment
- A multicultural and anti-racist curriculum
- Multicultural literature circles

Welcomes and Introductions

The following strategies make the transition to a new classroom easier for newcomers and help everyone feel welcome.

- *Introduce newcomers as speakers of their first language and point out that they are also learning English.* Avoid referring to a new student as someone who doesn't speak English. No one likes to be described in terms of what he or she cannot (yet) do. Every student arrives with at least one language already established, and it is important to acknowledge this. Write the student's name and the name of the language on the chalkboard and point out her or his country of origin on a world map, or ask the student newcomer to do so.

- *Learn how to pronounce the new student's name.* As you say it, write it on the chalkboard so that all students learn it. If the name is long, you might ask the student to write and say it slowly so that you can

Who Is in Our Group?

1. Interview your partner.

   What is your name?

   _____

   (Learn to spell and pronounce your partner's name.)

   Where were you born?

   _____

   How long have you or your family been in this country?

   _____

   What language(s) do you speak?

   _____

   Tell me something interesting about your name.

   _____
   _____
   _____

   Write two or three more questions to ask your partner.

   _____
   _____
   _____

2. Introduce your partner to the group.

   This is _____. He (she) was born in _____. She (he) speaks _____. I can tell you something interesting about _____.

3. Be ready to introduce the members of your group to the class.

learn to say it. Repeat the name several times to fix it in your memory. Some long names consist of two or three words with separate meanings, and it is easier to learn how to say them if the students show you the component words.

- *Seat newcomers or beginning learners of English beside someone who speaks their first language.* For the first few weeks, this provides a sense of security for newcomers and helps them understand what's going on.

- *Organize structured group interviews to help students introduce themselves to one another* at the beginning of the year or whenever classroom groupings change. Interviews will be more successful if you model the process by inviting a student to interview you. Distribute questions like those shown on this page to use as a guide. Beginning learners of English can participate in this activity with the help of a bilingual peer.

- *Make time for personal contact with new students* at least once during every lesson. Check that new students are involved in meaningful learning tasks, even if these are not the same as those other students are working on. See Chapter 13 for advice on how to adapt the program for English language learners.

Class Photographs

Photographs of the students can be used to create a class display or photo album, as well as for other purposes. You will, however, need a parent's permission to display photographs of students under 18. Those older than 18 can sign their own releases. Consult the principal to find out whether your school or jurisdiction has standard release forms and whether these are available in various languages. A blanket release that covers the entire school year or an entire semester can be sent home at the outset. When new students arrive, this form can be completed during the initial reception interview.

When taking photographs, use a digital camera if possible, so that you and the students can use the pictures for other purposes. They might, for example, be displayed on a class Web site or used to embellish students' projects.

This web is an alternative way of sharing information. Each fact is circled with a colored marker according to category (Home, Family, etc.).

- *Photograph every student in the class.* You can do this while the students are interviewing each other. If you use a digital or Polaroid camera, the pictures will be ready by the time students have finished the interviews. Remember to include a photo of yourself.
- *Encourage students to write a mini-biography to go with their photograph* by creating one to accompany your own picture. In your biography, share the kind of information that you want students to include in theirs. Some students may be able to produce bilingual biographies, while newcomers may be able to write only in their own language. You or another student might write an English version for them.
- *Create a permanent display of the photographs* and encourage students to add to the information about themselves as the year or semester progresses. Newcomers may appreciate this opportunity to demonstrate their progress in learning English. Arrange the photographs to match classroom groups and rearrange them whenever groupings change. Remember to add photographs of newcomers as they arrive.

Questionnaires and Language Surveys

Questionnaires and surveys enable you to learn about the linguistic and cultural background of students and help students learn about one another.

Questionnaires

Questionnaires help lay the groundwork for individual conversations with students. To help you learn about their linguistic and cultural background, as well as how they feel about school and the subject(s) you teach, ask students to fill them out at the beginning of the year or semester.

The questions shown on this page can be adapted to suit students of any age and level of English proficiency. If you are working with younger children, shorten the questionnaire and simplify the questions. Learners who are new to English may need the help of a bilingual peer to complete the questionnaire. Mainstream teachers who work with the same group of students for most of the day might conduct the survey orally over several days. Don't forget to survey students who arrive later in the term.

Language Surveys

Later in the year or semester, language surveys can be used to explore linguistic diversity in greater depth.

- *Begin by sharing demographic information* about your city, neighborhood, or school (e.g., percentage of English speakers, percentage of speakers of other languages, and percentage of immigrants). Ask students to identify evidence of linguistic and cultural diversity they have observed in the school, the community, or the media, and invite them to bring examples to class (e.g., books, magazines, newspapers, flyers, and announcements printed in various

Getting to Know You

- What is your name?
- Where were you born?
- If you were not born in this country, when did you come to this country?
- What language do you usually speak at home?
- What language do you usually speak with your friends?
- What language(s) can you read?
- Which language do you read best?
- If English is not your first language, which language do you prefer to use for thinking and problem solving?
- Have you been to school in any other country?
- What do you like most about school?
- Is there anything you don't like about school?
- How do you feel about this subject?
- Are you involved in school activities or sports teams?
- What are your interests outside school?
- What else would you like me to know about you?

languages; information about community events; samples of their work in an international languages class; and labels from packaged foods). Display this material in the classroom or hallway. Ask older students questions that encourage critical thinking (e.g., Is there a correspondence between the language backgrounds of students and teachers in the school? If not, is this a problem? If so, what can be done about it? How can students of various backgrounds be persuaded to consider a career in teaching?).

- *Create and distribute a language survey* like the one shown on this page and ask students to administer the survey to a partner or to respond privately in a journal. This survey encourages students to reflect on the contexts in which they choose to use one or another of their languages. The results can be fascinating. Some children may, for example, use different languages with different family members. Others may prefer to use one of their languages in specific situations, such as counting, telling jokes or stories, reading poetry, and singing. Learning about their classmates' language backgrounds encourages monolingual English-speaking children to become interested in languages and helps promote a positive approach to learning new languages.

- *Integrate mathematics.* Encourage groups to represent the survey data on graphs, charts, and tables and to create percentage and ratio problems for other groups to solve. A group might, for example, create a graph showing the languages spoken by class members. Before drawing the graph, discuss the criteria for including a language (e.g., Will the graph include only languages students learned as babies or all the languages students now know? Will it include languages that students can speak but not read and write or languages that they are just beginning to learn?).

- *Display the survey data* in the classroom or hallway. This display could become a school project if one class or a group of classes surveys other classes or uses data from a school profile to create a display at the school's main entrance.

Roots and Routes

Displaying interest in students' roots affirms that their cultural background is valued and helps dispel notions that learning English means abandoning their own heritage.

- *Trace students' roots* on a world map that is permanently displayed in the classroom. Make a name tag for each student — or have students make their own — and place these on their country or countries of origin.

- *Add newcomers to the map* as they arrive. Students can point out their home country on the map, and if they already know some English, tell you or the class something about it.

Language(s) in Your Life

1. Is English your first language?
2. How long have you been learning English?
3. What other language(s) do you speak and understand?
4. What other language(s) can you read or write?
5. What is your strongest language?
6. What language(s) do you use with your parents?
7. What language(s) do you use with your brothers and sisters?
8. What language(s) do you use with your grandparents?
9. What language(s) do you use with your friends?
10. Are you learning any languages now?
11. What language(s) do you think you might learn in the future?
12. What are some advantages of knowing more than one language?

Caution!

Issues relating to immigration may be troubling for some students. They may, for example, have left their homeland in difficult circumstances and some may even have lost family members. Be sensitive to this and prepare an alternative assignment for those who prefer not to participate. These students might, for example, report on less personal information about their country or countries of origin.

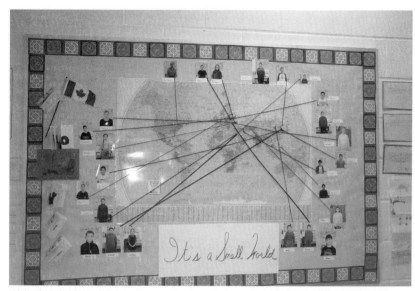

This display uses pushpins and colored thread to link photographs of students to their countries of origin on a wall map.

- *Ask students to interview each other* about how, when, and why they, their parents, or their ancestors immigrated. Some students may need to consult family members to discover this information, and some may wish to bring family photos or artifacts to show the class.

Inclusive Displays

The visual environment of the classroom transmits important messages about students' membership in the classroom community. Students are more likely to feel a sense of ownership and inclusion if classroom exhibits reflect their lives and work, as well as their contributions.

- *Include material in languages other than English*, such as signs and labels, students' writing, and items from community newspapers.

- *Change displays regularly*. Exhibits may focus on topics or events explored in class. Invite all students to contribute to displays relating to general themes, such as food and nutrition, people who make a difference, and mathematics in architecture. At the appropriate time, students from specific ethnocultural groups might enjoy preparing a display featuring a special day or holiday.

- *Involve students in creating displays*. Groups that have worked together for an extended period might, for example, be asked to create a display. Group members can then explain how the display reflects who they are or the work they have been doing.

- *Don't insist on perfection*. Learning a second language involves making mistakes, and these mistakes reflect learners' current stage of development. If you make students correct all their language errors, the work is no longer theirs; moreover, second language

Student-created displays like this need not be perfect. They are evidence of learning in progress.

learners learn little from this kind of correction. See chapters 8 and 10 for more information on errors and feedback.

- *Be creative about finding space for displays.* Don't limit displays to bulletin boards. You might, for example, suspend material on clotheslines strung across the classroom. And don't forget hallways! If you are a middle or secondary school teacher working with classes that rotate through the same classroom or if you share a classroom with teachers, creating displays is more challenging — but not impossible. Consider creating mobile displays on poster boards or in binders that can be put away between classes.

Peer Tutors and Partners

A system of peer tutors and same-language partners helps meet the needs of diverse groups of learners and can be especially helpful in providing extra help and support to newcomers. The research on peer tutoring suggests that tutors also benefit from the experience. They develop their social and leadership skills, feel a sense of accomplishment, and often enhance their own understanding of concepts after explaining them to someone else.

- *Provide same-language partners for newcomers.* Students who are just beginning to learn English benefit from the support of a bilingual partner for the first few weeks. If no one speaks the newcomer's language, select a friendly student who is sensitive to the needs of others.

- *Organize a peer-tutoring program.* Students who already speak some English appreciate the support of a friendly English speaker. The peer tutor may be from the same class or another class and the tutoring may take place in or outside the classroom.

- *Assign specific tasks to peer tutors and partners.* A student might be asked, for example, to work with an English language learner on a mathematics problem. When the language learner can describe each step orally in English, both students have successfully completed their assigned task.

- *Collaborate with staff in nearby schools* to link elementary children with adolescents who can act as mentors, tutors, and role models. If they speak the same language, so much the better, but this is not essential. In some jurisdictions, doing this kind of work enables secondary students to earn cooperative education credits or fulfill community service requirements.

- *Recognize the important contribution of peer tutors and partners* through a letter of commendation (in a language that parents understand), a visit and a handshake from a school administrator, or a presentation in a school assembly. The school might also present an award to the partner or tutor of the year. When setting up the program, explain the benefits to participating students. It is often said, for example, that those who teach learn the most.

This peer tutor is helping a newcomer. When selecting peer tutors, social skills are more important than academic skills.

Support for the Efforts of Language Learners

Help students who are learning English by recognizing and supporting their efforts and enlisting the support of all students in the class.

- *Explain that every classroom is a language classroom* as well as a place for learning mathematics, social studies, or other subjects. Explain the importance of a supportive environment in which language learners feel comfortable speaking English without fear of ridicule or criticism.

- *Show English-speaking students how they can actively help classmates* who are learning English (e.g., by repeating or rephrasing, using gestures and drawings to help explain something, writing a word, and using effective strategies for seeking clarification and confirming comprehension). Encourage students to follow your example when communicating with second language learners.

- *Communicate a positive attitude toward language learning.* The task is not overwhelming, especially in a supportive environment with positive motivation. Anyone who has acquired one language can acquire another. Point out role models — other students, teachers, and public figures — who have successfully acquired English as a second or additional language.

- *Communicate a positive attitude toward second language learners.* Students who are learning English are not "experiencing language difficulties"; they are becoming linguistically enriched. Bilingualism is an admirable goal, and people who are fully bilingual are an asset to their community and country. English language learners in your class can provide positive role models for learning another language.

A Multilingual Classroom Environment

Students in multilingual classrooms benefit when teachers and classmates value linguistic diversity.

- *Communicate a positive attitude toward linguistic diversity* by, for example, displaying slogans that support language learning and encouraging students to invent additional slogans.

- *Incorporate other languages and other varieties of English* into the classroom and the curriculum by creating multilingual displays and signs, comparing how various languages express ideas, and producing dual-language versions of projects and assignments. Encourage students to consult adults. This will help students expand their knowledge of their first languages and provide parents with opportunities to become involved in their children's education. See Chapter 10 for more suggestions for incorporating students' languages into the program.

- *Learn simple expressions in students' languages.* Students will appreciate your efforts even if you learn only a few greetings. You might

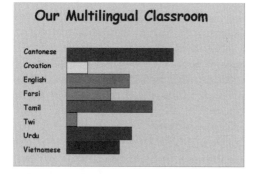

Celebrating linguistic diversity helps all students feel valued.

Students created this multilingual greeting.

even take a course in a language spoken by a significant number of students in the school.

- *Encourage students to learn words and phrases in one another's languages.* Every week, for example, you might ask a student or group of students who speak the same language to teach you and the class a greeting in their language. Then everyone in the class will use it for the rest of the week.

- *Provide multilingual reading material* in school and classroom libraries. Though monolingual books in other languages may be available in community bookstores or public libraries, dual-language materials are especially useful. Some popular children's books are available in dual-language editions.

- *Involve parents.* Ask parents and other community members to help find material in their language, and involve parents of primary children in creating simple picture books. You might also develop homework activities — with instructions for parents printed in their language — that children can participate in with their parents.

A Multicultural and Anti-Racist Curriculum

It is important to prepare all students to live and work effectively in the culturally diverse communities and workplaces that are increasingly common in Western countries. All students, even those in schools with a homogeneous student population, benefit from a curriculum that encourages them to

- value linguistic and cultural diversity
- enrich their store of cultural knowledge
- expand their world view and understand perspectives and experiences different from their own
- recognize and challenge bias and discrimination whenever and wherever they experience or witness them

Though schools can take the first steps toward achieving these goals by introducing a model of **multicultural education** that celebrates cultural differences, this does not go far enough. To help students accept differing points of view and challenge racism and discrimination, **anti-racist education** is also necessary.

Multicultural education, which consists of educational practices that recognize the experiences and contributions of diverse cultural groups, is often regarded as a developmental stage on the path toward anti-racist education. Anti-racist education consists of institutional practices intended to reduce prejudice and discrimination, promote academic equity, and develop in all students the skills necessary to interact effectively in a racially and culturally diverse society.

As the chart on the following page illustrates, many schools promote multicultural education by offering special events and learning experiences that celebrate cultural differences (the heroes-and-holidays approach), and many teachers integrate multicultural content by focusing on topics that highlight non-dominant cultures (the

Multicultural and Anti-Racist Education: A Continuum

Multicultural Education →   → **Anti-Racist Education**

	Heroes-and-Holidays Approach	Multiculturalism-as-a-Subject Approach	Multiple-Perspectives Approach	Social-Action Approach
Examples	• School concerts featuring music, dance, and traditional clothing of various cultures. • Multicultural feasts featuring food contributed by parents. • Special displays for Chinese New Year.	• Stand-alone units focusing on specific cultures (e.g., black inventors and scientists, the contributions of specific groups).	• Multicultural content is integrated naturally into curriculum. • Diverse perspectives are recognized (e.g., consequences of arrival of Europeans in Americas from point of view of Aboriginal peoples, Europeans, and contemporary environ-mentalists).	• Curriculum deals directly with bias, prejudice, and discrimination. • Students examine taken-for-granted institutions, practices, and beliefs. • Students learn how to challenge inequity.
Benefits	• Events can be a lot of fun. • A low-risk starting point for schools that have never paid attention to cultural diversity.	• Multiculturalism gains credibility when included in curriculum.	• Sends message that diversity is normal. • Students recognize fundamental commonalities and interesting differences. • Students' cultural experience and knowledge become a resource. • They learn about contributions of all groups to human development and knowledge.	• Students develop critical thinking skills and sense of control (e.g., believe they can help change the world). • Students are prepared to participate in a democracy. • Fighting racism is seen as everyone's work.
Concerns	• Events are separate from curriculum. • Events are based on a limited concept of *culture.* • Focus is on cultures viewed as different from the mainstream, which is considered "normal."	• Multicultural content is an add-on to curriculum. • Examples may promote stereotypes (e.g., houses in North America and huts in Africa as examples of homes). • Mainstream perspectives may dominate (e.g., *To Kill a Mockingbird* addresses racism from a white perspective).	• Members of the dominant cultural group may feel that their heritage is threatened. • Resources are not always readily available.	• Care must be taken not to polarize students. • Teachers need anti-racism training.

multiculturalism-as-a-subject approach). These are positive ways to begin raising everyone's awareness of cultural diversity.

It is important, however, to keep moving along the path toward anti-racist education by helping students see events from varying perspectives (the multiple-perspectives approach) and helping them develop the skills and knowledge needed to take action (the social-action approach). Only then will young people be prepared to help create a just and equitable society in which people of all linguistic, cultural, and racial backgrounds are able to reach their full potential.

Multicultural Literature Circles

Multicultural literature circles integrate varying cultural perspectives into the curriculum and help students develop a problem-solving approach to racism and other forms of inequity. The approach is modeled on book or literature circles, in which people who have read or are reading the same book meet to talk about it. For many adults, book circles are a way of socializing while expanding their intellectual and cultural horizons, and book circles have become so popular that some adult fiction is now published with accompanying discussion guides.

You can organize book circles — with a multicultural emphasis — in your own classroom. If books are well chosen and appropriate support is provided, this approach can promote reading as a pleasurable way to spend private time. It also encourages students to share ideas and experiences with others.

Reading and discussing multicultural literature enhances the multicultural climate of the classroom, expands everyone's store of cultural knowledge, and enables students to view the world through perspectives other than their own. Multicultural literature circles can be adapted for use at any grade level.

Organizing Multicultural Literature Circles

1. *Choose the books.* To validate cultural diversity and broaden students' cultural literacy, select a variety of books that deal with a particular theme in various cultural contexts. With older students, short stories can also be used. Depending on the size of the class, you may need four to six copies of several different books or stories. Choose books or stories at various readability levels to accommodate students' needs.

Choose themes addressed in the mainstream English or language arts curriculum or that relate to other subjects such as social studies and science. Possible themes include journeys, friendship, adventure, making peace, escape, growing up, family, overcoming adversity, identity, and dreams. Biographies related to themes such as freedom fighters, great writers, and inventors can also be chosen.

Ask the school's teacher-librarian or a librarian in your community's public library for help in researching suitable literature. Other resources are mentioned in "To Learn More ..." at the end of this chapter.

2. *Model the activity.* Choose a book and show students the cover and some of the illustrations, or read the information on the jacket. Encourage students to brainstorm questions and predictions about the book. Read the book aloud. If you have copies, students can follow along as you read. Lead and model the kind of discussion you want students to

engage in as they read in their circles. To do this, use prompts such as, "What do you think is going to happen next?" "Why did ____ do that?" "Can you guess what the word _____ means?" and "What would you do in this situation?" Introduce concepts such as character, setting, problem, and resolution.

Provide prompts for journal responses that encourage students to retell, relate, and reflect on the book. See Chapter 12 for more information on keeping journals.

3. *Organize the circles and guide the discussions.* Divide the class into groups of four to six students and assign a different book to each group, matching students' reading levels to the books available.

Though groups may need only one or two class periods and meetings to read and discuss children's picture books, longer books may require several periods of discussion and some at-home reading.

Circulate among the groups to participate in their discussions and provide additional support when needed. You might even read aloud some sections of the book.

Provide prompts and guiding questions like the following to encourage students to relate events in the story to their own experiences and to talk about how the events might be perceived from other points of view. The first few times, it may be helpful to assign each group member a specific role, such as discussion leader, recorder, reporter, and so on.

With older students, intersperse group discussions with teacher-led discussions of various literary concepts and terms.

As students read and discuss books in multicultural literature circles, it is important to provide support and guidance.

Examples of Discussion Prompts	
Fiction: Journeys	**Biography**
Where does the story take place?	When (where) was this person born?
Who are the main characters?	
Why do they leave their country or community?	What key events happened in her or his life?
What problem do the characters face? How do they solve it?	What difficulties did he or she overcome?
Would you do the same thing in that situation? Why?	What was her or his main achievement?
What was your favorite part of the story?	What was the most interesting part of the story?
What does this story remind you of in your own life?	Why is it important for us to know about this person's life?
	What does this person's story mean to you?

4. *Showcase the books.* Suggest to students some ways of promoting their book to their classmates. These presentations are different from traditional book talks. Remind students that their purpose is not to tell the story but to reveal just enough to entice others to choose this book for independent reading.

Provide some models of the various ways students might present their books. Here are some examples:

Suggestions for Showcasing Books	
Fiction	**Biography**
Dramatize a scene or simulate an interview with characters.	Present key events in the subject's life through role plays or simulated interviews.
Create a book jacket, bookmark, or captioned illustrations.	Write letters to and from the subject.
Write reviews or present TV commercials.	Create posters or epitaphs to commemorate the person.
Write and illustrate a story on a similar theme. These stories can be collected into a class anthology and shared with other classes and teachers. Some students may be able to produce bilingual versions of their stories. Parents may be able to help.	Write a letter to the principal, explaining why the person's life and achievements should be commemorated in a specific way (e.g., through an award for a student or group working toward similar goals).

5. *Assign independent reading.* Encourage every student to choose one of the books to read individually. Some students may choose to read them all!

Don't always require the students to complete follow-up work after reading. This turns reading into a chore. The purpose of literature circles is to encourage students to read as many books as possible and to think and talk about them so that they develop a lifelong love of reading that will expand their horizons and enrich their lives.

6. *Choose another theme and start again!* Use multicultural literature circles regularly to foster a love of reading, introduce differing cultural perspectives, and address problems related to racism and discrimination in literature and in students' daily lives. Reorganize the groups periodically so that students make connections with as many other students as possible.

To Learn More ...

Books and Articles

Banks, J.A. *An Introduction to Multicultural Education*. 2nd ed. Boston, Mass.: Allyn and Bacon, 1999.
Overview of concepts and practices in multicultural and anti-racist education.

Coelho, E. *Teaching and Learning in Multicultural Schools: An Integrated Approach*. Clevedon, U.K.: Multilingual Matters, 1998.
Examines schools and classrooms as cultural and linguistic environments and provides practical strategies for integrating diverse languages and cultures into mainstream programs.

Cummins, J., Bismilla, V., Chow, P., Cohen, S., Giampapa, F., Leoni, L., Sandhu, P., and Sastri, P. Affirming Identity in Multilingual Classrooms. *Educational Leadership* Vol. **63** | No. **1**, September 2005: 38-43.
This article explains the value of incorporating students' home languages and cultures into the classroom program, and describes some projects that use linguistic and cultural diversity as an asset.

Daniels, H. *Literature Circles: Voice and Choice in the Student-Centered Classroom*. York, Me.: Stenhouse Publishers, 1994.
Guidelines for setting up and managing literature study circles using the principles of cooperative learning. Staff development video is also available.

Derman-Sparks, L., and the ABC Task Force. *Anti-Bias Curriculum: Tools for Empowering Young Children*. Washington, D.C.: National Association for the Education of Young Children, 1989.
Classic handbook provides practical advice for implementing an anti-bias curriculum. Includes a list of useful resources.

Edwards, V. *The Other Languages: A Guide to Multilingual Classrooms*. Reading, U.K.: National Centre for Language and Literacy, 1996.
Helpful information includes suggestions for working with children to enhance the multilingual climate of the school, as well as models of language surveys.

Edwards, V. *The Power of Babel: Teaching and Learning in Multilingual Classrooms*. Reading, U.K.: National Centre for Language and Literacy, 1998.
Recounts experiences of teachers, parents, and students working together on multilingual projects that enable all children to participate in a rich multilingual environment.

Hill, B.C., N.J. Johnson, and K.L.S. Noe. *Literature Circles and Response*. Norwood, Mass.: Christopher Gordon Publishers, 1995.
Collection of articles providing a rationale for literature circles and practical advice on implementing this approach.

Kezwer, P., *Worlds of Wonder: Resources for Multicultural Children's Literature*. Toronto, Ont.: Pippin, 1995.
Detailed listings of more than 320 multicultural titles from picture books to young adult novels.

Lee, E., D. Menkart, and M. Okazawa-Rey, eds. *Beyond Heroes and Holidays: A Practical Guide to K-12 Anti-Racist, Multicultural Education and Staff Development*. Washington, D.C.: Network of Educators on the Americas, 1998.
Provides readings, practical examples, and a comprehensive resource guide.

Muse, D., ed. *Multicultural Resources for Young Readers*. New York: New Press, 1997.
Guide to multicultural literature for students in Kindergarten to Grade 8 includes more than 1,000 book reviews, organized thematically, as well as teaching suggestions, essays on multicultural education and information on videos and CD-ROMs. An essential resource for school librarians.

Samway, K.D., and G. Whang. *Literature Study Circles in a Multicultural Classroom*. York, Me.: Stenhouse Publishers, 1996.
Detailed advice on using literature study circles. Includes bibliographies of children's literature and lists of authors from various cultural backgrounds.

Samway, K.D., G. Whang, and M. Pippitt. *Buddy Reading: Cross-Age Tutoring in a Multicultural School*. Portsmouth, N.H.: Heinemann, 1995.
Authors recount their experiences with cross-grade tutoring in an elementary setting. Suggestions for setting up the program and training tutors are helpful at all levels.

Schecter, S., and J. Cummins, eds. *Multilingual Education in Practice: Using Diversity As a Resource*. Portsmouth, N.H.: Heinemann, 2003.
Suggestions for incorporating students' linguistic and cultural knowledge into the school environment. Includes classroom stories with photographs and many examples of students' writing and artwork.

Schniedewind, N., and E. Davidson. *Open Minds to Equality: A Sourcebook of Learning Activities to Promote Race, Sex, Class and Age Equity*. 2nd ed. Englewood Cliffs, N.J.: Prentice-Hall (now Pearson Education), 1997.
Cooperative learning activities that help students recognize and change inequities based on race, gender, class, age, language, sexual orientation, disability, and religion.

Walker, S., V. Edwards, and H. Leonard. *Write around the World*. Reading, U.K.: National Centre for Language and Literacy, 1998.
Practical ideas for producing bilingual resources in the classroom.

Zaslavsky, C. *The Multicultural Math Classroom: Bringing in the World*. Portsmouth, N.H.: Heinemann, 1996.
Practical suggestions for topics and activities that help students learn about mathematical applications and inventions from many cultures. For information on other multicultural mathematics resources by the same author: <www.math.binghampton.edu/zaslav/cz.html>

Videos

Many Voices. TV Ontario, 1991.
Series of problem-solving dramas related to racism and discrimination. For students in Grades 6 to 9.

Playing Fair. National Film Board of Canada, 1992.
Four video dramas designed to promote discussion of racism and prejudice. For students in Grades 2 to 6.

Reflections: Suggestions for an Antiracist Curriculum. Toronto, Ont.: Metropolitan Toronto School Board (now Toronto District School Board), 1996.
Practical ways of integrating anti-racist education across the curriculum at all grade levels.

Websites and Online Resources

Another Story <www.anotherstory.ca>.
This Toronto bookstore specializes in multicultural books and diverse perspectives, including children's picture books, biographies, and young adult fiction. Staff will locate books that support specific themes or link with topics in the curriculum, such as medieval times, ancient history, communities, and Canadian history.

Center for Multilingual Multicultural Education at the University of Southern California. <www.usc.edu/dept/education/CMMR>.
Information on research, publications,

Dual Language Showcase: <http://thornwood.peelschools.org/Dual>.
This school-based site shows m any examples of dual language books written by children. training, and public services. Provides links to articles on current education issues.

International Children's Digital Library. <www.icdlbooks. org>.
This organization is creating a digital library of outstanding children's books from all over the world. The materials are presented in the original languages in which they were published, reflecting cultural diversity around the world.

Mantralingua. <www.mantralingua.com>.
U.K.-based publishing house specializing in multilingual children's books, CDs, and display materials.

Multi-Cultural Books and Videos. <www.multiculbv.com>.
A large selection of books, videos, audiocassettes, educational materials and computer software. Dual-language books are available in many languages, and a catalogue is available on request.

The Multiliteracy Project. <www.multiliteracies.ca>.
This site documents a three-year Canadian research study about literacy and pedagogy in a pluralistic, technological society. The sample projects include dual language books written by students.

National Centre for Language and Literacy <www.ncll. org.uk>.
Website includes a database of multicultural resources and information about books on multilingual schools and classrooms.

Rethinking Schools. <www.rethinkingschools.org>.
Offers an online journal as well as advice and resources for teachers interested in developing anti-racist and social-justice education. Special publications include *Rethinking Our Classrooms*, 1994; *Rethinking Columbus: The Next 500 Years*, 1998; and *Rethinking Our Classrooms, Volume 2*, 2001.

II   How English Works

Teaching in multilingual schools requires a special awareness of language. In addition to teaching a particular level or subject(s), teachers in multilingual schools are important linguistic models and informants for students who are learning English or who may speak a variety of English other than standard English. Most native speakers of English, however, pay little conscious attention to the way they put together the specific sounds, words, and sentences that make up the language.

In addition, many English speakers have little knowledge of how other languages differ from English. As a result, teachers are sometimes puzzled by the problems students experience when learning English and find it difficult to help them.

The chapters in this section are about the English language and how it works. Designed for teachers who may have little or no background in linguistics, the chapters present explicit information about language in general, and English in particular. This information includes basic terms and concepts relating to the sound system of English, its grammar system, its writing system, the origin and structure of words, and how language is used in various real-life contexts, including the school.

Each chapter focuses on several general concepts of language study and presents examples of elements of English that often cause difficulty for language learners — and sometimes native speakers, as well. Throughout, the differences between English and other languages are highlighted to help you become more aware of students' needs. Each chapter concludes with suggestions for language teaching and further reading.

For ESL teachers, a knowledge of how English works is as fundamental as a knowledge of how mathematics works is for math teachers. Refer to the information in this section regularly and, if your goal is to become an expert language teacher, continue to read and study in this area. If you are a classroom or subject teacher, an awareness of some of the complexities of English and some of the common difficulties experienced by language learners will help you understand what is involved in learning a second language — and prepare you to help the students in your classroom.

For more detailed information for language teachers and teachers of English language learners, see:

Fillmore, L.W., and C.E. Snow. What Teachers Need to Know About Language. *ERIC Clearinghouse on Languages and Linguistics*, 2000.
This article and several related articles are available at <www.cal.org/ericcll/teachers>.

Freeman, D.E. and Y.S. Freeman. *Essential Linguistics: What you Need to Know to Teach Reading, ESL, Spelling, Phonics, and Grammar.* Portsmouth, NH: Heinemann.
Introduction to basic concepts of linguistics for teachers, with practical examples of classroom application.

3 I Say Tomato: The Sound System of English

Helping students who are struggling to produce the sounds of English requires knowledge of the English sound system, as well as of the difficulties learners often encounter as they try to speak English. This chapter introduces important elements of the English sound system and provides information to help improve your "ear" for the sounds of language, making it easier to understand your students and identify specific problems they may have. The chapter also suggests strategies for helping students who are having trouble reproducing some English sounds.

Phonology: The Sounds of Language

These students are receiving help from a specialist ESL teacher.

Every language uses a specific set of sounds that is not exactly the same as the set of sounds used in any other language. These sounds, and the patterns used to combine them into words and sentences, make up the **phonological system** of a language. **Phonology** is the study of the sounds of language.

Children who are learning their first language acquire its phonological system very early in their development, long before they even begin to say words. This explains why most people find it difficult to produce new sounds when they try to learn a new language later in life and why they often retain accents that mark them as non-native speakers.

When second language learners encounter sounds or phonological patterns that are different from those of their first language, they often substitute a sound or apply a pattern that exists in their own language. This is what causes a second language learner's accent. English speakers who are learning French, for example, may have trouble pronouncing the *r* sound, which is produced at the back of the mouth in many dialects of French. They often substitute the English version of the sound, which isn't produced as far back. Similarly, the English sound represented by the letters *th* in words like *thin* occurs in few other languages, and learners of English may pronounce this word as "tin," "fin," or "sin." In addition, learners sometimes have problems when a sound that does exist in their own language is used differently. The *g* of the English word *go*, for example, exists in Russian but never appears at the end of a word. As a result, many Russian speakers pronounce a word like *bag* as "back."

Everyone speaks with an accent, in their own language as well as in languages they have learned later in life. In his lyrics for the song "Let's Call the Whole Thing Off," songwriter Ira Gershwin poked gentle fun at the differences among English accents by highlighting the varying pronunciation of words such as *tomato* (*tomahto*).

Some accents, such as Australian, Jamaican, Southern American, Maritime Canadian, or Northern English, are regional, while others are linked to social class, so that people of similar social standing speak the language more or less the same way. The Queen of England has an accent, as do the prime minister of Canada and the president of the United States. For more information on accents and language variety, see Chapter 6.

When an accent doesn't interfere with communication, it is simply an interesting aspect of a person's speech and may even be considered sophisticated, charming, or cute. Learners of English from some language backgrounds, however, tend to have specific difficulties with some sounds of English, and these difficulties may interfere with communication or create a negative impression among listeners. In these cases, it is important to provide pronunciation instruction and practice.

The Sounds of English

The phonological system of a language consists of its individual speech sounds, as well as its stress, rhythm, and intonation patterns. Understanding these can help you become more aware of the task facing the second language learners in your classroom.

Phonemes

A **phoneme** is the smallest unit of sound that can affect meaning in a language. For example, the English sounds represented in print by *th* and *t* are phonemes because, although they are produced by moving the tongue, teeth, and lips in somewhat similar ways, experienced English speakers can perceive the difference between words such as *thin* and *tin*, and *tenth* and *tent*.

In phonology, vowels and consonants are not letters of the alphabet, but sounds. Though the English alphabet has 26 letters, for example, English speakers produce more than 40 sounds. The exact number of sounds depends on the variety of English spoken. Some other languages have more sounds than English, and some have fewer.

Knotty Problems in English

Using symbols to represent the sounds of English is especially helpful for language learners because of the large number of homographs and homophones that exist in the language.

Homographs are words that are spelled the same but pronounced differently depending on their meaning.

- *read* and *read* (present and past tense)
- *lead* and *lead* (the verb and the metallic element)

Homophones, which are also called homonyms, are words that sound the same but are spelled differently.

- *red* and *read* (past tense)
- *bare* and *bear*
- *meet* and *meat*
- *their*, *there*, and *they're*
- *knotty* and *naughty* (in most varieties of North American English)

In print, the sounds of English are represented by letters and letter combinations, and one letter may represent several sounds. The letter *a*, for example, represents different sounds in the words *ban*, *bane*, and *ball*, and *c* represents different sounds in the words *can't* and *cent* — and is not pronounced at all in *scent*. In addition, one sound may be represented in print by several different letters or letter combinations (e.g., the letters *s* and *c* represent the same sounds in *sent* and *cent*).

Because spelling is not always an accurate guide to pronunciation, most dictionaries provide a pronunciation guide. Some dictionaries use respelling (e.g., puh-tay-toe for *potato*), while others use phonetic symbols to represent the various sounds. Though the English alphabet has only 26 letters, 40 or more symbols are used to represent its sounds.

Most technical books for language teachers use phonetic symbols to represent English sounds and to describe the difficulties that learners may encounter when trying to produce these sounds (see the charts on the following pages). Dictionaries also use phonetic symbols. The symbols used vary from reference to reference, however. This is why it is always important to check the symbols used in the reference books you consult.

The Phonemes of English

The charts on the following pages show symbols that are often used to represent the phonemes of North American English. Many of the symbols are taken from the International Phonetic Alphabet, which is a much larger set of symbols that can be used to transcribe any language or to show pronunciation variations among different speakers of the same language.

The charts also include words shown in conventional print to illustrate how the sound represented by each symbol is *usually* pronounced in North America. These words are intended as a general guide only. The pronunciation of words varies, and a particular word may be pronounced differently in your region. In most areas of North America, for example, *knotty* and *naughty* sound exactly the same. In other varieties of English, especially British English, the vowel sounds are different. When dealing with the examples given in any pronunciation guide, regional variations must always be taken into account.

To distinguish English phonemes from alphabetic letters, phonemes are usually enclosed between two slashes. For example, /s/ represents the phoneme that may be spelled *s* as in *sip*, *ss* as in *hiss*, *ps* as in *psychology*, *c* as in *cent*, *sc* as in *scent*, and so on. The word *cent* is represented as /sɛnt/.

As you review the charts, read aloud each example word to hear how it sounds. If this is the first time you have done this, you may be surprised at how many ways there are of representing some sounds. Language teachers may need to refer to this chart — or another similar one — regularly to identify the specific sounds that are causing difficulty for some students.

Learning the Sounds of English

Most problems with pronunciation in a second language are the result of **interference** from the first language. Interference refers to a learner's transfer of features of the sound system of her or his first language to the

Consonants

Many of the symbols for the consonant sounds of English are the same as the letters of the alphabet that represent the sounds. Others are different because no letter accurately represents them.

Symbol	Examples
b	bite, rumble, object, table, rib
k	keep, akin, bark, bike, ink, coil, question, chorus, acknowledge, anchor, back
d	do, radio, undo, did, bend, water, butter, metal, medal, waiting, wading
f	fill, roofing, after, life, shelf, phone, trophy, cough
g	give, begin, ingrown, leg, rogue, song, exact, examine, example
h	have, hold, ahead, unholy, whole
l	list, please, allow, cool, apple
m	map, hammer, impure, time, comb, thumb
n	next, runner, anvil, rain, plane, pneumatic, mnemonic, knot
p	pig, open, staple, stop, pump
r	run, arrange, unrest, car, wrist, wrench, awry, unwritten
s	sent, also, assent, list, kiss, cent, scent, ascent, listen, ice, locks, lox, psychology
t	take, attack, cat, can't, ptomaine, ptarmigan, Ptolemy
v	van, avail, envy, give, delve
w	well, wait, await, unwilling, what, while, one, anguish, language, Ouija
y	you, yawn, soya, unyielding, use, usual, ewes, amuse, few
z	zoo, razor, ozone, ooze, prize, comprise, prison, gives, lies, loses, exact
tʃ	child, achieve, inch, future
dʒ	jump, enjoy, giant, agile, engine, lodge, sponge, exaggerate
ʃ	shut, ashes, motion, tissue, conscious, ancient, fuchsia, rush, microfiche
θ	think, ether, anthem, tooth, ninth, length
ð	these, either, rhythm, smooth, soothe
ʒ	genre, measure, occasion, azure, presume, unusual, beige
ŋ	angle, anguish, language, English, ring, boring

Voiced and Unvoiced Consonants

Consonants are voiced or unvoiced. To see the difference, hold the tips of your fingers against your throat and make the sound [z]. You will feel your vocal chords vibrate. Now make the sound [s]. You will feel no vibration in your vocal chords. The phoneme /z/ is voiced, and /s/ is unvoiced.

Voiced		Unvoiced	
b	bat	p	pat
d	den	t	ten
g	gate	k	Kate
v	vine	f	fine
z	zip	s	sip
ð	thy	θ	thigh
ʒ	vision	ʃ	fission
dʒ	joke	tʃ	choke

Vowels and Diphthongs

In print, the letters *a, e, i, o, u,* and *y* are used in a variety of combinations to represent the vowel sounds of English. Though the number of English vowel phonemes varies among dialects and regions, the following are the most common.

ɪ	it, bit, crystal, exact, women
ɛ	end, pen, correct
æ	angle, man, meringue, can, can't, bath
ɑ	pot, got, bought, father, law, cot, caught, offal, awful, shone, Sean, clod, clawed
ʊ	put, pudding, foot, look, could
o	bore, four, for, fore, door
ʌ	up, but, jump, butter, undo
ə	about, rotten, forget, sofa, the, Roman, father This is the most common vowel sound in English. It is sometimes called a schwa.

Some vowel sounds are diphthongs, which combine two vowel sounds:

iy	evil, eat, meat, meet, meter, thief, receive
ey	ate, day, rain, rein, reign, weight, hay, hey, plate
uw	too, two, to, cruise, tune, noon, neutral, through, threw, true, blue
ow	ode, boat, alone, though, so, sow, sew, potato, toe
ay	by, buy, mine, lie, fly, find, fine, site, sight, sign, high, height
aw	cow, out, bough
oy	boy, oil, join, Freud

new language. This occurs because the sounds of the first language are imprinted very early in a child's development. Most children are born with the vocal equipment to produce the sounds of any language. At the babbling stage, however, babies begin to tune their repertoire of sounds, patterning their production on the sounds they hear around them. Most infants stop producing — and gradually lose the ability to produce — sounds that are not part of their language environment. As a result, it is often difficult later on for second language learners to produce sounds or combinations of sounds that do not exist in their own language.

Individual Sounds and Combinations of Sounds

Some sounds of English are especially difficult for speakers of other languages. For example, the sound /θ/ in *think* and its voiced equivalent, /ð/, in *then*, are uncommon in the languages of the world. As a result, many learners of English produce the closest match from their own language. Thus, *think* may be pronounced as "tink" or "sink," while *then* may be pronounced as "den" or "zen."

Some vowel sounds pose problems as well. English, for example, distinguishes between the sounds /iy/, as in *seat*, and /ɪ/, as in *sit*. Many languages include only one of these sounds, so that students may have trouble distinguishing them in spoken language and may pronounce them the same way. This problem can also affect spelling.

Just as individual sounds differ among languages, so does the way sounds are combined. English, for example, includes many **consonant clusters**, a term that refers to two or more consonants appearing in a row, as in *desks, split, cluster*. Some languages, such as Cantonese and Vietnamese, have no consonant clusters; others use consonant clusters differently from English. In English, for example, the consonant cluster /kn/, in which both [k] and [n] are pronounced, sometimes appears in the middle of words (e.g., *acknowledge*), but never at the beginning of words. In Russian and some other Slavic languages, this cluster occurs at the beginning of words (e.g., *kniga — book*).

Learners of English often experience difficulty with consonant clusters and develop a variety of strategies for dealing with these difficult sound combinations. In Spanish, for example, clusters beginning with [s] do not begin words. As a result, Spanish speakers often pronounce a word like *street* as /ɛstriyt/. And in Farsi, every consonant is paired with a vowel. As a result, Farsi speakers often try to add a lax, or weak, vowel either before or in the middle of English consonant clusters. As a result, they may pronounce a word like *place* as /pɛleys/. They may have special difficulty with clusters of three consonants and often try to insert two additional vowel sounds, so that word like *street* may be pronounced /ɛstɛriyt/. Cantonese and Vietnamese speakers, by contrast, may eliminate one of the consonant sounds in a cluster, so *street* may be pronounced /sriyt/. At the end of a word, they may pronounce only the first sound in a cluster, so that a word like *fast* is pronounced as /fæs/.

Stressed and Unstressed Syllables

Stress refers to the degree of force with which a syllable is uttered. In all English words of more than one syllable, one of the syllables is uttered with stronger stress, or emphasis, than others (e.g., **syl**lable). Though no infallible rule governs which syllable is stressed, some useful generalizations can be made.

Why Are These Sentences ~~Sew Sow~~ So Hard ~~two too~~ to ~~Reed~~ Read ~~Allowed~~ Aloud?

We polish the Polish furniture.

He could lead if he would get the lead out.

A farm can produce produce.

The dump was so full it had to refuse refuse.

The soldier decided to desert in the desert.

The present is a good time to present the present.

At the army base, a sea bass was painted on the head of a bass drum.

The dove dove into the bushes.

I did not object to the object.

The insurance for the invalid was invalid.

The bandage was wound around the wound.

There was a row among the oarsmen about how to row.

They were too close to the door to close it.

The buck does funny things when the does are present.

They sent a sewer down to stitch the tear in the sewer line.

To help with planting, the farmer taught his sow to sow.

The wind was too strong to wind the sail.

After a number of anesthetic injections, my jaw got number.

I shed a tear when I saw the tear in my clothes.

I had to subject the subject to a series of tests.

How can I intimate this to my most intimate friend?

I spent last evening evening out a pile of dirt.

Syllable Stress in English	
Generalization	Examples
In about 75 percent of two-syllable words, the first syllable is stressed.	**lan**guage **ac**cent **stu**dent **Eng**lish **tea**cher
In some two-syllable words, the second syllable is stressed.	pro**nounce** be**come** ap**ply**
Some two-syllable words can be used as nouns or verbs. When the word is a noun, the first syllable is stressed; when it is a verb, the second is stressed.	Keep a **re**cord of the experiment. Re**cord** every step of the procedure.
Words of three or more syllables usually include a major stress, a minor stress, and one or more unstressed syllables. In the examples, the major stress is in boldface and the minor stress is underlined.	**dif**fi<u>cult</u> <u>un</u>der**stand** pro<u>nun</u>ciation <u>bio</u>**log**ical <u>per</u>se**ver**ance
An important characteristic of English is the reduction of the vowel sound in unstressed syllables. The vowel in unstressed syllables is usually pronounced /ə/ (e.g., *written* — /rɪtən/).	for**get** con**nect** al**ter** a**round** pro**nounce** stu**dent**
In some words, the unstressed syllable is pronounced /ɪ/ (e.g., depend — /dɪpɛnd/).	**want**ed ex**am**ple **lan**guage
In compound nouns, the major stress is on the first part of the word.	**hand**bag **news**paper **fire**fighter **wa**tershed
In compound verbs, the major stress is on the second part of the word, and the minor stress is on the first part.	over**come** under**stand** under**mine** over**look**
When a suffix is added to a word, the stress pattern doesn't usually change.	**dif**ficult — **dif**ficulty under**stand** — under**stand**able
When a suffix is added to a word ending in *-tion*, *-sion*, *-ic*, *-ical*, or *-ity*, the major stress is usually on the syllable that precedes the suffix.	e**volve** — evolution phonology — phono**log**ical

These generalizations apply only to English. Stress patterns are different in other languages. In French, for example, the final syllable of a word is usually stressed. In other languages, such as Jamaican Creole, all syllables are stressed equally. As a result, many learners of English find it very hard at first to even hear unstressed syllables in an English sentence. To many learners, it sounds as if English speakers are swallowing their words. As a result, it may be very difficult for learners to understand what is being said.

When speaking, English language learners often stress syllables that are usually unstressed in English, which tends to make some words almost unintelligible to English-speaking listeners. For this reason, it is extremely important to provide opportunities for students to hear and practice saying new words.

Rhythm

English speech has a characteristic **rhythm**, or stress pattern, that is different from that of many other languages. In connected English speech, the stresses or beats are spaced evenly through sentences. All sentences with the same number of major stresses take about the same amount of time to utter because the time between stressed syllables is the same, no matter how many minor stresses and unstressed syllables separate these syllables. The unstressed words and syllables are compressed or reduced to make this possible.

Read the following sentences aloud:

●	●	●
John	**speaks**	**French.**
John is	**speak**ing	**Eng**lish.
Jonathan is	**speak**ing	**Roma**nian.

All three sentences take about the same amount of time to say, although the second and third have more syllables than the first. The unstressed syllables are compressed and de-emphasized to make this possible. In many other languages, equal stress is placed on all the syllables in words. When speakers of those languages attempt to give equal time or emphasis to every syllable in an English word or sentence, the effect is strange to the ears of English speakers. Some students need to hear and repeat new words, on their own and in longer phrases and sentences, to distinguish and produce the stress patterns of English.

SENTENCE STRESS

In an English sentence, the words that carry the most information are stressed. These are often called content words. Words that carry less information are usually unstressed, even though they perform grammatical work — unless the speaker wishes to create a particular emphasis. These words are often called function words.

Because the characteristic rhythm of English affects the way words are pronounced in connected speech, beginning learners of English often have trouble understanding speech, even though they may recognize the same words in isolation or when they are carefully enunciated.

- The reduction of function words can cause phrases to sound like single words. In normal speech, for example, the individual words in the following phrases are not distinct:

fish and chips	sounds like	/fɪʃəntʃɪps/
a jug of milk	sounds like	/ədʒʌgəmɪlk/
all of them	sounds like	/ɑləvəm/
going to	sounds like	/gɑnə/
got to	sounds like	/gɑdə/
What do you mean?	sounds like	/wɑdəyəmiyn/

- Contractions are common in connected speech. Beginning learners may have difficulty recognizing contractions in both speech and writing.

Stressed and Unstressed Words	
Content Words (stressed)	Function Words (unstressed)
Nouns	Articles: *a, an, the*
Main verbs	Prepositions: *to, of, on, in*, etc.
Adverbs	Auxiliary verbs: *is, are, have, has, do, does*, etc.
Adjectives	
Question words: *why, when*, etc.	Modal auxiliary verbs: *can, will, must*, etc.
Demonstratives: *this, these*, etc.	Conjunctions: *but, so, and*, etc.
	Relative pronouns: *which, that*, etc.
	pronouns: *I, you, it, us*, etc.

Full Form	Usual Pronunciation	Written Contraction	Example
we have	/wiyv/	we've	We've done it.
I will	/ayəl/	I'll	I'll do it.
we are	/wiyər/	we're	We're going to be late.

- Some contracted forms are indistinguishable from one another, which may confuse learners.

Full Form	Usual Pronunciation	Written Contraction	Example
he would	/hiyd/	he'd	He said he'd do it.
he had	/hiyd/	he'd	He said he'd done it.
she has	/ʃiyz/	she's	She's already left.
she is	/ʃiyz/	she's	She's leaving.

- In connected speech, individual sounds may be omitted, especially when they occur in consonant clusters. For example, the word *next* is usually pronounced without the final [t] when the following word begins with a consonant, so that *next month* sounds like *necks month*. The omission of this final consonant often makes it difficult for learners to hear grammatical endings, such as past-tense verb endings, in English. Say the following pairs of sentences aloud in a normal way, noticing what happens to some of the past tense endings:

We watch TV.	We watched TV.
Education can open doors for you.	Education opened doors for me.
Stop talking!	They stopped talking.

Intonation

Intonation refers to characteristic patterns of rise and fall in pitch. English has three basic levels of tone: high, mid, and low. These are used in two main intonation patterns: rising-falling and rising.

- A rising-falling intonation pattern is used for most statements, as well as for questions that begin with a question-word, such as *who* or *what*. The pitch of the voice rises to a high tone at the major stress in the sentence, then falls through the rest of the sentence to end at a pitch lower than that of the first part of the sentence. Say the following sentence aloud and listen to the way your voice begins at mid-tone, rises to a high tone, then falls to a low tone.

I had to go to the | **su** | permarket.

- A rising-falling intonation is used in each clause of a complex sentence, dropping lower still at the end of the final clause.

Although he | **came** | l ate, he | **fin** | ished the work.

- A rising-falling intonation is also used in tag questions when the intent is to seek agreement.

She's a good | **teach** | er, | **is** | n't she?

- A rising intonation is used in questions that require a yes-or-no answer. The pitch begins to rise on the major sentence stress — and continues rising.

Is it **rain**ing?

Do you speak **Eng**lish?

- A rising intonation marks the end of statements that express doubt, seek clarification, or ask a question.

It's **rain**ing? You speak **Eng**lish?

- Arising intonation is also used within sentences to indicate continuation (e.g., when reciting words in a list or series).

She speaks **Eng**lish, **Span**ish, **Ital**ian, and **Ger**man.

- A rising intonation is used in tag questions when the intent is to seek information.

She speaks **Eng**lish, **doesn't** she?

In English, intonation is also used to communicate meanings that may be quite different from the surface meaning of an utterance. "Yeah, right!" may indicate agreement or sarcastic disagreement, for example. Intonation is also used to communicate emotions or moods such as boredom, enthusiasm, surprise, anger, and affection. When uttered a certain way, an expression like "Oh, you fool!" can be a term of endearment, for example. This emotional content can be very difficult for learners of English to detect.

The intonation patterns of other languages are different from those of English. In some languages, more changes in pitch occur. In **tone languages**, such as Cantonese and Vietnamese, individual words may be spoken at a different pitch or tone. These languages include many homophones, and only the tone enables listeners to distinguish the meaning of two or more otherwise identical words. In Vietnamese, for example, the word *ba* may mean six different things, depending on the tone used.

When the intonation patterns of a language with a greater range of pitch are applied to English, the effect may be disconcerting to English speakers. Speakers of languages that mark statements and questions differently from English, for example, may use a rising pitch when English would use a falling tone and vice versa. As a result, statements may sound like questions. To English speakers, inappropriate intonation may sometimes sound abrupt or impolite because the wrong word is emphasized. At the same time, speakers of languages in which the range of pitch is narrower than in English may sound bored or uninvolved — to English speakers. Many learners need focused instruction on the English intonation patterns used to ask questions and make polite requests and suggestions.

An important feature of English intonation is its use of higher pitch and volume to signal emphasis. Emphasizing a particular word changes the meaning of a sentence, as the following examples show:

I didn't give the book to Mei. (Someone else gave her the book.)
I **didn't** give the book to Mei. (… although you think I did.)
I didn't **give** the book to Mei. (I only lent it to her, or she took it from me.)
I didn't give the **book** to Mei. (I gave her something else.)
I didn't give the book to **Mei**. (I gave it to someone else.)

Some languages indicate emphasis by changing the order of the words in sentences, rather than through intonation. As a result, some learners of English need to practice listening to contrasting emphatic utterances in order to help them distinguish the emphasis and understand its meaning.

Teaching Pronunciation

Younger children who are learning English seldom need a great deal of help with pronunciation, although some sounds may be difficult for some students. Learners older than 11 or 12 are more likely to have trouble with specific words, sounds, and intonation patterns and will probably need focused instruction in some areas. Listen carefully as students speak or read aloud. You may notice that individual students or members of specific language groups have specific pronunciation difficulties. Some students whose first language does not include [w], for example, may substitute [v], so that *wet* sounds like *vet*; on the other hand, students whose first language includes [w] sound but no [v] may do the opposite.

When to Teach Pronunciation

Avoid interrupting or correcting a student's speech in front of the class. If the student's speech is so unclear that other students do not understand, repeat or paraphrase without drawing direct attention to the problem. Make a note of the problem so that you can provide focused instruction individually or with a small group at an appropriate time. Because students of different language backgrounds have different problems with the pronunciation of English, it is not always appropriate to deal with a specific pronunciation problem with the whole class — even an ESL class — unless the whole class shares a common first language.

Do not expect all students to end up sounding like native speakers of English. Most children who begin learning English before puberty will acquire a local accent, but this is neither a realistic nor a desirable goal for most adolescents and adults. Learning the sound system of a new language tends to be more difficult for older students, who are often more self-conscious than young children about experimenting with a new language and using their tongue and lips in unfamiliar ways. They may feel awkward and embarrassed. In addition, some may feel that striving to speak English without an accent implies giving up their own cultural identity.

For all students, the goal should be to speak English intelligibly, to communicate accurately, and to avoid forms of pronunciation that may be stigmatized in the wider society. As a result, it is important to provide focused instruction when

- a student confuses or distorts specific sounds that may interfere with listeners' comprehension. It can be confusing, for example, if a speaker pronounces the [iy] in *seat* as the /ɪ/ in *sit* and vice versa.
- a student uses pronunciations that may be stigmatized by native speakers. Some learners substitute [t] for /θ/, for example, so that *three* sounds like *tree*. Among English speakers, this pronunciation is associated with very young children who are learning to talk. When older children and adults pronounce [θ] as [t], English

speakers may subconsciously view their speech — and by association, their intellect — as childish or undeveloped.

- a student distorts the pronunciation of words by stressing the wrong syllable, or by giving unstressed syllables equal emphasis. The word *examine*, for example, is normally pronounced /ɪgzæmɪn/, with the major stress on the second syllable. The word becomes unintelligible if it is pronounced as /ɛksəmayn/, with the major stress on the first syllable, the second syllable unstressed, and the final vowel sound pronounced as it is in words like *mine*, *line*, and *fine*.
- inappropriate intonation leads to a mistaken conclusion that the student is bored, tentative, deferential, overbearing, or aggressive.

How to Teach Pronunciation

Second language learners may have difficulty not only in *producing* some of the sounds of English, but also in *hearing* the difference between the way they produce a sound and the way the sound is produced by a native speaker of English. For this reason, instruction in pronunciation begins with helping students develop their **phonemic awareness**: the ability to perceive sounds and subtle differences among sounds.

The following strategies help raise students' phonemic awareness and improve their articulation and intonation of English words and phrases:

- Read aloud often so that students become familiar with the rhythm and intonation patterns of English.
- Read the same statement several different ways, using intonation to communicate different meanings. Invite students to figure out the differences in meaning.
- Encourage students to listen to books on tape while they follow along in a printed text. They can rewind when they hear a new or difficult word. For more ideas on using books on tape, see Chapter 11.
- Choose language arts software that allows students to point to or click on specific items to hear how the words are pronounced. Make sure that the voice quality of the program is true to life: much computer speech lacks stress and intonation, and you don't want your students to sound like robots!
- Lead students in choral readings of sentences and paragraphs to help them produce the stress and intonation patterns of English. Jazz chants that set common expressions and sentence patterns to music are especially effective in helping learners of all ages internalize stress and intonation patterns, as well as common expressions and grammatical patterns. For more information about jazz chants, see "To Learn More …" at the end of this chapter.
- Introduce **minimal pairs** to help students perceive differences between sounds. Minimal pairs are pairs of words that are identical except for one specific vowel or consonant sound (e.g., *sit* and *seat*, *slip* and *sleep*). Always use real words and, as far as possible, use words that students already know. For younger children or beginning language learners, draw a picture to illustrate each word.

    Ask students to listen as you say each word while pointing to an appropriate picture. Be sure to pronounce each word in the pair with exactly the same intonation: the two should sound identical

Recognizing rhyme is an important aspect of phonemic awareness.

except for the specific vowel or consonant contrast you are focusing on. In normal spoken English, the second word of each pair would be spoken with a falling intonation, which may cause students from tone-language backgrounds to assume that the tone, rather than the sound, distinguishes the words. You may need to pay special attention in order to produce "toneless" intonation for this activity.

You can also read the pairs, some with the same and some with different sounds, and ask students to identify which are the same and different.

Minimal Pairs

These examples of minimal pairs can be used to contrast the pronunciation of /θ/ and /t/ at the beginning and end of words.

thin	tin
thick	tick
thank	tank
three	tree
through	true
thread	tread
hearth	heart
tenth	tent
both	boat
bath	bat

- Distribute a list of minimal pairs or a set of pictures that represent the words. Read aloud one word from each pair and ask students to circle the appropriate word or picture. You may need to repeat this activity several times on different days — as well as individually with some students — until they can really *hear* the difference.

- When students can hear the difference between the two words in minimal pairs, they are ready to practice producing the sounds. Ask them to say a pair of words so that the difference is clearly heard. Do this chorally at first, then individually. To help students produce some sounds, you may need to show them how to position the tongue, lips, and teeth. Mirrors and diagrams may help show the position of the lips, teeth, and tongue, and a feather can demonstrate how air escapes on plosive sounds, such as [p]. Try to make this experience fun, not embarrassing!

- Make up a few sentences that include words containing the contrasting sounds (e.g., Sit in your seat and eat your dinner!) and ask students to read them aloud chorally, then individually.

- Encourage students to create illustrated posters or booklets featuring specific sounds, such as [θ] and [t]. Students of the same language background often experience similar pronunciation problems and could work together on this project. They can take the booklet home to practice or work with a peer tutor. Each day listen to one or two students as they read some of the captions aloud.

- When introducing new words during a lesson, always include pronunciation practice. Say the word, articulating clearly, and write it on the chalkboard. Then say it again, articulating slowly, pointing to each syllable, and emphasizing the main stress on polysyllabic words, such as *evolution*. Point out how the stress shifts when different forms of the word are used (e.g., *evolve* and *evolution*, *photograph* and *photographer*, *examine* and *examination*).

  Say the word again in a more natural way and instruct students to repeat it, both chorally and individually. The next time students enter the room, ask them to pronounce words they learned during the previous lesson.

- Teach older students how to use pronunciation guides. Show students how to find these in various resources, such as dictionaries, and point out that many different systems are used.

- Invite students to rehearse, then read aloud, short passages from familiar texts.

- Distribute a list of minimal pairs and encourage students to create a skit that includes some of the words.

To Learn More ...

Books and Audio Materials

Avery, P., and S. Ehrlich. *Teaching American English Pronunciation*. Oxford, U.K.: Oxford University Press, 1992.
Readable and comprehensive introduction to the sound system of English. Includes helpful information about the specific difficulties of students of various language backgrounds, as well as suggestions for teaching pronunciation.

Baker, A., and B. Goldstein. *Pronunciation Pairs*. Cambridge, U.K.: Cambridge University Press, 1990.
Student's book, audiotapes, and teacher's guide provide exercises and communicative activities for specific sounds, stress patterns, and intonation patterns of North American English. Teacher's guide includes a diagnostic test that can be used to identify specific problems.

Celce-Murcia, M., D.M. Brinton, and J.M. Goodwin. *Teaching Pronunciation: A Reference for Teachers of English to Speakers of Other Languages*. Cambridge, U.K.: Cambridge University Press, 1996.
Comprehensive reference work for ESL teachers. Accompanying audiocassette provides oral language samples for practice in assessing learners' needs.

Chernen, J. *Interactive Pronunciation Games*. Vancouver, B.C.: Vancouver Community College, 2000.
Activities focus on distinguishing minimal pairs, intonation, word stress, and sentence stress and reinforce useful vocabulary and clarification language. Can be photocopied and adapted to the needs of learners of various ages.

English Language Learning and Instruction System. ELLIS Master Pronunciation. <http://ellis.com >.
Software that helps learners improve pronunciation and listening comprehension.

Encomium Publications. Pronunciation Power. <http://encomium.com/pp/en/products.html>.
CD-ROMs use sound samples, photographs, and diagrams to teach the sounds of English.

Fairfield Language Technologies. The Rosetta Stone. <www.RosettaStone.com/ESL/index.html>.
ESL software package includes a speech recognition component.

Gilbert, J. *Clear Speech: Pronunciation and Listening Comprehension in American English*. 2nd ed. Cambridge, U.K.: Cambridge University Press, 1993.
Student's book, audiocassettes, and teacher's manual provide clear explanations and practice activities with a strong emphasis on intonation, stress, and rhythm.

Gilbert, J. *Clear Speech from the Start: Basic Pronunciation and Listening Comprehension in American English*. Cambridge, U.K.: Cambridge University Press, 2000.
Text and accompanying audiotape help beginning English language learners recognize and produce the sounds, intonation, and stress patterns necessary to communicate intelligibly with English speakers.

Graham, C. *Jazz Chants: Rhythms of American English for Students of English as a Second Language*. New York: Oxford University Press, 1978.
An enduring classic that introduced a series of titles. Available in book and audiocassette format, the chants use jazz rhythms to help students improve pronunciation and intonation and practice specific grammar patterns.

Grant, L. *Well Said: Pronunciation for Clear Communication*. 2nd ed. Boston, Mass.: Heinle and Heinle, 2000.
Designed for use with adult learners, book is a useful resource for all language teachers and can be used by older secondary students for independent study. Audiotape is also available.

Laroy, C. *Pronunciation*. Oxford, U.K.: Oxford University Press, 1995.
Includes many ideas for improving rhythm, stress, and intonation, as well as the articulation of individual sounds.

Swan, M., and B. Smith. *Learner English: A Teacher's Guide to Interference and Other Problems*. 2nd ed. Cambridge, U.K.: Cambridge University Press, 2001.
Information about the phonological system and grammatical structure of more than 20 languages, as well as specific difficulties that may be experienced by speakers of those languages. Audiocassette and CD are also available.

Weinstein, N. *Whaddaya Say: Guided Practice in Relaxed Speech*. 2nd ed. White Plains, N.Y.: Addison-Wesley, 2000.
Activities to help learners recognize and begin to produce the most common reduced forms of spoken English, such as *gonna*, *wanna*, etc. Audiocassette is available.

Websites and Online Resources

Office of English Language and Writing Support, University of Toronto. <www.sgs.utoronto.ca/english/pd/pronunciation.htm>.
Designed to support graduate students at the University of Toronto, site provides links to Web-based resources on various aspects of language use, including pronunciation. Good background material for teachers.

New Okanagan College. English Pronunciation. <http://international.ouc.bc.ca/pronunciation>.
Uses sound samples and graphics to demonstrate pronunciation. Online practice exercises also available.

4 No More Red Pen: Teaching English Grammar

Do you sometimes feel overwhelmed by the many grammatical errors made by second language learners? Do you have trouble understanding why students make these errors? Are you sometimes uncertain about how to explain the correct forms? In response to problems such as these, teachers sometimes resort to the red-pen approach, correcting and circling all errors in students' work in the hope that they will learn from this. The practice of using codes such as *sp* to indicate spelling errors and *gr* to indicate grammar errors has been described as "spitting and growling in the margin."

This chapter discusses some of the features of English grammar that can be difficult for English language learners. It also presents approaches to grammar instruction and feedback that can be integrated into daily lessons. These approaches enable teachers to set aside the red pen, stop spitting and growling, and provide effective instruction and supportive feedback.

The Rules of Language

Breaking the Rules?

Winston Churchill, the former prime minister of the United Kingdom, was noted for his skilled use of language. When a report he was reading contained a particularly stilted sentence written to avoid placing a preposition at the end, Churchill is said to have scribbled this famous comment in the margin: "This is the sort of bloody nonsense up with which I will not put!"

Many of the traditional grammar rules that people learned in school are prescriptive and proscriptive, describing what English speakers *should* and *should not* say or write if they expect to be viewed as polite or educated. You may have learned, for example, that *whom* is the correct form to use as the object of a preposition and that sentences should not end with prepositions. According to these rules, it is correct to say, "To whom do you think you're talking?" and incorrect to say, "Who do you think you're talking to?" Many of these rules apply only in the most formal situations, however; in most contexts, following them sounds forced and pedantic. Most native speakers of English actually say, "Who do you think you're talking to?"

Early prescriptive and proscriptive rules sometimes applied the conventions of Latin grammar to English. Because these rules took into account neither language change nor stylistic and regional variations, however, they did not necessarily reflect the way English was actually spoken. Few second language learners wish to end up sounding like a grammar book; they want to learn the language as it is really used — in both formal and informal settings, and in speech and writing — by native speakers of English.

This chapter takes a *descriptive* approach to language conventions. It describes what native speakers do when they use English. Consider the following conventions:

- The article *a* is used before nouns beginning with a consonant sound, and *an* is used before nouns beginning with a vowel sound.
- The simple past tense of *go* is *went*.

Most native speakers of English follow these conventions with little or no conscious awareness, and some may not even be able to state them when asked. Instead, they do what "sounds" right because they have internalized the patterns without explicit instruction. Indeed, children acquire most of the grammar of their first language before they even start school.

It takes many years, however, for second language learners to acquire all the patterns or conventions of English grammar. To plan an effective instructional program, teachers, and especially language teachers, must have an awareness of English grammar and the difficulties that learners may encounter.

What Is Grammar?

Grammar refers to the language patterns that indicate relationships among words in sentences. Take, for example, the English words *give, book, teacher,* and *student*. These words can be combined in many different ways to create a sentence that makes sense in English — and the way they are combined indicates the relationship among the words. Who gives the book? When? To whom? Which book, teacher, or student? How many books, students, or teachers? Is this a question or a statement?

The following are some of the ways in which these words can be organized or transformed grammatically:

The teacher gave the book to the student.

The teacher gave the book to a student.

The teacher will give a book to the student.

The teacher gave the books to the student.

A student's book was given to the teacher.

Did the teacher give the book to the student?

Has the teacher given the book to a student?

Will (would, can, may, could, should) the teacher give a book to the student?

The student gave (will give, has given, etc.) the books to the teacher.

The teacher was given some students' books.

Elements of English Grammar

The study of English grammar usually includes both **morphology** and **syntax**. Morphology refers to the study of word structure, while syntax involves the study of word combinations or sentence structure.

Morphology

As the smallest contrastive unit of grammar, **morphemes** are the building blocks of words. The word *words*, for example, is made up of two morphemes: the first is *word*, and the second is the suffix -s, which means more than one.

Morphemes are different from syllables. Some single-syllable words, such as *word*, do consist of one morpheme. This is not always the case, however. *Words*, for example, is a single-syllable word that consists of two morphemes.

Derivational morphemes are affixes (prefixes or suffixes) that are added to words to form new words (e.g., *possible — impossible, impossibility*). To learn more about derivational morphemes, see Chapter 5.

Inflectional morphemes provide grammatical information about gender, number, person, case, degree, and verb form. Though most inflectional morphemes are suffixes, some irregular forms do exist (e.g., *men* is the plural of *man*).

GENDER

In many languages, nouns are assigned a **gender**. They are masculine, feminine, or in some languages, neuter. Grammatical gender often has little to do with biological gender, however. In French, for example, *girl* is feminine (*la fille*), while it is neuter in German (*das Mädchen*). *Table* is feminine in French (*la table*) and masculine in German (*der Tisch*). English does not make this distinction, though cars and boats are sometimes referred to as "she" or "her."

In some languages, different forms of a word indicate whether a person is male or female (e.g., *le directeur* and *la directrice* in French). English, too, sometimes uses different forms to indicate biological gender, especially when describing occupations (e.g., *waiter* and *waitress*). Recently, however, gender-neutral forms, such as *server*, have become more common.

Some English pronouns also indicate gender (e.g., *he-she, him-her, his-her*, and *his-hers*), while others do not (e.g., *I, you,* and *we*). In some languages, gender distinctions are made in all pronoun forms; in others, no distinctions exist.

Learner Errors

Learners who have not yet acquired all the forms of the English pronoun system may produce errors such as, *I like Sara. He is very kind.* This may happen even among those who are at very advanced levels of learning English.

NUMBER

In English grammar, **number** refers to the distinction between one (singular) and more than one (plural).

The plural of English nouns is usually formed by adding an inflectional suffix, which is written as *-s* or *-es* and pronounced /s/ as in *books*, /z/ as in *pencils*, or /ɪz/ as in *boxes*. Some irregular plurals (e.g., *men*, *women*, and *children*) also exist, and some plurals are the same as the singular form (e.g., *sheep*); others change the final consonant before adding the plural suffix (e.g., *knives*).

English pronouns also have plural and singular forms (e.g., *I-we* and *she-they*).

In English, countable, or count, nouns are handled differently from uncountable, or non-count, nouns. Count nouns, such as *boy* and *book*, have plural forms (*boys* and *books*), while non-count nouns, such as *milk*, are always singular and have no plural form. English speakers do not say *several milks*, for example. Though the concept of count and non-count nouns is not unknown in other languages, it may not apply to the same words as it does in English.

Learner Errors

Learners may omit plural suffixes, especially when the context supports the concept. They may, for example, produce phrases something like *a man with blue eye*. Beginning learners may also have difficulty with irregular plural forms, producing things like *two mans* or *three mices*.

Learners may also have trouble with count and non-count nouns. *Rice*, for example, is a non-count noun in English but a count noun in other languages. As a result, English language learners may say something like, "Wash your rices."

PERSON

Person is a grammatical form that applies to pronouns and affects the form of verbs. Pronouns may be first, second, or third person, as shown on the following chart.

Pronouns		
Person	**Singular**	**Plural**
First	I	we
Second	you	you
Third	he, she, it	they

Though the form of verbs does change to indicate, among other things, the time of an action, only one form of regular verbs — the present-tense, third-person singular — changes to indicate person by adding an -*s* or -*es* (e.g., *she plays, he sings, it rains, she passes*). In spoken English, this suffix may be pronounced /s/ (e.g., *she wants*), /z/ (e.g., *it rains*), or /ɪz/ (e.g., *she passes*). This feature of English is called subject-verb agreement.

English also includes many verbs that do not follow an established pattern, however. The third-person, present-tense singular form of *have* is *has*, for example, and the verb *be* has many different forms in the present and past tenses, as shown on the following chart.

Conjugation of *Be*				
	Present Tense		**Past Tense**	
Person	**Singular**	**Plural**	**Singular**	**Plural**
First	I am	we are	I was	we were
Second	you are	you are	you were	you were
Third	he (she, it) is	they are	he (she, it) was	they were

Learner Errors

Subject-verb agreement is a continuing source of difficulty for second language learners, even at advanced levels. Students may produce errors such as, *She never come here, They was very late,* and *Why don't he like it?*

CASE

In English grammar, **case** refers to noun and pronoun forms that indicate grammatical relationships to other words.

English nouns have only one morphological case, indicating possession. This is indicated in writing by adding the suffix -'*s* or -*s*' (e.g., *the boy's books, the boys' books,* and *a summer's day*). This suffix may be pronounced /s/ (e.g., *the cat's basket* and *the cats' basket*), /z/ (e.g., *the boy's book* and *the boys' book*), or /ɪz/ (e.g., *the fox's den* and *the foxes' den*).

English pronouns have three cases: subjective, objective, and possessive, as shown on the following chart.

Case of English Pronouns		
Subjective	**Objective**	**Possessive**
I	me	my, mine
you	you	your, yours
he	him	his
she	her	her, hers
you	you	your, yours
we	us	our, ours
they	them	their, theirs

Learner Errors

English language learners often experience difficulty learning pronoun forms, especially in the early stages. As a result, beginners may produce errors such as, *This is yours book.* They may also omit the possessive suffix on nouns, as in, *I like Aresh picture.*

DEGREE

To express degrees of comparison, English uses the suffixes *-er, -est,* or separate words such as *more* and *less.* The basic patterns are as follows:

- Most one-syllable regular adjectives and adverbs add *-er* to create the comparative form and *-est* to create the superlative (e.g., *tall, taller, tallest* and *fast, faster, fastest*).
- One-syllable adjectives consisting of a consonant-vowel-consonant "sandwich" double the final consonant when adding a suffix: (e.g., *big, bigger, biggest*).
- Most two-syllable regular adjectives ending in *-y, -ly,* and *-le* also add *-er* and *–est* (e.g., *happy, happier, happiest* [note spelling change]; *friendly, friendlier, friendliest*; and *simple, simpler, simplest*).
- The comparative and superlative forms of most regular adjectives of two or more syllables are created by using *more* and *most* or *less* and *least* (e.g., *intelligent, more [less] intelligent, most [least] intelligent*).
- The comparative and superlative forms of all adverbs ending in *-ly* are created by using *more* and *most* or *less* and *least* (e.g., *easily, more [less] easily, most [least] easily*).
- Other adverbs have irregular forms, as shown on the chart.

Comparison of Irregular Adjectives and Adverbs		
Adjective or Adverb	**Comparative Form**	**Superlative Form**
good	better	best
bad	worse	worst
little	less	least
few	fewer	fewest
much	more	most
many	more	most
well	better	best
badly	worse	worst

Learner Errors

Learners may overgeneralize the use of *-er* and *-est,* producing constructions such as, *She is the intelligentest student in the class.* Learners may also omit the definite article in superlative forms, as in, *He is tallest student.* Many second language learners — and some English speakers — confuse *less* and *fewer,* as well as *least* and *fewest.* They may produce errors such as, *I have less books than you do,* or *This one costs the fewest money.*

VERB FORMS

The form of the verb may indicate tense (past, present, or future) or concepts such as completion or continuation. Verb forms may also be active or passive. For example:

Simple Past Tense:

In spoken English, the simple past tense form of regular verbs is indicated by a suffix which is represented in print as -d or -ed, as in *lived, kissed, wanted*. The ending is pronounced /t/ as in *finished*, /d/ as in *moved*, or /ɪd/ as in *wanted*. Some verbs have irregular past tense forms (e.g., *go/went, see/saw*). Some past tense forms are the same as the present (e.g., *put, let, cut*).

Auxiliary Verbs:

Some verb forms are created by combining the auxiliary verbs *be, have,* or *do*, with some form of the main verb, as in *she is studying, I have studied*, or *did you study?* The form of the auxiliary verb changes to indicate the tense, as in *she was studying, she will be studying,* or *she had been studying.*

Present Participle:

Some verbs forms use the present participle, such as *going* or *teaching*, in combination with some form of the auxiliary verb *be*, as in *I am going, she was teaching.* The present participle is also used as an adjective, as in *an interesting lesson, a boring lesson, a charming person.*

Past Participle:

Some forms of regular verbs use the past participle (e.g., *wanted, moved, kissed*). The suffix is pronounced /ɪd/, /d/, and /t/). Some past participles are irregular, as in *broken, written, seen.* Past participles may be used in combination with some form of the auxiliary verb *have*, as in *I have finished, she has moved,* or *they have gone.* Past participles are also used in combination with some form of the auxiliary verb *be* to form the passive voice (e.g., *the homework is done, the homework will be done, the homework was done*). Another use of the past participle is as an adjective, as in *a bored student, a used car, a broken window.*

Learner Errors

English verb forms are complex and even advanced learners make errors when using them. They may:

- use present-tense forms instead of the past, especially in the early stages of learning English, producing sentences such as *I see him last night.*
- over-generalize regular past tense endings, as in *I forgetted to do my homework.*
- have difficulty with the written form of some *-ing* forms, where the final consonant of a root must be doubled before adding the suffix, as in *run/running.*
- take a long time to learn the forms of irregular verbs, and produce errors such as *I have broke it.*
- confuse the use of present and past participles when used as adjectives, as in *I was very boring in that lesson* or *I am not very interesting in that.*
- pronounce the past tense suffix incorrectly, so that words such as *moved* or *breathed* are pronounced as two syllables (as they were in Shakespeare's time!).

Syntax

Syntax refers to the way words are organized in sentences to create meaning. Many second language learners have difficulty with specific features of English sentence structure, especially when the syntactic conventions of English differ from those of their first language. A complete discussion of English syntax is beyond the scope of this book. The following sections deal with some of the difficulties second language learners may encounter.

WORD ORDER

In English, word order is very important and is more rigid than it is in many other languages. Word order is used to distinguish subject from object, nouns from verbs, adjectives from nouns, and so on. Changing the order of words in a sentence can change the meaning of the sentence.

The typical word order in English is subject + verb + object.

Subject	Verb	Object
Lee	kissed	Mary.
Mary	kissed	Lee.

In English, adjectives usually precede nouns.

	Adjective	Noun
a	fair	school
a	school	fair

Learner Errors

Speakers of other languages may mix up or misinterpret word order in English, especially in the beginning stages. German speakers, for example, may place the verb at the end of the sentence, as is the rule in German (e.g., *I have the homework not finished*), and Spanish speakers may place adjectives after nouns (e.g., *a flower pretty*). Furthermore, learners of all language backgrounds may not perceive differences in meaning when the order of words is subtly rearranged (e.g., *She had her hair cut* and *She had cut her hair*).

DETERMINERS

Determiners precede nouns and add meaning in some way. As shown on the chart, they may give information about number and quantity or answer the question, Which?

Determiner	Examples
Indefinite articles: *a* and *an*	I saw a child (an adult).
Definite article: *the*	I saw the child (the children).
Demonstrative pronouns: *this, that, these, those*	I saw this child (these children, etc.).
Possessive pronouns: *my, your, his, her, its, our, their*	I saw my child (her children, etc.).
Quantifiers: *some, any*	I saw some children. I didn't see any children. I have some time. I don't have any time.

Because the conventions governing the use of determiners are very complex, beginning English language learners often produce errors like, *I don't have child, I have headache, I saw that children, The life is precious, I don't have some time,* and *The humans have been on earth for more than a million years.*

Deciding when to use articles is especially difficult for second language learners because not all languages use articles the same way as English. Farsi, for example, distinguishes between definite and indefinite by adding a suffix to nouns rather than by inserting a word before the noun. South Asian languages, such as Hindi, Punjabi or Gujarati, have no equivalent of *the* and, in some cases, use a word meaning *one* where an indefinite article might be used in English. As a result, speakers of these languages often omit articles entirely or use *one* instead of *a* or *an.* And because some languages, such as Russian, include no separate articles, speakers of these languages may omit them (e.g., *May I have book?*) or use them incorrectly (e.g., *I have the headache*).

THE VERB SYSTEM

As the following chart shows, English verbs can be classified as lexical, auxiliary, or modal, depending on their function.

Students used magnetic letters to practice using the verb form shown on this magnetic board.

Verbs		
Category	**Function**	**Examples**
Lexical	Main verbs that carry meaning	She **arrived** late. I **live** in Toronto. I **work** on Tuesdays.
Auxiliary	*Be, have,* and *do* combine with lexical verbs to create new forms	She **didn't** arrive on time. I **have** lived here for three years. I **am** working tonight. **Do** you speak English?
Modal	*Can, could, will, would, shall, should, may, might,* and *must* combine with lexical verbs to convey important nuances of meaning	I **may** arrive late. I **could** live here forever. I **should** work tonight.

Verb forms in English usually indicate tense, or time. English has three "simple" tenses: the simple past, simple present, and simple future.

- Verbs in the simple present and the simple past tense consist of one word (e.g., *go/went)*.
- The simple future consists of the modal verb *will* and the base form of the lexical verb (e.g., *will go*).

Some verb forms indicate other concepts as well as past, present, or future. For example:

- The auxiliary verb *be* is used with the present participle of the lexical verb to indicate "action in progress" or "continuing action," as in *I am reading, they were sleeping, she will be working.* These verb forms are called the "progressive" or "continuous" tenses.
- The "perfect" forms of verbs, consisting of the auxiliary verb *have* and the past participle of the main verb, communicate the concept of "completed action with a continued effect." For example: *I have studied for this test* (implication: I am ready for the test now); *he had slept for only a few hours* (implication: he was very tired the next day). The future perfect combines *will* with *have* and the past participle of the lexical verb or *have been* and the present participle of the lexical verb (e.g., *They will have traveled around the world, They will have been traveling for six months*).

These and other verb forms are used unconsciously by native English speakers, and many would not be able to explain how they are formed or used. Learners of English often have difficulty with the verb system of English, because other languages do not have verb forms that are exactly comparable.

English Verb Forms		
Form	**Simple**	**Continuous (progressive)**
Present	live (lives)	am (is, are) living
Past	lived	was (were) living
Future	will live	will be living
Present perfect	has (have) lived	has (have) been living
Past perfect	had lived	had been living
Future perfect	will have lived	will have been living

Some languages have more verb forms than English. In Russian, the ending on past tense forms changes to match the subject: a different form for I, you, we, etc. Other languages have fewer verb forms. In Chinese, verbs never change form. Tense is either implicit in the context or indicated by an adverbial expression such as *yesterday* or *long ago*.

An additional problem for many learners of English is that the grammatical tense of a verb does not always match its meaning. For instance, it is correct, but somewhat unusual, to ask, *What will you do tonight?* Most English speakers would probably ask, *What are you doing tonight?* Similarly, most English speakers do not say, *The train will arrive at eight o'clock.* They are more likely to say, *The train arrives at eight o'clock.* In addition, *going to* is used more often than *will* to indicate a planned or expected event (e.g., *I am going to graduate at the end of June*).

Learner Errors

Learners of English often have difficulty with the verb system of English because the verb forms in their first language are different.

- Some languages do not distinguish between the simple present (e.g., *I eat*) and present continuous forms (e.g., *I am eating*). As a result, learners of English may say, *I eat my dinner now.*

- Learners may also rely on adverbial expressions such as *yesterday* or *last week* to indicate past time (e.g., *I see him yesterday*)
- Some students omit auxiliary verbs (e.g., *She sleeping*).
- Many learners of English, even at advanced stages, have trouble producing complex forms accurately (e.g., *I have never go there*).

LINKING VERBS

The verb *be* performs many roles in English. It functions as an auxiliary in continuous forms (e.g., *I am working*) and in passive-voice forms (e.g., *The money was stolen*). *Be* also functions as a linking, or copular, verb that couples or links a subject to a complement that may be a noun, adjective, or prepositional phrase (e.g., *She is a teacher, We are tired*, and *It's in my bag*).

Learner Errors

Many other languages either have no equivalent of *be* or they use it in different ways, especially in the present tense. As a result, second language learners often omit this verb and produce sentences such as, *I too tired to study last night* or *She in the garden now*.

MODAL VERBS

The verbs *can, could, will, would, shall, should, may, might, ought to*, and *must* are modal verbs. Modal verbs convey important nuances of meaning, such as permission or prohibition, intent, obligation, ability or possibility, probability, and certainty.

Consider the meaning of the following sentences in which modal verbs indicate the degree of certainty:

- It might rain tonight. She could have done it. (possible)
- It may rain tonight. She may have done it. (probable)
- It will rain tonight. She must have done it. (certain)

Modal verbs also signal important differences between suggestions, advice, and orders, as the following sentences illustrate:

- You could go tonight. You might rewrite that. (a suggestion)
- You should go tonight. You should rewrite that. (advice)
- You must go tonight. You will rewrite that. (an order)

Modal verbs do not have many forms. For example, *must* has no past-tense form: the past-tense equivalent of *he must go* is *he had to go*. Negative statements with modal verbs are formed by inserting *not* (e.g., *You must not go* and *Can't you finish that?*).

The meaning of modal verbs varies with the context. Though *must*, for example, usually indicates obligation or compulsion (e.g., *he must go*), it has an entirely different meaning in an expression like *he must be in love*, in which it indicates certainty on the part of the speaker. Similarly, *may* in a sentence like, *You may go*, indicates permission, whereas *You may do well on this test* indicates possibility.

Learner Errors

The irregular forms and nuances of meaning of modal verbs present many difficulties for learners of English who may produce errors like, *I will must go*, and *I must went*.

Because other languages often use different structures to convey the ideas expressed in English by modals, many learners produce sentences such as, *She can to do that*, and *You should going there*. Forming questions with modal verbs also poses problems for learners who often apply the conventional patterns to produce sentences such as, *Do I must go?* In addition, learners may apply the patterns to negative statements and produce sentences such as, *You don't must go*, or *I don't can finish that.*

Language learners may also have trouble sorting out the subtle shades of meaning conveyed by modal verbs and may deliver a stronger or weaker message than intended. An eager student might, for example, unintentionally give offense by saying, *You must mark my work tonight*, in a situation where a native speaker would say, *I would appreciate it if you could mark my work tonight*, or *Do you think you might have time to mark my work tonight?*

PASSIVE VOICE

Verbs in the passive voice are formed by combining a form of the auxiliary *be* with the past participle of a lexical verb. As the chart shows, the passive voice can occur in any tense, even though the past participle is used in all forms.

Academic and bureaucratic writing often makes greater use of the passive voice than other styles.

As the following sentences show, the passive voice is used when the focus is on the persons or objects affected by an action rather than on who carried out the action.

- Active voice: The army *surrounded* the enemy forces. (Focus is on what the army did.)
- Passive voice: The army *was surrounded by* the enemy forces. (Focus is on what happened to the army.)

The passive voice is also used when the agent is unknown and to avoid identifying the agent.

- Many European cities *were destroyed* during World War II.
- Millions of Africans *were captured* and *transported* to Europe and the Americas.

Passive-voice verbs are also frequently used to describe processes and systems and in administrative language.

- The experiment *was carried out.*
- The trees *are felled*, and the logs *are floated* downstream.
- The use of calculators *is* not *allowed* during tests.
- The examination *will be written* in the gym.
- The project *is to be completed* and *handed in* on February 6.

Passive Voice Verbs				
Subject	**Form of *Be***	**Past Participle**	**Additional Information**	**Agent**
The common cold	is	caused		by a virus.
The fox	is being	chased		by the hound.
The car	was	hit		by a truck.
A decision	has been	reached.		Unknown or unstated
Wheat	is	grown	in Alberta.	Unknown or unstated
Millions of dollars	were	cut	from the budget.	Unknown or unstated
The exam	will be	written	tomorrow.	Unknown or unstated

Some languages have no passive voice, and even in English, use of the passive is often limited to formal or academic contexts. As a result, it may take years for students to become proficient in using passive verbs.

This means that learners may have difficulty recognizing the difference in meaning between passive and active forms. They may not, for example, understand the difference between sentences like, *The car hit the truck* and *The car was hit by the truck*. Learners may also produce constructions such as, *The water heat* or *The water was heat*, instead of, *The water was heated*.

QUESTIONS

Questions in English often involve complex verb transformations using auxiliary verbs. Questions fall into two main categories: yes-no questions and question-word questions. The chart shows the transformations that occur when the affirmative statement *She speaks English* is changed into a yes-no question and a question-word question.

Transforming Statements into Questions					
Kind of Sentence	**Question Word**	**Auxiliary Verb**	**Subject**	**Main Verb**	**Object**
Affirmative statement			She	speaks	English.
Yes-no question		Does	she	speak	English?
Question-word question	When	does	she	speak	English?
	How well	does	she	speak	English?

Learner Errors

In many languages, questions are formed by switching the place of subject and verb. As a result, many learners of English ask questions such as, *Like you pizza?* Though this form was acceptable centuries ago, including in Shakespeare's time, it is no longer used.

In some languages, questions are communicated simply through the use of rising intonation. Though this technique is also used in English, it occurs only when someone is seeking confirmation (e.g., *She speaks English?*).

In addition, questions are formed in some languages by adding a question word at the beginning or end of a sentence — without changing the form of the verb. As a result, many second language learners produce questions such as *Where she lives?*

NEGATIVE STATEMENTS

As the chart shows, negatives are usually formed in English by inserting an auxiliary verb and the adverb *not* before the main verb.

Transforming an Affirmative Statement into a Negative					
Kind of Statement	**Subject**	**Auxiliary Verb**	**Adverb**	**Main Verb**	**Object**
Affirmative	She			speaks	English
Negative	She	does	not	speak	English

Negative statements that use words other than *not* require no auxiliary verb (e.g., *She never speaks English, She speaks no English*).

Learner Errors

In many languages, negatives are formed by simply adding a word that is the equivalent of *not*. As a result, it is very common for second language learners to produce sentences such as, *I not see him* or *I no see him*. In addition, the double negative (e.g., *I don't have no homework*) — a highly stigmatized form in contemporary standard English — is the usual form in many languages and in some varieties of contemporary English. Both *ne* and *pas* are negative words in French, for example, and are used together in standard French statements like, *Je ne parle pas anglais*, which translates literally as *I not speak no English*.

NEGATIVE QUESTIONS

Negative questions are formed by changing the word order of a negative statement. A negative statement such as *She doesn't speak English* can be transformed into a negative question as follows:

- Doesn't she speak English?

Learner Errors

Even after spending many years in an English-speaking environment, second language learners often have trouble responding to negative questions, such as *Don't you like tomatoes?* In English, a negative response agrees with the negative sense of the question: *No, I don't [like tomatoes]*. An affirmative response contradicts or disagrees with the negative sense of the question: *Yes, I do [like tomatoes]*. In many other languages, answering yes to a negative question means, *Yes, I don't like tomatoes*.

TAG QUESTIONS

Tag questions are tacked to the end of statements, usually to elicit agreement or confirmation. As indicated on the chart, if the statement is affirmative, the question tag is usually negative, though it may be affirmative; if the statement is negative, the tag is always affirmative. The response, if required, agrees or disagrees with the main statement.

Tag Questions and Responses			
Statement	**Tag Question**	**Agree**	**Disagree**
She speaks English,	doesn't she?	Yes (she does).	No (she doesn't).
She doesn't speak English,	does she?	No (she doesn't).	Yes (she does).
They speak English,	don't they?	Yes (they do).	No (they don't).
They speak English,	do they?	Yes (they do).	No (they don't).
They don't speak English,	do they?	No (they don't).	Yes (they do).

Because some other languages add one word as a tag, often the equivalent of *no*, many second language learners reproduce this pattern, which is unusual in English (e.g., *She speaks English, no?*). Learners may also be unsure about how to respond to tag questions, especially when the main statement is negative (e.g., *She doesn't speak English, does she? Yes,* [*she doesn't*]).

PHRASAL VERBS

Phrasal verbs are verbs that combine a verb and an adverb or a preposition (e.g., *get up, put on, take out, get away with, give in to*). Together, the two — and sometimes more — words form a verb that means something different from the separate meaning of the individual words. Consider the following sentences:

- Tiko called up his friend.
- Tiko called up the stairs.

Though phrasal verbs are common in languages that are closely related to English (e.g., German, Dutch, Swedish, Danish, and Norwegian), they are rare in other languages. As a result, learners often have trouble understanding the differences between phrasal verbs such as *put off, put out, put on,* and *put down,* and even more trouble sorting out the difference between expressions such as, *Let's put it off until tomorrow* and *His manner puts me off.*

Phrasal verbs also present difficulties because the words in some are separable; in others, they are not. If the words are separable, the parts of the phrasal *may* be separated, and they are always separated when the direct object of a sentence is a pronoun (e.g., *I put on my coat, I put my coat on, I put it on* — not *I put on it*). If the two words are inseparable, they are never separated (e.g., *I got over my disappointment, I got over it* — not *I got it over*).

Learner Errors

Much exposure and practice are required to internalize the rules about which phrasal verbs are separable and which are not. Though native speakers acquire these rules at an early age and use them automatically, it is not unusual for learners to produce sentences such as, *I read on it up in the encyclopedia,* or *I ran him into at the library.*

Learners of English may also have difficulty understanding the differences between *I stood up to him, I stood him up,* and *I stood up for him.* They may fail to communicate effectively if they produce a sentence such as, *I saw through him,* when the intended meaning is *I saw him through.*

INFINITIVES AND GERUNDS

An infinitive is the base form of a verb and is often combined with *to* to form the *to*-infinitive (e.g., *to eat, to go, to live*). Like participles, gerunds are *-ing* verb forms, but they differ from participles because they are used as nouns (e.g., *healthy eating, rough going, easy living*). As the chart shows, infinitives and gerunds perform many functions in sentences.

No easy rule explains which verbs are followed by infinitives (e.g., *want, expect, hope, decide,* and *refuse*) and which are followed by gerunds (e.g., *enjoy, avoid, risk, finish,* and *deny*). To add to the difficulty for learners, some verbs (e.g., *like, begin, start,* and *remember*) may be followed by either, depending on the specific meaning to be conveyed. Saying, *I*

Function of Infinitives and Gerunds		
Infinitive	I want to go.	I expect to go.
Object + infinitive	I want you to go.	I expect them to go.
Object + infinitive – to	I will let you go.	I can't make you go.
Gerund	I enjoy reading.	I avoid reading.
Possessive + gerund	I appreciate your being here.	I can't bear your leaving.

remembered to do it, for example, is different from saying, *I remembered doing it*.

Learner Errors

Most languages have no gerunds, though most do use infinitives. In addition, infinitives occur more frequently than gerunds in spoken English. As a result, learners encounter infinitives more often than gerunds and may overgeneralize their use to produce errors such as, *I enjoy to read*.

Learners may also overgeneralize the use of the *to*-infinitive, as this is the most common pattern in English (e.g., *I want to go, I hope to go*, and *Please allow me to go*). As a result, learners may produce sentences such as, *Please let me to go*.

INDIRECT SPEECH

Sometimes called reported speech, indirect speech causes great confusion for learners because of the complex rules governing the sequence of tenses. Other changes may also be necessary when transferring direct to indirect speech.

- Indirect speech requires the backshifting of tenses.

Direct Speech	Indirect Speech
I will do it.	I told her (that) I would do it.
I have never met him.	She said (that) she had never met him.
I don't like him.	She said (that) she didn't like him.
What did you eat?	The doctor asked what he had eaten.

- Indirect speech also involves changes in pronouns.

Direct Speech	Indirect Speech
Why won't you do it for me?	She asked why he wouldn't do it for her.
I will love you forever.	He said (that) he would love me forever.
We must leave at once.	She said (that) they must leave at once.

- Possessive and demonstrative pronouns may also change.

Direct Speech	Indirect Speech
I will read my book.	He said that he would read his book.
I've never seen this man before.	She said (that) she had never seen that man before.
I like these shoes the best.	He said (that) he liked those shoes the best.

- Imperatives become infinitives.

Direct Speech	Indirect Speech
Have supper with us.	They invited me to have supper with them.
Go home!	She told them to go home.

- Expressions related to time and space may change.

Direct Speech	Indirect Speech
I'll do it tomorrow.	He said (that) he would do it the next day.
I ate here last night.	He said (that) he had eaten there the previous evening.
Come back later this evening.	She told them to go back later that evening.

- In indirect questions requiring a yes-or-no answer, *if* or *whether* introduces the question and the verb is no longer in question form.

Direct Speech	Indirect Speech
Is everything okay?	She asked if everything was okay.
Do you want to eat here?	She asked whether I wanted to eat there.
Do you want tea or coffee?	She asked whether I wanted tea or coffee.

- In indirect questions introduced by a question word, the question word remains, but the verb is no longer in question form.

Direct Speech	Indirect Speech
What time will they be here?	She wanted to know what time they would be there.
Where are you going?	He asked her where she was going.

Learner Errors

Because the distinction between direct and indirect speech is more sharply defined in English than in many other languages, learners may produce errors such as *She told me she will come early* instead of *She told me she would come early*.

The rules governing indirect questions are especially confusing. After learning how to use question forms, students must learn *not* to use them in indirect questions. As a result, they may produce statements such as, *She asked me how old am I*, and *He asked her where was she going*.

Learners must also learn *not* to apply the rules for question formation in embedded questions such as *I'd like to know what time the train arrives* and *I wonder how old she is*. Learners may say, *I'd like to know what time does the train arrive*, and *I wonder how old is she*.

PRONOUN REFERENCE

Pronouns such as *it, he, this, which,* and *whose* refer to antecedents, which are words that have appeared earlier in a sentence or paragraph. The greater the distance between an antecedent and pronoun, the more difficult it is for a listener — or reader — to keep the antecedent in short-term memory. Consider the words *them, most,* and *they* in the final sentence of the following paragraph, for example. What is their antecedent?

Strangely, of the eighty pyramids built on the west bank of the Nile, not a single body has been found in any of *them. Most,* including the Great

Pyramid, contain a granite sarcophagus — the outer casing of the coffin — but empty *they* remain.

Learner Errors

Students may find it difficult to understand text that includes many sentences like the one in the example in the preceding section. Note that *sarcophagus* causes no difficulty because this word is defined in context; rather, the problem is caused by the need to track the antecedents of *them, most,* and *they.*

LITERARY STYLE

Some academic and literary texts are written in a style that involves variations from the usual word order of English. Consider this sentence: "Most, including the Great Pyramid, contain a granite sarcophagus — the outer casing of the coffin — but empty they remain." The more usual word order for the final phrase is *they remain empty.*

Even young children encounter unusual syntax in the literature they read and that is read to them. Word order such as that shown on the chart can confuse second language learners and native speakers alike.

Literary Style and Normal Communication	
Literary	**Normal**
Down came a spider …	A spider came down …
In the palace lived a wise old king.	A wise old king lived in the palace.
So poor were they that …	They were so poor that …
But for the King's refusal to …	If the King had not refused …
Had they known …	If they had known …
Should you need assistance …	If you need assistance …
Were they to discover …	If they discovered …

Learner Errors

Though students may understand every word in expressions like those shown on the chart, they may have difficulty figuring out the meaning of the sentence. They may, for example, expect sentences that begin with words in reverse order (e.g., *Should you* …) to be questions.

EMBEDDING AND SUBORDINATION

Embedding refers to the inclusion of a linguistic unit in another linguistic unit. This may involve separating the main verb from its subject by adding one or more phrases (e.g., Canada, unlike the United States, has a parliamentary form of government). **Subordination** refers to the joining of a subordinate clause to a clause of higher value often by using connectors (e.g., You can go as long as you have finished your homework). Academic and literary texts often contain complex sentences that embed elements that distance the verb from the main subject and include one or more subordinate clauses. The following example is from an economics textbook:

Subject	The monopolist,
Embedded phrase	just like a firm in a competitive market structure,
Main verb	will attempt to maximize profit
Embedded phrase	by producing extra units of output
Subordinate clause	so long as the additional revenue exceeds the additional cost.

Learner Errors

Texts that feature many complex sentences are very demanding for readers. As a result, less proficient readers and English language learners may find it difficult to extract meaning from what they are reading.

CONDITIONAL SENTENCES

Conditional sentences express a relationship in which one situation depends on another. Often introduced by *if* statements, they express three kinds of condition: real or possible conditions, hypothetical conditions, and impossible or unrealized conditions. As the chart indicates, these conditions may refer to the past, present, or future.

Conditional Sentences	
Kind of Condition	**Example**
Present real condition	If you cut your finger, it bleeds.
Past real condition	If I saw him in the street, I always crossed to the other side.
Future possible condition	If I have time tonight, I'll finish the essay.
Present hypothetical condition	If I won the lottery, I would still keep my job.
Present impossible condition	If I were a bird, I would fly to India.
Past unrealized condition	If I had studied harder, I would have passed the test.

Conditional sentences are among the most difficult structures for second language learners to master because the grammatical tense of the verb does not always match the meaning. For example, *if I have time tonight* is a present-tense form that refers to a future possibility, and *if I won the lottery* uses a past-tense form to describe something that hasn't happened yet — and may never happen.

Though conditions are often expressed using *if*, other forms are also used (e.g., *Had penicillin not been invented …, But for the invention of penicillin …, Should you require assistance …,* and *Were she to die while in office …*).

Learner Errors

Because some conditional verb forms are very complex, even native speakers sometimes have difficulty with them. As a result, it is not unusual for second language learners and native speakers alike to produce errors such as, *If I would have known that ...,* and *If you would have told me ....* In addition, they may also mis-hear the spoken elision of *would have* into *would've,* so that they produce *would of* (e.g., *I would of bought it*).

LONG NOUN GROUPS

In English, it is possible to string together a set of nouns such as *government energy-conservation project, water-cycle diagram,* and *food-chain chart.* These expressions are very dense. To draw meaning from them, learners must understand not only every word, but also that only the last word actually functions as a noun. The preceding nouns function as adjectives.

Learner Errors

English language learners may have great difficulty unpacking expressions like *student council election committee meeting.* A helpful technique is to begin at the end by assuming that the final noun in the string is the central concept and that the rest function as adjectives. *Student council election committee meeting,* for example, can be unpacked as *a meeting of a committee for the election of a new council of students.*

CONDENSED SYNTAX

Technical, academic, and administrative prose often contains condensed expressions and reduced forms that cause tremendous difficulty for English language learners. Reduced relative clauses, such as *air under pressure* (i.e., *air that is under pressure*) and *articles left in lockers* (i.e., *articles that students have left in their lockers*) can be especially troublesome.

Learner errors

English language learners may misinterpret some of these expressions. They may, for example, understand a phrase like *organisms found in water* as *organisms found water.* Note that even in their expanded form, these expressions often use passive verbs, which themselves pose difficulties for many students.

Teaching Grammar

Research has shown that grammar instruction in isolation has little effect on learners' ability to create grammatically correct sentences. Though students may be able to identify the correct form in grammar exercises that focus on specific forms, they may be unable to transfer these uses to real communication. For more information on the effects of instruction, see Chapter 8.

When planning instruction to help students recognize and internalize new grammatical patterns, keep the following principles in mind:

- Grammar is best taught and practiced in an authentic context. A new structure is more likely to stick in learners' minds if they have immediate and frequent opportunities to use it in real

Get Rid of the Red Pen!

Supportive feedback does *not* consist of correcting or circling every error in a student's work. This can be overwhelming for the student, who may have little understanding of why a particular item has been corrected or circled. Instead, look for consistent errors of a specific type and provide feedback on these.

communicative contexts. As a result, specific grammar structures should be taught and practiced in contexts in which it is natural or necessary to use the structure repeatedly. If students need to use passive verbs to write science lab reports, for example, use model lab reports to highlight and explain the structure.

- Supportive feedback is more helpful than overt correction (see Chapter 8).
- New structures will not stick unless they are appropriate to students' current level of development. There is little point, for example, in expecting students to learn passive constructions, such as *The water was heated*, if they have not yet acquired the active form, *We heated the water*.
- Students may need many opportunities to hear, read, and practice a new structure for months or even years before they internalize it thoroughly enough to produce it on their own.

The following strategies support the preceding principles and can be incorporated into daily lessons in various subject areas. They enable students to learn the curriculum at the same time as they focus on specific features of English grammar.

- *Use material and plan activities that feature repeated language patterns.* Repetition of a grammatical structure in a meaningful context helps learners recognize and understand the pattern. Songs, chants, games, and children's books often feature repetitive patterns. Eric Hill's picture book, *Where's Spot?*, for example, repeats prepositions (e.g., *in*, *on*, and *under*), interrogative forms of the third-person singular of *be* (e.g., *Is he in the...?*), and negative forms of the third person singular of *be* (e.g., *He isn't under the ...*).

  The chants in Carolyn Graham's Jazz Chants series are based on repeated patterns and provide a change of pace in a lesson.

  Students can also create their own books and chants, following a pattern introduced in a song, chant, or picture book.

- *Use the content of lessons to introduce grammar concepts.* Look for repeated patterns that occur naturally in textbooks and lessons, such as past-tense verb forms in history and passive forms in science lab reports. Highlight a specific language feature rather than attempt to deal with all students' grammar errors and problems at once. Encourage students to use this feature independently by incorporating it into other learning tasks, such as journal writing.

  Provide opportunities for supported practice based on the content of a lesson or activity. You might, for example, introduce cloze passages that require students to use the target structure. For more information about journals, cloze passages, and other writing scaffolds, see Chapter 12.

- *Provide learners with the tools they need to talk about language.* Students need a basic vocabulary about language if they are to discuss and ask questions about the language patterns they are having trouble with. By the time they are nine or 10 years old, most children can learn and understand basic terms, such as noun, verb, adjective, adverb, preposition; singular and plural; verb tense; and suffix and prefix. Older learners can be introduced to concepts such as subject, verb, object; active and passive verbs; articles; relative clauses and so on. You can teach these concepts by using

What Did You Do Last Night?

Ms. Vega planned today's lessons.
Ms. Vega had dinner at her friend's house.
Samantha went to the supermarket with her mother.
Sanjay played video games.
Van Bao called his brother in Sydney.
Nobody went to the library.
Almost everybody watched television.
Alfonso wrote a letter to his sister.
Everyone went to bed before midnight.
Only four people did the math homework!

Verbs in Math Problems

The regular price of a popsicle *is* 50 cents but the store *has* a special sale price of 40 cents on Mondays. If Leroy *buys* 2 popsicles on Saturday and 3 on Monday, what *is* the average price of each popsicle?

sentences from a story or text that you have been reading with the class, student-generated sentences, or sentences about things that happen in the class.

Instead of teaching parts of speech and other language concepts by teaching a rule or definition first, try providing examples from which learners can figure out a rule or pattern. To introduce the concept of verbs, for example, follow these steps over a period of several days.

– Ask students to make statements, such as those shown on this page, about what they did the previous night. Write these on the chalkboard or chart paper.

– Highlight or underline the verb in each sentence. Point to each verb and say, "This word is a verb."

– Erase the verbs and ask students to suggest a verb to complete each sentence. Be sure to use the word *verb* many times. There may be several alternatives for the verbs in some sentences (e.g., *Ms. Vega ate [had, enjoyed] dinner at her friend's house*).

– Next day, write the sentences again, without highlighting or underlining the verbs. Point to various words and ask, "Is this a verb?" Then ask individual students to identify a verb by pointing to a word and saying, "This is a verb."

– Write the nouns and verbs from the sentences on flash cards. As you display each card, ask students to say, "Yes (it's a verb)," or "No (it isn't a verb)."

– During the next few days, write sentences that use simple present or past-tense verbs to describe the content of lessons and ask students to identify the verbs.

– Use material related to the content of lessons to gradually expand the concept of what a verb is. Mathematics word problems like the one shown on this page, for example, often use *is* and *are* or *have* and *has* to describe the context. To introduce abstract verbs such as *want, need, like, think, have, expect, hope,* and *be*, you can also use examples from fiction and sentences about the students. Gradually introduce negative forms and forms other than simple present and simple past tenses.

– Use terms taught in class when you discuss writing with students. Make suggestions like, "Can you add some really interesting adjectives to describe how you felt?" or "If this happened last week, the verbs need to be in the past tense."

• *Take a long-term view!* Remember that learners need hundreds, perhaps even thousands, of opportunities to hear, read, and use the target grammatical structure, as well as supportive feedback, before they fully internalize English language forms. Be patient. Your modeling, instruction, and feedback will contribute to students' long-term language development and, as long as other teachers provide similar support, will bear fruit, though this may not be evident for several years.

To Learn More …

Reference Books for Teachers

Celce-Murcia, M., and D. Larsen-Freeman. *The Grammar Book: An ESL/EFL Teacher's Course*. 2nd ed. Boston, Mass.: Heinle & Heinle, 1999.

An essential reference for language teachers who wish to become expert in pedagogical grammar.

Crystal, D. *The Cambridge Encyclopedia of Language*. 2nd ed. Cambridge, U.K.: Cambridge University Press, 1997.

A wide-ranging reference that explains how English and other languages work.

Eastwood, J. *The Oxford Guide to English Grammar*. Oxford, U.K.: Oxford University Press, 1994.

Useful guide to English grammar includes discussion of differences between British and American English and between English and other languages.

Lock, G. *Functional English Grammar: An introduction for second language teachers*. Cambridge: Cambridge University Press, 1996.

This book describes English grammar as a communicative system. Useful for language teachers.

Palmer, F. *Grammar*. Harmondsworth, U.K.: Penguin Books, 1971.

A much-reprinted classic. Provides an overview of important concepts in grammar and is especially helpful in dealing with notions of "correctness."

Parrott, M. *Grammar For English Language Teachers*. Cambridge: Cambridge University Press, 2000.

An introduction to the grammar system of English, with information about typical learner problems and suggestions for teaching. Online resources also available at <www.cup.cam.ca.uk/elt>.

Ur, P. *Grammar Practice Activities: A practical guide for teachers*. Cambridge: Cambridge University Press, 1988.

The grammar practice activities in this book provide models for the teacher to develop activities based on the content of specific lessons or subject areas.

Yule, G. *Explaining English Grammar*. Oxford, U.K.: Oxford University Press, 1998.

Each chapter focuses on a problem area and provides explanations, authentic examples, and teaching suggestions.

Websites and Online Resources

These websites were designed to support English language learners at the post-secondary level but they also provide useful information for teachers.

Guide to grammar and Writing. Capital Community College. </www.ccc.commnet.edu>.

Grammar Help. <www.ruthvilmi.net/hut/LangHelp/Grammar/>.

Online Writing Lab at Purdue University. <owl.english.purdue.edu/handouts/grammar/index.html>

Writing at the University of Toronto: Advice on Academic Writing. <www.utoronto.ca/writing/advise.html>.

5 In Other Words: The Power of English Vocabulary

Vocabulary knowledge is an extremely important factor in reading comprehension and academic achievement: the more words you know, the higher your level of reading comprehension — and the higher your level of reading comprehension, the higher your level of academic achievement.

Acquiring English vocabulary presents a major challenge to English language learners. The varied origins of English words have given rise to a huge lexicon that includes many synonyms and near-synonyms that convey subtle differences in meaning. In addition, English words can be transformed in a variety of ways to create additional word forms.

This chapter begins with a summary of the origins of English words. This is followed by a discussion of the vocabulary that English language learners must acquire to catch up to their age peers. The third section describes the structure of English words, and the chapter ends with recommendations for teaching vocabulary. For more detailed suggestions, see Chapter 12.

Where Do English Words Come From?

English is sometimes called a promiscuous language because it embraces so many words from other languages. Only about 10 percent of English words are actually English, or Anglo-Saxon, in origin. During its history, English has come into contact with many other languages and has adopted words from many of them. Though most of the additions were borrowed from Latin and Greek — either directly from those languages or through French — English has also borrowed words from other European languages, as well as from the languages of South Asia (e.g., *bungalow* and *jodhpur*), the Americas (e.g., *tobacco*, *tomato*, and *potato*), and Africa (e.g., *zebra*).

The chart on the following pages shows an approximate chronology of English language and its borrowings from other languages.

How Many Words?

The adoption by English of hundreds of thousands of words from other languages has produced a vocabulary unequalled in size by any other language. The *Oxford English Dictionary* lists more than 500,000 words and does not include hundreds of thousands of scientific and technical terms. By comparison, German has about 185,000 words, and French 100,000.

No single person can know all the words of English. The standard reference dictionary found in most school libraries lists more than 100,000 words, but most are **low-frequency words** that are rarely used. Others are **subject-specific words**, likely to be used only within a specific field of work or study. Only about 2,000 to 3,000 are **high-frequency words** that are used constantly in many different contexts.

The Average English Speaker's Vocabulary

Because experts disagree about what constitutes a word, it is difficult to count the number of words people know. The simple word *run*, for example, can be transformed by adding suffixes to produce the nouns *runner* and *running*. Are these distinct words? In addition, *run* has many meanings. Does each meaning count as a different word?

Knowledge of the various connotations of a word depends to a large extent on experience and education. English-speaking children, for example, know the meaning of *run* as a verb of motion when they enter school. By the time they're nine, they know the meaning of *run* as a baseball term, and by the time they're 11, they probably understand its use in political contexts, such as *run for office*. By 13, they understand the word in *run a business*, and by 18, in *a run on the dollar*.

Estimates of an individual's word knowledge must also consider the difference between **active vocabulary** — the words a person can use — and passive or **receptive vocabulary** — the words a person can recognize or understand in print or when other speakers use them. The receptive vocabulary of native speakers and second language learners alike is much larger than their active vocabulary. Should a count of the number of words a person knows include only the words he uses or all the words in his receptive vocabulary?

Some studies suggest that by the time they start Kindergarten, English-speaking children know about 1,000 words and add to this total at the rate of about 1,000 words a year. By the age of eight, most students have a vocabulary of 4,000 to 5,000 words. According to some estimates, the average undergraduate enrolling at university has acquired a vocabulary of about 15,000 **word families**, which are related words such as *educate, education, educated,* and *educational*.

Setting Goals for English Language Learners

Students who are learning English as a second language must learn the vocabulary necessary to catch up to their peers, who sometimes have a huge head start. A newcomer who first enters an English school environment at the age of eight, for example, must learn 4,000 to 5,000 words to catch up to English-speaking eight-year-olds. This cannot be done in a year. In fact, it would take several years for the newcomer to acquire this many words. And because English-speaking children are adding about 1,000 words a year to their vocabularies, the second language learner is constantly attempting to catch up. She must learn the words her peers already know, as well as 1,000 more a year until she catches up.

Most students who arrive in their new school environment with good skills in their first language and a solid educational background, who approach the task of acquiring English with confidence, and who

---

Running into New Words …

In each of the following examples, *run* has a different meaning and could therefore be counted as a separate word. Nevertheless, the meanings are related, even if only figuratively, so that they could also be counted as various forms of a single word.

- Contextualized meanings such as *run a race, run a company, salmon run,* and *run cold*.
- Phrasal verbs such as *run in, run on, run out, run out of, run up against, run into, run up, run down, run through,* and *run over*.
- Fixed idiomatic expressions such as *run wild, run late, run short, run aground, run for office,* and *run-of-the-mill*.
- Compound words and phrases such as *runway, runoff, run-in, run-through, runner-up, drug runner, running mate,* and *dog run*.

A Chronology of the Development of English	
400 BCE	First Celts arrive in Ireland and begin settling the British Isles.
	As a result, the first languages spoken in what is now England were not English at all, but varieties of Celtic.
55 BCE	Roman legions begin invading and conquer Britannia, launching four centuries of Roman occupation that end in the 5th century CE.
	The linguistic effect of the occupation was minimal and is evident today mainly in place names, such as London (from *Londinium*) and Manchester (the suffix derives from *castellum*, the Latin word for *fort*).
449 CE	Groups of Angles, Saxons, and Jutes from what is now northern Germany begin invading Britain, pushing Celts into present-day Scotland, Wales, and Cornwall.
	Over the next two centuries, England (from *Englaland* — land of the Angles) gradually became a country. The English spoken during this period is known as Anglo-Saxon or Old English and is the basis of contemporary English sentence structure and vocabulary. Fundamental words such as *man, woman, child, brother, sister, house, eat, drink,* and *sleep*, as well as nearly all function words, such as *to, for, but, and, the,* and *or*, are Anglo-Saxon in origin. Without these words, it would be impossible to construct an English sentence.
597 CE	Anglo-Saxons begin converting to Christianity, which paves the way for Latin, the language of the Roman Catholic Church, to become the language of religion and scholarship.
	Over the next centuries, many Latin words related to religion and law entered Old English, and the Latin alphabet was adapted to represent Old English, replacing most of the runic characters used in early English writing. Because the sounds of Latin and English were not exactly the same, however, some runic characters were retained. The symbol Þ, for example, was retained to represent the initial sound in words like *thick* and *this*. By the late middle ages, this character had evolved and was similar in appearance to the letter Y. This is the origin of some present-day commercial uses, such as Ye (The) Olde Tea Shoppe. By the end of the Middle Ages, Latin letters had replaced all runic characters.
792	Vikings from Scandinavia begin to invade and settle in Britain.
	A century later, most of northern England belonged to the Danes, and many Scandinavian words became part of the language, providing many of the synonyms that exist today, such *skill* for *craft* and *skin* for *hide*. Some of the new words came from the same source as Old English but had changed in pronunciation (e.g., *skirt-shirt* and *wake-watch*). This led to significant dialectal differences between northern and southern varieties of English, differences that continue to exist today.
1066	Normans, the French-speaking descendants of Vikings or Norsemen who had settled in the part of France known as Normandy, begin their conquest of England.
	This event sparked the next major stage in the evolution of English. For the next several centuries, England was multilingual: Norman French was the language of court and the courts, Latin of religion and education, and English of the common folk, who were in the majority. Welsh and

	A Chronology of the Development of English
1066 (cont'd.)	Celtic languages were also spoken in some areas. During this Middle English period, about 10,000 French words entered English, transforming it from a Germanic language to a language of mixed Germanic and Romance ancestry. Many of the new words were synonyms for existing words (e.g., *malady* was added but did not replace the English words *sickness* and *illness*) and reveal the feudal hierarchy of the time. Anglo-Saxons who raised animals called them cows or oxen, pigs, and sheep, for example. The French-speaking nobles, whose main experience with these animals was as meat cooked and served at the table, ate beef, pork, and mutton (*boeuf, porc*, and *mouton* in modern French).
1337	The Hundred Years War between England and France begins. This war accelerated the decline of French in England, and English became more widely used. It replaced Latin as the language of instruction in schools, and writers such as Geoffrey Chaucer chose to write in English rather than French. Over the next centuries, the printing press was influential in stabilizing English, though spelling and vocabulary continued to vary from region to region.
1450	The stage known as Early Modern English begins. Though the precise dates of this phase in the evolution of English are disputed, it is often identified as the 250-year period between 1450 and 1700. This was a time of great change. Latin was still an important language of higher education, as was Greek, and many words from both languages entered English at this time. As a result, it is now possible to express many concepts in English using expressions rooted in either Anglo-Saxon or in Latin. Many Greek and Latin words were also adopted to express new concepts in science and technology, medicine, navigation and astronomy, and the arts. Words were also borrowed from other languages as English speakers came into contact with them through commerce, maritime exploration, and conquest and colonization. At the same time, English began its journey toward becoming a world language. The Bible was translated into English, and Shakespeare wrote during this period. The language was still very different from the English used today, as all who have studied Shakespeare know.
1700	The stage known as Modern English begins. Although the language continued to change, English began to displace the Celtic languages in much of Ireland, Scotland, and Wales, and became established in North America, India, Australia, and many parts of Africa. The language developed differently in various areas, resulting in many new varieties of English. During this period, English continued to gain new vocabulary from increased contact with other peoples.
Today	As a result of the many borrowings, English has a much larger lexicon than any other language. Most of these words have come into English from other languages, and about 200,000 are in regular use. Though widespread literacy and the mass media have helped stabilize English, the language continues to evolve. New words are continually added — and the meanings of old ones change — to express new or changing concepts. Today, most new words are formed by compounding (e.g., *photocopy, screensaver*, and *spellchecker*).

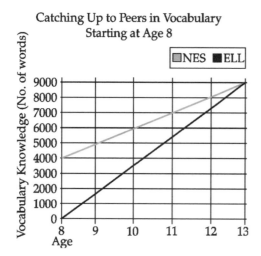

Catching Up to Peers in Vocabulary Starting at Age 8

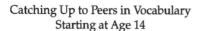

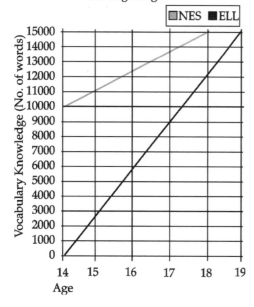

Catching Up to Peers in Vocabulary Starting at Age 14

receive appropriate support need at least five years to catch up to their English-speaking peers. The graph represents the task facing an eight-year-old English language learner (ELL). To catch up to her native English-speaking peers (NES) within five years, she must learn 9,000 to 10,000 words, or about 2,000 new words a year. This is double the rate of her English-speaking peers and means that she must learn an average of about 10 new words or word families every school day. Students who arrive with limited previous schooling need more support for a longer time.

Though an eight-year-old may catch up by the time she enters high school, the task of acquiring English is even more challenging for those who are older when they arrive. A 10-year-old won't be able to catch up to his peers before moving on to secondary school, and as the second graph indicates, beginning learners of English who arrive when they are 14 must spend an additional year in high school and learn about 3,000 words a year — triple the rate of their peers — to acquire the 15,000 words that their university-bound native English-speaking peers know by the time they are 18. These students need ESL support throughout the five-year period, and even then, their vocabulary may lag behind that of their English-speaking peers by the time they are of an age to enter post-secondary institutions.

Students who have studied some English in their home country may progress more quickly, and those who speak European languages that include words with Greek and Latin roots have an advantage when it comes to learning low-frequency English words (e.g., the word *machine* is similar in many European languages). Students who speak languages that are completely unrelated to English, such as Chinese, however, often have a harder time learning these words.

For all English language learners, acquiring an English vocabulary is a challenging task. For this reason, it is as important to teach students strategies for handling unfamiliar words as it is to add to their store of known words. For more information on how long it takes English language learners to catch up to their English-speaking peers, see Chapter 8. Information about vocabulary instruction is found in Chapter 12.

Which Words?

Though your instructional goals may include helping students learn 2,000 to 3,000 new words a year, this does not mean that you should try to *teach* all these words. Students will acquire many high-frequency words incidentally, through daily activities, meaningful classroom activities, and regular interaction with more proficient English speakers. Low-frequency words and subject-specific vocabulary require more direct attention, however. Students may also need assistance to expand their repertoire of **connectives**, the words and phrases that link ideas (e.g., *prior to* and *subsequently*).

High-Frequency Words

To communicate in English, language learners must acquire the high-frequency words that are used every day in a variety of contexts. These include common nouns, such as *boy, girl, mother, father, school,* and *teacher*; common verbs, such as *live, like, run, eat, have, is* and *are*; and function words, such as *the, in, but,* and *you*. English-speaking children acquire most of these words before starting school, and like them, English language learners will learn high-frequency vocabulary through involvement in engaging and meaningful activities that enable them to encounter and use basic words over and over again. For suggested activities, see chapters 10 and 12.

Most high-frequency words are of Anglo-Saxon origin. The *General Service List*, developed by Michael West and published in 1953, lists 2,000 high-frequency words in English. Although the list is dated and does not contain contemporary high-frequency words such as *computer*, it remains a useful guide for teachers interested in vocabulary development. Many language-teaching materials, such as graded readers, are based on this list. The vocabulary in standardized reading tests from pre-primer to Grade 3 corresponds to the first 1,000 words on this list.

At first, most students learn only the most common and literal meanings of these words. For this reason, they may have difficulty understanding a common word when it appears in a specialized setting (e.g., the meaning of *face* in geometry is different from the common meaning). Learners may also have trouble understanding idiomatic expressions, such as *run that by me again*.

Low-Frequency Words

When students are beyond the beginning stage of learning English, teachers must focus on low-frequency words and word families that are more likely to be learned and used in school than in daily life. Most of these words, which are also known as **general academic vocabulary**, are based in Latin (e.g., *accurate, analyze,* and *consequently*), though some are from Greek (e.g., *chronological* and *technological*). Many of these words are not essential for communication; high-frequency words can be used to express most of the same concepts. In general, people of higher socioeconomic status and greater education tend to use more Latin-derived vocabulary in daily conversation (e.g., *vocabulary* instead of *words, possess* instead of *own, register* instead of *sign up, participate in* instead of *join in,* and *converse* instead of *talk*).

The academic word list, developed by the School of Linguistics and Applied Language Studies at Victoria University of Wellington, New Zealand, was published in 2000 and, in addition to the words on the general service list, contains 570 word families that are frequently used in academic texts. These words begin to appear in the Grade 4 curriculum. Only about 25 percent of the words on standardized reading tests for Grade 4 are high-frequency words found on the general service list; the other 75 percent are academic or low-frequency words.

The graded word lists on the following page show the dramatic shift that occurs between grades 3 and 4. Until Grade 3, the lists consist of basic high-frequency words; by Grade 4, nearly all the words are low-frequency Latin-based words.

Knowledge of general academic vocabulary is essential for reading school texts and writing school assignments. In addition, the use of these words is often associated with education, intelligence, and high social status. Students must learn not only what these words mean, but also when it is appropriate to use them. Though these words may create a favorable impression in academic contexts, using too many in informal settings may create an unfavorable impression of pomposity and verbosity.

Like the meanings of the 2,000 most common words, the meanings of some low-frequency words vary according to the subject area. The word *balance*, for example, has a special meaning in business and accounting courses. In history, a student may encounter the expression *balance of power*; in environmental studies, *balance of nature* describes an ecological concept; in law and civics, *balance of mind* refers to a legal notion of criminal responsibility; in economics, *balance of trade* is an important concept; in physical education, *balance* is a physical skill; in developing an argument in many subject areas, a *balanced* view is desirable; in physics, *balance* is both a concept and a tool; and in the arts, *balance* refers to harmony in the way the elements of a composition relate to one another.

A general-purpose academic vocabulary can be developed by reading aloud to students and by involving them in extensive independent reading, as well as through focused instruction. Students must also develop effective vocabulary acquisition strategies (e.g., using context or word analysis to figure out meaning and using dictionaries effectively) to help them deal with unknown words. To learn more about these strategies, see Chapter 12.

Subject-Specific Words

Subject-specific or technical terms, such as *photosynthesis*, *denominator*, *equilateral*, *metaphor*, and *biome*, occur only in a limited range of contexts or subject areas. These words derive from Latin and, especially in science and technology, from Greek. English language learners at all stages must learn important subject vocabulary. A 16-year-old beginning learner, for example, may need to learn the word *trigonometry* before *kitten*.

Learning subject-specific words is important if students are to achieve success in science courses.

Graded Word Lists

Pre-Primer	Primer	Grade 1	Grade 2	Grade 3	Grade 4*
1. a	1. all	1. after	1. also	1. air	1. amused
2. at	2. am	2. again	2. always	2. cold	2. ancient
3. back	3. any	3. book	3. around	3. dear	3. award
4. big	4. came	4. boy	4. best	4. drink	4. cemetery
5. can	5. day	5. come	5. box	5. every	5. echo
6. do	6. find	6. hand	6. color	6. food	6. elastic
7. for	7. had	7. how	7. fall	7. hold	7. flock
8. go	8. into	8. keep	8. five	8. learn	8. government
9. have	9. now	9. long	9. grow	9. move	9. invade
10. help	10. out	10. many	10. head	10. number	10. jealous
11. I	11. put	11. never	11. light	11. often	11. lizard
12. in	12. ran	12. next	12. made	12. several	12. mechanic
13. jump	13. say	13. once	13. part	13. start	13. mysterious
14. of	14. soon	14. open	14. people	14. such	14. portion
15. one	15. there	15. room	15. read	15. table	15. savage
16. play	16. two	16. school	16. same	16. today	16. scarlet
17. said	17. well	17. them	17. small	17. try	17. signal
18. see	18. what	18. think	18. town	18. wash	18. statue
19. she	19. with	19. up	19. turn	19. wrong	19. stout
20. that	20. yes	20. where	20. wish	20. yellow	20. vicious

*Note the dramatic shift in Grade 4 from everyday words of Anglo-Saxon origin, to more academic Latin-based words.

Although subject-specific words may appear to be hard to learn, they are often less challenging than general academic words, because teachers pay attention to teaching new technical terms when they introduce concepts. In addition, subject-specific vocabulary is usually defined or explained in textbooks, which often provide a glossary. It is important, however, to help students see links among words. This may help when they encounter new words that contain the same roots or affixes, such as *photo*, *bio*, and *chlor*.

Some subjects — especially science — involve so many subject-specific terms that the task of learning them may be overwhelming for English speakers and English learners alike. So much attention may be paid to these words that some of the more generally useful vocabulary may be neglected. Many of the specialized terms students must learn in some subjects are not fully internalized and may be forgotten as soon as the course is finished. As a result, it is important to focus on essential conceptual words. If students do not need a word to understand the big idea, the word is probably not important enough to take up space on the vocabulary agenda.

The Structure of English Words

Possessing a rich vocabulary depends not only on knowing many words, but also on understanding how words can be transformed to create new or related words. To help students analyze the structure of English words and recognize relationships among words, teachers must understand **word classes**, traditionally known as parts of speech, as well as morphemes.

Word Classes

Linguists often group English words into the word classes shown on the chart on this page. Students must learn to recognize which words in a sentence are nouns, verbs, and so on. Understanding these concepts and using the terms as labels is helpful to first and second language learners alike, especially adolescents. Rather than teaching these concepts by definition, it may be more helpful to teach through example and to encourage students to label examples of nouns, verbs, and so on in samples of real language. For a model lesson, see Chapter 12.

Roots and Derivational Morphemes

English words are made up of morphemes, which are combined in various ways to transform the meaning or function of words. Morphemes are classified into three categories: word roots, also known as stems; inflectional morphemes; and derivational morphemes. The word *prefixes*, for example, contains one derivational morpheme (*pre-*), one word root (*fix*), and one inflectional morpheme (*-es*).

WORD ROOTS

Every word contains at least one root that carries its basic meaning. The words *form*, *formal*, *formation*, *information*, and *informational*, for example, all contain the root *form*.

Some roots, such as *form*, *word*, *root*, and *Canada*, are **free morphemes** that can stand alone as individual words. Some words contain more

Word Classes	
Class	**Examples**
Nouns	child, English, language, swimming, truth
Pronouns	I, you, we, they, him, us, which, who, that
Verbs	run, jump, sleep, think, have, be, die
Auxiliary verbs	have, be, do (e.g., she has gone, she is going, did she go?)
Modal verbs	will, may, can (e.g., I will go, I may go)
Prepositions	in, on, over, through, beneath
Conjunctions	and, because, if, so, whereas

than one free morpheme. Compound nouns such as *blackboard*, *textbook*, and *notebook*, for example, consist of two roots, as do compound verbs such as *understand* and *overlook*.

Some roots are **bound morphemes** that cannot stand alone. The root *duc*, for example, derives from a Latin word meaning *to lead* and can be used only in combination with other morphemes (e.g., *reduce*, *educate*, and *conduct*).

Knowledge of low-frequency words is critically important to understanding textbooks and other academic material. Most low-frequency words contain Latin or Greek roots. The chart on this page shows 20 of the most common of these word roots in English. Knowledge of these helps unlock the meaning of thousands of words in English.

These roots should be taught as they arise in daily lessons rather than in isolation. If the word *extensive* occurs in a lesson, for example, ask students to think of examples of other words that use the same root, add a few more examples if necessary, and explain the meaning of the root. As similar words occur in lessons, post them on a chart as a reference for students.

Common Roots in English		
Root	**Meaning**	**Examples**
ceive, cept	take, seize	receive, conceive, concept, intercept
dic	speak	dictionary, dictate, contradict, predict, verdict
duc	lead	educate, produce, conduct, reduce
fac, fic, fec	make, do	factual, perfect, manufacture, fiction, efficient, defect
fer	carry, bear	offer, defer, confer, prefer
graph, gram	write	graph, monograph, autograph, telegram,
loc	place	location, dislocate, allocate, local
log	word, study	dialogue, epilogue, logic, geology
meter, metre	measure	barometer, thermometer, centimeter
mit, miss	send	transmit, submit, intermittent, mission
phon	sound	phonology, symphony, phonics, telephone
plic, plex, ply	fold	implicate, complicated, complex, perplex, multiply
pos, pon	put, place	position, dispose, compose, deposit, opposite, opponent
spec, spic	see, look	aspect, spectator, inspect, respect, conspicuous
scribe, script	write	inscribe, script, description, manuscript
sta, st	stand	station, status, insist, persist, protest
tain, ten (1)	hold, have, keep	detain, retain, contain, tenacious, maintenance
tele	far	telephone, television, telepathy, telegram
ten (2)	stretch	extend, extent, intend, intense, tension, tense
vis, vid	see	vision, visible, evidence, provide

The English affix system is very productive in forming new words. Some words have both prefixes and suffixes (e.g., information and informed), and some have more than one of each (e.g., misinformation and informational). This productivity may create difficulties for learners, many of whom may not perceive the underlying relationships among words such as act, actor, active, react, reaction, and reactionary.

Prefixes change or add to the meaning of a word (e.g., *view* and *preview*), while most suffixes signal the word class (e.g., noun, verb, and so on) and may add meaning. The charts on the following pages show the most common prefixes and suffixes in English.

For students of some language backgrounds, creating new words by adding affixes is an entirely new concept. Most Chinese words, for example, serve many purposes without changing form. The same word may function as a verb, noun, adjective, and adverb. Because the Chinese words for *difficult* and *difficulty* are the same, learners may not distinguish between these words in English, saying "This test is very difficulty," or "I have difficult in this test."

It may take a long time and much guidance for English language learners to become proficient in the morphological patterns of English. Teachers can help students recognize roots and affixes — the building blocks of words — when they encounter new words. This can dramatically improve students' reading comprehension and enhance their ability to use new words appropriately.

Learning New Words

English language learners must expand their vocabulary at twice or three times the rate of their English-speaking peers. To help them achieve this, an effective vocabulary program includes three components.

- Extensive reading of student-selected material
- Explicit instruction focusing on vocabulary that arises within the context of lessons
- Demonstration and modeling of vocabulary acquisition skills

Extensive Reading

According to Stephen Krashen, an expert in second language acquisition, reading extensively is the best way to promote vocabulary development, increase awareness of sentence structure, and encourage a life-long love of reading. Some researchers suggest that students pick up new words 10 times faster through reading than through explicit vocabulary instruction.

Most native speakers of English with large vocabularies developed their knowledge of words through extensive reading. In addition, people who read a lot are likely to improve their spelling without any focused spelling instruction. As long as the text is interesting and contains no more than five percent new words, reading can be a pleasurable way of expanding vocabulary, learning about life in North America and about other cultures, enhancing awareness of English sentence structure, and developing awareness of various writing styles.

Reading extensively is a powerful way to expand vocabulary.

Common English Prefixes			
Prefix	Other Forms	Meaning	Examples
ab-	a-, an-	from, away, up, out, not	abnormal, abolish, abduct, atheist, abstract, absent, anarchy
ad-	a-, ac-, af-, ag-, al-, an-, as-, at-	to, toward	add, admit, address, advertise, adhere, accept, affix, affluent, affiliate, agree, allegiance, announce, ascend, attach
com-	co-, col-, con-, cor-	with, together	combine, cooperate, collect, contain, correct
de-		from, down, away	defend, depend, decline, deceive, descend, deduct
dis-	di-, dif-	not; apart, away	disagree, dislike, distasteful; distance, diffuse, different
ex-	e-, ef-	out, beyond	extract, expand, exceed, educate, erase, effluent
in-(1)	ig-, im-, il-, ir-	not	inactive, indecent, incomplete, ignorant, ignoble, impossible, illogical, illegal, irreversible, irreparable
in-(2)	im-, il-, ir-	into	include, inform, invite, inhale, infect, import, immigrate, illuminate, illustrate, irradiate
inter-		between, among	interview, interfere, intervene, international
mis-		bad, wrong	mistake, misbehave, mislead, misrepresent
non-		not	nonviolent, nondescript, nonconformist
ob-	op-, of-, oc-	against, toward	objection, obtain, opposite, oppose, offer, offend, occasion, occur, occult
over-		above, too much	oversee, overpower, overwhelming
per-		through	perceive, perfect, perform, persuade, pervasive
pre-		before	prevent, predict, prefix, preview, prejudice
pro-		forward, in favor	progress, prosperity, produce, protect, proactive
re-		again, back	reform, review, return, reduce, reflect
sub-	suc-, suf-, sug-, sup-, sur-, sus-	under, close to	submerge, subvert, succeed, suffix, suffer, suggest, support, surround, suspect
trans-		across, beyond	transport, transfer, translate, transcribe
un-		not	unhappy, unlike, undo, unable

Common English Suffixes		
Suffixes	**Word Class (Meaning)**	**Examples**
-al	adjective	usual, bilingual, fundamental, critical
-ic	adjective	economic, linguistic, public, poetic
-y	adjective	easy, sunny, funny, cheesy, watery, icy
-ant, -ent (1)	adjective	pleasant, defiant, diligent, excellent
-ive	adjective	active, passive, negative, furtive
-ous	adjective	dangerous, marvelous, joyous
-ble	adjective: able to	portable, possible, credible
-ward	adjective: direction	toward, forward, backward, westward, upward
-ern	adjective: direction	southern, western
-ful	adjective: full of	resourceful, helpful, useful
-less	adjective: without	useless, hopeless, worthless, careless
-ly	adverb	easily, usually, linguistically
-ion, -tion, -sion	noun (abstract)	union, education, confederation, expansion
-ment	noun (abstract)	government, judgment, announcement
-ty, -ity	noun (abstract)	safety, beauty, loyalty, unity, charity, necessity
-ance, -ence	noun (abstract)	repentance, ignorance, violence, absence
-ship	noun (abstract)	hardship, friendship, fellowship, citizenship
-ism	noun (abstract): belief	Hinduism, Judaism, socialism, racism, sexism
-ant, -ent (2)	noun: person	immigrant, assistant, student, superintendent
-ian	noun: person	historian, physician, mathematician, musician
-ist	noun: person	biologist, pharmacist, specialist, dentist , racist
-er, -or	noun: person or instrument	teacher, ruler, hanger, doctor, actor, protractor
-ate	verb	indicate, immigrate, communicate
-ize	verb	symbolize, realize, organize
-en	verb	tighten, loosen, moisten, fasten, frighten

How to Promote Extensive Reading

- *Set aside a regular time* for free reading.

- *Encourage students to choose their own material* at a suitable reading level. Offer help to those who have difficulty choosing and always allow students to abandon a book that is not holding their interest.

- *Provide a variety of fiction and non-fiction materials* that appeal to students' interests, including magazines, comic books, children's picture books, romance novels, young adult fiction, newspapers, and how-to manuals.

- *Provide plenty of material at each student's independent reading level* (about 95 percent known words, other than names).

- *Provide recorded books for students at the beginning level* (see Chapter 11).

- *Focus on volume.* Encourage students to read as much — and as widely — as possible. Students can keep a reading record of the number of pages or books read.

- *Make the experience pleasurable.* Do not require students to write book reports or subject them to comprehension quizzes. Follow-up activities should focus on the learner's personal response to the selected material and give students choices. Most students enjoy discussing a book with a partner who has read the same book, for example, but they should not be required to do this with every book. Students may also enjoy reading aloud favorite sections to a cross-grade tutor or presenting a one-minute oral review to the class. From time to time, encourage students to write journal responses.

Encourage students to choose their own reading material: the purpose is to read freely and extensively, not necessarily to read fine literature or uplifting material. You can provide a selection of graded readers developed for English language learners, as well as other high-interest, low-vocabulary materials, though some students may prefer to read informational books, magazines, and newspapers. Picture books can also be used with students of various ages as long as the content is not too immature for older students.

Various publishers offer graded readers especially written or adapted for English language learners. Some readers retell classic or traditional stories, while others present simplified versions of contemporary adult fiction by authors such as John Grisham. Sentence structure is controlled so that books for beginners use only the most basic sentence structures while those at the higher levels are more complex. Vocabulary is also graded. Materials at the beginning level are based on the first 300 to 400 words of English, while those at higher levels include a vocabulary of 2,500 words or more. Do not insist that students read every title at each level; encourage them to choose titles that interest them and to move on to the next level as soon as they can read with ease. (For a list of resources, please see page 213.)

Emphasize reading for pleasure, and do not worry if students don't choose quality literature. They can learn an amazing number of low-frequency words, such as *nemesis*, *villain*, and *heroic*, from comic books. Quality literature can be introduced through teacher-directed activities such as literature circles (see Chapter 2) and guided reading activities (see Chapter 12).

English language learners enjoy reading simple books as long as the content and illustrations are appropriate to their maturity level. Some older students, however, may prefer not to reveal the kind of books they're reading to their English-speaking peers. As a result, it may be a good idea to keep these books in the ESL classroom rather than in the school library. Other students may be reluctant to read simple books because their pressing need is to read a science textbook or other complex material. Show these students how the books are graded and explain that if they work diligently through the levels, they will learn important vocabulary that will enable them to read textbooks. In addition, explain that the program will also include some intensive reading of more difficult textbook-style material.

Listening to books on tape is also helpful. Unless commercially produced recordings are developed specifically for language learners, the books are usually too difficult and the speech on the recordings is too fast. Try enlisting colleagues or senior students to help you create suitable recordings for students. You might also pair students with cross-grade tutors who will work with them regularly, reading aloud and explaining new words and concepts.

Some ESL graded readers include vocabulary practice exercises, but it is not a good idea to require students to do so much work that reading becomes a chore. Some students, however, may wish to complete vocabulary and other follow-up exercises because this fits their image of language learning. Allow them to do so. At the same time, you may wish to point out that experts such as Stephen Krashen suggest that students learn more words by reading another book than by completing exercises.

The main purpose of extensive reading is to instill a love of reading. Encouraging students to read material they enjoy will keep them motivated and moving forward. From time to time, ask students to meet in informal literature circles to share information about the books they are reading or meet students individually to talk about the books. Students might also enjoy sharing information about their books through drama or art activities. For more ideas for follow-ups, see chapters 2 and 12.

Focused Instruction

Students also require focused instruction on new vocabulary as it arises in daily lessons in various subject areas. This enables them to learn academic vocabulary in a meaningful context and provides opportunities for them to use new words immediately. For specific strategies such as word walls, cloze activities, and vocabulary notebooks, see Chapter 12.

Vocabulary Acquisition Skills

Second language learners must develop strategies for dealing with new or challenging vocabulary when they are reading independently. Use the guided reading process, described in Chapter 12, to demonstrate effective strategies for dealing with unfamiliar words in textbooks and other learning resources. These strategies are also useful when students are reading questions on tests and exams, including standardized literacy tests or the TOEFL (Test of English as a Foreign Language). A satisfactory score on the TOEFL is required by many universities before they will admit non-native speakers of English. You can also teach students how to use a vocabulary notebook and how to use dictionaries effectively (see Chapter 12).

To Learn More …

Books and Articles

Allen, J. *Words, Words, Words: Teaching Vocabulary in Grades 4-12*. York, Maine: Stenhouse Publishers, 1999.
Practical, research-based activities to enrich students' vocabulary with words drawn from reading and from various subject areas.

Bragg, M. *The Adventure of English: the biography of a language*. London: Hodder and Stoughton, 2003.
Entertaining story of the origins of the language and its spread around the world. The book builds on the U.K. television series of the same title.

Coxhead, A. "A New Academic Word List." *TESOL Quarterly*. Vol. 34, no. 2 (2000), pp. 213–238.
This word list is available online: <www.vuw.ac.nz/lals/research/awl>.

Crystal, D. *English as a Global Language*. 2nd ed. Cambridge University Press, 2003.
Interesting story of the origins and spread of English and the development of various forms of English around the world.

Day, R.R., and Bamford, J. *Extensive Reading in the Second Language Classroom*. Cambridge; Cambridge University Press, 1998.
Examines the research base for extensive reading as a way to develop vocabulary and other aspects of linguistic competence. Offers detailed practical advice on setting up an extensive reading program.

Fry, E., J. Kress, and D.L. Fountoukidis. *The Reading Teacher's Book of Lists*. 4th ed. West Nyack, N.Y.: Center for Applied Research in Education (now Jossey-Bass), 2000.
Compendium of lists (e.g., mathematics vocabulary, prefixes, and Greek and Latin roots) that are helpful when planning lessons.

Gairns, R., and Redman, S. *Working with Words: A guide to teaching and learning vocabulary*. Cambridge: Cambridge University Press, 1986.
Useful guide on vocabulary instruction..

Krashen, S. *The Power of Reading: Insights from the Research*. Englewood, Colo.: Libraries Unlimited, 1993.
Discusses the benefits of extensive reading on overall language development, including vocabulary and spelling.

Kress, J. *The ESL Teacher's Book of Lists*. West Nyack, N.Y.: Center for Applied Research in Education (now Jossey-Bass), 1993.
Another compendium of lists that include general and academic vocabulary. Useful reference for language teachers.

McArthur, T., ed. *The Oxford Companion to the English Language*. Oxford, U.K.: Oxford University Press, 1996.
An essential reference, filled with interesting information about the English language.

McCrum, R., W. Cran, and R. MacNeil. *The Story of English*. Revised ed. London: Faber and Faber, 1992.
This comprehensive overview of the development of English was originally published to accompany the BBC television series of the same name.

McWilliam, N. *What's in a Word? vocabulary development in multilingual classrooms*. Stoke on Trent, UK, 1998.
This book has a strong emphasis on school language, academic vocabulary, and academic success of English language learners. Includes many examples of children's language and classroom talk.

Nation, I.S.P. *Teaching and Learning Vocabulary*. Boston, Mass.: Heinle & Heinle, 1990.
Includes answers to many questions that teachers ask, such as, How many words does a second language learner need? and What should I do when there are unknown words in a text?

Nation, P., ed. *New Ways in Teaching Vocabulary*. Alexandria, VA: Teachers of English to Speakers of Other Languages, Inc., 1994.
A variety of classroom activities to introduce and practise vocabulary, and develop vocabulary acquisition skills.

Pilgreen, J.L. *The SSR Handbook: How to Organize and Manage a Sustained Silent Reading Program*. Portsmouth, N.H.: Heinemann, 2000.
Practical advice on setting up an extensive reading program. Includes suggestions for resources.

Richler, H.A. *Bawdy Language: How a Second-Rate Language Slept Its Way to the Top*. Toronto, Ont.: Stoddart, 1999.
An entertaining and informative look at the ever-changing English language.

Schmitt, N., and McCarthy, M. *Vocabulary: Description, Acquisition, and Pedagogy*. Cambridge: Cambridge University Press, 1998.
The articles in this collection provide a thorough treatment of vocabulary, for those who intend to become expert language teachers.

Schmitt, N. *Vocabulary in Language Teaching*. Cambridge: Cambridge University Press, 2000.
Provides research-based information for language teachers, as well as suggestions for classroom practice. Includes a word list of academic vocabulary and a vocabulary test.

Various authors. *Vocabulary in Use*. Cambridge: Cambridge University Press, various dates.
Series of student books at several levels, suitable for self study for students at the secondary level; also useful as a model for designing content-based vocabulary activities. The series can be ordered in British or North American versions. Similar books on idioms and phrasal verbs are also available. <www.cambridge.org/elt/inuse/vocabulary>

West, M. *A General Service List of English Words*. London: Longman, Green, 1953.
This list of the most frequent 2,000 words in English is out of print and hard to find, but it is available online at <jbauman.com/index.html>.

Wright, J. *Dictionaries*. Oxford, U.K.: Oxford University Press, 1998.
Many classroom activities designed to teach effective dictionary skills, learning strategies, and memory techniques.

6 English in Real Life: Communicative Competence

The concept of **communicative competence** was developed by Dell Hymes in the 1970s, and although the term has been adopted — and adapted — by others, it continues to refer to the ability to communicate effectively in real situations.

The previous chapters in this section presented information about English pronunciation, grammar, and vocabulary. These aspects of language performance are often called **structural competence**. Though structural competence is essential, effective communication requires more than learning new words, pronouncing them correctly, and stringing them together in grammatical sequences. These sentences — and the ideas they convey — must also be combined into a coherent whole. This aspect of language performance is called **discourse competence**.

Another important component of language performance is **sociolinguistic competence**, which refers to the ability to recognize and produce language that is appropriate in various social contexts and relationships. Equally important is **strategic competence**, which involves the ability to employ a variety of verbal and nonverbal strategies that are essential to participating effectively in conversations.

The chart on this page is a simple model of communicative competence. This chapter provides an overview of discourse competence, sociolinguistic competence, and strategic competence.

Communicative Competence			
Structural Competence	**Discourse Competence**	**Sociolinguistic Competence**	**Strategic Competence**
Pronunciation Grammar Vocabulary	Coherence and cohesion Genres of writing	Style (register) Cultural norms Language variety	Communication strategies Conversational strategies

Discourse Competence

Discourse competence involves the ability to understand and produce utterances or writing, such as stories, conversations, and reports, that are longer than sentences. It includes the effective use of reference words, understanding and using a wide variety of connective words and phrases, and the ability to recognize and produce specific forms or genres of language.

Examples of Connectives

- *To indicate generalizations*
Generally speaking, in my opinion, it is evident that, it can be argued that, some scientists (historians, experts, etc.) believe

- *To add examples or details*
For example, for instance, one example of this is, for one thing, such as

- *To add information or evidence*
In addition, moreover, furthermore, also

- *To identify a conclusion*
In conclusion, finally, to sum up, therefore, for these reasons, in the final analysis

- *To identify cause and effect*
Consequently, accordingly, thus, therefore, in order to, for this reason, because (of), as a result (of)

- *To compare or contrast*
Also, likewise, the same, similar, equally, both, neither, too, as well, parallel, in common
More, less, fewer, the most (least, fewest), bigger (biggest), smaller (smallest)
Twice as much as, twice as many as, half as much as, a quarter of
Second highest, third largest
Three times as many as, three times more than, three times larger than
Ten percent more than, five percent less than
Alternatively, by contrast, but, yet, whereas, on the other hand, however, nevertheless, conversely
Unless, otherwise, instead (of)
Despite, in spite of, although, even though, inasmuch as, notwithstanding

- *To indicate time and sequence*
First, second, third
Before, after, subsequently, prior to, next, then, after that, finally
While, meanwhile, simultaneously, contemporaneously, during
Invariably, always, usually, often, sometimes, occasionally, seldom, rarely, hardly, never
Briefly, temporarily, permanently, forever, for the time being, for the foreseeable future, for the next 10 years

- *To illustrate spatial organization*
By, in, on, over, up, down, into, beside, below, along, across, through, above
Next to, equidistant from, parallel to, attached to
Bisecting, bisected by, intersecting, intersected by

Reference Words

Reference words, such as *it, he, this, which, whose, the former,* and *the latter,* promote cohesion by linking ideas from one sentence to the next. The following examples are from a history textbook:

> In 1939, Mackenzie King promised Britain and France that Canada would support the war effort by sending military equipment and supplies. To do this, ...

In this example, *this* is a convenient way of referring to *sending military equipment and supplies* without repeating the phrase.

> Canadian scientists played a small role in helping the Americans develop the atomic bomb. On August 6, 1945, the United States Air Force dropped the first atomic bomb on Hiroshima in Japan. The Americans dropped a second bomb on Nagasaki on August 9, 1945. The destruction caused by these two bombs had never been seen before. The bomb dropped on Hiroshima killed 70 000 people. Most were civilians. The second bomb dropped on Nagasaki killed 40 000 people. Many more died later as a result of the effects of radiation.

The underlined words and phrases help link the ideas in this paragraph by referring to ideas mentioned earlier. In addition, the expressions, *the destruction caused* and *the bomb dropped,* are reduced versions of the longer forms, *the destruction that was caused* and *the bomb that was dropped.* Reduced references like these are common in academic text.

Connectives

In connected speech and organized writing, certain words and phrases promote coherence by showing the logical organization of ideas. For instance, the connective phrase *for example* indicates that an example of a previously stated idea is being cited. As students progress in school, they must acquire an increasingly sophisticated repertoire of connectives to understand academic text and organize their own ideas in speech and writing.

A typical written academic argument in English requires an opening statement of fact or opinion. This is supported by a series of arguments or examples and concludes with a closing statement that restates the initial assertion.

Specific connectives are used to advance a thesis or argument, separate main ideas from examples or details, and identify conclusions. Other connectives link ideas among and within sentences and paragraphs in specific, logical ways. They may be used to identify cause and effect, to compare or contrast, to indicate time and sequence, and to illustrate spatial organization.

Many learners of English must expand their repertoire of connective expressions so that they can recognize and use these expressions in formal academic writing.

Genres of Language

In all cultures, oral and written communication is shaped in accepted ways according to the audience and the purpose. These forms of communication can be classified as genres, each with specific identifiable features. A typical informal conversation in English, for example, is marked by hesitations, false starts, fillers (e.g., *um, you know*), grammar errors, and idiomatic expressions. By contrast, a newsreader uses careful speech that has been rehearsed to eliminate the hesitations, redundancies, and errors that are typical of informal conversation. Other genres of oral language include small talk, speeches, job interviews, talk-show interviews, and telephone conversations.

English language learners may be unfamiliar with the conventions that apply to various genres. They may not know, for example, that speeches in English traditionally begin with "Ladies and gentlemen." For this reason, they must be exposed to many examples of formal and informal oral language and encouraged to use the features of each. For more information about the features of oral language, see Chapter 7.

Specific textual features also mark the genres of written language. In news stories, for example, an inverted pyramid structure is typical. The first one or two paragraphs summarize the essential information: who, what, when, and where. The most important details follow immediately; those that are less important are provided later. This means that, if necessary, the bottom of the story can be cut without deleting important information or requiring a complete rewrite. It also means that editors can squeeze more attention-grabbing stories on to the front page and continue each on inside pages. Readers can then decide which to read in more depth. This style is also common in Web publishing because it enables readers to skim the main points and decide whether to click on a link to read more.

Other written genres include fairy tales, poems, science lab reports, essays, and journal entries. For more information on the written genres used in schools, see Chapter 7.

How Teachers Can Help

- Obtain the necessary permissions and make video- or audio tapes of various genres of oral communication, such as radio and TV news programs, public address announcements in the school, recorded telephone messages, and so on. Encourage students to discuss their similarities and differences. Students can also create short skits or role plays using one of the genres.
- Present samples of various genres of formal and informal written communication (e.g., formal business letters, friendly letters, and e-mail messages) and encourage students to discuss their similarities and differences.
- Use the guided reading process to draw students' attention to reference words and connectives in instructional text. See chapters 7 and 12.
- Use modeled and guided writing to encourage students to produce writing in various genres. See chapters 7 and 12.

Sociolinguistic Competence

Sociolinguistic competence, also known as sociocultural competence, involves speaking or writing at an appropriate level of formality for the situation, observing cultural norms with respect to conventions such as forms of address and nonverbal language, and recognizing or using varieties or dialects of English. Sociolinguistic competence is as important as accuracy in grammar, pronunciation, and word choice because

- students may use language that is grammatically correct but nevertheless inappropriate in a specific context. They may, for example, address their teachers in a style that is too familiar, too formal, or too forthright. They may also misinterpret messages they receive.
- learners may be unaware of cultural norms, such as the appropriate form of address for a teacher or the importance of making eye contact and using specific gestures.
- students whose first language is a non-standard variety of English, such as Jamaican Creole, may have difficulty recognizing differences between the variety they speak and the variety required to achieve success in school.

Language Style or Register

The **language style** or register that people use varies according to purpose, situation, and relationships. Everyone has many styles of speaking — and writing — and everyone varies his or her style to match the audience. In English and many other languages, for example, social characteristics, such as gender and the social status of the listener, may affect the style of the participants in a conversation. Age is another important variable: people speak differently to older and younger listeners. In some languages, these differences are very marked. In Korean, for example, children use various honorifics to address elders and older siblings.

The language style selected also depends on the speaker's relationship with other participants in a conversation. The way you speak to your friends and family, for example, may be quite different from the way you speak at school. And even at school, the way you speak to an individual student about an assignment may be different from the way you speak to the whole class, and the way you speak to the class may be different from the way you address a school assembly. Your style may also change when you speak to the principal — and may be more formal with a new principal than with a principal you have worked and socialized with for several years. Your style also varies according to your purpose. You probably use a different style to converse informally, to scold, to tell a story, to instruct, to entertain, and to make a speech.

To be successful in school, students must become competent in choosing and using the appropriate language style for specific purposes. Though it might be appropriate, for example, for a student to say to a peer, "Hey, gimme my ball back, okay?" it would be inappropriate to say, "Hey, gimme my essay back, okay?" to a teacher who has been slow to return an assignment. In day-to-day conversation, it is factually accurate and grammatically correct to say, "It rains a lot in Vancouver"; in the context of a high school geography course, however, the student

What Is Register?

Style is often referred to as register, although some linguists reserve *register* for the special ways that language is used in certain occupations. Teachers, for example, have a language of their own, both formal (e.g., *learning outcomes*, *curriculum expectations*, and *assessment rubrics*) and informal (e.g., *a spare* and *special ed*).

Register can also refer to the way language is used in various socioeconomic groups. The term *luncheon*, for example, may be considered more elevated than *lunch*. Through their choice of register, people may reveal their social origins or aspirations.

who can write, "Vancouver has a higher rate of precipitation than most other Canadian cities," will probably earn higher marks.

Second language learners may not perceive these differences in style, or they may have had insufficient exposure to English to develop a range of styles. As a result, they may misinterpret messages or communicate unintended messages.

Problems may arise when teachers and students from differing cultural backgrounds have different expectations about the style of communication between teachers and students. Over the past 50 years, North American classrooms have become much less formal, and the teacher-student relationship is much less authoritarian than it is in many other countries. It is also much less strict than adult-child relationships in some cultural and socio-economic groups. Rather than issuing commands, for example, teachers in North America often express directions and warnings as indirect requests or suggestions. At the end of a lesson, a teacher might say, "I like the way Ranjit is putting away all his crayons," as a cue for other children to put away their crayons, or "Where do the crayons belong, Ayesha?" as a veiled command to an individual child.

This kind of indirectness may be misinterpreted by students from backgrounds in which instructions, warnings, and rules are delivered in a much more direct and explicit manner. These students might respond more appropriately if the teacher said, "I want you all to put away your crayons now," or "Ayesha, put the crayons away now."

How Teachers Can Help

- Find a supportive and non-judgmental way to let students know they have used language in a socially inappropriate way, whether this involves sounding too deferential or abrupt and rude. To the student shown in the cartoon, for example, you might say, "I understand that you want me to look at your paper as soon as I can, but the way you said it is not the best way to speak to a teacher. Instead, you could say, 'Mr. ____, I worked hard on my assignment, and I really want to know how I did. I hope you'll have a chance to look at it soon.'"

Formal and Informal Expressions

Formal	Informal
Could you speak up, please?	Speak up!
	What?
Would you mind speaking more loudly?	Come again?
	What did you say?
You are speaking too softly.	Whassat?
	Huh?
I'm sorry, I can't hear you.	Eh?
	Eh?
It's very noisy in here.	
Sorry, I missed that.	
I think we have a bad line.	
Sorry, you're breaking up.	

- In English or language arts classes, expose students to language at various levels of formality and encourage them to identify differences. For example, after obtaining the appropriate permissions, show video clips from interviews and talk shows on local public television stations and compare these with material from shows that appeal to different audiences.
- Encourage students to read and listen to famous speeches, such as Martin Luther King's "I Have a Dream" speech, and identify some of the elements of oratorical style.
- Invite speakers to make presentations of various kinds. The president of the students' council or representatives of clubs, for example, might provide information and solicit support for activities, or the principal might visit to welcome newcomers and talk about the school's approach to cultural diversity. Afterwards, discuss how elements of the speaker's style differ from conversational speech with a friend.
- Help students develop a repertoire of formal and informal ways of expressing the same message. Display a list of expressions like those shown on this page and talk about situations in which each is appropriate. Discuss factors such as the relationship between the speakers (e.g., whether they know each other and whether one is older or in a position of authority). Point out that the medium of communication is also important. An expression like, "I think we have a bad line," is appropriate only when speaking on the telephone, and "Sorry, you're breaking up," is specific to a conversation on a cellular phone.
- Involve students in role plays that encourage them to practice adjusting their speech to the social context. Pairs might be assigned an expression from the list on this page, for example, and instructed to create a short dialogue using it in an appropriate situation.
- Provide opportunities for students to "translate" formal language into a more relaxed style and vice versa. Students might listen to a formal announcement on the public address system, for example, and translate this into the style of a conversation among friends in the cafeteria.
- Do not be embarrassed to deal with vulgar or obscene language. Language learners sometimes use inappropriate expressions that they have learned in the schoolyard and elsewhere. Rather than ignoring these expressions, explain what is considered appropriate in English. A more proficient bilingual peer can sometimes help with the explanation. In the case of anatomical expressions, it is important to help students distinguish between vulgar terms, everyday terms, and the words that might be used in a doctor's office.
- At the beginning of the year or course, give instructions that are as clear and direct as possible. Make sure all students can see and hear you. Because students may also interact with other teachers whose style is more indirect, however, gradually start using this style yourself, but remember to decode it for the students. You might say, for example, "The next class needs a clean and tidy classroom. This means that you must clean up now." To an individual student, you might say, "I think you can improve this assignment. This means that I want you to redo it, following the suggestions I have given you, and show it to me tomorrow."

- When students appear to ignore or misunderstand instructions, treat this as a linguistic problem. You might say something like, "Yesterday, I said that it might be a good idea to revise the last paragraph of your report. What do you think I wanted you to do?"

Cultural Norms in Language Use

In every language, unstated social rules or norms govern how language is used in various social contexts. The following factors may affect communication:

- The context or setting may determine who may initiate a conversation, especially when differences in age, sex, or social status are involved. Some newcomers, for example, may have been schooled in an environment in which students seldom initiate discussions or ask questions; rather, they wait for the teacher to call on them.
- The relationship among speakers may affect word choice. In French, for example, *tu* is the familiar form of *you* and would be used by an adult, such as a teacher, to address a child; the more formal *vous*, however, is used to address strangers and authority figures.
- In some cultures, addressing a teacher as "Teacher" is a sign of respect, but this is not so among English speakers. In some North American schools, it is more usual to address teachers as "Sir" or "Miss." In other schools, students are required to address teachers by name (e.g., "Mr. Arnold," "Ms. Weinstein"), and in some alternative schools, students are encouraged to use teachers' first names.
- Naming practices vary across cultures. If you address Lam Van Bao's mother as "Mrs. Bao," for example, you are addressing her by her son's given name, which is like calling Billy Smith's mother "Mrs. Billy."
- In some languages, such as Japanese and Korean, several levels of formality exist and the level chosen depends on the relative status of the speakers. By comparison, it may seem easy to make choices in English. Still, when you address someone in English, you must decide whether to use the person's given name, nickname, pet name, family name, or an honorific, such as Mr. or Ms, and the family name. Many learners of English are taken aback by the apparent easy familiarity of many North Americans and often misjudge their response. To make the matter even more complex, a person addressed by his first name cannot assume that he is free to reply in kind, even if both speakers are adults. What if the person is his professor or supervisor at work?
- Using *please* and *thank you* is very important in English. It is also common to acknowledge thanks by saying, "You're welcome." Because these expressions — or their equivalents — are not as commonly used by speakers of many other languages, some language learners may sound unintentionally abrupt. And in some languages, the equivalent expressions may be used in somewhat different ways. In French, for example, *merci*, which means thank you, sometimes indicates refusal and is the equivalent of saying "No, thank you," in English.
- English speakers are often uncomfortable with conversational silences that last more than a few seconds and hasten to fill them. When a student does not respond immediately to a question, the teacher may move on to another student or ask another question. In other cultures, silence may indicate thought or that a reply is not

considered necessary. In the classroom, second language learners often need more time to compose a response.

- In many cultures, it is polite to decline an offer of food the first two or three times it is offered — and accept it only on the third or fourth offer. People from Bulgaria, for example, would be astonished and offended if, after a first refusal, food is not offered to them again. This is just one example of the importance of cultural as well as linguistic knowledge in cross-cultural communication.

Nonverbal Language

Nonverbal language consists of body language, such as gestures, eye contact, facial expressions, and body posture or movement, as well as less visible but equally important behavior, such as the use of silence and the use of physical space. Nonverbal language varies from culture to culture. The following examples of differences in nonverbal language may sometimes lead to miscommunication.

- Most English speakers beckon with the hand palm up; in other cultures, this may be insulting. In some, it is usual to beckon with the hand held palm down, which may look similar to the rather dismissive English gesture that means go away.
- Rules governing eye contact often vary. Many English speakers interpret looking someone in the eye as a sign of trustworthiness, sincerity, or interest. In some cultures, however, it is considered impolite to make or maintain eye contact for more than a fraction of a second, especially when the social status of the participants in a conversation is different. It may be considered rude, for example, for a child to sustain eye contact with a teacher or other adult.
- The interpretation of facial gestures, such as winking, raising the eyebrows, rolling the eyes, looking upward, and smiling, may vary from culture to culture. In some cultures, displaying an open mouth is considered rude, which is why some students — especially females — may attempt to conceal a smile or laugh behind their hands.
- Handshaking, where it is practiced at all, may be restricted to persons of the same sex, to certain age groups, or to a particular kind of relationship or situation. The handshake may also be gentler than in North America, where a firm handshake is often considered a sign of forthrightness and strength of character.
- Head movements that indicate yes and no are not universal. In Bulgaria, for example, a brief shake of the head means yes, and a sharp toss of the head upwards indicates no. English speakers may completely misinterpret these gestures.
- North American hand gestures, such as thumbs up or circling the thumb and forefinger to indicate okay, are considered obscene in some cultures.
- In some cultures, formalized body movements communicate respect. In Japan, for example, students may have a repertoire of bows, while South Asian students may join their hands in front of the body and bow their heads.
- The physical distance that speakers maintain during conversation varies. In some cultures, standing close to a conversation partner is usual; in others, more personal space is required. Without being aware of it, speakers from various cultures may move toward or away from each other to regain their own position of comfort.

- In North America, physical touching is generally restricted to family members, close friends, or those involved in intimate relationships. In many other cultures, it is common to maintain fleeting physical contact during conversation with, for example, a touch of the hand on the arm.
- In many English-speaking countries, public displays of affection, such as handholding and kissing, are common. In many other cultures, however, physical intimacy between males and females is a private matter, although friends of the same sex may hold hands or walk arm-in-arm in public.

How Teachers Can Help

- Discuss student-teacher relationships and encourage students to compare aspects of school culture in their new country with their previous experience and expectations.
- Ask students to go outside the classroom to observe and document unwritten cultural norms for forms of address, polite forms, and nonverbal language. Students might, for example, visit a fast-food restaurant or the school office to observe examples of polite language and behavior, such as saying, "Good morning," "May I help you?" "Thank you," and "You're welcome." They might also observe how far apart people stand when engaged in conversation, how loudly they speak, and how they distribute themselves in cafeterias, restaurants, elevators, buses, and other public places. Teenagers will be especially interested in observing how couples and friends behave in public. Discuss students' observations and make cross-cultural comparisons.
- Explore cultural differences through drama. Students might, for example, create a role play showing how a situation might unfold in their new culture and their country of origin.
- Ask students how names work in their home language and culture and how you should address their parents. The class might create a display comparing naming practices and explaining the meaning or origin of their own names.
- Show students how to use the firm North American handshake and set up role plays in which they can practice using it (e.g., during introductions, parent-teacher interviews, or job interviews).
- Discuss nonverbal language as an important mode of communication and explain how cultural miscues may convey mistaken impressions. Validate the cultural norms students are accustomed to, but explain that they must also learn how to relate effectively to people raised in English-speaking countries. Students can practice using various forms of nonverbal communication in skits and role plays.
- If you use a gesture that causes consternation or hilarity among some students, explain what it means and ask whether its meaning is different in their culture. Similarly, if a student uses a gesture that puzzles you, ask what it means and show him or her an equivalent gesture.

Language Variety and Standard English

All languages evolve differently in different locations and among various social groups, and English is no exception. Differing varieties of

English evolved in the days before mass communication, when groups of English speakers were often physically isolated from one another and when contact among people of different social classes was limited. English also traveled with explorers, empire builders, colonial administrators, and British settlers to countries all over the world — and the language evolved differently in all these places.

Regional and social-class variations survive today, despite mass media and communication systems that enable people to interact with one another across vast distances. Even though populations today are highly mobile, moving easily from one speech community to another, linguistic variation thrives. Pressures that encourage homogenization are counterbalanced by pressures within speech communities to assert their cultural and social identity by maintaining distinct speech patterns.

Language is more than a means of communication; it is also an important marker of identity and social status. The variety of language a person speaks sometimes reveals a great deal about his or her geographic origin, and socioeconomic status. Some varieties of English enjoy greater prestige than others. The preferred or more prestigious variety is associated with superior education and social standing and is often referred to as **standard English**.

People who speak standard English are often considered well-spoken. Other varieties of English are more likely to be associated with low social standing, lack of sophistication, or undesirable character traits. As a result, speakers of other varieties of English are more likely to be judged to speak poorly. These attitudes are based on linguistic prejudice, rather than the intrinsic superiority of standard English.

Though standard English is not superior to other varieties of English, it does have a special place as the language of school. To be academically successful, all students must become proficient in standard English and the special ways it used at school. At the same time, other varieties of English should be respected. Jamaican Creole, for example, is a valid means of communication among Jamaicans and an important source of cultural identity and self-esteem.

To work effectively with students who speak various forms of English, teachers must understand regional and social variety in English and how the variety known as standard English acquired its status. It is also important to respond to language variety in the classroom in ways that are respectful and helpful to students who need to add standard English to their language repertoire.

WHAT IS STANDARD ENGLISH?

Standard English is a dialect. Once known as the King's or Queen's English, it evolved from the dialect spoken at court and among the powerful in London. William Caxton chose to represent this dialect in print when he printed the first books in English, and its use as the printed form of the language helped establish it as the standard.

The term *standard* is often used as if it were synonymous with *correct*; in fact, all varieties of English are equally correct, and standard English owes its status more to might than right. "A language is a dialect with an army and a navy" is a famous saying among linguists. The standard dialect is the one spoken by those in authority and those with education; as a result, it has special currency as the dialect of prestige and power. Those of higher socioeconomic status — and those who aspire to this — usually speak the standard dialect. Many people also speak a local or

Caribbean English Creole: Language or Dialect?

Analysis has shown that the grammar and phonological rules of Caribbean English Creole can be described as systematically as those of any other language, including English. Furthermore, Caribbean English Creole is as distinct from English as French and Spanish are from Latin.

Whether it is a language or a dialect, Caribbean English Creole coexists with standard English in the Caribbean and in the English-speaking countries where Caribbean immigrants and their children and grandchildren live. Often stigmatized because it is associated with slavery, poverty, lack of schooling, and lower socioeconomic status, Creole may be viewed, even by those who speak it, as inferior to standard English, which is the official language and the language of power and education.

Most speakers of Caribbean English Creole can switch between Creole and standard English, as well as intermediate forms between the two. At the same time, however, they may retain some distinctive features of Creole grammar. They may mark past-tense and plural forms inconsistently, for example, saying things like, "She give me some book to read." Pronunciation may also differ; the sounds represented in print by *th*, for example, may be pronounced so that *thin* sounds like *tin* and *those* sounds like *doze*.

When students of Caribbean background attend schools in English-speaking countries, they may need explicit instruction in certain forms of standard English. At the same time, however, it is important to acknowledge their variety of English as a valid form of communication that provides them with an enriched language repertoire. They are bilingual — or potentially bilingual — in the same way as, for example, their Vietnamese- or Spanish-speaking peers. The kind of language instruction they need is not the same, however. Students who speak Caribbean English Creole may already possess a large English vocabulary, for example, and are often receptively competent in English. Instruction should therefore focus on specific forms that cause difficulty and use a contrastive approach to make explicit the differences between the two varieties of English.

social-class variety, switching between their two dialects depending on the context.

Standard English is not limited to a specific geographic region; it may be spoken anywhere, often with a regional accent. Standard British English, standard Canadian English, standard American English, standard Australian English, standard Jamaican English, and many other forms of standard English are spoken with different accents. Vocabulary differences also mark the varieties; for example, *lorries* in British English are *trucks* in North America, and *kinfolk* in the Southern United States are *relatives* elsewhere. No matter where it is spoken, however, the sentence structure of standard English is nearly identical.

REGIONAL VARIATION

Regional **dialects** are spoken in various geographic areas, such as London, Liverpool, Glasgow, New York, Atlanta, the Appalachian region of the United States, Newfoundland, Singapore, New Delhi, Lagos, and many other cities and rural areas in countries around the world. Regional differences in English are sometimes so great that speakers of different varieties need subtitles to understand one another. Jamaican and Scottish films, for example, as well as films made in some English cities, such as Manchester and Liverpool, are often subtitled for North American distribution.

A dialect is more than an accent. An accent is simply the way people pronounce the sounds of a language and is most marked on vowel sounds (e.g., *bath* may be pronounced /bæθ/ or /bɑθ/). Everyone speaks with an accent, and there is no accent-free way to pronounce words, although some accents have greater prestige than others.

Dialects are marked by grammar differences as well as a distinctive accent. In many parts of Northern England, for example, *he were* is the third-person singular, past-tense form of *be*; *tha* and *ta*, derived from the archaic form *thou*, are used for you; and the forms *thee*, *thy*, and *thine* are common in some rural areas. In Newfoundland, *youse* is a common plural form of *you*, while in the southern United States, *you-all* — or *y'all* — is a commonly accepted plural form.

The grammar of some regional dialects diverges from standard English more dramatically than others. The grammar of Caribbean English Creole, such as Jamaican Creole and Trinidadian Creole, is different from that of standard English in many ways, including plural markers, verb tenses, and the pronoun system. *The Oxford Companion to the English Language* notes 11 grammatical features that identify Black English vernacular, also known as Ebonics. Versions of this dialect are spoken by many African Americans.

The vocabulary of regional dialects also varies. Some words in Black English vernacular, such as *yam* and *tote*, trace their ancestry to the languages of West Africa, and Caribbean English Creole languages also include words of West African origin. The Jamaican word *nyam*, for example, means eat and probably derives from Twi, the language of the Ashanti people of Ghana.

Vocabulary differences among dialects can lead to comprehension difficulties and are sometimes so great that speakers of different dialects have trouble understanding one another. Nevertheless, speakers of regional dialects usually refer to their language as English, and speakers of different dialects generally use standard written forms.

A regional dialect is not an incomplete or deficient version of standard English. For reasons that have more to do with linguistic prejudice

Social-Class Variations in English

- Dropping aitches. Upper-class speakers in all regions of the United Kingdom usually pronounce the *h* in words such as *house*, while people in the lowest social groups seldom do. Interestingly, dropping the *h* in some words of French origin (e.g., *an hotel* and *an historic occasion*) is sometimes associated with upper-class speech in British English.
- Dropping the *g* in *-ing* endings and pronounce these as *in*. Until a few generations ago, this was also a fashionable affectation among the British landed gentry, who were very fond of *huntin, shootin,* and *fishin.*
- Using *ain't*. This word is, however, sometimes used by educated speakers as an affectation. Interestingly, the question form *aren't I?* was probably adopted as a result of the strong social stigma against the use of *ain't I?*
- Using *me, him,* and *her* as subjective pronouns (e.g., *James and me went to the movies*).
- Using double negatives (e.g., *She didn't give me none* and *I never saw nobody*). In some other languages, however, double negatives are common (e.g., *ne ... pas* and *ne ... jamais* in French).
- Using different verb forms (e.g., *I been there, I seen it, she done it, it's broke, he give it to me last week,*).
- Using *them* as a demonstrative pronoun (e.g., *Give me them books*).
- Using *don't* and *was* with all persons (e.g., *She don't like it* and *We was there*).

than with the utility of the dialect in question, however, most regional dialects do not have the same status as standard English. Because standard English is the language of education, schools have a special responsibility to help students learn standard English in addition to their own dialect.

SOCIAL-CLASS VARIATION

Language is as much a badge of social class as it is of geographic origin. Throughout the English-speaking world, varieties of language related to social class are often called **sociolects**. Like dialects, sociolects differ in accent, grammar, and some vocabulary. Because social differences affect some of the most commonly used forms of the language, it is easy to listen to someone and "place" him or her socially within seconds. In *Pygmalion*, both Henry Higgins and Eliza Doolitle knew that the way Eliza spoke identified her origins in a poor, working-class London neighborhood and that she would be accepted by members of the upper classes only if she learned to speak like them.

The examples shown on this page illustrate linguistic variations that are commonly stigmatized as incorrect. These examples are in no way inferior to standard forms in terms of efficiency of communication and are considered incorrect or sloppy only because they are generally associated with lower socio-economic status and lower education levels. In fact, some of these stigmatized forms may be used by more English speakers than so-called correct forms. I *seen it* and *I done it*, for example, may be more common than the standard English forms *I saw it* and *I did it*. If these forms are more widely used than the standard version, who is to say which is correct?

Nevertheless, these forms — and other features of non-standard English or working-class speech — are frowned on in schools, and students who use them in their writing are nearly certain to have their papers heavily marked in red ink and to receive lower marks. Generations of teachers have spent so much time and energy correcting children who use these non-standard forms that many people now hypercorrect by applying rules inappropriately. Many educated people say, for example, "Between you and I ..." when the objective form, *me*, is the correct choice as the object of the preposition *between*.

To be successful in school, children whose home language is a socially stigmatized variety of English must learn the standard English forms that are accepted in the school setting. These students need an awareness of the pragmatic value of standard English, not as a superior version of language, but as a version that is associated with success in the wider society.

How Teachers Can Help

Teachers in socially and culturally diverse schools must provide explicit instruction in features of standard English and school language that many learners may not be exposed to every day. Without this instruction, students whose home language does not match that of the school may never acquire some important features of literary and academic language. At the same time, however, it is important to validate other languages and other varieties of English spoken in the community and to ensure that all students develop positive attitudes toward linguistic diversity and language variety.

The following approaches help students develop a pragmatic awareness of the benefits of learning the language of the school and become proficient in that language at the same time as they maintain and value their own linguistic heritage and identity.

- Incorporate literature that includes different varieties of English. Much Caribbean literature, for example, uses standard English in the narrative and Creole for dialogue.
- Obtain the appropriate permissions and show video clips of people using various English dialects. For example, the British soap operas *EastEnders* and *Coronation Street* are set in working-class districts in London and Northern England respectively.
- Develop students' critical language awareness, helping them understand that though standard English is no more correct than other varieties of English, it is more closely associated with power and success than others. A useful way to explain this is to say that to change unfair rules, you must be able to speak the same language as those who make the rules. Someone who is able to say, "Them rules ain't fair, so let's change 'em!" as well as, "The existing rules are unjust, for the following reasons.... The following changes are recommended ...." is more likely to receive a respectful hearing.
- Provide explicit instruction in standard English forms and school language. Use a content-based approach to integrate this instruction into the curriculum. For examples of content-based instruction, see Chapter 12.
- Provide supportive and formative feedback. Do not correct every error a student makes; rather, note persistent errors made by individuals or groups and provide short, focused mini-lessons to those students, either later in the lesson or the next day. And rather than correcting students' errors yourself, help students understand and correct their own errors. For more information on responding to students' errors, see chapters 8 and 10.

Strategic Competence

Confident language learners use a range of **communication strategies** to compensate for their incomplete knowledge of English and maintain communication, even when the level of conversation is significantly beyond their level of proficiency. Some English language learners may be so anxious about getting things right, however, that they cannot speak fluently or respond quickly enough in conversation or in classroom discussions.

Confident language learners also use a variety of **conversational strategies**, which are semi-fixed expressions that help people initiate or enter a conversation, steer it in the direction they want to go, and terminate it smoothly. Less confident students may be able to respond to questions and prompts but lack the strategies required to initiate or "steer" a conversation. As a result, they do not participate as much or as effectively as they would like.

Communication Strategies

Second language learners must learn to use specific communication strategies when communication is difficult. These strategies include

- paraphrasing to confirm comprehension (e.g., Do you mean that I have to finish it this week?)
- seeking clarification (e.g., Can you give me an example of what you mean?)
- finding an alternative way to express an idea. A student who knows the word *gloves* but not *mittens* might say, "Like gloves, you know, without fingers."
- substituting an all-purpose word, such as *things* or *stuff*, for an unknown word in the target language
- asking for help (e.g., Would you repeat that? or What does ___ mean?)
- repeating, with rising intonation (e.g., I must finish it this week?)
- guessing at the meaning of a word based on the context or by analogy with other known words or cognates
- using nonverbal signals (e.g., mime, gestures, and facial expressions) or drawing a picture to illustrate an unknown word
- approximation (e.g., substituting "beautiful red flower" for "rose")
- creating a word, following a known pattern (e.g., *hateable* for *hateful*)

Some learners avoid certain topics or situations that are especially difficult. Many students become very frustrated when they want or need to communicate their ideas on abstract or complex topics but are unable to do so. Some English language learners in secondary school avoid entire subjects, especially in the humanities, because they fear the language load will be too great. Other less drastic avoidance strategies include changing the subject, pretending not to understand a question, and simply falling silent in a discussion.

How Teachers Can Help

- Do not over-emphasize correctness, as this may inhibit communication. Accept that mistakes are part of the language learning process and encourage students to continue talking even when they know they are making mistakes. For more on errors and error correction, see chapters 8 and 10.
- Involve language learners in engaging group tasks and problem-solving activities that promote interaction among students. For suggestions on structuring group activities, see Chapter 10.
- Ensure that other students are sensitive to the needs of second language learners. Show by your own example how they can help the English language learner remain involved in discussions (e.g., by repeating or rephrasing the learner's utterance in a non-judgmental way).
- Comment favorably when students keep a conversation going (e.g., Did you notice what Kim did when she didn't know the word *mittens*?).
- Encourage students to guess the meaning of new words, using context, illustrations, and other cues.
- Help students expand their repertoire of conversational strategies.

Conversational Strategies

Think of your last meeting with your principal or another administrator. One of you may have initiated the conversation by saying something like, "Hi, thanks for coming in," or "Thanks for finding the time to see me." Then one of you may have presented the topic by saying, "I wanted to talk to you about (get your ideas on) ...." Perhaps one of you disagreed with the other, saying, "Well, I don't really see it that way," and one of you may have negotiated consensus: "Can we agree that ...?" Finally, someone probably ended the conversation with words like, "Well, thanks for your help (input, time, etc.)."

Expressions like these perform important functions. Conversational strategies not only help guide conversations, but they also give the participants a second or two of thinking time. Without a repertoire of these strategies, many English language learners are unable to participate as effectively as they would like in classroom discussions or one-on-one conversations. Conversations become awkward and stilted, with uncomfortable gaps and moments of uncertainty, and some speakers may never have an opportunity to say what is on their minds.

Some conversational strategies are especially important in classroom interactions. Students need a repertoire of expressions to, for example, seek attention or help, take a turn in a conversation or offer someone else a turn, seek clarification or repetition, check comprehension, express an opinion, indicate disagreement, keep the discussion on track, and show appreciation. Proficiency in using these expressions greatly enhances students' fluency and confidence.

To seek the attention of a teacher, for example, it is appropriate to say something like, "Excuse me, Ms _____, do you have a minute?" In another situation, however, "Hey!" or "Yo!" might be more appropriate. Students need a wide repertoire of these expressions, as well as the language awareness necessary to choose the expression that is most appropriate in a specific situation.

A repertoire of conversational strategies enables students to exert greater control over their daily language transactions and learning experiences. The chart on the following page shows examples of expressions that students can use to improve classroom communication.

How Teachers Can Help

- Involve students in role plays focusing on the use of expressions for a specific function. To practice interrupting politely, for example, pairs of students might role play going to the office to get help for a friend who is ill, asking for help from a teacher who is busy planning a lesson, going to the staffroom to ask to see a specific teacher, or asking for help in a store where two clerks are engaged in conversation.

- Use cooperative learning to focus on specific behavior and conversational strategies that support the group process. During group activities, observe how students use nonverbal behavior and conversational strategies to take turns, disagree, keep the group on task, and so on. If students are discussing a controversial topic, for example, observe how they express disagreement. Do they use strategies that promote continued discussion and negotiation and communicate respect for one another's ideas? If students are not managing disagreement effectively, focus attention on this topic

Conversational Strategies	
Intent of Speaker	**Strategy**
Get attention or help	Excuse me. Do you have a moment? Pardon me for interrupting. Sorry to interrupt, but … I wonder if you can help me. Can you help me? Can I bother you for a moment? May I have some help over here?
Take (or offer) a turn	I'd like to say (add, suggest, ask) … I have an idea (point, comment, question). Can I get a word in? Let me suggest (explain, add). Do you have any suggestions (ideas)? What about you? Let's hear from _____. (We haven't heard from _____.
Seek clarification or repetition	Sorry, I didn't get that. Would you explain it again? Did you say …? Would you run that by me again? Would you repeat that? Would you go over that again? Come again? Pre…storic? (repetition with rising intonation)
Express an opinion	In my opinion, … My view is … You may not agree with me, but … I strongly (honestly, really, etc.) believe (think) that … As I see it, … It seems to me that … It's clear (obvious) to me that …
Indicate disagreement	I don't really see it that way. I don't agree. I disagree. I don't see eye to eye with you on that. I have another point of view. Look at it this way. We're not on the same wavelength.
Keep the discussion on track	Let's get back to … Can we focus on …? Going back to … Let's stay on topic (task). We are off topic.
Show appreciation	Thanks (thank you) (for your help, time, etc.). I appreciate your help (support, etc.). You have been very helpful (kind, supportive, etc.). That's a good idea (suggestion, etc.). You have been a big help.

once the group task is finished. You might say, "When we disagree with someone, it's important to keep discussion going and show respect for other people's opinions. What are some things we can say and do to manage disagreement and ensure that no one's feelings are hurt?"

Ask the groups to brainstorm possible answers and synthesize students' ideas into a class agreement that can be posted as a reminder to students the next time they are discussing a controversial topic. Continue adding to the agreement as necessary during the year and generate new agreements as required. Though you may need to draw students' attention to the agreement many times during the year, they will eventually begin to integrate the strategies and expressions into their repertoire in a more natural way. For more on cooperative learning, see Chapter 10.

To Learn More ...

Books and Articles

Brown, H.D. *Principles of Language Learning and Teaching*. 4th ed. White Plains, N.Y.: Addison-Wesley Longman (now Pearson Education), 2000.

A standard in TESL training programs. Chapter 7 discusses sociocultural factors that affect language learning, and Chapter 9 provides an overview of communicative competence and communicative language teaching.

Bryson, B. *The Mother Tongue: English and How It Got That Way*. New York: William Morrow, 1990.

An entertaining and informative book about the English language.

Burridge, K. *Blooming English: Observations on the roots, cultivation, and hybrids of the English language*. Cambridge: Cambridge University Press, 2004.

A collection of short articles on many interesting aspects of the English language, including word origins, "bad language", and spelling reform.

Chaika, E. *Language: The Social Mirror*. 3rd ed. Boston, Mass.: Heinle and Heinle, 1994.

Introduction to sociolinguistics, with helpful and interesting chapters on styles of speech, nonverbal language, dialects, and social attitudes to language.

Claire, E. *Dangerous English 2000: An Indispensable Guide for Language Learners and Others*. McHenry, Ill.: Delta Systems, 1998.

Updated version of a classic ESL text designed to help students avoid embarrassment and insulting others, learn correct terms for the doctor's office, and understand street language.

Coelho, E. *Caribbean Students in Canadian Schools, Book 2*. Toronto, Ont.: Pippin Publishing, 1991.

Background information on Caribbean English Creole and suggestions for helping Creole speakers add standard English to their language repertoire.

Coelho, E. *Jigsaw*. Toronto, Ont.: Pippin Publishing, 1991.

Content-based reading and discussion tasks and problem-solving activities for English language learners in middle and secondary school.

Coelho, E., and L. Winer. *Jigsaw Plus*. Toronto, Ont.: Pippin Publishing, 1991.

More content-based reading and discussion tasks and problem-solving activities.

Coelho, E. *Learning Together in the Multicultural Classroom*. Toronto, Ont.: Pippin Publishing, 1994.

How to promote oral interaction through cooperative learning activities.

Corson, D. *Language, Minority Education, and Gender*. Toronto, Ont.: Ontario Institute for Studies in Education (now University of Toronto Press), 1993.

Sociopolitical perspective on language and power focuses on students whose use of language has traditionally been stigmatized.

Crystal, D. *The Cambridge Encyclopedia of Language*. Cambridge, U.K.: Cambridge University Press, 1987.

An introduction to many topics in language, including language variety and register.

Delpit, L. *Other People's Children: Cultural Conflict in the Classroom*. New York, N.Y.: New Press, 1995.

Includes commentary on teaching standard English to speakers of other varieties, such as Black English Vernacular.

Hadfield, J. *Classroom Dynamics*. Oxford, U.K.: Oxford University Press, 1992.

Activities for creating a classroom environment in which students interact comfortably with one another to complete group tasks.

Helmer, S., and C. Eddy. *Look at Me When I Talk to You: ESL Learners in Non-ESL Classrooms*. Rev. ed. Toronto, Ont.: Pippin Publishing, 2003.

Outlines areas of cultural difference and potential conflict. Essential reading for teachers in multilingual and multicultural classrooms.

Hymes, D. "On Communicative Competence." In J.B. Pride and J. Holmes, eds., *Sociolinguistics*. Harmondsworth, U.K.: Penguin, 1972.

Ideas in this article have influenced linguistics and language teaching for more than 30 years.

Jerald, M., and R.C. Clark. *Experiential Language Teaching Techniques: Out-of-Class Language Acquisition and Cultural Awareness Activities*. Brattleboro, Vt.: Pro Lingua Associates, 1994.

Thirty structured contact assignments to help students use English in real-life situations.

Keller, E., and S.T. Warner. *Conversation Gambits*. Hove, U.K.: Language Teaching Publications, 1988.

Originally developed for use by francophone civil servants in Canada, the activities in this book help students acquire a range of conversational strategies.

Lynch, T. *Communication in the Language Classroom*. Oxford, U.K.: Oxford University Press, 1996.

The first part of this book provides a rationale for communicative language teaching; the second sets out communicative activities that promote interaction in the classroom.

Maley, A., and A. Duff. *Drama Techniques in Language Learning: A Resource Book of Communication Activities for Language Teachers*. 2nd ed. Cambridge, U.K.: Cambridge University Press, 1982.

Communicative tasks that promote fluency and enable learners to practice using language in real-life situations.

McArthur, T., ed. *The Oxford Companion to the English Language*. Oxford, U.K.: Oxford University Press, 1992.

An essential reference filled with interesting information about the English language.

McCrum, R., W. Cran, and R. MacNeil. *The Story of English*. Revised ed. London: Faber and Faber, 1992.

Overview of the development of English was originally published to accompany the BBC television series of the same name.

Mendelsohn, D., and J. Rubin, eds. *A Guide for the Teaching of Second Language Listening*. San Diego, Calif.: Dominie Press, 1995.

Theoretical and practical articles on teaching effective listening strategies focus on academic language. Especially useful for secondary school teachers.

Morgan, J., and M. Rinvolucri. *Once Upon a Time*: *Using Stories in the Language Classroom*. Cambridge, U.K.: Cambridge University Press, 1984.

Storytelling activities that promote genuine language interaction.

Porter Ladousse, G. *Roleplay*. Oxford, U.K.: Oxford University Press, 1987.

Practical ideas for using role plays in language classrooms. Some activities may need to be adapted for use in North American schools.

Richler, H. *A Bawdy Language: How a Second-Rate Language Slept Its Way to the Top*. Toronto, Ont.: Stoddart, 1999.

Entertaining and informative look at the ever-changing English language.

Shameen, N., and M. Tickoo, eds. *New Ways in Using Communicative Games in Language Teaching*. Alexandria, Va.: Teachers of English to Speakers of Other Languages, 1999.

Language games that promote oral fluency.

White, G. *Listening*. Oxford, U.K.: Oxford University Press, 1998.

Activities that foster effective listening strategies for use in real-life situations.

Whiteson, V., ed. *New Ways of Using Drama and Literature in Language Teaching*. Alexandria, Va.: Teachers of English to Speakers of Other Languages, 1996.

Drama techniques and literature-based communication activities for the language classroom.

Videos

University of California. Nonverbal Communication. Video series. <www.berkeleymedia.com>.

Two videos in the series focus on cross-cultural communication: *A World of Gestures: Culture and Nonverbal Communication*, 1991; and *A World of Differences: Understanding Cross-Cultural Communication*, 1997.

Websites and Online Resources

Ethnologue.com. <www.ethnologue.com>.

Owned by SIL International, this site has up-to-date information on the languages of the world. Click on LinguaLinks and go to the Lingualinks Library for reference materials on languages and linguistics.

Perry, T., and L. Delpit, eds. "The Real Ebonics Debate: Power, Language, and the Education of African-American Children." *Rethinking Schools* Online. Vol. 12, no. 1 (1997). <www.rethinkingschools.org/archive>.

Thought-provoking articles on language variety in the classroom.

Virtual Language Center of Southwest Missouri State University. <www.missouristate.edu/vlc>.

Information about language and language learning.

7 The Ritn Wird: Reading and Writing in English

Writing probably began as a system of accounting and later evolved into a method of recording information by using visual symbols that have accepted meanings in a specific language community. The scripts used vary from language to language and may or may not represent the sounds of the language. In some languages — especially English — learning to spell is an important aspect of learning to write. Over the centuries, written language has evolved into a medium of communication quite distinct from speech. In all languages, styles of writing may be influenced by cultural factors. As a result, reading and writing in a second language may require the learning of not only a new script, but also a new way of organizing ideas. This chapter discusses the challenges written English presents to language learners and offers suggestions for instruction.

Differences between Writing and Speech

For centuries, knowledge of reading writing was the preserve of the privileged and highly educated. Written language had special status as the means of preserving and communicating traditions in law, government, and religion. Consequently, written language was regarded as superior to oral language, and many of the prescriptive rules governing language use were drawn from written texts. In standard English, for example, the *-ing* ending in words such as *going* is pronounced /ɪŋ/. The *g* is added in print because the English alphabet is based on the Latin alphabet, which possessed no symbol for the nasalized [ŋ]. The influence of the written form has led some teachers — and others — to insist on pronouncing the *g*, often in exaggerated form, so that many people believe that this is the only correct pronunciation.

Oral language has existed much longer than written language, and most people speak more often than they read or write. Children learn to speak naturally, without instruction, whereas writing must be taught. In some respects, oral language can be regarded as more "real" or "fundamental" than written language. After all, it is possible to live as a member of a language community without reading and writing, but oral language — or its signed equivalent — is essential for communicating with others.

Rather than viewing one medium of communication as better, more correct, or superior to the other, it is more useful to regard oral and written language as distinct, but equally important, methods of communication. To participate fully in contemporary society, it is not enough to use oral language alone; it is also necessary to be literate.

Oral language and written language are fundamentally different ways of communicating. If you have ever tried to transcribe oral language, you may have been surprised at how little resemblance it bears to the organized sentences and paragraphs of written text. Even fluent speakers and gifted orators do not produce oral language that can be transcribed exactly into ordered written prose. Most written language is not oral language written down, and the purposes of written and oral language are usually very different.

The chart on the next page shows some of the differences between oral language and written text.

Writing Systems around the World

Writing systems around the world evolved independently at different times. The earliest writing systems consisted of **pictographs**, which usually represented concrete objects in the real world. A sea or a river, for example, might be represented by a symbol like this: ≋. Pictographs like those shown on this page are still used today on road signs and in other public places. They are understood by people around the world.

Logograms, which are symbols or characters that represent whole words or concepts, are another kind of visual representation that can be read in many languages. The mathematical symbols +, $, %, &, and =, for example, can be understood in any language, although the spoken words vary from language to language. Mathematics and science make extensive use of logograms to express specific logical relationships.

Some modern writing systems, such as Chinese, are **ideographic**: each symbol or combination of symbols represents a concept or a whole word rather than a sound. Most writing systems, including the English system, however, are **phonological**: the graphic symbols represent the spoken sounds of the language. Some phonological systems are **syllabic**, using symbols to represent spoken syllables, which are usually consonant-vowel combinations. Others are **alphabetic**, using symbols to represent discrete phonemes. Though some alphabetic systems are very regular and predictable, English is notorious for its irregularity.

Ideographic Writing Systems

The Chinese writing system is based almost completely on ideographic characters that represent concepts. The earliest characters were pictographs that represented concrete objects (e.g., a circle with a dot in the centre represented the sun). In time, the characters evolved into ideographs that could also represent more abstract concepts. When the two characters that represent *moon* and *sun* are combined, for example, they make up a new character that means bright. Today, Chinese characters and combinations of characters represent morphemes and whole words that may have different oral counterparts in various Chinese languages.

The advantage of this system is that the symbols can be understood by speakers of different Chinese languages, such as Mandarin, Cantonese, and Hakka. This means that speakers can communicate with one another in print even if they do not speak the same language. The disadvantage is that basic literacy requires knowledge of about 2,000

日   月   明

sun   moon   bright

Differences between Oral and Written Language	
Oral language …	Written language …
… is ephemeral. Listeners must grasp the message right away. Although speech may be recorded, the intent of the speaker is usually to be understood here and now by a specific listener or group of listeners.	… is relatively permanent and available for reference. Readers can take their time processing and re-processing a text. The writer can predict neither exactly who readers will be nor when and where the text might be read.
… is interactive. Listeners and speakers can seek immediate clarification or check each other's comprehension. Local and personal references (e.g., expressions such as *this one*) are used frequently.	… provides no opportunity for the reader to question the writer. Because the writer must communicate across time and space, vagueness and ambiguity are avoided. Vocabulary is carefully selected and sentences are carefully constructed to convey the writer's exact meaning.
… uses stress, intonation, and pauses to distinguish between questions and statements, provide emphasis, and divide utterances into manageable chunks. Many of these features cannot be represented in print.	… uses layout and punctuation to organize ideas, distinguish between questions and statements, and provide emphasis.
… is usually unedited and full of pauses, fillers (e.g., *um, well, you know*), sentence fragments, false starts, and repetition and redundancies. These features actually support comprehension, giving the listener time to process the message and hear important words and ideas more than once. Although there are times when oral language is formal and delivered in complete sentences, this is often rehearsed language, probably from notes or a script: it is really written language read aloud.	… is much more dense, consisting of complete sentences and featuring little repetition or redundancy. Each sentence must usually be understood in order to follow the text. The writer composes carefully, often in a series of stages, rereading and polishing the text until it is judged finished.
… is usually informal, especially when unrehearsed. It consists of relatively short declarative sentences and questions, and uses common vocabulary. The level of formality depends on the audience and purpose. A request to a peer, for example, might be phrased differently from a request to a stranger or authority figure.	… is more formal, especially in textbooks. It consists of longer sentences, featuring more embedding and subordination, greater use of impersonal structures, such as the passive voice, and Latin-based vocabulary that is less common in day-to-day interactions. The level of formality depends on the kind of writing; e-mail messages may not be written in carefully crafted prose, and computer-based interactions are especially likely to be informal.
… has a regional or social class accent or dialect that may help or hinder comprehension, depending on whether the speakers are familiar with each other's accent or dialect.	… is usually in the standard dialect and has no accent, unless the writer wishes to represent different kinds of speech in print.

characters and thousands of characters must be learned. Children begin practicing the strokes that make up characters at a very young age, before even attempting to write simple characters. As a result, many Chinese-speaking students have well-developed fine motor skills and a strong visual sense that helps them perceive English words as entire graphic images.

Syllabic Writing Systems

In syllabic writing systems, a phonological relationship links symbols and spoken language. Each symbol represents a syllable, usually a consonant followed by a vowel, or a vowel alone. Syllabic systems require fewer symbols than ideographic systems.

Cree and other Algonkian languages use a syllabic system, as does Japanese. Japanese, however, also uses *kanji*, ideographic characters that represent concepts rather than sounds, and a third system, called *katakana*. *Katakana* is a syllabary used mainly for transcribing foreign words.

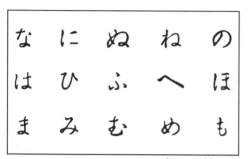

Japanese hiragana

Tamil uses a syllabic writing system. Each of the characters shown represents a complete syllable consisting of one vowel and one consonant sound.

ரொறன்ரோ மாவட்ட பாடசாலைச் சபையின் பாலர் வகுப்பு வரவேற்கிறது

பெற்றார் ஆகிய நீங்களே உங்கள் பிள்ளையினது அதி முக்கியம் வாய்ந்த ஆசிரியர். பாடசாலை ஆசிரியர்களாகிய நாம், பெற்றோர்களுடன் நெருக்கமாக சேர்ந்து செயற்படும் பொழுது பிள்ளைகள் மிகச் சிறந்த பெறுபேறுகளை எட்டுகின்றனர் என்பதனாலேயே, உங்கள் பிள்ளையினுடைய பாடசாலையுடனும் அங்கு செயற் படும் காரியத் திட்டங்கள் ஒவ்வொன்றிலும் உங்களையும் ஈடுபடு மாறு அழைக்கிறோம்.

உங்கள் பிள்ளை பெறவுள்ள பாலர் வகுப்புக் காரியத் திட்டம் பற்றிய விபரங்கள் இச் சிறு நூலில் தரப் பட்டுள்ளது. எமது ஆசிரியர்கள் செயலூக்கமுள்ளதும் எதிர்பார்ப்புக்கள் உள்ளதுமான கற்றல் சூழல் ஒன்றினைத் தருவார்கள். அதனால், வெவ்வேறு வகை அனுபவங்கள் கிடைக்கின்றதுடன், அங்குள்ள சாதனங்கள் பிள்ளைகளை முழுமையாக ஈடுபட வைக்கும், ஒவ்வொரு செயற்பாடும் பிள்ளையின் வளர்ச்சியைக் கட்டி எழுப்பும் நோக்குடனேயே அமையும்.

In syllabic writing systems, the sound-symbol correspondence is very strong; each written symbol always represents the same sound. Most languages that use syllabic systems possess between 50 and several hundred symbols. English has about 5,000 spoken syllables, however, a feature that makes a syllabic system impractical.

Alphabetic Writing Systems

Like syllabic systems, alphabetic writing systems are based on a relationship between symbol and sound, but they break down the sound units even more. The advantage is that a relatively small number of symbols must be learned. The English alphabet has 26 symbols, for example, and the Khmer 74. Some alphabets also use accents, or diacritical marks, such as ~ and `, to indicate the quality of a particular sound.

귀 자녀의 교육에 적극적으로 참여 하십시요.

＊ 귀자녀와 함께 책과 이야기를 즐기며

＊ 귀자녀에게 질문을 함으로써

＊ 학교교장선생님과 담임교사와 이야기함으로써

＊ 학부모 교사 인터뷰에 참여함으로서써

귀자녀가 성공적이 되도록 도우십시요.

Somali uses the same Roman alphabet as English, with the exception of *p*, *v*, and *z*. The letters occur in different combinations, however, and do not always represent the same sounds as they do in English.

Ku so Dhawow Dugsiga Xannaanada Caruurta ee Golaha Waxbarashada ee Degmada Toronto

Waalid ahaan, waxa aad tahay baraha kowaad ee ilmaha ugu muhiimsan. Waxannu kugu martiqaadaynaa in aad gacan ku yeelato howl kasta oo khusaysa barnaamijyada iyo dugsiga ilmahaaga, waayo waxa aannu og nahay in ilmuhu ku guuleystaan waxbarashadooda marka aannu, macallimiin ahaan, waalidka ilmaha si weyn ula shaqayno.

Buuggani wuxu tafaasiil ka bixinayaa barnaamijyada ilmahaaga la siin doono. Waxay shaqaalahayagu u huri doonaan ilmaha degaan ku salaysan firfircooni iyo halgan waxbaarasho. Waaya-aragnimadu way kala duwanaan doontaa, qalabkuna wuxu noqon doonaa mid xiiso leh, loolanka koritaankuna wuxu ka sal yeelan doonaa xubin kasta oo wax qabad.

Hints on Pronunciation for Foreigners

This poem is from a letter, signed T.S.W. and published in The Sunday Times *of London on January 3, 1965.*

I take it you already know
Of tough and bough and cough and dough?
Others may stumble but not you,
On hiccough, thorough, rough and through.
Well done! And now you wish, perhaps,
To learn of less familiar traps?

Beware of heard, a dreadful word,
That looks like beard and sounds like bird,
And dead: it's said like bed, not bead?
For goodness' sake, don't call it "deed!"
Watch out for meat and great and threat
(They rhyme with suite and straight and debt).

A moth is not a moth in mother
Nor both in bother, broth in brother,
And here is not a match for there
Nor dear and fear for bear and pear,
And then there's dose and rose and lose?
Just look them up — and goose and choose,
And cork and work and card and ward,
And font and front and word and sword,
And do and go and thwart and cart —
Come, come, I've hardly made a start!
A dreadful language? Man alive,
I'd mastered it when I was five!

THE IRREGULARITIES OF ENGLISH SPELLING

Some alphabetic writing systems, such as Spanish and Arabic, are very regular, with a nearly one-to-one sound-symbol correspondence. English is widely regarded as the most irregular or unpredictable of all the alphabetic systems, and this irregularity sometimes causes nearly as much difficulty for native speakers as it does for those learning English as a second language.

Fortunately, English is not entirely irregular, or no one would be able to read it. In fact, English spelling is about 75 percent regular. The irregularly spelled words, however, include many of the most frequently used words in the language and are the words that young children and second language learners learn first. As a result, second language learners who have already learned to read and write a highly regular alphabetic system, such as Spanish, may experience considerable difficulty decoding and spelling English words, pronouncing them as they look and spelling them as they sound.

WHY IS ENGLISH SPELLING SO ~~WEARD~~ ~~WEERD~~ ~~WERED~~ ~~WIERD~~ ~~WEYERD~~ WEIRD?

Many of the anomalies of English spelling originate in the history of the language. Some of these oddities, such as the changes that occurred when the Latin alphabet was imposed on the Old English sound system, were mentioned in the previous chapter. Other changes also occurred.

- After the Norman conquest of Britain, French scribes respelled many English words. They introduced the *qu-* convention, for example, so that the Old English spelling *cwene* became *queen*, as well as the *ou* combination to represent the vowel sound in words such as *mouse* and *house*, which rhymed with *loose* at the time.

- Spelling was extremely flexible for several centuries. *Where* was spelled several different ways, for example, and Shakespeare signed his own name with several different spellings.
- The first printers spelled according to their own pronunciation, which depended on the dialect they spoke. The *gh* in *right*, for example, reflects the 15th-century pronunciation of a sound that no longer exists in English except in loan words, such as *loch*. Many of the printers were from Europe, especially Holland, and this further complicated English spelling.
- The English spelling system has not kept pace with pronunciation shifts and often reflects earlier pronunciations. Though printing eventually standardized many spellings, the spoken language continued to change. In Chaucer's time, for example, the final *e* on many words was pronounced, not silent, as was initial *k* in words such as *knee* in Shakespeare's day.
- In the 16th century, when Latin and Greek were valued as the languages of scholarship, the spelling of many words was altered to reflect their Latin or Greek roots. A *b* was added to *debt*, for example, to reflect its origin in the Latin word *debitum*. This development led to some interesting mistakes. The word *island*, for example, has an *s* because the word was thought to derive from the Latin *insula*; in fact, *island* comes from the Anglo-Saxon word *igland*.
- About 400 years ago, many new words entered English from other languages, such as French, Latin, Greek, Spanish, Italian, and Portuguese. Along with the words came new spelling patterns, such as *bizarre*, *canoe*, *epitome*, *grotesque*, *harass*, *pneumonia*, and *vogue*.
- New varieties of English evolved as the language began to spread around the world through the process of conquest and colonization. English no longer belonged exclusively to the English, and in the United States, new spelling rules evolved, largely as a result of the work of Noah Webster in the late 18th century. Contemporary American English spelling rules include a single, rather than a double, *l* before a suffix in words such as *traveling* and *modeled*, *-or* instead of *-our* in words such as *color*, and *-er* instead of *-re* in *theater* and *center*. Many individual words, such as *plow* and *plough*, *gray* and *grey*, and *jail* and *gaol*, are also spelled differently in American and British English. Canadian spellings are something of a hybrid of English and American spellings.

Over the years, many attempts have been made to reform English spellings. Bills proposing spelling reform have twice been presented to the British Parliament, for example, but neither passed. For the English sound-symbol correspondence to be perfect, more than 40 symbols — similar to those shown on the chart in Chapter 3 — would be needed to represent the sounds of the language. Though a system like this would reduce the number of spelling rules and irregularities people must memorize, it would be difficult to reach agreement on which variety of English should become the "standard" reflected in spellings.

In addition, important relationships among words would be less evident in print. If the silent *g* were eliminated from *sign*, for example, its relationship to *significant* would be less evident, as would its link with similar words in other European languages, such as the French *signifier*. Moreover, great effort and expense would be required to translate all existing print materials to the new system, as well as to teach everyone

Catching a Ghoti?

Commenting on the irregularities of English spelling, George Bernard Shaw once noted that *fish* could be spelled *ghoti: gh* as in *cough*, *o* as in *women*, and *ti* as in *nation*.

to read and write in the new system. In any case, the weight of tradition makes major spelling reform unlikely.

Capitalization and Punctuation

Rules governing capitalization and punctuation differ among languages. The scripts of Middle Eastern languages, such as Arabic and Farsi, and of South Asian languages, such as Gujarati or Punjabi, either have no capital letters or use them differently from English. Even languages related to English do not use capital letters in the same way. German, for example, capitalizes all nouns, while days of the week, names of months, and names of languages are not capitalized in French or Italian.

Some languages either use different punctuation symbols or symbols that are familiar to English speakers in different ways. In Spanish, for example, question marks and exclamation marks appear at the beginning and end of a question or exclamation, and the first symbol is inverted: ¿ and ¡. In Greek, a semicolon indicates questions.

Direct speech is also indicated in many different ways: " … " in English; < ….> in Greek and French; „ … " in Russian and German; and — … in Vietnamese. In some languages, no punctuation sets off direct speech or quotations.

Some languages use a comma where English does not. In Russian and German, for example, a comma precedes all subordinate clauses, so that learners may produce English sentences such as *I expect, that she will come soon.* In West African languages such as Twi, a comma is placed after the equivalent of *that* in reported speech, so that learners may write English sentences such as *She said that, she would be late.*

The concept of what constitutes a sentence also differs. Thai, for example, includes no punctuation marks at all and inserts spaces between groups of words to indicate pauses. And in Arabic, sentences usually start with the equivalent of *and*, *but*, and *so*. As a result, Arabic speakers writing in English may produce long sentences linked by commas and several *and*s.

Direction of Print

Many languages, such as Hebrew, Farsi, and Arabic, are written — and read — from right to left. Chinese may be written from top to bottom or left to right.

This Farsi text is read from right to left.

به کودکستان در آموزش و پرورش منطقه تورانتو   خوش آمدید

شما در مقام پدر و مادر مهمترین آموزگاران کودک هستید.   زیرا کودکان وقتی بهترین موفقیت را بدست می آورند که ما

آموزگاران با والدین همکاری نزدیک داشته باشیم .

از شما دعوت می کنیم که در همه جوانب برنامه های مدرسه کودکتان مشارکت نمائید.

این جزوه همه برنامه های کودکستانی را که برای کودک شما فراهم گردیده توضیح می‌دهد. کارکنان ما محیط آموزشی

فعال و رقابت آمیزی تدارک می بینند. تجربیات متنوع و مواد آموزشی مشغول کننده خواهد بود و امکانات رشد در

هریک از فعالیتها منظور گردیده است .

Many learners of English must learn not only a new alphabet, but also to read and write in a different direction. In the early stages, this may slow their progress. They may confuse letters — such as *p* and *q* or *d* and *b* — that have mirror opposites or misread sequences of letters, confusing words like *from* and *form*, and *top* and *pot*. The handwriting of some may appear undeveloped, partly because they are writing against the grain and learning new fine motor skills.

Horizontal Alignment

Students may have trouble writing on the lines if the script of their home language does not include letters of varying height or depth or if the letters hang from a line rather than sit on it, as is the case in many of the languages of India.

Punjabi script hangs from a horizontal line.

ਟੋਰਾਂਟੋ ਡਿਸਟ੍ਰਿਕ ਸਕੂਲ ਬੋਰਡ ਦੇ ਕਿੰਡਰਗਾਰਟਨ ਵਲੋਂ ਆਪਦਾ ਸੁਆਗਤ!

ਮਾਂ ਬਾਪ ਦੇ ਨਾਤੇ ਤੁਸੀਂ ਆਪਣੇ ਬੱਚੇ ਦੇ ਅਤੀ ਮਹਤਵਪੂਰਨ ਅਧਿਆਪਕ ਹੋ. ਜਦੋਂ ਮਾਂ ਬਾਪ ਅਤੇ ਅਧਿਆਪਕ ਮਿਲ ਕੇ ਕੰਮ ਕਰਨ ਤਾਂ ਬੱਚੇ ਬੜੀ ਉਚੀ ਸਫਲਤਾ ਪ੍ਰਾਪਤ ਕਰ ਸਕਦੇ ਹਨ. ਅਸੀਂ ਤੁਹਾਨੂੰ ਆਪਣੇ ਬੱਚੇ ਦੇ ਸਕੂਲ ਅਤੇ ਉਸਦੇ ਹਰ ਪ੍ਰੋਗਰਾਮ ਵਿਚ ਹਿੱਸਾ ਲੈਣ ਲਈ ਸੱਦਾ ਦੇਂਦੇ ਹਾਂ. ਇਸ ਕਿਤਾਬ ਵਿਚ ਉਸ ਕਿੰਡਰਗਾਰਟਨ ਪ੍ਰੋਗਰਾਮ ਦਾ ਪੂਰਾ ਵੇਰਵਾ ਹੈ ਜਿਹੜਾ ਤੁਹਾਡੇ ਬੱਚੇ ਨੂੰ ਦਿੱਤਾ ਜਾਵੇਗਾ. ਸਾਡਾ ਸਟਾਫ ਬੜਾ ਯੋਗ, ਚੁਣੌਤੀ ਭਰਪੂਰ ਅਤੇ ਸਿਖਿਆਰਥੀ ਪ੍ਰੋਗਰਾਮ ਪ੍ਰਦਾਨ ਕਰੇਗਾ. ਹਰ ਇਕ ਕਿਰਿਆ ਭਿੰਨ ਭਿੰਨ ਤਜਰਬਿਆਂ ਨਾਲ ਭਰਪੂਰ ਹੋਵੇਗੀ, ਸਾਮਗ੍ਰੀ ਰੁਚੇਵੀ ਹੋਵੇਗੀ ਅਤੇ ਤੁਹਾਡੇ ਬੱਚੇ ਦੇ ਵਿਕਾਸ ਵਿਚ ਵਾਧਾ ਕਰੇਗੀ.

Chinese characters are the same height.

歡迎加入多倫多區學校

作爲家長，你是你孩子的重要教師。要孩子有更高的成就，作爲學校教師的我們，必須和家長緊密合作，。我們誠意邀請你參與孩子在學校及課程的各方面活動。

這小冊子是介紹你孩子將會參與的幼稚園課程。我們教職員將會提供一個活動及具挑戰性的學習環境。得到的經驗將會多樣化，教材將會具吸引力，每一項的活動都會配合孩子成長中的挑戰。

In Arabic, the tall and hanging letters are aligned.

مرحبا بكم فى حضانة منطقة الإدارة التعليمية بتورنتو

كولى أمر أنت تعتبر أهم معلم لطفلك لان الأطفال عاده يحققون درجة عالية من النجاح عندما يكون هناك اتصال دائم ومباشر بين المدرسين وأولياء الأمور . ولهذا فإننا ندعوكم للاشتراك فى كل أوجه برامج وأنشطة مدرسة أطفالكم

هذه الملزمة ستشرح لكم برنامج الحضانة الذي سوف يقدم لأطفالكم . تقدم لكم هيئة التدريس بيئة تعليمية شيقة تتناسب مع تفاوت القدرات . كما أن المواد المستخدمة متنوعة وجذابة ، وأيضا الأنشطة المقدمة مصممة بطريقة تشجع الطفل على التقدم فى التعليم .

Arabic speakers may write through the ruled lines on a page because they are accustomed to using the lines to align the tops and bottoms of the tall or hanging letters, as well as diacritical marks. And because Arabic text includes little or no margin, Arabic-speaking English language learners may write into the margins.

Printed and Cursive Script

Because the printed and cursive forms of many scripts, such as Arabic, are the same, speakers of those languages may have great difficulty reading English handwriting, such as notes on the chalkboard or comments on a paper. When a teacher's handwriting is idiosyncratic, the problem becomes even worse.

Students who are used to a single script may print in English and avoid using cursive script. As long as their printing is legible, this is not something to worry about. For important assignments and projects, however, these students need access to computers to give them an equal chance of handing in work that looks attractive.

Reading and Writing in English

Mastering a new script is only one of the challenges some English language learners face in learning to read and write English effectively. Written language is much more than oral language recorded on paper. There are many differences between spoken and written English, and students who speak fluently may, nevertheless, have considerable difficulty reading material that is cognitively demanding. They may also have trouble producing the kind of written language required to successfully complete school assignments and tests.

Success at school depends on an ability to comprehend **instructional texts** — textbooks and other learning resources — that are often written at a readability level significantly higher than the independent reading level of most English language learners — and many native speakers of English. Instructional text not only instructs, but also requires the support and guidance of an instructor to help students use it effectively.

School success also depends on proficiency in using various genres or forms of writing, such as narration, recounting, reporting, and explaining, for specific purposes.

Features of Instructional Text

Instructional text is challenging because it includes many low-frequency words that may be unfamiliar, as well as complex sentence structures. Students may not recognize how the text is organized, and they may not understand some of the connectives that indicate how ideas are linked. In addition, the text may contain references to background knowledge and cultural information that many English language learners may not possess.

Reading instructional text requires readers to use a variety of strategies that many English language learners can use effectively in their first language. They may process English text ineffectively, however, because they are so anxious to comprehend every word that they lose the sense of the text as a whole. They may consult a dictionary every

Features of Instructional Text

Vocabulary	Grammar	Organization	Cultural Knowledge
Low-frequency words, mostly Latin-based (e.g., *comprehend*) Various forms of words (e.g., *vertebrate* and *invertebrate; colony, colonize, colonist, colonial, colonialism*) Subject-specific vocabulary (e.g., *photosynthesis, numerator, stanza*) Context-defined vocabulary (e.g., *balance, mass, power, face, product*) Abstract nouns: (e.g., *democracy, consumption, distribution, erosion, notoriety*) Noun clusters (e.g., *government energy-conservation project, water-cycle diagram*) Figurative language (e.g., *fall by the wayside, fall flat, fall into disuse, fall from grace, fall into the hands of, fall on deaf ears, fall on hard times, fall short [of], fall prey to*)	Passive voice (e.g., *The logs are floated downstream*) Condensed expressions (e.g., *work selected for display*) Embedding and subordination (e.g., *Keeping track of the main idea in sentences in which the subject and verb are surrounded or separated by other information can be very difficult.*) Reference words referring to antecedents in previous sentences (e.g., *All the bird species look different. Some, such as vultures and eagles, are huge. Others, such as hummingbirds and sparrows, are only about as big as mice. Some have startling and beautiful colors. Others are brown and drab-looking.*) Literary style and word order (e.g., *In the castle, there lived …*)	Paragraph and essay structure • topic statement (thesis) • examples, details, evidence • summary (conclusion, restatement) Genres of writing (e.g., recounting, reporting, defining procedure, explaining, persuading, and discussing) Patterns of thinking and connectives (e.g., however, nevertheless, first, in conclusion) • generalization and example, detail, or evidence • spatial organization • classification and definition • components • quantity • time and sequence • comparison and contrast • cause and effect	Textbooks sometimes refer to or build on assumed knowledge or experience (e.g., camping in a national park). Students of various cultural and socioeconomic backgrounds may come to school with different background knowledge and experiences. Newcomers may be at a disadvantage when concepts are introduced or explained with reference to • traditional stories (whose tradition?) • Bible stories and characters • European mythology • Western history and personalities • literary references • national history, current events, places, and personalities • sports • art forms • popular culture

time they encounter an unknown word, so that by the time they finish reading a paragraph, they may have translated several words but have little sense of the main idea. Their anxiety may even interfere with their ability to use helpful textual features, such as headings, visual material, and chapter summaries.

The chart on the previous page summarizes the features of instructional text that pose special challenges for English language learners. Although the focus here is on learning resources such as a textbook, a journal article, a reference book, or other instructional print material, students face similar challenges when dealing with instructional videos and other audio-visual media.

Genres of Writing

In the early elementary school years, most writing is expressive, narrative or poetic. As students move into Grade 4, however, this begins to change and they are also required to produce writing in various non-fiction genres. By the time they reach high school, most of their writing consists of non-fiction.

Non-fiction genres, such as recounting, reporting, explaining a process, describing a procedure, persuading, and discussing, are organized according to conventions that are not necessarily universal. In English, for example, persuasive writing argues a particular point of view and usually begins with a thesis or statement of opinion, goes on to provide evidence, and concludes by restating the thesis. In some languages, such as Chinese, to begin by stating a point of view may be considered arrogant and opinionated. It is more usual to provide evidence and expect the reader to come to the desired conclusion without ever actually stating a personal opinion. English-speaking teachers might respond to writing like this by asking, "What's your point?"

In English, the writer is also expected to focus on one main point. In Russian and other Slavic languages, however, it is usual for a writer to allude to other interesting related information which, in English, would be deemed irrelevant or off topic.

Many English language learners have learned to write according to the conventions of their own language and culture. Though their understanding of how writing should be organized is not wrong, they do need to learn some of the most important ways of organizing ideas in a persuasive piece and other common non-fiction genres. Here are key characteristics of six common non-fiction genres in English.

CHARACTERISTICS OF COMMON ENGLISH NON-FICTION WRITING GENRES

Recounting

- Setting the scene (e.g., Last week, we went to the museum)
- Recounting events, usually in chronological order (First, ... Next, ... Then, ...). Usually uses past tense.
- Closing, usually a commentary on the experience (e.g., I enjoyed our visit to the museum because..., or I learned ...).

Reporting

- Identifying the topic, often with some kind of classification (e.g., Whales are huge mammals that live in the sea. There are many different kinds of whales, such as ...).
- Describing components, functions, characteristics, behavior, etc., usually in the present tense, as well as using prepositional phrases (e.g., On top of the head is a ...) and comparing or contrasting.

Explaining a Process

- Introduction (e.g., Manufacturing paper involves several steps)
- Sequential description of stages or steps in the process (e.g., First, ... Next, ...), using present-tense verbs, often in passive voice (e.g., The trees are felled). Differs from recounting in that it focuses on explaining how or why and uses causal connectives (e.g., as a result)
- Closing. Usually reiterates the opening (e.g., This is how ...)

Describing a Procedure

- Statement of purpose (e.g., To find the boiling point of water ...)
- List of materials or equipment
- Often includes diagrams or other illustrations
- Sequenced steps in the process, often numbered. Recipes and instructions omit articles and reference words (e.g., Add milk, Beat until frothy). Science experiments feature passive verbs (e.g., The temperature was measured)
- Concluding statement (e.g., Serves 6, Water boils at 100°C)

Persuading (exposition of a point of view)

- Thesis presenting writer's point of view (e.g., In my opinion, budget cuts are harming education)
- Arguments and evidence (e.g., One result of budget cuts is that students do not have adequate access to computers. For example, in our school, ... Another problem is, ... In addition, ...)
- Restatement of thesis (e.g., For these reasons, I believe that ...). May include a recommendation (e.g., Therefore, the board of education should ...)

Discussing (exposition of various points of view)

- Statement of issue or problem and preview of main arguments (e.g., Our school is developing a dress code. Some people believe that this would improve the image of the school. Others believe that it would limit the rights of students)
- Arguments for one point of view, with supporting evidence (e.g., Some people believe ... For example, ... In addition, ...)
- Arguments for opposing point of view, with supporting evidence (e.g., Others argue that ... For example, ... In addition, ... Furthermore, ...)
- Statement of opinion (recommendations), with rationale (e.g., In my opinion, ... Because ...)

Developing Reading and Writing Skills in English

To understand how English non-fiction text is organized and to learn to use specific reading strategies, English language learners — as well as many native speakers of English — need a teacher's support and guidance. Though immersion in narrative fiction and high-interest non-fiction helps students develop their vocabulary and knowledge of sentence structure, extensive reading alone won't enable students to read challenging instructional material. English language learners are understandably anxious about keeping up with their peers, and most are integrated into mainstream classrooms for at least part of the school day. Therefore, reading instruction should occur in the context of the curriculum, using textbooks and other classroom resource material.

English language learners also need guidance and practice to learn how to produce various genres of writing for specific audiences and purposes — and instruction should be provided through guided writing activities related to the curriculum. For example, students should learn how to write a procedure such as a science experiment when they are required to do so in science class.

The following chart shows how teachers can help students develop specific reading and writing skills. Acting as an expert and guide, the teacher helps students achieve independence. From a students' point of view, this model of teaching and learning can be summarized as a four-step process.

- Show me what it is.
- Show me how to do it.
- Help me do it.
- Let me try it on my own.

Detailed instructions for some of the strategies such as using key visuals, guided reading, and writing scaffolds appear in Chapter 12.

How to Support Developing Readers and Writers		
	Developing Readers …	**Developing Writers …**
Exploration — Show me what it is	… examine two or three textbook chapters or articles on the same topic. … identify features that make the material challenging (e.g., vocabulary and sentence length) and features that may be helpful (e.g., chapter summaries, headings, and glossary).	… examine several models of a particular genre (e.g., letters to the editor as models of persuasive writing). … rank the effectiveness of the models and identify common elements and specific features, such as word choice, that make some more effective than others.
Modeled and shared reading and writing — Show me how to do it	… observe an expert (the teacher) as she thinks aloud while reading text. In order to demonstrate strategies, such as skimming, scanning, skipping unknown words, and inferring meaning from context. … can be invited to make suggestions (e.g., "I wonder what ___ means. Is there anything in the paragraph that can help me figure it out?").	… observe an expert (the teacher) as he thinks aloud while composing a piece of writing in the same genre and focuses attention on key vocabulary and grammatical structures. … can be invited to suggest ideas, words, and sentences to complete the piece (e.g., "I don't think *mad* is the best word to use here. I'd like to use a better word. Any ideas?").
Guided practice or scaffolding — Help me do it	… read text with the support of key visuals and guided reading activities. These supports are scaffolds that enable students to handle challenging text that they would not be able to read independently.	… may complete practice activities that highlight key vocabulary or sentence patterns. … write a piece modeled on the example composed by the teacher. They may do so with the support of key visuals and other scaffolds.
Independent work — Let me try it on my own	… gradually receive less support as they begin to use specific strategies independently.	… develop other pieces in the same genre, using the writing process to develop and refine their work. … receive feedback from peers or the teacher or both.

To Learn More ...

Books, Articles, and Videos

Cappellini, M. *Balancing Reading and Language Learning: A Resource for Teaching English Language Learners, K–5*. York, Me.: Stenhouse Publishers, 2005.

Practical advice on shared reading, guided reading, independent reading, and literature circles with English language learners.

Carasquillo, A., Kuker, S.B., and Abrams, R. *Beyond the Beginnings: Literacy Interventions for Upper Elementary English Language Learners*. Clevedon: UK: Multilingual Matters, 2004.

The authors offer detailed suggestions on literacy practices for English language learners who have acquired conversational fluency and basic literacy skills in English but need support in developing academic language skills.

Center for Applied Linguistics. *Why Reading is Hard*. McHenry, Illinois: Center for Applied Linguistics, 2001.

Video and viewing guide provide important insights about the task facing English language learners as they read school texts. Best viewed and discussed in segments with study groups. For more information: <www.whyreadingishard.com>

Crystal, D. *The Cambridge Encyclopedia of Language*. 2nd ed. Cambridge, U.K.: Cambridge University Press, 1997.

Comprehensive introduction to many topics in language includes a history of writing systems.

Feathers, K.M. *Infotext: Reading and Learning*. Toronto, Ont.: Pippin Publishing, 2004.

Helpful introduction to teaching reading in all subject areas.

Franklin, E., ed. *Reading and Writing in More Than One Language*. Alexandria, Va.: Teachers of English to Speakers of Other Languages, 1999.

Uses classroom scenarios to illustrate effective literacy practices in multilingual K-12 classrooms. Strong focus on using students' first languages as an asset in learning to read and write in English.

Freeman, Y., and D. Freeman. *Teaching Reading in Multilingual Classrooms*. Portsmouth, N.H.: Heinemann, 2000.

Overview of best practices in reading instruction for English language learners. Illustrated with examples from elementary and secondary classrooms.

Garcia, G., ed. *English Learners: Reaching the Highest Level of English Literacy*. Newark, Del.: I.R.A., 2003.

Articles focus on reading instruction for English language learners.

Harvey, S., and A. Goudvis. *Strategies That Work: Teaching Comprehension to Enhance Understanding*. York, Me.: Stenhouse Publishers, 2000.

How to teach reading strategies to K-8 students. Strong emphasis on teacher modeling and guided reading.

Katzmer, K. *The Languages of the World*. Rev. ed. London: Routledge & Kegan Paul, 1986.

Provides an overview of language families and individual languages, with samples of written script.

Lewis, M., and D. Wray. *Writing Frames: Scaffolding Children's Writing in a Range of Genres*. Reading, U.K National Centre for Language and Literacy, 1996.

Outlines characteristics of six non-fiction genres of writing and provides blank templates to help scaffold children's writing. <www.ncll.org.uk>.

Lewis, M., and D. Wray. *Writing across the Curriculum: Frames to Support Learning*. Reading, U.K.: National Centre for Language and Literacy, 1998.

More ideas for using writing frames to support students' writing in a variety of subject areas. Contact the National Centre for Language and Literacy at <www.ncll.org.uk>.

Manguel, M. *A History of Reading*. Toronto: Vintage, 1998.

Interesting facts and stories about reading, such as how scientists explain reading, and how some women in ancient cultures managed to learn to read and write.

Peregoy, S., and O. Boyle. *Reading, Writing, and Learning in ESL: A Resource Book for K-12 Teachers*. 2nd ed. Reading, Mass.: Longman, 1997.

Useful resource for all aspects of second language teaching. Several chapters focus on reading and writing.

Sacks, D. *Language Visible: Unravelling the Mystery of the Alphabet from A to Z*. Toronto: Alfred A. Knopf, 2003.

The history of the alphabet and of literacy, recounting interesting facts about the significance of individual letters in the Roman alphabet; for example, why the word for "Mother" begins with the sound of the letter M in so many languages.

Shemesh, R., and Waller, S. *Teaching English Spelling: A practical guide*. Cambridge: Cambridge University Press, 2000.

Each unit in this book focuses on an English sound and the common spelling(s) associated with it, and contains teaching suggestions and activities.

Spangenberg-Urbschat, K., and R. Pritchard, eds. *Kids Come in All Languages: Reading Instruction for English Language Learners*. Newark, Del.: International Reading Association, 1994.

Collection of articles provides practical advice on language learning and literacy development in all classrooms.

Wilhelm, J.D., T.N. Baker, and J. Dube. *Strategic Reading: Guiding Students to Lifelong Literacy 6-12*. Portsmouth, N.H.: Heinemann, 2001.

How to teach reading skills in middle and secondary schools. Strong emphasis on guided and scaffolded reading.

Young, T.A., and Hadaway, N.L., eds. *Supporting the Literacy Development of English Learners: Increasing Success in All Classrooms*.

Practical advice for mainstream classroom teachers, K-12.

Websites and Online Resources

International Reading Association <www.reading.org/focus/langdiv_articles.html>.

Online resources on literacy include a collection of articles on linguistic and cultural diversity.

III   The Language Learning Environment

This section is about language learning and how teachers can provide programs, create an environment, and develop activities that promote language learning.

Chapter 8 begins by discussing how children learn their first language and how acquiring additional languages is both similar to and different from this process. The chapter then outlines ideal conditions for promoting language acquisition and answers frequently asked questions about how this process is affected by factors such as the learner's age, the length of time learners have been in an English-language environment, their motivation, and the effects of instruction and correction.

Chapter 9 provides an overview of how schools and school districts commonly organize second-language instruction and discusses some of the advantages and disadvantages of the various models.

Chapter 10 describes practical ways of establishing a classroom environment that promotes language learning while validating students' linguistic backgrounds. These strategies are equally appropriate in mainstream and ESL settings.

Chapter 11 describes language-teaching techniques for students who are just beginning to learn English or who are just beginning to learn to read and write.

8 Understanding Second Language Acquisition

Nearly all children succeed in learning at least one language. Most children have learned the sound system of their first language, as well as most of its grammar and a vocabulary of 1,000 or more words by the time they start Kindergarten — with no formal language instruction. Children raised in bilingual families achieve this feat in two languages.

How do they do this? And why does it seem to be so much harder to learn another language later in life? Do young children learn a new language more easily than adolescents and adults? How long does it take? This chapter answers these questions and many more.

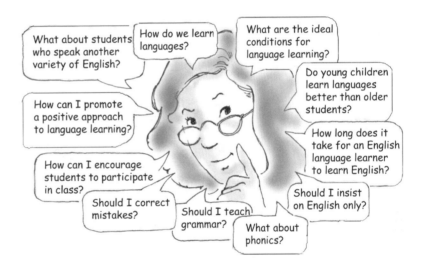

How Do People Acquire Language(s)?

Language theorists have proposed three major theories to explain how language is acquired.

- Language is learned through imitation and habit formation.
- Language is learned through an innate cognitive process.
- Language is learned through a process of social interaction.

Each theoretical perspective explains at least part of the language learning process. Though each is based on the way children acquire their first language, the same processes are involved in acquiring a second language.

Language Learning through Imitation and Habit Formation

Behaviorists such as B.F. Skinner maintain that learning language is a process that involves input, imitation, and habit formation through repetition. This view emphasizes the importance of the language environment: children imitate the language they hear and receive positive reinforcement in the form of praise or the satisfaction of achieving communication. This reinforcement encourages children to continue reproducing language patterns until these become automatic or conditioned language habits.

IMITATION AND HABIT FORMATION IN FIRST LANGUAGE ACQUISITION

Children are born with the physical ability to produce the sounds of any language, as their early babbling shows. At this stage, babies around the world sound alike. By the time they are a year old, however, infants have begun to restrict their language production to the sounds they hear around them. They imitate the sounds that are reinforced in their language environment, so that their babbling often consists of repeated syllables such as "ma-ma-ma" or "da-da-da." Thrilled parents provide positive reinforcement for these sounds, repeating them to their children. *Mama, Dada,* and similar-sounding words are used in many of the world's languages because generations of parents have attributed the same meaning to these early syllables in their children's speech.

Eventually, a child's repertoire of sounds becomes restricted to those heard in her or his own language environment. Children raised in an English-language environment, for example, produce only the sounds of English, while those raised in a French-language environment produce only the sounds of French. When they subsequently try to learn each other's language, it is difficult for the English speaker to re-learn how to produce the French *r* sound and just as difficult for the French speaker to re-learn how to pronounce the sounds represented by *th* in English.

Imitation and habit formation through repetition do not, however, account for the learning of grammar. If they were the only processes involved in acquiring a language, children would never make mistakes because they would produce only the sentence patterns modeled and reinforced in their language environment. But children do produce forms they have never heard. English-speaking children, for example, often go through a stage when they produce forms such as, "I brang it." The verb form *brang* cannot be the result of imitation, because adults do not say this. In fact, all children learning their first language — as well as second language learners of all ages — produce many utterances that they cannot have learned by imitation. In addition, learners are not exposed to enough examples of every possible grammatical pattern to enable them to acquire all patterns as habits.

Though imitation is an important element of language acquisition, especially in the early stages and especially in learning the sound system and words, it is only one of the processes involved in language development.

IMITATION AND HABIT FORMATION IN SECOND LANGUAGE ACQUISITION

Second language learners learn to pronounce the sounds and words of the new language in the same way as they learned to utter the sounds of their first language: through imitation. Because they have already refined their production of sounds to match the language environment in which they first learned to talk, however, they may have difficulty recognizing and producing some of the sounds of a new language. Most people who begin learning another language after puberty will always have an "accent" in the new language.

When English language learners try to imitate some English sounds, the sound system of their first language may cause interference that prevents their hearing the English sound accurately. Moving their mouths and tongues in unfamiliar ways can also be very difficult. As a result, English language learners may encounter difficulty with language features like the following:

- the sounds represented by *th* in *thin* and *this*: These are difficult for most learners of English because these sounds are rare in the world's languages. Learners may actually hear these sounds as /t/ and /d/.
- the sounds represented by the letters *v* and *w*: Distinguishing between these is difficult for students whose first languages do not include one of these sounds.
- the sounds represented by the letters *l* and *r*: Distinguishing between these is difficult for students whose first languages either do not include one of these sounds or include a different version of the sound.

The self-consciousness felt by many learners when they attempt to imitate the sounds of a new language may also make acquiring new sounds difficult. In addition, learners may neither wish nor need to sound like native English speakers. Learner motivation is discussed later in this chapter.

Though imitation and repetition help improve pronunciation, students do not automatically use these strategies. For this reason, ESL instruction increasingly emphasizes strategy training to help students improve their language learning. Language-learning strategies are discussed later in this chapter.

Language Learning as an Innate Cognitive Process

The **innatist** view of language learning is associated with the linguist Noam Chomsky, who suggests that children learn language because it is in their nature to do so. Children begin learning language from the day they are born, and possibly even earlier. Chomsky theorized the existence of a language-acquisition device, an innate predisposition for language learning that enables children to discover the patterns or conventions of language on the basis of the language in their environment.

INNATE COGNITIVE PROCESSES IN FIRST LANGUAGE ACQUISITION

Children appear to seek patterns subconsciously, to test the validity of the patterns by reproducing them in their own utterances, and to modify their patterns in response to feedback and further linguistic input. This process, known as hypothesis testing, appears to be fundamental in learning the grammatical patterns of a language.

The hypothesis-testing process is evident in the way young English speakers acquire the past tense forms of irregular verbs such as *bring*. At first, a child does not mark the past tense at all. He might say, for example, "Nana bring me home [yesterday]." Gradually, he acquires some irregular verb forms but may overgeneralize a pattern, saying, for example, "Nana brang me." This hypothesis is the result of his forming an analogy with the past-tense forms of verbs such as *ring* (*rang*) and *sing* (*sang*). Later, the child perceives the less obvious but more common pattern of adding a suffix to mark past time (e.g., *wanted* and *moved*). At this stage, the child may say, "Nana bringed me." Later, he may even say, "Nana broughted me."

Eventually, after repeated interaction with adults and many opportunities to experiment, the child acquires the adult form, "Nana brought me." The forms *brang*, *bringed*, and *broughted* are the child's approximations of the adult model *brought*. These forms are not learned by imitation, because adults do not use them.

The innatist view of language development is further supported by the fact that language is acquired with little or no overt teaching and no careful sequencing of input (e.g., exposure to regular verbs before irregular ones). In fact, when parents do intervene to correct their children's speech, the effect is usually minimal and may result in an exchange like this, which was recorded by Martin Braine and cited by Jay Ingram in his book, *Talk, Talk, Talk*.

CHILD: Want other one spoon, Daddy.
PARENT: You mean, you want the other spoon.
CHILD: Yes I want the other one spoon, please Daddy.
PARENT: Can you say, "The other spoon"?
CHILD: Other … one … spoon.
PARENT: Say "other."
CHILD: Other.
PARENT: "Spoon."
CHILD: Spoon.
PARENT: "Other spoon."
CHILD: Other … spoon. Now give me other one spoon?

One reason young children do not pick up on instruction or correction is that language is acquired in a predictable order. Children learning English as their first language, for example, acquire the plural suffix (e.g., *boys*) relatively early, whereas the possessive suffix (e.g., *boy's*) is acquired much later — even though it sounds exactly the same. The suffix for present-tense subject-verb agreement (e.g., *she buys*) is acquired later still. The order of acquisition suggests that language learning is associated with the maturation of the brain, a theory that further supports the innatist view of language acquisition.

INNATE COGNITIVE PROCESSES IN SECOND LANGUAGE ACQUISITION

In the same way as they initially developed their first language, second language learners listen to the language they hear around them and subconsciously seek patterns, test the validity of the patterns by reproducing them in their own speech, and over an extended period, modify their patterns in response to feedback and further linguistic input. **Overgeneralization** is a characteristic feature of second language development. In a natural language environment, for example, the simple present tense form *go* occurs much more often than the third-person singular form *goes*. As a result, most second language learners use *go* for all persons and may take several years to acquire and consistently use, "She goes," or "He goes."

The intermediate forms that learners produce are known as **interlanguage**. Many interlanguage patterns are common among learners of all language backgrounds, suggesting that they are developmental in nature; that is, they are a result of the language-learning process and represent one of the stages that learners must go through. Speakers of languages as distinct as Cantonese, Arabic, Spanish, Farsi, Vietnamese, and Somali all produce the form *she go* when learning English.

ESL teachers help learners acquire specific forms of English by presenting many examples of a pattern and providing many opportunities for students to use the pattern in meaningful contexts. Like children learning English as a first language, however, learners acquire some forms, such as *goes*, much later than others.

Sometimes, an interlanguage pattern such as *he go* remains static even after several years. This phenomenon is known as **fossilization**. What prevents the learner from developing full proficiency? Several factors may be involved.

- Some linguists suggest that there is a critical period for language acquisition and that the innate ability to learn language diminishes after puberty.
- Unlike first language learners, most second language learners require explicit instruction.
- Some students need training to become active listeners and observers who pay attention not only to the meaning of what is said but also to the form.
- Some students may neither need nor wish to sound like native speakers.

Instruction and feedback, learning strategies, and learner motivation are discussed later in this chapter.

Language Learning through Social Interaction

Interactionists believe that language development results from the interaction between the learner and the language environment, assisted by innate cognitive processes. Children learn language by interacting with others and by using it as a tool to do something else, such as listen to a story, play a game, or learn something new and interesting, especially when they are involved in this activity with adults and older children who are proficient speakers.

SOCIAL INTERACTION IN FIRST LANGUAGE ACQUISITION

Adults tend to address young children using **modified input**. They might say "cars and trucks," for example, rather than "vehicles." The language they use is also rooted in the here-and-now and is related to what the child and parent are doing or can see at the time. So if the adult says, "Let's get in the car and go shopping," and the two then get into the car and go shopping, the child has strong contextual support to understand the meaning of *get in*, *car*, and *go shopping*, although she cannot yet produce a complete sentence. The parent's intention is to communicate with the child, not to teach language. Language learning takes place because the parent presents language that relates to something meaningful within the child's direct experience, even if the words and phrases are slightly beyond her developmental level.

Adults also support language development by expanding on what children say. A child at the one-word stage, for example, may look at a photograph and say, "Car!" When his parent replies, "Yes, that's our car," the parent has presented language that the child can understand with the help of context, even if he cannot yet produce the phrase independently.

Through frequent involvement in interactions like this, children eventually acquire new words and develop their ability to produce longer sentences independently.

Providing temporary supports that enable learners to perform at a higher level than they would be able to without support is called **scaffolding**. When adults and older children modify their output, for example, they enable young children to focus on a restricted repertoire of language. This helps children recognize repeated sounds and words and begin to understand language. As the children's level of comprehension and production increases, the adults move their output level slightly higher, just as construction workers build the scaffolding of a building higher and higher until the building is strong enough to stand alone.

The social or interactionist view of language learning is associated with Lev Vygotsky's concept of the **zone of proximal development**. Vygotsky theorized that learning takes place when adults or more proficient peers interact with a child within the child's zone of proximal development, which is a level slightly beyond the child's current level of development. This level eventually becomes the child's independent level of performance.

SOCIAL INTERACTION IN SECOND LANGUAGE ACQUISITION

Many people have difficulty learning a foreign language because they have little or no opportunity to interact with proficient speakers of the target language. In English-speaking parts of Canada, for example, most students in French classes have little or no contact with native speakers of French and little need or opportunity to use French.

Like children learning a first language, second language learners need frequent opportunities to engage in extended, purposeful interaction in the target language with adults or more proficient peers. Simply immersing second language learners in an English-language environment is not likely to be effective, however. Just like young children learning their first language, second language learners need modified input to make sense of the language.

Stephen Krashen, a theorist and researcher in second language acquisition, takes this idea farther. According to Krashen, second language acquisition occurs when learners receive **comprehensible input**. This means that

- the language presented is not too far above learners' current level of development. In Vygotskian terms, the language is within the learners' zone of proximal development; that is, just a little beyond their current level of competence.
- the meaning of new words or grammatical forms can be easily inferred (e.g., learners are able to use previous knowledge and experience to help them figure out the meaning; other cues such as pictures or concrete objects are available; and the activity is meaningful).

In classrooms, learners must have enough background knowledge in the subject area to be able to relate to the context, and the language level of the text or lesson must not be too far above the learner's current level of development. Teachers can provide scaffolds to help students understand and produce language that is beyond their current independent level by

- expanding on the language that learners produce
- providing prompts
- involving students in chants and songs
- encouraging students to chime in when familiar or patterned stories are read aloud
- providing models, templates, visual organizers, and other supports
- organizing structured group activities

Chapter 10 discusses how to make the language environment comprehensible to second language learners.

Merrill Swain, another language-acquisition researcher, says that input alone is not enough; it is also necessary for learners to produce **meaningful output** and receive feedback that will enable them to refine their language use. Therefore, opportunities for genuine two-way communication in the target language are essential. Students need to be involved in small-group activities that push them to participate orally, rather than simply listen, observe, and follow directions.

Keep in mind, however, that most students who have received some of their education in other countries before arriving in Canada may have limited experience with group work. Introduce and structure group work very carefully, using cooperative learning methods, and include instruction on the group process itself. Chapter 10 sets out suggestions for structuring group work in the classroom.

Summing It Up

The behaviorist, innatist, and interactionist models of language acquisition are not necessarily mutually exclusive or competing. Children and second language learners acquire some aspects of their first language — especially the sound system — through imitation and practice. At the same time, they acquire grammar by using innate cognitive processes to seek patterns, generate and test hypotheses about these patterns, and refine their hypotheses until they eventually produce the adult form. To use these processes effectively, they must engage in social interactions with more proficient language users.

What Are the Ideal Conditions for Language Learning?

The ideal conditions for language learning are the conditions under which young children learn their first language. Providing similar conditions for English language learners in the classroom helps them acquire a second language. Here are some key characteristics of young children's language-learning experiences.

- *They are exposed to vast quantities of language.* They hear language, both formal and informal, used in many different contexts. They hear adults and older children talking to each other; they are introduced to the language of literature by listening to stories that are told or read to them; they hear formal, ritualized, and sometimes archaic language in places of worship and at ceremonial events; their older siblings introduce them to the language of an older peer group; and they are exposed to many kinds of language on radio and TV. Though most of this language is beyond their comprehension, this rich environment provides input from which they can learn the language. They begin to recognize the sounds, then the words, and then the grammatical patterns of their first language.

Interacting with more proficient English speakers helps language learners.

- *They have many opportunities to interact with more proficient language users.* Parents, preschool teachers, other adults, and older siblings usually enjoy talking to young children, playing with sounds, reading and telling them stories, playing word games, and teaching them songs, rhymes, and chants. Through these activities, children not only hear the sounds, words, and rhythms of English, but they also produce output of their own. Children are also initiators. As infants, they constantly babble to themselves, and later, they talk to themselves, to each other, and to their parents and older children.

- *They are not expected to understand or produce language that is too far beyond their current stage of development.* In fact, until they are about a year old, children are not expected to produce language at all. Parents and other adults recognize that children go through developmental stages when learning to talk, and as a result, they modify their own language and expectations when interacting with young children.

- *Language directed to them is simplified.* Parents and other adults, or older siblings, alter the way they speak when addressing young children. They provide modified input by using shorter sentences, speaking more slowly, raising the pitch and tone of their voice, repeating words and phrases, and using simple vocabulary. This language is sometimes called motherese or caretaker language.

- *Language directed to them is strongly linked to the context.* Conversation is usually rooted in the children's immediate reality and needs, and they can usually see, feel, taste, smell, or hear whatever the adult is talking about. For example, when a parent takes the snowsuit out of the closet and says, "Let's put on your snowsuit," the child sees the snowsuit, a familiar object, and is physically engaged in putting it on. This **contextual support** enables children to attach meaning to new words and phrases.

- *Adults seldom point out or criticize young children's language errors.* Parents are thrilled with their children's early attempts to communicate and value nearly everything they say, including, or even especially, their **developmental errors**. All parents cherish examples of their children's early language development, such as the child who refers to her forehead as her "threehead" because she is only three years old. The child will eventually learn the word *forehead* with no intervention by adults.

- *Adults seldom correct children's speech.* Instead, they often rephrase children's utterances, responding to the message but providing a model of the correct utterance. If a child says, for example, "I drawed you a picture!" the delighted parent may reply, "Let me see what you drew," offer praise, and go on to ask questions about the child's drawing. In this way, the parent provides a model of the adult form of the language while responding to the child's message.

- *Adults expand on children's utterances.* Adults and older children promote language development in younger children by providing models of language just beyond their current stage of development. When a child points and says, "Car! Car!" the adult may respond, "Yes, it's a big red car." After many interactions and over a period of several months, the child will begin producing two-word utterances, such as, "Big car!" or "Red car!" Later, the child will begin using sentences. At first, these will be telegraphic, missing some function words such as *a* or *the*, as in, "That our car!" or "Give me red car!"

- *They learn language through purposeful use.* Children learning their first language do not study it. They use it for purposes that are important to them, such as listening to a song or story, playing a game, naming the objects around them, asking for something they need, and requesting information. Language learning happens as a result of their engagement in a meaningful activity or interaction.

How Is Learning a Second Language Different from Learning a First Language?

Anyone who has learned one language can learn another, or several others. Unfortunately, the conditions under which most of us learn a new language seldom resemble the ideal conditions under which we learned our first language. Most English speakers, for example, learn a foreign language, such as French or Spanish, in school and have little or no exposure to the language outside the language classroom. Depending on the language-teaching method used, the emphasis may be on memorizing vocabulary and grammar rules rather than on using language purposefully. Errors may be corrected and penalized.

This scenario hardly resembles the ideal conditions described in the previous section and partially explains why most people find learning a new language more challenging than learning their first. Other factors, such as age and motivation, may also be at work and are described later in this chapter.

For a number of reasons, conditions are even more challenging for most English language learners.

- The stakes are much higher. Their education and, indeed, their entire future may depend on learning English.
- English language learners are dealing with the additional pressure of learning the curriculum at the same time as they are learning the language of instruction.
- English language learners are attempting to catch up to peers who may be five, 10, 15, or more years ahead in developing their English language skills. A 15-year-old newcomer, for example, who is beginning to learn English must catch up to students who have been learning English for 15 years. Most English language learners make great strides, gaining the equivalent of two or more years of language development in one calendar year. As they do this, however, their peer group's skills are also developing. English-speaking students continue to develop their vocabulary, reading skills, and ability to construct complex sentences and organize their ideas into paragraphs and longer forms of writing all the way through school.

These adolescent language learners must catch up to others who may have been speaking English all their lives.

- English language learners are often expected to understand and produce language that is beyond their current stage of development. Depending on local resources, they may or may not receive ESL instruction appropriate to their needs. In mainstream classrooms, where most English language learners spend at least part of the school day, some teachers may be unwilling or unable to modify input, offer alternative resources, or adapt assessment and evaluation strategies and criteria.
- English language learners may be penalized for making errors. Marks may be deducted for word choice, spelling, or grammar inaccuracies that are a normal part of the language acquisition process.
- Although English language learners do have the advantage of being exposed to great quantities of English at school, in the community, and in the media, their opportunities to interact with proficient English speakers may be limited. This depends on how they are integrated into mainstream classes and how the classroom is organized.

Summing It Up

For students who are learning English as an additional language, many of the conditions that support first-language learning may be missing. Teachers can, however, transform classrooms into supportive language-learning environments by replicating as closely as possible the nurturing and supportive conditions in which young children learn a first language helps learners acquire a second language. Chapter 10 describes strategies for achieving this.

Do Young Children Learn Languages Better Than Older Students?

Research has shown that younger children acquire the sound system of English more quickly than those who are older.

Many people believe that young second language learners have an advantage because they are still able to draw on many of the innate, intuitive strategies that they used to learn their first language. Research has shown, for example, that children who begin learning a second language before puberty acquire the sound system of the new language relatively quickly and soon speak with the same accent as local native speakers. In contrast, most students who arrive in an English-speaking environment after puberty will probably never sound like native speakers.

In addition, some older language learners seem to reach a stage at which their performance fossilizes, so that some aspects of their English language use never sound quite right. Some theorists have suggested that early childhood is a critical period for second language acquisition. This theory has been the basis of considerable argument about the best age for starting foreign-language instruction.

On the other hand, the cognitive abilities and greater first-language development of older learners give them an advantage in learning English vocabulary and grammar. They have a greater store of general language knowledge to draw on, and many appear to approach language learning in a more conscious way than young children. They are more likely to request explanations and benefit from explicit instruction about how the language works. Indeed, in the early stages, older students are more efficient at acquiring the grammatical forms of a new language. Nevertheless, children's performance in acquiring a second language surpasses that of adolescents and adults in the long run.

No definitive research demonstrates that changes in the brain at puberty prevent older students from reaching a high level of proficiency, however. Other factors often coincide with the age of the learner and make it difficult to identify age as the critical factor. For example, beginning at about the age of nine, students are required to deal with more complex, decontextualized language and challenging content in situations where the stakes are much higher. The pressure to keep up with the curriculum becomes more intense, and peer relationships are often more competitive and less supportive. Learners may be ridiculed by their peers when they make errors that are a normal part of the language-learning process, and they may lose marks for written work that contains these errors.

Stephen Krashen says that these pressures create an emotional barrier that may prevent adolescent or adult learners from acquiring language in the natural, unselfconscious way of children. Krashen calls this barrier the **affective filter**. If Krashen is correct, it is the affective filter, rather than the physical maturation of the brain, that causes older students to experience more difficulty in acquiring a second language. They may be anxious about performance and afraid of making mistakes or drawing attention to themselves by participating in classroom discussions or taking the risks required to learn a language. In contrast, young children are at an advantage because they are much more likely to be immersed in an English environment that in many ways resembles the nurturing, non-judgmental conditions in which they learned their first language.

Summing It Up

- Older students have an initial advantage in learning vocabulary and grammar because they can draw on their greater knowledge of language.

- Young children learn the sound system of a new language much more effectively, and in the long run, their overall performance surpasses that of students who begin later.

- Experts disagree whether it is the maturation of the brain or the learning environment that places older language learners at a disadvantage.

- Unlike their younger brothers and sisters, students who are nine and older require explicit guidance to learn vocabulary and specific structural features of English. See Chapter 12.

- Like younger children, older students will learn a second language more effectively in a nurturing and supportive language-learning environment. See Chapter 10.

How Long Does It Take an English Language Learner to Learn English?

Most English language learners need *at least five years* to become academically proficient in their second language — and many need much longer. Most North American-born children of immigrants with first languages other than English, for example, do not catch up to their English-speaking North American peers in academic achievement and language development until the age of 13. Immigrant children who are adjusting to a new cultural environment or who may have missed some schooling in their own country may need more time and more support than North American-born English language learners.

Jim Cummins, an expert on second language acquisition among school-aged students, distinguishes between two important aspects of second language development: **Basic Interpersonal Communication Skills** (BICS) and **Cognitive Academic Language Proficiency** (CALP).

- Basic interpersonal communication skills refers to conversational fluency. Most students develop basic interpersonal communication skills within the first two years of immersion in an English language environment
- Cognitive academic language proficiency refers to the kind of language required to achieve academic success. English language learners typically need at least five years to develop age-appropriate CALP levels.

The chart on the following page describes these two aspects of language proficiency in more detail.

Basic Interpersonal Communication Skills	Cognitive Academic Language Proficiency
Consist predominantly of oral language used for social communication and meeting day-to-day needs (e.g., playing a game, talking about personal experiences, shopping, and using public transit).	The level of competence required to understand "teacher talk," lectures, and other educational presentations, as well as to read textbooks, write reports, and complete research projects and other academic tasks.
Learners use BICS in familiar, supported contexts. There may be a personal relationship between the speakers, or they may be interacting in familiar and practiced roles. The interaction is often face-to-face, providing an opportunity to ask questions and clarify meaning. The content is usually familiar and conceptually undemanding. Sentence structure is simple and vocabulary consists of common one- and two-syllable everyday words (e.g., *word*, *childish*, *later*, and *homework*).	Learners are required to use CALP in more formal situations, often with no opportunity for interaction (e.g., when listening to a lecture or reading a textbook). The content is often unfamiliar and conceptually demanding. Instructional English is impersonal and abstract, and usually includes many multi-syllable words of Latin and Greek origin. Chapters 4, 5, and 7 discuss various aspects of instructional English.
According to Cummins, many students achieve basic interpersonal communication skills within two or three years. Research has shown, however, that teachers may be misled by a student's proficiency in BICS, however, perceiving them to be more proficient in English than they really are. This means that many students do not receive support or accommodation for language learning after the first year or two.	Most English language learners learn English very fast, but their English-speaking peers are also constantly improving their own language development as they mature and move through school. Thus, although the gap narrows from year to year, it can take five to 10 years for second language learners to catch up. Students who arrive with limited literacy development in their first language may take even longer — and many never catch up.

Wayne Thomas and Virginia Collier are American researchers who have found that the CALP of many English language learners never catches up to that of their peers, so that they never reach the same levels of academic achievement. They note that most ESL and bilingual education programs are not sustained long enough for students to close the gap. Most English language learners are fully integrated into the mainstream after two or three years. After this, the rate of acquisition slows and becomes the same as that of their English-speaking peers. English language learners who are still significantly behind their age peers at this point may never close the gap. The implication is clear: Most English language learners need more support over a longer time than most school districts provide.

Thomas and Collier also found that progress is faster and academic performance significantly improves when students are schooled in their first language as well as English. Bilingual models of education are discussed in Chapter 10.

Summing It Up

- Most students acquire the basic interpersonal communication skills required to meet their day-to-day needs within the first year or two.

- Most students need five or more years to develop the same cognitive academic language proficiency as their English-speaking age peers.

- In order to acquire CALP, English language learners need the help of all their teachers to understand academic text, expand their vocabulary, and develop more complex sentence patterns.

- Bilingual education can accelerate language acquisition and enhance academic achievement.

Should I Insist on English Only?

It is important to encourage students to maintain and continue to develop their own languages while they are learning English. A learner's first language is

- the foundation for second language learning
- an important tool for learning
- an important component of personal and cultural identity.

The First Language as a Foundation for Second Language Learning

Second language acquisition is most effective when a learner's first language is well developed. Children who can already read in one language, for example, need not rediscover the principle of reading when they learn a new language, although they may be required to learn a new script and how to read in a different direction. Learners who understand concepts such as rhyme and figurative language will more readily recognize and learn to use these features in the new language. And students who already have some explicit knowledge of language,

Linguistic or Legal Abuse?

Teachers in multilingual schools may need to counteract uninformed attitudes about the value of children's first languages. In 1995, for example, *Maclean's* magazine reported on a Texas child custody case in which the judge accused a mother of abusing her daughter by speaking Spanish at home. The judge threatened to remove the child unless the woman started speaking English to her.

The judge said,

If [the child] starts first grade with the other children and cannot even speak the language that the teachers and others speak, and she's a full-blooded American citizen, you're abusing that child and you're relegating her to the position of housemaid. Now, get this straight: you start speaking English to that child, because if she doesn't do good [sic] in school, then I can remove her because it's not in her best interest to be ignorant.

You are real big [sic] about talking about what's best for your daughter, but you won't even teach a five-year-old how to speak English. And then you expect her to go off to school and educate herself and be able to learn how to make a living. Now, that's bordering on abuse.

Note the two occurrences of [*sic*]. Both were added by the editors of *Maclean's*.

such as the concept of verb tenses, have a useful tool when they are learning a new language.

Teachers can support first-language development by encouraging parents to provide a rich first-language environment at home (e.g., by telling stories and reading to children in their first language, participating in formal and informal first-language community events, watching and discussing current affairs programs on TV, and reading first-language newspapers). Teachers can also encourage parents to enroll their children in heritage or international language programs and can show support for these programs by visiting classes and developing links with the teachers. In addition, teachers who make an effort to learn a few expressions in students' languages show that they are committed to the concept of a multilingual society and model their willingness to take the risks necessary to learn another language.

The First Language as a Tool for Learning

Learners' first language can be an important learning tool as they catch up to their peers in the second language. Some experts warn that students who stop developing their first language before they have acquired considerable competence in the second may not possess sufficient proficiency in either language to carry out some academic tasks. Continued development of the first language supports linguistic and cognitive development in English, enabling students to think, talk, read, and write at a higher level than if they were restricted to using English only.

Teachers can provide opportunities for English language learners to develop ideas in their first language by encouraging them to use their first language to produce their first writing samples, clarify concepts, discuss problems, and plan group tasks, as well as to write notes, outlines, and first drafts. This is a preliminary step toward producing work in English and contributes to an improved product. Chapters 2 and 10 include suggestions for using students' first languages in the classroom.

First Language as a Component of Identity

Learners' first languages are an important component of their identity and a source of cultural pride, and students may resist completely acquiring English if they believe that doing so will threaten their sense of identity or self-esteem. Students' cultural identity may be threatened, for example, if they are encouraged to abandon their own linguistic and cultural background to embrace English and assimilate into the dominant culture. Their self-esteem may also be threatened if the second language appears to be more valued by the wider community than their first language. Students who feel marginalized in the wider society may reject opportunities for linguistic and social integration and bond exclusively with members of their own cultural and linguistic group.

Other students may respond differently, rejecting their first language and culture. From the day they enter an English language school, development in their first language may cease. Many children begin to use English at home, becoming less and less able to discuss ideas and experiences with family members. This can have negative effects on students' relationships with relatives and with other members of their cultural community.

Learning a second language or another variety of English need not threaten students' first language. Schools can ensure that students' own languages and cultures are accorded equal status with English, while helping students understand the pragmatic value of becoming proficient in English, the language of school and the language of power in the wider society. Ideas for incorporating students' languages into the school environment and into the classroom program are included in chapters 2 and 10.

Summing It Up

- The continued development of students' first language supports a higher level of development in English.

- Students' languages have a place alongside English in the classroom.

- Students' languages support their sense of identity and help maintain effective communication within the family and the community.

Should I Teach Grammar?

Most students require a certain amount of explicit instruction to help them figure out some of the rules of English grammar. The older students are, the less likely they are to intuitively pick up the patterns of English and the more formal instruction they may require. Even young children and beginning learners of English can understand the concepts "one" and "more than one" when learning the plural endings of nouns, such as *books* — as long as they are talking about real books. Providing instruction about specific patterns of English grammar is important — as long as the focus of the lesson is within the reach of the learner's current stage of development, as long as the lesson is based on meaningful content, and as long as the lesson involves real communication.

Developmentally Appropriate Instruction

Research has shown that learners of all ages and language backgrounds acquire the grammatical structures of English in a fairly predictable order, with or without formal instruction. Fairly early in their exposure to English, most students can, for example, accurately use the progressive *-ing* verb form, the auxiliary *be*, and the plural *-s* form of nouns. It takes longer, however, to accurately use articles (*a*, *an*, and *the*) and irregular past-tense verb forms (e.g., *went* and *saw*). It takes even longer to develop accuracy in using the regular past tense (e.g., *wanted* and *looked*) and third-person *–s* forms (e.g., *he goes*, *she likes*, and *it rains*).

Formal instruction is not likely to work if the target structure is too far beyond the learners' level of development. It would be inappropriate, for example, to focus on subject-verb agreement or passive verbs with beginning learners of English.

A Meaningful Context

Grammar instruction can help students use English more accurately. Teachers who use isolated pattern drills and decontextualized practice are often disappointed with the results, however. Students involved in this kind of pattern practice may display increased accuracy while their attention is focused on a specific structure (e.g., during a drill or grammar test) — but may be unable to reproduce these patterns in spontaneous or real-life communication.

To learn a new grammar structure, students must be exposed to many examples of the target structure in a realistic context. They then need guided practice in using the new structure to say or write something of real importance. For a particular grammar pattern to stick, students also need frequent and extended opportunities to use the target structure in a natural way. In addition, the same structure must be taught many times in different contexts.

Summing It Up

Grammar instruction works when it focuses on patterns that are developmentally appropriate and when new forms of language are taught and practiced in meaningful contexts.

What about Phonics?

Phonics refers to the teaching of specific sound-symbol correspondences so that children can sound out words. Children learn, for example, that a silent *e* at the end of a word causes the preceding vowel to say its name. Children who recognize the sounds represented by certain letters or letter combinations are able to decode print into sounds and synthesize these sounds into words.

According to Jim Cummins, decoding is one of several discrete language skills, which are specific literacy skills and concepts that are taught in the early grades. These skills and concepts include the direction of print, upper- and lower-case letters, the alphabet and alphabetical order, recognition of the most common words (often called **sight words**), and spelling rules. Some children — especially those from educated families and those raised in a rich literacy environment — have already developed some of these skills by the time they start school.

Discrete language skills receive a great deal of attention in the early grades. English language learners can develop these skills as they learn their first words and begin to communicate in English. Acquiring these skills, however, does not guarantee that students will develop the cognitive academic language proficiency that is essential to achieve success in school.

Phonics rules, for example, work very well for the 75 percent of English words that are regular in spelling and pronunciation. However, many of the most common English words — the words readers need to learn to recognize first — are irregular (e.g., *the, have, they, you, would, there, their,* and *one*). This is why these words must be learned as sight words.

In addition, sounding out words does not necessarily lead to an understanding of their meaning. English language learners, in particular, may not know the meanings of the words they are sounding out. In fact, some students are able to decode fluently, yet understand little of what they read.

Phonics is a useful skill that enables learners to pronounce many new words they see in print, but studies have shown that teaching phonics has little long-term effect on reading comprehension. Reading comprehension and academic success depend on understanding and the ability to use the vocabulary of textbooks and teacher talk.

Though discrete language skills are an important aspect of overall literacy development, proficiency in these skills does not guarantee academic success. Experts have noted that many students — especially low-income and minority language students — begin falling behind in academic achievement from Grade 4 onward. In North America, this phenomenon is sometimes called the fourth-grade slump. Children whose discrete language skills have been at grade level start losing ground because academic success comes to depend increasingly on reading comprehension, which in turn depends on vocabulary and background knowledge. Many low-income and minority language students lack this kind of knowledge, which is sometimes called **cultural capital**.

Many learners who do not possess the cultural capital that the children of educated families may bring to school need specific instructional support — beyond the teaching of discrete language skills — to develop this knowledge in school. They are unlikely to pick up the background knowledge and vocabulary they need in any other way.

For learners of all backgrounds, the research clearly links the development of vocabulary and reading comprehension skills with academic success. Vocabulary and reading comprehension skills are developed through:

- opportunities to read extensively. See Chapter 5.
- explicit and sustained instruction in vocabulary and comprehension skills. See chapters 5 and 12.

Summing It Up

Discrete language skills such as phonics have a place in the overall language program. These skills do not, however, guarantee the development of the vocabulary knowledge, background knowledge, and comprehension skills that are required to achieve academic success. This knowledge is best developed by reading extensively and through explicit instruction in vocabulary and comprehension skills.

Should I Correct Students' Mistakes?

All language learners make mistakes. Some errors are the result of carelessness, fatigue, or anxiety and are made by both native speakers and second language learners. These errors are often momentary lapses and seldom recur. If a particular error does not recur, it is not worth worrying about.

Teachers worry much more about recurrent errors in students' speech and writing. It is important to recognize, however, that these errors may indicate that learning is taking place. They may be the result of faulty or incomplete hypotheses about how English works.

"What Would Happen If...People Can Fly". Errors like these are a normal part of the language acquisition process.

When learning a new language, learners sometimes make transfer errors based on interference from the first language. The learner's accent in a second language, for example, can be the result of interference from the sound system of the first language. This means, for example, that students whose first language has no /w/, may pronounce *went* as *vent*.

Transfer errors also show up in grammar. A learner who says, *You should always wash your rices*, for example, is treating *rice* as a count noun, like *bean*, because this is how *rice* is treated in her own language. Sometimes students base their word order on the patterns of the first language. A Spanish speaker might, for example, place an adjective after a noun in English, as he would in Spanish. Learners may also experience difficulty with features of the new language that have no parallel in their first language. Students whose first languages have no prefixes and suffixes, for example, may have special difficulty with these features of English.

Most mistakes are very similar among students of all language backgrounds, however, and are the result of overgeneralizing a pattern in English. The student who says, *My foots are cold*, has over-generalized the pattern for making nouns plural and has not yet learned the exceptions. The student who says, *I enjoy to go swimming*, is treating the verb *enjoy* like the verbs *like*, *love*, and *want*. And the student who says, *I go to bed late last night*, has not yet internalized the past-tense forms of verbs. These are developmental errors that indicate that students are at a particular stage in acquiring English.

For teachers, understanding the source of a specific error is not as important as knowing how to respond. You may remember that your own language teachers seemed to point out and correct your errors constantly. How did that make you feel? Perhaps you responded negatively, feeling intimidated and reluctant to speak. Or perhaps you responded positively, believing that your teachers were providing sound guidance. English language learners may also respond positively and negatively to correction.

Research has discovered no positive link between correction and the speed or accuracy with which students learn English. In fact, constant correction can have a negative effect. If teachers point out and correct every error, some students may become anxious and discouraged, and their accuracy may actually decline. Others may play it safe, limiting their language production to what they know is correct, rather than reaching for language that is beyond their current level. A student may, for example, write a very short and superficial response rather than risk making errors in a longer, more imaginative piece.

Insisting on correct form can also limit students' oral participation. By the time they have figured out how to correctly say what they wanted to, the opportunity to speak may be lost. In addition, constant interruption is frustrating. Students may feel that the teacher is attending only to their errors and paying no attention to the content of what they are saying or writing. In written work especially, so many errors may be circled and corrected that student may be unable to understand the reasons for the corrections.

At the same time, many English language learners and their parents come from educational backgrounds that place great value on correctness. Some students may lose confidence in a teacher who seldom corrects errors. They may think that the teacher doesn't know enough English to be a good teacher! Other students may complain that they are not receiving enough guidance. And still others may ask the teacher to correct every error in their written work.

As a compromise, think about errors not as problems, but as markers on the path to proficiency in English. If a student's errors show that he is going in the wrong direction, provide some helpful information but don't get in his way. Here are some suggestions to help you do this.

- *Always respond to the message first.* The most important part of any communication is the information conveyed.

- *Be selective in deciding which errors to respond to,* providing a model rather than an explanation. Focus on errors that interfere with communication, cause embarrassment, or indicate that a student is not applying something that has recently been practiced in class.

  If a student says, "You can't imagine how I was scare," his meaning is clear, and there is no need to intervene. He will acquire the correct word order and word ending eventually, as long as the conditions for language learning are met. If he pronounces *scare* as *scar*, however, you might respond by saying, "I'm sure you were very scared. I would be scared, too."

  One student wrote in her journal: "Intercourse with English speaker is very difficulty for English language learner." Errors in word choice are common when students look up words in bilingual dictionaries. In a situation like this, privately explain connotations that may cause embarrassment or confusion.

  If you have recently been practicing the uses of *there is* and *there are* and a student says, "It have ten province in Canada," you might respond: "Yes, that's right, but can you say that again, using *there are*?"

Respond positively to every student's attempts to communicate.

- *Focus on one error at a time,* even if a student makes several in one sentence.

- *Don't expect students to use the correct form right away.* Students may need to be exposed to hundreds of models and receive feedback hundreds of times over a period of months or years before they acquire some structures.

- *Don't be dismayed if students seem to forget something they appeared to know a few days earlier.* If they are learning new concepts or working on complex tasks, they cannot focus on language production at the same time. Language learning is not neatly linear, and learners sometimes go back a step or two before they fully internalize new structures.

Summing It Up

- Making errors is part of the language-acquisition process.

- Constant correction may limit participation and increase anxiety, thus limiting development.

- Respond to errors judiciously and respectfully, providing necessary feedback without embarrassing students.

How Can I Encourage Students to Participate in Class?

Although social interaction is important in second language acquisition, do not insist that beginning language learners start speaking English right away. In the very early stages, many students — especially younger children — pass through a silent period. They say very little, and what they do say may consist of memorized phrases rather than original utterances.

During this period, they are absorbing language at an amazing rate and will start to produce it when they feel that they have figured out some of the rules. For some learners, this period is very brief; for others, it may last several months. It is important not to push beginners to produce language before they are ready. During this time, some language teachers use the Total Physical Response (TPR) method, which allows beginners to remain silent for a significant period. Chapter 9 describes TPR in more detail.

Students who are too intimidated to speak up in class may feel more secure about talking in a small group, where the audience consists of only two or three other students. This works best if you teach all students how to work effectively in small groups by making sure everyone has a turn at speaking, knows how to seek clarification, knows how to help English language learners learn new words, and so on. Chapter 10 describes cooperative learning in more detail.

If you are very concerned about a student who seldom speaks, even after several months, consulting with the parents and, if possible, arranging a first-language assessment (see Chapter 1) are good ideas.

At all stages in the language acquisition process, learners' **receptive competence** — their ability to understand oral language and written

These students understand much more in English than they are able to express.

text — is considerably more developed than their **productive competence** — their speaking and writing. This means that English language learners can understand language at a higher level of complexity than the language they can produce and nearly always know more than they can show in English. You can help by providing alternative ways for students to demonstrate their learning (e.g., by giving them a graphic organizer to complete rather than asking them to produce a long written answer).

Summing It Up

- Many learners need a silent period when they are not pressured to speak in class.

- Cooperative learning strategies encourage students to talk.

- Students' receptive competence is usually significantly higher than their productive competence.

How Can I Promote a Positive Approach to Language Learning?

Students will approach the task of learning English more positively if they have a genuine desire or motivation to learn the language, a sense of confidence in their ability to do so, and some effective learning strategies to draw on.

Motivation

The learner's motivation is critically important in acquiring a second language. Students who are willing to put forth the persistent effort needed to become bilingual have an **integrative motivation** for language learning. Other learners may focus on learning as much language as they need for a specific purpose, but otherwise seem satisfied with a more limited level of proficiency. This orientation is called **instrumental motivation.** Some students seem to care little about learning the language and may actually resist doing so.

INTEGRATIVE MOTIVATION

Integrative motivation refers to a desire to interact effectively with native speakers of the new language in many situations: academic, social, in the workplace, and so on. Integratively motivated students display positive attitudes toward speakers of the target language, ask questions about the language, read English books on their own, seek opportunities to use English with peers and adults, have friends who are native English speakers, and are interested in learning the latest English phrases and jokes.

To develop integrative motivation, learners must have positive experiences with native speakers. They must feel welcomed, included, and respected. You can make this happen by providing structured opportunities for students to make cross-cultural connections and friendships (e.g., by organizing cooperative learning groups and helping students become involved in extracurricular activities). Integrative motivation is also enhanced by involving students in a wide variety of language experiences beyond the school — in other institutional settings and in the community — and by demonstrating respect and support for all languages and for second language learners in the classroom and in the school.

INSTRUMENTAL MOTIVATION

Instrumental motivation refers to acquiring a new language for a specific purpose. Learners who take this practical approach regard English as a tool, or instrument, that will help them reach a goal, whether this is to participate successfully in mathematics and science programs or to pass a language test for university entrance, such as the Test of English as a Foreign Language (TOEFL). Instrumentally motivated students relate positively to language programs that connect clearly with the academic program by focusing on the language and study skills required in specific subject areas or by teaching and practicing typical test items.

Though instrumentally motivated students may succeed in achieving their goal, they may be less proficient in social interactions and other contexts. Some adolescents may, for example, choose courses with English requirements that they believe to be less demanding. They may choose courses such as math and computer studies, rather than drama or media studies — and score high marks. They may experience difficulty, however, in making presentations or participating in seminars, which are requirements of college and university courses. They may also have trouble socializing in English, which could hinder their advancement in the workplace. Helping these students develop a more integrative motivation toward learning English is a good idea.

RESISTANCE

Some students resist acquiring English completely for reasons related to identity and self-esteem. They may feel that their sense of identity is threatened by pressure to abandon their linguistic and cultural background in order to embrace English and assimilate into the dominant culture. Students' self-esteem may also be threatened if the second language appears to be more valued by the wider community than the first.

Students who are isolated from the mainstream, who find it hard to fit in, and who feel culturally rejected by teachers or peers are unlikely to develop positive attitudes toward the new language — and may actively avoid the kind of contact that supports acquiring English. They may bond exclusively with members of their own cultural and linguistic group, for example. This behavior may be viewed negatively by peers and teachers and may further isolate these students from opportunities for linguistic and social integration.

To encourage resisting students to develop a more positive attitude toward English, teachers must show respect for their language and culture, allow space for their language to co-exist with English in the school, and provide many opportunities for them to interact positively with English speakers.

Confidence

Some students are intimidated by the idea of learning English and cannot imagine ever learning the language well enough to be successful in school. If the situation is threatening — if there is a risk of ridicule for pronouncing words incorrectly, for example, or if students are required to make oral presentations with inadequate preparation and support —

Many students feel more confident speaking to a partner than to the whole class.

their anxiety levels are likely to rise. As a result, their performance may suffer, and they may be reluctant to participate in similar activities in the future.

You can increase students' confidence in themselves as language learners by

- providing conditions that promote language learning
- setting tasks appropriate to the learner's present level of language proficiency
- providing supportive feedback rather than constant correction
- introducing them to others who have successfully learned English and are achieving academic success
- ensuring that no student is criticized or ridiculed for making the language errors that are a necessary part of the language-learning process

Learning Strategies

Learning strategies are the mental or cognitive activities that students engage in when they are learning a new language, or anything else. Recitation, for example, is a strategy that many people use to help them memorize things.

Successful language learners employ a variety of learning strategies — and these can be taught. Students can be taught, for example, how to use a learner dictionary effectively, how to use context to infer the meaning of unfamiliar words, and how to use word stems and affixes to figure out relationships among words. Modeling, thinking aloud, and guided reading are important ways of demonstrating how to use these strategies. You can also help students become more aware of effective learning strategies by encouraging them to engage in **metacognition**: thinking about how they learn. You might, for example, encourage them to talk about how they completed a task or write about the process in a learning log or journal.

Using specific learning strategies helps students become more active, self-directed learners who can take control of their own learning. All students can benefit from **cognitive strategy instruction**, especially as many strategies are transferable to other learning tasks. The chart on the following page shows six learning strategies and examples of each.

Summing It Up

- The attitude of English language learners will be more positive if they have positive experiences with English speakers.

- Students will feel more confident of their ability to learn English if the learning environment is supportive and they have strong role models.

- Students will develop a more positive attitude toward learning English and take some control of their own learning if they learn to use effective language learning strategies.

Learning Strategies	
Strategy	**Examples**
Memory strategies … help learners remember new information (e.g., vocabulary).	Recitation and repetition Mnemonic devices, such as acronyms, concept maps, and visual imagery
Cognitive strategies … help learners understand and produce the language.	Recognizing and producing patterns Practicing in natural contexts Analyzing Creating analogies and comparisons
Compensation strategies … help learners communicate despite gaps in knowledge (e.g., when they don't know a word).	Inferring meaning from context Using gestures Using synonyms or circumlocutions (e.g., saying, "Things you wear on hands when it's cold," for *gloves*)
Social strategies … help learners interact with others in the target language.	Cooperating with others in the classroom Using language to keep the communication process going (e.g., asking for clarification)
Affective strategies … help learners maintain the self-confidence and motivation necessary to acquire a second language.	Lowering stress and anxiety Self-encouragement Keeping a language-learning journal
Metacognitive strategies … help learners plan and monitor their own learning.	Setting goals and objectives Monitoring personal progress Learning about language learning

What about Students Who Speak Another Variety of English?

Some students speak varieties — or dialects — of English that differ significantly from standard English. Many students of Caribbean background, for example, speak an English-related creole language that is so different from standard English that many linguists classify it as a distinct language. Most students from the English-speaking Caribbean, however, consider themselves to be English speakers and have usually had much more exposure to standard English, in both their home country and their new country, than their peers from other language backgrounds. Though these students may appear to understand more English than their peers from non-English-speaking countries, however, they may still need help to acquire local forms of standard English.

Summing It Up

It is important for teachers to respect the linguistic background of all students and to provide instruction and feedback in a way that does not threaten students' self-esteem and sense of identity.

To Learn More …

Books and Articles

Association for Supervision and Curriculum Development. (2004) *Educating Language Learners. Educational Leadership,* Vol. 62 | No. 4, December 2004/January 2005.
This issue of the journal is entirely devoted to the topic of English language learners. Includes articles on language learning, differentiated instruction for English language learners, and affirming students' linguistic and cultural identities.

Bartram, M., and R. Walton. *Correction: A Positive Approach to Language Mistakes.* Hove, U.K.: Language Teaching Publications, 1991.
Helpful advice on how to respond to students' mistakes in oral and written language.

Brown, H.D. *Principles of Language Learning and Teaching.* 4th ed. White Plains, N.Y.: Addison Wesley Longman (now Pearson Education), 2000.
A standard in TESL training programs. Provides a thorough overview of second language acquisition.

Chamot, A.U., S. Barnhardt, P.B. El-Dinary, and J. Robbins. *The Learning Strategies Handbook.* White Plains, N.Y.: Addison Wesley Longman (now Pearson Education), 1999.
Practical guidance on teaching learning strategies to English language learners.

Chomsky, N. Review of *Verbal Behavior* by B.F. Skinner. *Language.* Vol. 35 (1959), pp. 26–58.
Noam Chomsky's response to B.F. Skinner's theories of language learning forms the foundation of the innatist view of language development.

Coelho, E. *Caribbean Students in Canadian Schools, Book 2.* Toronto, Ont.: Pippin Publishing, 1991.
Discusses the relationship between Caribbean English Creole and standard English and describes instructional approaches and strategies for teaching standard English.

Cummins, J., Bismilla, V., Chow, P., Cohen, S., Giampapa, F., Leoni, L., Sandhu, P., and Sastri, P. (2005) Affirming Identity in Multilingual Classrooms. *Educational Leadership* Vol. 63, No. 1, September: 38-43.
This article explains the value of incorporating students' home languages and cultures into the classroom program, and describes some projects that use linguistic and cultural diversity as an asset. Cummins, J.

Cummins, J. "Reading and the ESL Student." *Orbit.* Vol. 33, no. 1, 2002, pp. 19–22.
Explains basic interpersonal skills, discrete language skills, and cognitive academic language proficiency, and recommends methods of improving reading comprehension and academic performance.

Cummins, J. *Language, Power and Pedagogy: Bilingual Children in the Crossfire.* Clevedon, England: Multilingual Matters Ltd, 2000.
Explains the distinction between conversational and academic language proficiency and the implications for instruction. Also suggests ways of raising the profile of students' languages.

Delpit, L. *Other People's Children: Cultural Conflicts in the Classroom.* New York: The New Press, 1995.
Includes a powerful rationale for teaching standard English while respecting the language backgrounds of students who speak other varieties of English.

Ellis, R. *Second Language Acquisition.* Oxford, U.K.: Oxford University Press, 1997.
An introduction to the field with an annotated list of additional readings on topics such as interlanguage and the role of instruction.

Freeman, D.E., and Y.S. Freeman. *Between Worlds: Access to Second Language Acquisition.* 2nd ed. Portsmouth, N.H.: Heinemann, 2001.
How teachers can help integrate the two worlds in which many minority language students live.

Ingram, J. *Talk, Talk, Talk.* Toronto, Ont.: Penguin Books, 1993.
A popular science writer explores language as a biological and social phenomenon.

Klesmer, H. "Assessment and Teacher Perceptions of English Language Learner Achievement." *English Quarterly.* Vol. 26, no. 3, 1994, pp. 8–11.
Results of a study of second language acquisition among school-aged children in Toronto, Ont.

Krashen, S. *Principles and Practice in Second Language Acquisition.* Oxford, U.K.: Pergamon Press, 1982.
Stephen Krashen's theories of second language acquisition are essential reading for all language teachers.

Lightbown, P., and N. Spada. *How Languages Are Learned.* 2nd ed. Oxford, U.K.: Oxford University Press, 1999.
Introduces first and second language acquisition and discusses the implications for second language instruction.

Lyster, R., P.M. Lightbown, and N. Spada. "Response to Truscott's 'What's Wrong with Oral Grammar Correction?'" *Canadian Modern Language Review.* Vol. 55, no. 4, 1999.
Article argues that recommendations to ignore students' oral errors are not based on evidence (see Truscott). Available online at <www.utpjournals.com>.

National Council of Teachers of English. *Teaching English Language Learners. Voices from the Middle,* Vol. 11, No. 14, May 2004.
This issue of the journal is entirely devoted to the topic of English language learners. Articles offer practical advice on working with English language learners in mainstream classrooms and for drawing on linguistic and cultural diversity in the class.

Oxford, R. *Language Learning Strategies: What Every Teacher Should Know.* Boston, Mass.: Heinle and Heinle, 1990.
Introduces six categories of language learning strategies and suggests activities that help learners develop these strategies.

Perry, T., and L. Delpit, eds. *The Real Ebonics Debate: Power, Language, and the Education of African-American Children.* Boston, Mass.: Beacon Press, 1998.
Articles on educating students whose home language is a non-standard variety of English.

Pinker, S. *The Language Instinct: How the Mind Creates Language.* New York, NY: Perennial Classics (Harper Collins), 2000.

Very readable yet learned book views language as a biological phenomenon, shared across cultures and languages.

Piper, T. *And Then There Were Two*. 2nd ed. Toronto, Ont.: Pippin Publishing, 2001.
Practical guide to second language acquisition among children.

Skinner, B.F. *Verbal Behavior*. New York: Appleton-Century-Crofts, 1957.
B.F. Skinner's theories of language learning as a conditioned response influenced the design of instructional programs and language labs in the 1960s and 1970s.

Solomon, P. *Black Resistance in the High School: Forging a Separatist Culture*. Albany, N.Y.: State University of New York Press, 1992.
Study of Canadian youth of Caribbean origin in a Toronto secondary school.

Swain, M. "Communicative Competence: Some Roles of Comprehensible Input and Comprehensible Output in Its Development." In S.M. Gass and C.G. Madden, eds., *Input in Second Language Acquisition*. Rowley, Mass.: Newbury House, 1986.
Complements Stephen Krashen's input theories by addressing the importance of providing opportunities for output or language production.

Swain, M., and B. Smith. *Learner English: A Teacher's Guide to Interference and Other Problems*. 2nd ed. Cambridge, U.K.: Cambridge University Press, 2001.
Provides information about the phonological system and grammatical structure of more than 20 languages and describes specific difficulties speakers encounter when learning English. Audiocassette and CD available.

Truscott, J. "What's Wrong with Oral Grammar Correction?" *Canadian Modern Language Review*. Vol. 55, no. 4, 1999, pp. 437–456. Available online at <www.utpjournals.com>.
Recommends abandoning oral grammar correction in light of research suggesting that correction does not improve learners' accuracy in oral language production.

Vygotsky, L.S. *Thought and Language*. Cambridge, Mass.: MIT Press, 1962.
Originally published in Russian in the 1930s, this book discusses theories that remain fundamental to the study of language development.

Wong Fillmore, L. "When Learning a Second Language Means Losing the First." *Early Childhood Research Quarterly*. Vol. 6, 1991, pp. 323–346.
Describes the negative consequences of first language loss and makes a strong case for maintaining the first language.

Websites and Online Resources

Center for Applied Linguistics. <www.cal.org>.
A wealth of information and links to sites on second language acquisition and bilingual education. Home to the ERIC Clearinghouse on Languages and Linguistics.

Center for Research on Educaton, Diversity, and Excellence. <www.crede.org>.
Research reports and other resources on second language acquisition and minority education, including "The Five Standards for Effective Pedagogy."

Collier, V.P. "The Effect of Age on Acquisition of a Second Language for School." *NCBE Occasional Papers in Bilingual Education*. No. 2. National Clearinghouse for Bilingual Education, 1988. <www.ncela.gwu.edu/pubs/classics/index.htm#books>.
Overview of literature on the relationship between age and second language acquisition.

Collier, V.P. "Acquiring a Second Language for School." *Directions in Language and Education*. Vol. 1, no. 4. National Clearinghouse for Bilingual Education, 1995. <www.ncela.gwu.edu/pubs/directions>.
Useful overview of research on second language acquisition. Especially relevant for those planning language education for school-aged students.

De Villiers, J. "Language Development." In Jerome Kagan, ed., *Gale Encyclopedia of Childhood and Adolescence*. Gale, 1997. <www.findarticles.com/p/articles/mi_g2602/is_0003/ai_2602000341>.
One of several interesting and readable articles on language acquisition.

Garcia, G. "Lessons from Research: What Is the Length of Time It Takes Limited English Proficient Students to Acquire English and Succeed in an All-English Classroom?" *NCBE Issue Brief No. 5*. National Clearinghouse for Bilingual Education, September 2000. < www.ncela.gwu.edu/pubs/issuebriefs/ib5.htm>.

National Clearinghouse for English Language Acquisition and Language Instruction Educational Programs (formerly National Clearinghouse for Bilingual Education). <www.ncela.gwu.edu>.
Information on second language acquisition and the education of language minority students. Click on Ask NCELA for answers to questions such as, Why is it important to maintain the native language?

Thomas, W.P., and V.P. Collier. *A National Study of School Effectiveness for Language Minority Students' Long-Term Academic Achievement*. Center for Research on Education, Diversity, and Excellence, 2002. <crede.berkeley.edu/research/llaa/1.1_final.html >.
Analyzes instructional programs and other factors that make a difference in second language acquisition and academic success. Essential reading.

Ursel, B. "Some Links on the Benefits of Learning Other Languages." Language Research Centre, Faculty of Humanities, University of Calgary. <fis.ucalgary.ca/alle/lllinks.html>.
Annotated list of useful online resources for teachers and parents.

Worswick, C. *School Performance of the Children of Immigrants in Canada, 1994–98*. Ottawa: Statistics Canada, 2001. <www.statcan.ca/bsolc/english/bsolc?catno=11F0019M2001178>.
Analysis of the academic achievement of Canadian-born English language learners.

9 Organizing Language Instruction

This chapter describes program models adopted by schools and school districts for providing language instruction and support to English language learners. It also provides an overview of methods of second language instruction that have been developed in response to various language-learning theories.

Organizing the Language Program

When language programs are designed, they sometimes focus exclusively on students' need to learn English. Though this need is immediate and obvious, a complete language program has two — and sometimes three — components.

- English language instruction
- heritage language instruction
- French language instruction (in Canada)

English Language Instruction

No single model for delivering language instruction is appropriate for all schools and all students. Effective second language programs make the best use of available resources, in accordance with what is known about how a second language is acquired.

Some jurisdictions contain large concentrations of students from two or three language communities and are able to provide **bilingual education** in the learners' own languages and in English. This model is most common in the United States. Other school districts in the U.S. and most schools and school districts in Canada, by contrast, offer various kinds of **English as a second language** programs, in which English is the sole language of instruction.

BILINGUAL EDUCATION

Children learn best in the language they know best. This is not a new concept: half a century ago, a UNESCO report identified the first language as the most effective medium of instruction for all children. In many countries, various models of bilingual education have been developed in accordance with this principle.

If the necessary resources and expertise were available in English-speaking countries, it would make sense to educate non-English-speaking children in their own language, at least until they are proficient in English. Bilingual programs — especially those designed

What about French Immersion?

The success of French immersion programs in Canada, where most of those enrolled are English speaking and most instruction is delivered in French, seems to belie the conclusion that learning in the first language is more effective than learning in a second language. Although most instruction is in French, anglophone students in French immersion programs do at least as well as — and often better than — their peers in monolingual English programs. A closer look at the way French immersion is delivered, however, confirms the importance of validating, maintaining, and developing the first language.

- The aim of French immersion programs is not to replace the first language with the second. On the contrary, the goal is to produce students who are equally proficient in Canada's two official languages: English and French.
- Because English is supported inside and outside the school, French immersion students' ability to develop their English language skills is not threatened. English is usually the dominant language of the community and is an official language of the country. As a result, most learners are immersed in English at home and in the community. To foster the development of their English skills, students receive specific instruction in *anglais*, as well as English language instruction in some subjects.
- French immersion teachers are bilingual, able to speak both English and French.
- Teachers are sensitive to the needs of students as second language learners and use second language teaching techniques to integrate language and content instruction.
- Most French immersion students are not newcomers. They are secure in the school's cultural environment, where their own background and experiences are validated and understood.

to promote full bilingualism — offer the best opportunities for students to achieve *all* the learning outcomes of a particular course and to learn the dominant language at the same time.

The goal of bilingual education is to enable students to progress academically at the same time as they are learning English. As a result, both the target language and the students' first language are used as the languages of instruction. Children who learn to read in their first language, for example, become more proficient readers and are able to transfer those skills into English as they learn the language. Some bilingual programs also aim to expand the linguistic abilities of all students to prepare them to live in a world where global communication and cooperation are increasingly important.

In the United States, where bilingual programs are most common, three models dominate. Each establishes specific goals for learners whose first language is not English.

- *Transitional bilingual education* provides instruction in the first language for a limited time, until students have acquired enough English to function in English only. The goals include continued academic development and eventual proficiency in English. Maintaining the first language beyond the transitional period is not a goal. Once instruction switches to English only, it is possible — even likely — that students will stop developing or lose proficiency in their first language.

- *Developmental bilingual education* is designed to maintain and develop proficiency in the first language while students learn English. Instruction is provided in both languages throughout the years of schooling. The goals include continued academic development and full bilingualism in English and the first language.

- *Two-way bilingual programs* include native speakers of English as well as learners of another language background, such as Spanish. Both languages are used for instruction. The goals include continued academic development and full bilingualism and biculturalism for all learners, including speakers of the dominant language. This means that Spanish speakers, for example, and English speakers in the same class would become equally proficient in the two languages at the same time as they develop an appreciation of one another's cultural perspectives.

Ideally, all English language learners would be involved in rich, curriculum-based bilingual programs that enable them to expand their knowledge, learn English, and continue to develop in their first languages at the same time.

Bilingual education is practical where large numbers of students of the same language group are congregated in the same area, as is the case in some parts of the United States. Bilingual education is also offered in some Canadian provinces. The 1978 Saskatchewan Education Act, for example, stipulates that a heritage language may be used as a language of instruction 100 percent of the time in Kindergarten and up to 50 percent of the time in grades 1 and 2.

It is difficult, however, to provide bilingual classes when students of a particular language group are scattered over a large geographic area or where students of many language backgrounds attend the same

What Is Bilingual Competence?

Though many people are proficient in more than one language, few are equally proficient in two or more languages in all contexts. Many bilingual people use their languages for different purposes and with different groups of people. They may, for example, think in their first language when working on specific tasks, such as counting or completing mathematical calculations. Some feel that one of their languages is more flexible or more effective when expressing some concepts or carrying out some activities, such as reading poetry or discussing politics.

When *Bilingual* Doesn't Mean Bilingual

Some so-called bilingual programs do not use the first language as a medium of instruction at all. In some jurisdictions, the term *bilingual* is used to describe all students whose first language is not the language of instruction, on the assumption that they will become bilingual when they learn the dominant language at school. This is unlikely to happen, however, unless special efforts are made to support the continued development of students' own language while they learn English. If no provision is made to maintain and develop students' first language, the result may be what Jim Cummins calls subtractive bilingualism.

Unless students' own languages are used alongside English as a language of instruction, it is a misnomer to call these programs bilingual.

school. Nevertheless, it is possible to centralize programs for specific language groups in designated schools. In Calgary, Alberta, for example, students can choose to attend a school where the curriculum is delivered in both Mandarin and English. Though this offers definite educational benefits, separating students from those of other linguistic and cultural backgrounds may have negative consequences.

In some areas where bilingual education might be a practical, common-sense option, the use of languages other than English (or French) as languages of instruction is not allowed. The Ontario Education Act, for example, states that the curriculum may be delivered only in French and English, Canada's two official languages. This means that even if all the children in a school speak Urdu and have little or no knowledge of English, they must be instructed in English or French only. So far, this legislation has not been challenged in the courts.

Even where bilingual education is well established and research studies have documented its benefits, opposing ideologies may prevail. Bilingual education has recently come under fire in some parts of the United States, for example. Critics argue that bilingual education causes children to become dependent on their first language and may inhibit their learning of English. In 1998, voters in California approved Proposition 227, which replaced bilingual programs with one-year, English-only programs. When the year is up, most students are fully mainstreamed and receive little or no continued support for acquiring English. Similar legislation was passed in Arizona in 2000, and initiatives are under way in other states. The debate is often acrimonious, pitting language acquisition researchers against organizations such as English First, which opposes providing services in languages other than English.

Though bilingual education may be neither practical nor politically feasible in many jurisdictions, it is difficult to argue against the notion that learning in a first language is more effective than learning in a second — at least until students' proficiency in the second language is adequate for learning the curriculum.

Where bilingual education is feasible, it is the least expensive way of supporting English language learners. They do not need additional classes or ESL teachers for English as a Second Language. They need only classroom teachers who are bilingual and trained in bilingual instruction. In addition, the need to provide a heritage language program is eliminated because students' first language is used as a language of instruction.

ESL PROGRAMS

In jurisdictions where bilingual education is not feasible, the next-best alternative is a strong ESL program that compensates for the fact that the students are learning in a language other than their own. **Self-contained ESL programs**, **ESL core programs**, **ESL resource support programs**, and **ESL integration programs** are common in school districts across Canada. Schools and school districts often provide more than one of these models, depending on local needs and resources.

Self-Contained ESL Programs

Self-contained ESL programs , which are sometimes called ESL reception programs, ESL reception centers, or ESL reception classes, concentrate resources and provide an intensive full-day program for newcomers as they adjust to their new academic and social environment and begin to learn English. Students may be enrolled for several months or, in some jurisdictions, a full school year. In areas of high immigration, nearly every school may provide such a program. In school districts where English language learners are distributed thinly, making it difficult to provide ESL support in every school, students may be congregated in a self-contained program in one or two designated schools. Students attend the congregated program until they are ready to enter their neighborhood school.

Two groups of newcomers benefit from self-contained programs.

- *Beginning learners of English*: These students may benefit from an intensive program of a few months' duration. During this time, they develop basic communication skills in English, learn about their new country, and are introduced to the educational and social environment they are about to enter.

- *Underschooled children*: Newcomers who have experienced significant gaps in their education would probably have difficulty relating to the mainstream program even if it were offered in their own language. These students are more likely to be successful if they initially receive intensive and specialized support in a program designed specifically to meet their needs. If possible, the students receive bilingual instruction, integrating language and literacy instruction with basic skills and concepts in mathematics, science, and social studies for a considerable time before they are completely mainstreamed.

A drawback of full-day, self-contained programs is that students may have no regular contact with English-speaking peers. As a result, they may be denied valuable language learning opportunities. In addition, many parents may be justifiably anxious if they perceive that their children are falling behind in the mainstream curriculum while they attend a reception program. And students who do not attend the neighborhood school may have no chance to make friends with whom they can socialize out of school.

During their time in a self-contained program, it is important to involve newcomers in activities with English-speaking students. This is not difficult if the program is located in a school where newcomers can participate in programs, such as physical education, alongside their English-speaking peers, or where they can be matched with peer tutors from other classes. This kind of contact is much more difficult to arrange, however, when the program is located at a stand-alone site.

It is also important to base the program's content on the content of the appropriate curriculum, so that students are exposed to the same curriculum as their age peers. Because students arrive with varying educational experiences, however, the curriculum must often be adapted to fill in gaps and provide essential background knowledge and skills. To ease the transition for students who are leaving a self-contained ESL program to go to a new school, teachers should establish strong links with neighborhood schools and ensure that each school has organized an effective reception and orientation plan.

ESL Core Programs

ESL core programs offer intensive support in neighborhood schools for students in the early stages of learning English. This model works well

Some newcomers benefit from a period of intensive support.

in schools with large numbers of English language learners. Teachers setting up ESL core programs should consider the following suggestions.

- Students in the early stages of learning English should be grouped in an ESL class for 50 percent or more of the school day.
- In elementary schools with large numbers of English language learners, English language learners should be grouped by grade level. In other schools, split-grade groupings (e.g., a Grade 1-2 class, a Grade 3-4 class) often make better use of resources.
- In elementary schools, the ESL program should be based on the core curriculum for the grade. This usually involves language arts, social studies, and mathematics, though science may also be included.
- In secondary schools, English language learners may be placed in special ESL classes instead of the English courses designed for native speakers of English. They may also be placed in special classes for history, geography, science, mathematics, and other compulsory courses — and receive academic credit for these courses. In Ontario, Canada, for example, a student who succeeds in an ESL Canadian history course is deemed to have earned the compulsory credit in Canadian history. Some schools also offer special classes in optional courses, such as drama.
- The program in the ESL core subjects should be adapted to meet the needs of the learners, in accordance with the principles of content-based language instruction. Content-based instruction is discussed later in this chapter.
- Students should be integrated into the mainstream program for the rest of the day. To make this possible, the mainstream timetable must be designed to provide the best opportunities for integration. If mainstream Grade 3 classes work on language arts and social studies at the same time as the Grade 3 ESL class, for example, English language learners can join their peers for other subjects with minimum disruption and maximum continuity.
- When English language learners are in mainstream classes, all teachers should be responsible for adapting the program to meet their needs, no matter what their stage of second language acquisition.
- Students' progress should be reviewed regularly. As soon as they are ready, students may move into the mainstream core program for longer periods, making room in the ESL core program for other newcomers.
- The program must be flexible. Some students may, for example, be ready for integration into mathematics soon after they arrive and should leave the core program to join their peers for this subject.
- Students who have moved out of core ESL programs need continued language support for several years after they leave. This support may be provided by an ESL teacher, if there is one, on a resource or withdrawal basis (see the following section). In addition, mainstream teachers must be aware of and responsive to the needs of English language learners.

Where ESL core programs are feasible, they offer significant advantages, especially for students in the early stages of learning English or of literacy development. Students in core programs develop knowledge and skills in academic subjects at the same time as they learn English.

ESL core programs are based on the grade-level curriculum.

The language program is clearly connected to the mainstream program and effectively prepares students for integration. At the same time, English language learners have opportunities to become involved in the mainstream program and interact with peers.

ESL Resource Support Programs

In ESL resource support programs, sometimes called pull-out or withdrawal programs, students are pulled out or withdrawn from the mainstream classroom to work with the ESL teacher for part of the school day. The time each student spends with the ESL teacher varies. Newcomers may spend a significant part of every day in the ESL class, while others may attend for only an hour or two a week.

The organization of ESL groupings often depends on when students can be withdrawn from the mainstream program. Some ESL teachers withdraw all students at the same level of English proficiency at the same time. Though this enables teachers to plan lessons for the whole group, it makes it difficult to match lessons to the maturity level of all learners and to coordinate the program with that in mainstream classrooms.

Other ESL teachers withdraw students according to grade level, which means that the group may include both beginners and more advanced English language learners. In this case, the teacher must provide several tasks — at various levels of difficulty — related to a particular topic. Grade-level groupings are more supportive of language acquisition than proficiency groupings because less advanced English speakers have opportunities to interact with their more proficient peers, who act as language models and informants. At the same time, the more advanced speakers gain practice and confidence as they rephrase, explain, and provide examples for their peers. Grade-level groupings also make it easier to coordinate the ESL program with the mainstream curriculum.

Most ESL teachers try to withdraw students when mainstream classes are involved in subjects, such as language arts and social studies, that are the most difficult for English language learners. As far as possible, these learners remain in the mainstream classroom for aspects of the program in which they can participate, such as physical education, the arts, and, in some cases, mathematics.

The program must also be flexible. As soon as students demonstrate a proficiency level that enables them to be successful in a curriculum area, they should rejoin the mainstream program for that subject. Many students from other countries are as proficient as — or even more proficient than — their age peers in mathematics, for example. As a result, withdrawing these students during the mathematics period may not be a good idea, especially if the math program uses manipulatives to facilitate comprehension and includes plenty of well-structured group work to promote meaningful language use.

Resource support programs work well in schools where the number of English language learners does not warrant establishing a core program or where students don't need the support of a core program. In school districts with a small and scattered population of English language learners, an itinerant ESL teacher may work with students for an hour or two a week to provide resource support in several schools.

The ESL setting provides a low-risk environment in which learners can begin speaking English, learn about their new environment, and make friends. The ESL teacher has opportunities to assess learners'

These children leave their grade level class to work with the ESL teacher for a short period each day.

needs and strengths and to tailor content and resources to these. As far as possible, the content should relate to the mainstream curriculum, and the ESL teacher should maintain close contact with classroom teachers.

ESL Integration Programs

Most English language learners, including beginners, should spend part of every school day in the mainstream classroom, where they can interact with English-speaking peers and become familiar with the grade-level curriculum. The mainstream classroom offers opportunities for second language acquisition, social integration, and academic growth that the ESL classroom alone does not. A second language is acquired most efficiently when it is used to achieve meaningful purposes, such as learning to play baseball, solving a mathematics problem, creating a dramatic retelling of a story, planning a class outing, and working on a group project. A well-planned integrated model also fosters positive intercultural attitudes among all the learners. For these reasons, the mainstream program is an important component of the ESL program.

Integration involves much more than assigning students a desk in the mainstream classroom. Without carefully planned program adaptations and support, failure is likely to be the result. In a multilingual school, where the learners are at various stages of proficiency in the language of instruction, it is important for all teachers to support successful integration by

- providing a learning environment that supports second language acquisition. Suggestions are included in Chapter 10.
- adapting curriculum and assessment, so that the learning outcomes are attainable and appropriate for students at various stages of proficiency in English. See Chapter 13.
- integrating language learning and content instruction. Strategies for achieving this are described later in this chapter and in Chapter 12.

Heritage Language Instruction

ESL programs should be complemented by a strong heritage language program that helps students maintain and continue to develop in their first language.

Attitudes toward students' first languages have changed considerably in the last two or three decades. Once considered detrimental to children's cognitive development and social integration, maintaining their first language is now recognized as an important factor in acquiring a second language and as a significant source of cultural pride and personal identity. For more on the importance of maintaining the first language, see Chapter 8.

Though in some school districts, students study their heritage language during the school day, most classes are held after school or on weekends. Many community groups also offer heritage language classes outside regular school hours. In these classes, students develop skills in their own language — or the language of their parents — and learn about the history, important leaders and personalities, traditions, and values of their cultural community.

Because heritage language classes are usually offered outside the regular school program, they are often perceived as less important than the "regular" curriculum. In addition, students may be reluctant to

This poster was created by a student in a Tamil heritage language class sponsored by the Toronto District School Board.

attend extra classes at times when they might otherwise be playing or socializing with friends. In many jurisdictions, heritage language teachers are not members of teachers' associations, are not required to meet the same professional standards as their mainstream counterparts, are paid less, and have less job security than classroom teachers. They may also have little contact with their mainstream colleagues. Some are relatively new immigrants themselves, and their teaching methods may be quite different from those learners are exposed to in mainstream programs. As a result, heritage language teachers may not be regarded as professionals in the same way as their mainstream colleagues.

Despite these difficulties, parents who recognize the benefits of maintaining their children's proficiency in their home language are eager to enroll their children in heritage language classes. These programs flourish in school districts across Canada, for example, often with little or no direct support from school districts or provincial education ministries. In British Columbia, about 150 organizations offer heritage language classes attended by 30,000 learners outside the school system. In Saskatchewan, 62 organizations teach 25 languages, and 45 languages are taught in Toronto's public schools, mostly outside school hours.

French Language Instruction

Students in English-speaking Canada are expected to develop some proficiency in speaking French. However, many newcomers arrive in Canada with little or no knowledge of French. Because their age peers may have already received several years of instruction, many immigrants need a French as second language program that will enable them to catch up to their peers.

Because learning English is the priority, delaying instruction in French until the newcomer has a good grasp of English may seem to make sense. In most cases, however, a delay is unnecessary, as long as the French teacher adapts the program for beginners. Ways of doing this are described in greater detail in Chapter 13.

Many newcomers are competent language learners. Their experience in acquiring an additional language helps them learn new sounds, acquire vocabulary, and perceive patterns in any language. In addition, many newcomers have already learned at least one additional language before starting to learn English. Many Punjabi speakers, for example, also speak Hindi; many Ukrainians know Russian; and many Cantonese speakers have learned Mandarin. For many newcomers, English is already a third or fourth language, and French is just one more.

In general, English language learners benefit from being placed in the French class alongside their age peers, as long as the program is adapted to accommodate them. Some secondary schools provide a beginner-level French course for newcomers, many of whom are subsequently able to continue learning French alongside their grade-level peers.

At the same time, a small number of newcomers may benefit from delaying instruction in French, or even, in exceptional cases, receiving a complete exemption, as long as a more appropriate program is available to replace it. Students who arrive with significant gaps in their schooling and limited literacy development in their own language, for example, might benefit from spending additional time in an ESL or literacy class, while newcomers who have clearly identified special needs might receive special education support instead of French instruction.

Methods of Second Language Instruction

Over the centuries, many approaches to second language teaching have been proposed and implemented. Recent approaches have been developed in direct response to theories of how languages are learned and to the needs of language learners.

Today, methods of second language instruction can be broadly classified as either **part-to-whole instruction** or **whole-to-part instruction**. Part-to-whole instruction focuses on form by breaking down language into its component parts, such as grammar rules or pronunciation patterns, and organizing these into a sequence of instruction. Practice drills and exercises are emphasized, and there is less emphasis on using language for meaningful communication. In contrast, whole-to-part instruction focuses on meaning and involves students in speaking, listening, reading, and writing activities designed to promote real communication. Instruction in specific features of the language is often secondary and is sometimes assumed to be unnecessary.

Most students who arrive in English-speaking countries with some previous instruction in English as a foreign language have probably been exposed to a part-to-whole approach. In countries where English is the dominant language, such as the United Kingdom, Australia, New Zealand, the United States, and English-speaking Canada, the emphasis in English as a second language instruction is increasingly on a whole-to-part approach. In practice, most second language teachers and programs adopt highly eclectic methods that combine elements of several approaches.

Students and parents who arrive in their new country with preconceived notions about what language instruction should be like may be highly uncomfortable in settings that do not match their expectations. In a communicative setting where the focus, at least initially, is on fluency rather than accuracy, students accustomed to learning rules and completing grammar exercises may feel that they are not receiving sufficient instruction. As a result, language teachers must be conscious of the rationale underlying instructional practices and prepared to explain this to students and parents. Stating the learning outcomes at the beginning of lessons and units helps students develop metacognitive awareness by providing opportunities for them to talk and write about the learning process. It is also important to be flexible. In some cases, this may involve incorporating some instructional strategies that learners are comfortable with, especially at the beginning.

Grammar-Translation Approach

The **grammar-translation approach**, the traditional method of language instruction, was perfected in the teaching of Latin and was also used in teaching modern languages. Depending on when and where you went to school, this may have been the way you were taught a foreign language. This method is still frequently used to teach English in non-English speaking countries where students usually share a first language.

Grammar-translation is a deductive approach that involves forming and applying rules. Lessons often consist of

- an explanation — and examples — of a grammar rule
- a list of new words, with translations
- a reading that includes applied examples of the grammar rule and the new words
- written exercises that require students to apply the grammar rule and use the vocabulary

The focus is on reading, often of literary excerpts or informational passages about the country and culture of the target language, and on written translation. Exercises are often unrelated to the content of the reading passage and may consist of transformations (e.g., changing all verbs to the past tense, converting statements into questions, or supplying the correct form of designated words in a sentence).

The language of instruction is usually students' first language rather than the target language. Where English is the language of instruction, for example, this means that the rules of French would be explained in English. Because students have little or no opportunity to converse with native speakers of French, many develop a large vocabulary, a knowledge of grammar, and reading comprehension skills that enable them to answer factual recall questions about a reading passage. At the same time, they may be unable to participate in simple oral discourse when they find themselves in a French-speaking environment or to adapt their approach to reading for different purposes.

Audiolingual Approach

The **audiolingual approach** was developed in reaction to grammar-translation, which had proven unsatisfactory in promoting proficiency in **authentic communication**, especially in oral language. Audiolingual methods were used in the armed forces during World War II, especially with intelligence personnel.

This part-to-whole approach, which is sometimes called the structural approach, is based on behaviorist psychology and descriptive linguistics. Behavioral psychologists, notably B.F. Skinner, viewed language development as conditioned behavior, and applied linguists developed descriptions of the patterns or structures of a given language based on scientific analysis of the language in use, rather than on using rules and terms based on Latin grammar.

Advocates of the audiolingual approach focus on habit formation and structural accuracy, with a strong emphasis on listening and speaking. The target language is the dominant language of instruction, and there is minimal description of grammar rules, which are to be acquired through induction: perceiving and learning a pattern by examining many examples.

Lessons often focus on grammatical structures, which are presented in a specific sequence. Present-tense verbs are taught before past-tense forms, for example, and modal auxiliaries are taught before conditional forms. The usual sequence of instruction is listening, speaking, reading, and writing, and students may spend time in a language lab, listening and responding to recorded dialogues and drills as the teacher monitors their performance.

Drilling for Accuracy

Substitution and transformation drills are usually important elements of the audiolingual approach.

Substitution Drill

Teacher provides the pattern: "This is a book."
Students repeat: "This is a book."
Teacher provides a cue: "Pencil."
Students respond: "This is a pencil."
Teacher provides another cue: "Pen."
A student (or group) responds: "This is a pen."
And so on, around the class.

Transformation Drill

Teacher provides a cue: "This is a book."
Teacher models the transformation: "These are books."
Students repeat: "These are books."
Teacher provides a second cue: "This is a pencil."
A student (or group) responds: "These are pencils."
Teacher provides another cue: "This is a pen."
A student responds: "These are pens."
And so on, around the class.

Lessons usually involve students in

- listening to a dialogue, often on audiotape, that features a target language structure, such as the simple present tense forms of *be*
- mimicking the dialogue, often with half of the class repeating one side of a two-person exchange as the teacher models correct pronunciation and intonation
- memorizing and practicing the dialogue with a partner or in small groups
- participating in oral pattern drills that usually involve substitutions or transformations for the purpose of making the language feature a conditioned response
- once certain structures and vocabulary are mastered, completing written exercises involving substitutions and transformations or reading a carefully selected or specially created passage that includes only previously learned structures and the new pattern, then responding to questions designed to elicit answers that use the new pattern

From the beginning, the audiolingual approach emphasizes producing and reinforcing "correct" utterances so that students do not fall into "bad habits." Because the emphasis is on correct form, learners end up manipulating linguistic structures rather than communicating genuine messages. Oral language takes priority, and reading and writing may not be introduced until students have learned a substantial corpus of grammar structures and vocabulary.

Total Physical Response Approach

The **Total Physical Response approach** (TPR) is a meaning-based, whole-to-part method that emphasizes listening comprehension and has proven effective with beginning language learners. In response to the teacher's commands, students carry out physical actions.

Here is an example of how TPR might be used with a class of beginning language learners.

- Teacher says, "Stand up," and stands, gesturing to students to do the same.
- Students stand but are not required to say anything.
- Teacher continues, giving more commands (e.g., "Sit down," and "Jump") and demonstrating the actions.
- The teacher gives the commands without demonstrating. Students demonstrate their comprehension by performing the required action.
- After several lessons, students begin to give some of the commands.
- The language gradually becomes more complex, and forms other than the imperative are introduced.

TPR emphasizes listening comprehension, followed by oral production of language, with very little reading and writing. Grammar is usually introduced in a specific sequence and is learned inductively, without explicit instruction.

Because students are not required to produce language in the early stages, this method lowers beginning learners' anxiety and meets the needs of those who are going through a silent period. The physical activity keeps everyone involved and interested and is especially well suited to the learning style of some students.

TPR's focus on what can be physically demonstrated limits its uses. Nevertheless, many second language teachers find it helpful to incorporate aspects of this approach into their program when working with beginners. TPR can also be applied outside the language classroom, such as in the physical education program or other subjects that emphasize hands-on activities, motor skills, and sensory involvement rather than — or as well as — learning content.

The Communicative Approach

The **communicative approach** moves from whole to part, emphasizing fluency and meaning before accuracy. The goal is to enable learners to communicate and understand real messages from the beginning. Grammar is usually learned inductively, as students are exposed to many examples of a structure and involved in communicative activities that require them to use it. With the help of the teacher, a rule may eventually be developed and made explicit. In foreign language teaching, the first language may be used to explain a rule.

Students are involved in practice aimed at developing accuracy as well as fluency. They work on tasks such as group problem solving, information-gap activities, role playing, games, and open-ended dialogues. Errors and interlanguage forms are tolerated, especially when dealing with language features that have not yet been formally introduced. Students respond to real messages in real conversations, and neither the students nor the teacher can predict exactly what the content or form of the next utterance will be.

Classroom activities are often designed to provide rehearsal for a **contact assignment** that requires students to use English with native speakers outside the classroom. A student might, for example, be required to conduct an interview or listen to a recorded announcement, then share the information with classmates or the teacher. Teachers organize field trips, inter-class projects, and other activities that bring together language learners and native speakers in supported contexts.

Students are also encouraged to record and reflect on their experiences and feelings in writing and to write for others, keeping dialogue journals or corresponding with "secret friends" in other classrooms. For more information on journals, see Chapter 12. The content of activities is usually geared to the needs and interests of the learners. Adolescents may be involved in talking, reading, and writing about issues relating to the social life of teenagers, for example, and younger children are often involved in literature-based programs using picture books and storytelling.

A communicative program may be sequenced according to **communicative functions** instead of, or in addition to, grammatical structures. This means that students may learn ways to apologize, interrupt, or agree before they know the grammatical rules underlying the structures of these expressions. Beginners may learn, for example, to introduce themselves, using expressions such as, "My name is ...," "I come from ...," and "I have been in this country for ...." In part-to-whole approaches, such as audiolingualism, students would not be exposed to the present perfect tense (e.g., *I have been*) at this stage; other tenses that are considered easier to teach and learn are introduced first.

The communicative approach emphasizes **needs assessment**: the program is designed to meet the specific needs of the learners. As a result, a beginner program for students who need to learn English for academic purposes is very different from a workplace program or a newcomer orientation program for adults, and the balance between reading and writing and listening and speaking depends on the learners' needs.

Content-Based Language Instruction

Content-based language instruction is a communicative approach based on the needs of those who are learning English to continue their education. Language teaching and content instruction are integrated so that learners develop knowledge and skills in a specific subject, such as science, or a particular occupational field, such as health care, at the same time as they develop their English language skills. Content-based instruction is widely used in elementary and secondary schools, college and university programs, and vocational training programs. In many school districts in the United States, content-based instruction is called **sheltered instruction**. In university settings, the approach is often referred to as English for academic purposes. In Canada, the approach has been widely implemented in French immersion as well as ESL programs.

LESSONS FROM FRENCH IMMERSION

In Canada, French immersion students whose first language is not French receive content-based French language instruction in most subjects, although in the beginning stages they often respond in English.

According to Fred Genesee, who has studied French immersion and second language instruction, research shows that

- integrating content and language instruction is likely to be more effective than teaching language in isolation
- instructional strategies and academic tasks that encourage purposeful classroom talk are likely to be especially beneficial for second language learning
- to maximize language learning, language development should be systematically integrated with academic development

INTEGRATING LANGUAGE AND CONTENT INSTRUCTION

Content is more than a vehicle for language learning; it is selected for its importance in students' overall education. The teacher's responsibility is to devise activities that help students develop specific language skills and practice using specific language features at the same time as they learn content. Students who are creating a bar graph comparing annual rainfall in various regions, for example, are engaged in the cognitive activity of finding the information and recording it on a graph. The language activity involves using language — both oral and written — to communicate information on the graph, (e.g., *twice as much as, half as much as, five times more than,* and *fifty percent more than*). The next lesson may continue with a description of the water cycle, and students may talk and write about a diagram of the cycle, using sequence markers such as *then, next, after that,* and *finally,* in addition to practicing subject-verb agreement in the simple present tense.

The content selected for the language program varies according to the learners' level of English proficiency and the expectations of the grade-level curriculum. Students in the very early stages of learning English need to deal with relatively undemanding content that relates to their immediate needs. Newcomers need to learn about the school system, for example, as well as festivals and holidays, and everyday topics such as food, clothing, sports, television, shopping, and transportation. Beyond the beginning stage, students work with more demanding content, including material selected from the mainstream curriculum. In addition, the program must focus on learner strategies for acquiring a second language, such as inferring meaning from context, using word roots and affixes, and consulting dictionaries.

Content-based instruction is a whole-to-part approach in which grammar is learned inductively, with help from the teacher. The grammar to be introduced is usually determined by the subject and the academic task involved. A geography lesson, for example, might involve using prepositions or comparative and superlative adjectives, while a history lesson might emphasize past tenses, and a science lesson might introduce passive verbs. Vocabulary is also determined by the demands of the subject area. Listening and speaking activities are balanced with reading and writing, and the program includes explicit instruction in specific academic skills and learning strategies.

Though content-based language instruction is used in classes consisting exclusively of English language learners, it is also useful in mainstream classrooms, where teachers have found that both English language learners and their English-speaking peers benefit from the increased attention paid to language and contextual support. Section 4 of this book, "Language Learning across the Curriculum," includes suggestions for planning curriculum and delivering lessons using a content-based approach.

Key Elements of Effective Content-Based Language Programs

- A comprehensible language environment
- Opportunities for interaction and purposeful language use
- Support for students' first language and cultural background
- Attention to students' social and emotional needs
- Strong links to the mainstream curriculum
- Instruction in specific language features that occur in specific contexts or subjects
- Instruction in effective learning strategies

To Learn More …

Books and Articles

Alladina, S. *Being Bilingual: A Guide for Parents, Teachers and Young People on Mother Tongue, Heritage Language and Bilingual Education*. Stoke-on-Trent, U.K.: Trentham Books, 1995.
Speaks directly to bilingual parents and children, as well as teachers. A suitable resource for discussions at parent-teacher meetings, this book could be used as a source of readings for adolescent English language learners.

Baker, C. *A Parents' and Teachers' Guide to Bilingualism*. Clevedon, U.K.: Multilingual Matters, 1995.
Helpful advice for parents and teachers on raising and teaching bilingual children, presented in question-and-answer format.

Baker, C. *Foundations of Bilingual Education and Bilingualism*. 3rd ed. Clevedon, U.K.: Multilingual Matters, 2002.
Thorough introduction to bilingual education and bilingualism.

Cenez, J., and F. Genesee, eds. *Beyond Bilingualism: Multilingualism and Multilingual Education*. Clevedon, U.K.: Multilingual Matters, 1998.
Helpful articles on content-based language teaching, as well as case studies of language programs in various countries.

Chamot, A.U., S. Barnhardt, P.B. El-Dinary, and J. Robbins. *The Learning Strategies Handbook*. White Plains, N.Y.: Addison-Wesley Longman (now Pearson Education), 1999.
Guide to teaching learning strategies to English language learners.

Chamot, A., and M. O'Malley. *The CALLA Handbook: Implementing the Cognitive Academic Language Learning Approach*. Reading, Mass.: Addison-Wesley, 1994. Resource book for content-based language instruction.

Clegg, J., ed. *Mainstreaming ESL: Case Studies in Integrating ESL Students into the Mainstream Curriculum*. Clevedon, U.K.: Multilingual Matters, 1996.
Articles from the United Kingdom, Canada, Australia, and the United States providing practical strategies for integrating language and content instruction in mainstream classrooms, as well as suggestions on school policy.

Cloud, N., F. Genesee, and E. Hamayan. *Dual Language Instruction: A Handbook for Enriched Education*. Boston, Mass.: Heinle & Heinle, 2000.
Source book for educators planning a bilingual program or teaching in a bilingual classroom.

Corson, D. *Language, Minority Education and Gender: Linking Social Justice and Power*. Clevedon, U.K.: Multilingual Matters, 1993.
Essential reading for educators involved in policy decisions or planning language programs for minority language students.

Cummins, J. *Language, Power and Pedagogy: Bilingual Children Caught in the Crossfire*. Clevedon, U.K.: Multilingual Matters, 2000.
Analyzes various approaches to ESL, heritage languages, and bilingual education. Explains how traditional educational practices are largely responsible for academic failure in some linguistic groups and suggests strategies for reversing this.

Echevarria, J., and A. Graves. *Sheltered Content Instruction: Teaching English-Language Learners with Diverse Abilities*. 2nd ed. Boston, Mass.: Allyn and Bacon, 2003.
Program models and instructional strategies for adapting instruction for English language learners.

Echevarria, J., M.E. Vogt, and D.J. Short. *Making Content Comprehensible for English Language Learners: The SIOP Model*. Boston, Mass.: Allyn & Bacon, 2000.
Presents the sheltered instruction observation protocol model (SIOP), which helps teachers provide comprehensible instruction for English language learners.

Freeman, Y., D. Freeman, and S. Mercuri. *Dual Language Essentials for Teachers and Administrators*. Portsmouth, N.H.: Heinemann, 2004.
Uses examples from schools and classrooms to show how how effective dual language programs programs can help all students develop high levels of academic achievement as they become bilingual.

Freeman, Y., D. Freeman, and S. Mercuri. *Closing the Achievement Gap: How to Reach Limited-Formal-Schooling and Long-Term English Learners*. Portsmouth, N.H.: Heinemann, 2002.
Advice on program development and classroom practice for English language learners who arrive with limited or interrupted schooling.

Garcia, G., ed. *English Learners: Reaching the Highest Level of English Literacy*. Newark, Del.: International Reading Association, 2003.
This book focuses on literacy instruction for English language learners. Includes articles by experts such as Jim Cummins and Stephen Krashen.

Genesee, F., ed. *Educating Second-Language Children: The Whole Child, the Whole Curriculum, the Whole Community*. New York: Cambridge University Press, 1994.
Articles about approaches to second language instruction and excellent examples of content-based instruction.

Kaufman, D., and Crandall, J. *Content-Based Instruction in Primary and Secondary School Settings*. Alexandria, Va.: Teachers of English to Speakers of Other Languages, Inc. 2005.
Practical approach to integrating language instruction with curriculum content.

Krashen, S. *Condemned without a Trial: Bogus Arguments against Bilingual Education*. Portsmouth, N.H.: Heinemann, 1997.
Analyzes arguments against bilingual education and provides useful research-based information and counter-arguments.

Larsen-Freeman, D. *Techniques and Principles in Language Teaching*. 2nd ed. Oxford, U.K.: Oxford University Press, 2000.
Overview of second-language instruction methods, including TPR, the communicative approach, content-based instruction, and learner strategy training. Provides many classroom examples.

Mace-Matluck, J., R. Alexander-Kasparik, and R. M. Queen. *Through the Golden Door: Educational Approaches for Immigrant Adolescents with Limited Schooling*. Washington, D.C.: Center for Applied Linguistics, 1998.

Describes the educational needs of newcomer youth with limited schooling and provides guidelines for developing educational programs for these students.

Mohan, B., C. Leung, and C. Davison. *English as a Second Language in the Mainstream: Teaching, Learning, and Identity*. Harlow, U.K.: Pearson Education, 2001.

Describes programs and policies for English language learners in Australia, Canada, and New Zealand. Several chapters on integrating language and content instruction.

Ovando, C.J., and V.P. Collier. *Bilingual and ESL Classrooms: Teaching in Multilingual Contexts*. 2nd ed. Columbus, Ohio: McGraw-Hill, 1998.

Updated edition of a classic text on ESL, bilingual, and multicultural education. Includes chapters on content-based instruction in specific subjects, as well as research on bilingual education and the English-only movement.

Rigg, P., and V.D. Allen, eds. *When They Don't All Speak English: Integrating the ESL Student into the Regular Classroom*. Urbana, Ill.: National Council of Teachers of English, 1989.

Articles on topics such as program design, creating an effective language learning environment, language variation, and language through content.

Roessingh, H., Kover, P., and Watt, D. Developing Cognitive Academic Language Proficiency: The Journey. *TESL Canada Journal*, 23, 1, 2005.

The study documented in this article has significant implications for policy development and program planning for English language learners, confirming that these students, including those who arrive at a young age, need focused language instruction for a significant period of time in order to reach their academic potential.

Schecter, S., and J. Cummins, eds. *Multilingual Education in Practice: Using Diversity as a Resource*. Portsmouth, N.H.: Heinemann, 2003.

Suggestions for developing language policies and preparing teachers to work effectively in linguistically and culturally diverse settings.

Short, D., and Boyson, B. *Creating Access: Language and Academic Programs for Secondary School Newcomers*. Washington, D.C.: Center for Applied Linguistics, 2004.

Reporting on a study of 115 middle and high school newcomer programs, this book identifies important implementation features and offers advice on setting up newcomer programs.

Walqui, A. *Access and Engagement: Program Design and Instructional Approaches for Immigrant Students in Secondary School*. Washington, D.C.: Center for Applied Linguistics, 2000.

Analyzes the special challenges faced by immigrant adolescents and describes the characteristics of schools and programs that effectively meet their educational needs.

Websites and Online Resources

Center for Applied Linguistics. <www.cal.org>.

Information and links on second language acquisition and bilingual education. Home to the ERIC Clearinghouse on Languages and Linguistics.

Center for Research on Education, Diversity and Excellence. <www.cal.org/crede>.

Funds research projects and disseminates information related to the education of diverse groups of students. The sheltered instruction observation protocol is of special interest. Video and manual available.

Genesee, F., ed. *Program Alternatives for Linguistically Diverse Students*. Center for Research on Education, Diversity and Excellence, 1999. <www.cal.org/crede/pubs/>.

Describes various programs for educating students from diverse linguistic and cultural backgrounds.

Genesee, F. *Integrating Language and Content: Lessons from Immersion*. National Center for Research on Cultural Diversity and Second Language Learning, 1994. <www.cal.org/resources/digest/ncrcds05.html>.

Discusses the implications of research into French immersion for the design and development of ESL programs.

International Reading Association. <www.reading.org>.

This organization has published many useful books and articles on programs and instructional approaches for English language learners.

National Clearinghouse for English Language Acquisition and Language Instruction Educational Programs (formerly National Clearinghouse for Bilingual Education). <www.ncela.gwu.edu>.

Information on research, publications, educational programs, and classroom activities for linguistically and culturally diverse learners.

National Council of Teachers of English. < www.ncte.org>.

This site has a collection of articles and reviews of books related to the needs of English language learners in K-12 classrooms.

Polyphony. <http://epe.lac-bac.gc.ca/100/205/301/ic/cdc/polyphony/index2.html>

Explores immigrant experiences through 8 different themes. The education theme includes several articles on heritage languages.

Ruiz-de-Velasco, J., Fix, M.E., and Clewell, B.C. *Overlooked and Underserved: Immigrant Students in U.S. Secondary Schools*.

This report focuses on students who arrive with disrupted schooling, and "long-term" English language learners who still have not caught up to age peers in literacy development. Washington, DC: Urban Institute, 2000. <www.urban.org/publications/310022.html>.

Urban Institute. <www.urban.org>.

This site has many reports and other publications focusing on the education of immigrant students and English language learners.

10 Creating a Supportive Language Learning Environment

Whether you are teaching an ESL class or a mainstream class that includes English language learners, it is important to establish a learning environment that supports second language acquisition. This chapter offers strategies designed to help you

- *provide comprehensible instruction* by using strategies that help students understand more of what is going on
- *provide supportive feedback* that encourages students to take risks and learn from their errors in using English
- *incorporate students' first languages* as a tool for learning and as a source of cultural enrichment for all students
- *use cooperative learning strategies* to promote the kind of oral interaction that supports language acquisition

Providing Comprehensible Instruction

Comprehensible input is fundamental to second language acquisition. Input (language) is comprehensible when students can use their prior knowledge, visual support, or context to infer the meaning of new words and expressions. Arabic numerals, for example, are used in most of the world, with some minor differences. Seeing the numerals and hearing them named enables English language learners to use their prior knowledge to make the connection between the numerals and their English names. If they also have an opportunity to watch and listen as you demonstrate addition, for example, on the chalkboard as you say each step (e.g., "Eight *plus* two *equals* 10"), they will also learn the words and expressions that describe the addition process.

You can make lessons comprehensible for second language learners by becoming more aware of how language is used in your classroom and by providing additional support for comprehension. Here are 20 strategies that will make the language used in your classroom more comprehensible.

1. *Simplify vocabulary.* Consider the difference between these two instructions: "Learn the new words" and "Review the new vocabulary." Most second language learners are likely to understand the first, but may have trouble with the second. In many subjects, the amount of Latin-derived vocabulary increases as the content becomes more complex and abstract, and it is important to explain concepts in simple language before introducing new words. To begin a unit on photosynthesis, for example, explain, "We are going to learn

about how plants make food." Teach the lesson, using visuals, models, and videos, and introduce the word *photosynthesis* only after students understand the process.

2. *Teach key words before the lesson.* Select a few key words from the text or lesson and teach their meaning by providing a picture, using gestures or mime, giving the word in the students' languages, providing synonyms, using the word in a highly supported context, or drawing an analogy.

3. *Repeat and rehearse new words.* When you introduce a new word, articulate clearly. Say the word again as you write it on the chalkboard or point to it on a classroom chart. Instruct students to repeat it chorally and add the word, as well as an example of its use, to a classroom word wall. Information on word walls and other approaches to vocabulary development are included in Chapter 12.

4. *Recycle new words* by reintroducing them in a new setting or use recently learned words to introduce or expand a concept. To internalize the meaning of new words, students need to hear and use the words several times in highly supported contexts.

5. *Print, rather than write.* Remember that cursive script may be especially difficult for students who are not familiar with the Roman alphabet.

6. *Provide plenty of concrete and visual support,* such as models, toys, math manipulatives, pictures, charts, flash cards, vocabulary lists, posters, and banners. Demonstrate and provide hands-on activities.

7. *Use key visuals to present key concepts.* Key visuals are teacher-developed graphic organizers such as T-charts, Venn diagrams, flow charts, concept maps, and timelines. Key visuals lower the language barrier, enabling students to see relationships among ideas and to develop thinking skills, such as classifying, connecting cause and effect, following sequence, and comparing or contrasting information. More detailed information on key visuals and their use is included in Chapter 12.

8. *Simplify sentence structure.* When making classroom presentations or engaging in classroom discussion, it is important to use direct, personal language and to avoid complex sentences and passive verbs as much as possible. Rather than saying, for example, "The homework must be completed and handed in by Friday," tell students: "You must finish the work and give it to me on Friday."

9. *Emphasize key ideas and instructions.* Pause before making an important point. Make sure all students can see you, use gestures for emphasis, raise the pitch and volume of your voice slightly, and repeat or rephrase — or ask a student to do so. Give students an opportunity to go over information and instructions orally in small groups by telling them to take one minute to make sure everyone in the group understands what to do next. You can also conduct random checks to make sure that everyone in a group understands.

10. *Use many nonverbal cues.* Gestures, facial expressions, and mime help learners understand what you are saying. Be aware, however, that the meaning of some gestures varies from culture to culture. Chapter 6 includes more information about nonverbal language.

11. *Make notes to signal key ideas, new words, and so on.* Use the chalkboard or make a chart for use during the lesson and for future reference. You can also provide summary sheets for students to refer to when studying at home.

12. *Give clear instructions.* Because language learners may be unable to process oral instructions quickly enough to understand fully, tell students to rehearse instructions in groups before they start a task. Provide clear and simply worded written instructions for homework and projects, and write page and exercise numbers on the chalkboard as you say them. Language learners may not recognize numbers when they are delivered in rapid speech and may have trouble distinguishing between numbers such as *fourteen* and *forty*. Without a written cue, they may completely misinterpret simple instructions. When you say, for example, "Do questions 1 to 6," they may hear this as, "Do questions 1, 2, 6," or "Do question 126."

13. *Encourage oral rehearsal of key ideas and words.* At the beginning of a lesson, you might say, for example, "Make sure everyone in the group knows four things about [key ideas from the previous lesson]," or "Make sure everyone understands these five words that we talked about yesterday." You can also use this technique to summarize key ideas at the end of a lesson.

14. *Check often for comprehension.* If you ask, "Do you understand?" some students may say yes simply to avoid embarrassment. Instead, test their understanding by conducting random checks. Say, "Tell me what you have to do next," or "Show me the pages you have to read for homework." Make all group members responsible for ensuring that everyone is on track.

15. *Speak naturally* and only slightly more slowly than you would when talking to native speakers of English. This way, students will learn to recognize the language as it is really spoken. It doesn't help if they understand you, but no one else! Explain contractions such as *don't* and spoken forms such as *gonna*, emphasizing the difference between oral and written forms of the language.

16. *Be aware of figurative and idiomatic language.* If you say, "Run that by me again," or "Take a stab at it!" some students may translate these expressions literally and be very confused. Avoid using idiomatic expressions with students who are in the early stages of learning

Notes on chart paper help signal key words and new ideas.

English. Once students have developed some oral competence and confidence in using English, however, take opportunities to teach the meaning and use of idioms. English language learners understand that these expressions add life and color to the language and help them sound more like English speakers. Rephrase or explain the idiom — or encourage other students to explain — and post a list of the week's idioms and figurative expressions on a bulletin board.

17. *Provide enough response time* when you question English language learners. They need time to think in their first language and compose a response in their second.

18. *Provide peer tutors.* These may be from the same class, or you may wish to set up a cross-grade tutoring program. Students in the early stages of learning English benefit from the help of bilingual peer tutors who can clarify instructions, provide translations of key words, and help you check comprehension. Even when they don't share a common language, peer tutors can be a valuable source of support to newcomers.

19. *Provide alternative resources.* If a textbook is too difficult, look for a resource that uses simpler language and more visual support. Work with colleagues to rewrite the textbook for language learners or provide a simple chapter summary. Some students may be able to "graduate" to the grade-level textbook after using the simplified version to develop background knowledge and basic concepts.

20. *Reduce anxiety levels.* English language learners carry a double load. At the same time as they are learning some of the content, they are also learning the language of instruction. They will understand more if they are not under stress. Focus on key concepts and skills rather than *all* the content, and acknowledge progress in language learning as well as content-based skills and knowledge.

Tutors develop their social and leadership skills, feel a sense of accomplishment, and often enhance their own understanding of a concept after explaining it simply to someone else.

Providing Supportive Feedback

Second language learners rely on feedback from English-speaking peers and teachers to help them learn English. It is important not to point out or correct every error, however, as this may provide too much feedback for the learners to deal with and may even inhibit them from producing as much language as they need to in order to progress.

Remember that making errors is an important part of the language acquisition process. Learners need supportive feedback to help them learn from their errors. You can help students by responding systematically to their errors as they use English, both orally and in writing.

Responding to Oral Errors

Language learners may make several errors in a single statement or question. When students are speaking, don't interrupt them to correct errors, as this may inhibit their language production. Most students — especially adolescents — quickly become very reluctant to speak up in front of peers if attention is drawn to their errors. Focus, instead, on understanding what the student is saying and on responding to the message. A student who says, for example, "We go a filltrip Tursday?" is communicating a comprehensible message, despite the errors in grammar and pronunciation. This does not mean that you should ignore all errors, however.

- *Provide indirect feedback* by modeling the correct form when you respond to the message and occasionally remind students to monitor their own output and your feedback. In response to the student who asked about the field trip, you might say, for example, "Yes, we are going on a field trip Thursday. Bring your lunch. Did your mother sign the permission form?" You can also provide prompts that keep an exchange going or expand on the student's utterance to provide a model of language that may be slightly beyond the learner's current level of competence.

  Here is an example of how a teacher might provide feedback and expand on a student's utterance while modeling the past tense form of *had*:

  > STUDENT: I no come school yesterday. I have hedeck.
  > TEACHER: You didn't come to school because you had a headache? Do you feel better today?
  > STUDENT: Yes, I feeling better today.

- *Note specific, habitual errors so that you can provide direct instruction later.* Unless all the students in the class share the same problem, however, it's often best deal with errors privately or with a small group.

- *Persist in your efforts to understand students.* Their efforts to communicate are important. If you do not understand what a student has said, ask her to repeat it. You might also try paraphrasing what you think you heard and checking this with the student. If this doesn't help, ask another class member who speaks the student's first language to translate. If this isn't possible, ask the student to meet you later and move on with the lesson. With practice, you will find that your ear for students' language will improve, and you will understand them more readily.

- *Enlist the support of the more proficient English speakers in the class* by emphasizing that every lesson is a language lesson as well as a lesson in science, music, mathematics, or another subject. Explain to the class some of the factors involved in learning a second language. Suggest that students watch how you deal with the errors learners make when they are speaking and follow your example when they interact with one another. Make this an expectation for classroom behavior.

Responding to Written Language

When students speak, you probably focus on the message rather than the form in which it's delivered and are, therefore, less likely to notice errors. This isn't true of written work. When you read students' writing, you have plenty of time to examine both its content and form. In addition, some errors, such as sentence fragments, incorrect punctuation, and misspellings, become evident only in writing. Here are some suggestions for repairing students' written errors.

- *Read past the mistakes.* To save yourself — and the student — from becoming overwhelmed by the errors, focus first on content before dealing with the language errors.

Focusing on Specific Errors

The following stories illustrate how teachers can help students focus on a single error rather than overwhelming them by flagging every mistake. In the first, the teacher has focused on possessives; in the second, on the formation of past tense verbs.

Method 1 (for beginners)

In April my sister get marry. We have big party in my <u>uncle</u> house, it was more than 100 peoples come there.

My <u>sister</u> name Deepa and her new husband name Hari. Hari have two sister, 14 and 16, I like Hari sister. Hari make good joke, I like him too.

<u>Hari</u> family in Hamilton so my sister leave home to live in Hamilton. I miss my sister but she call me every day. Last weekend I go my <u>sister</u> house in Hamilton. I go on bus.

Method 2 (for more proficient learners)

Yesterday we went on field trip to museum. This
* was first time I ever visit museum in Canada. We
* saw dinosaurs who live million of years ago. There are not any dinosaur in the world now, because they all died in Ice Age. Dinosaurs are extinct. I saw one movie about dinosaurs that came back to life, it was Jurassic Park, I hope that never really will happen. It was beautiful day and we had
* launch outside, I very enjoy our trip to museum.

- *Be selective.* As with oral language, don't try to deal with every error a student makes. If you draw attention to every error, students may decide to play it safe by handing in short, unimaginative pieces. In addition, the traditional margin comments or symbols may not provide enough information to help students understand or correct their errors, while flagging every error with a detailed marking code or explanation may confuse students with too much information.

- *Focus on a consistent error of a specific type.* Some errors may show that students have either not acquired a particular language pattern, such as plural endings or subject-verb agreement, or have adopted a faulty or incomplete pattern. Many students, for example, go through a stage of generalizing the regular past tense *-ed* ending and applying it to most verbs. They may write things like, "She gived it to me."

  In deciding which errors to focus on, select a language convention that is comprehensible at the student's present stage of development. For example, a student who records in a lab report, "We heat (the) water," "We hot (the) water," or "Water hot" is not ready for a lesson on passive verbs ("The water was heated"). Still, he has successfully communicated one step in the scientific process.

  In responding to students' written work, focus your attention on the target error only and ignore the others. Doing this can be difficult at first, because a teacher's instinct is often to "fix" things.

- *Select common errors as the language feature of the week* and flag them for explicit instruction and practice. Post a chart of examples on the classroom wall for reference. Encourage students to edit their own work carefully, paying special attention to the featured structure. Recognize that students may need repeated instruction and practice over a period of months or years to acquire some patterns.

- *Don't correct students' errors for them!* Learners learn little when others correct their work. It is more beneficial if they make the corrections themselves. When reviewing students' writing, select a specific error and flag it every time it occurs. With beginning students, underline the error, as illustrated. With more proficient students, place an asterisk or other symbol in the margin next to the line in which the error occurs.

  Hold a conference with individual students or teach a mini-lesson to a group, giving explicit instruction about the specific language feature you flagged. Older students may be able to understand written explanations. At the end of the conference or mini-lesson, encourage students to return to their piece of writing, find the errors you marked, and correct them using what they have learned about the language feature.

- *Incorporate the writing process into the classroom program.* As students become more proficient, encourage them to keep their own editing checklist containing examples of errors and corrections from their own work. They can refer to the checklist during the editing stage of the writing process. For more information on the writing process, see Chapter 12.

Ideas for Dual-Language Assignments

Geography or Civics: Prepare a bilingual booklet designed to help people applying for citizenship. Each group's booklet will be on a different topic — government, geography, economy, politics, etc.

Language arts or literature: Create a poster to celebrate an author who wrote in a language other than English. Include some quotations, with translations.

Geography: Make a bilingual advertisement to attract visitors to your country or region.

Science: Make a dual-language picture book about a human biological process. You will share your book with a younger child.

Mathematics or visual arts: Create a poster showing the geometric shapes present in real-life objects (e.g., textiles, buildings, and household objects). You can draw the objects or use magazine pictures, photographs, pieces of fabric, and so on. Label your poster in two languages.

These students are using their first language to clarify information before they switch to English.

- *Be patient!* Although students may be able to correct their own errors with your guidance in controlled situations, do not expect instant or permanent results. Some language features, such as subject-verb agreement, are acquired relatively late in the language learning process, which may take five years or more. In the meantime, your consistent, persistent, and supportive feedback, as well as that of your colleagues, will help raise students' awareness of how English works and their own language learning processes. It will also encourage students to continue monitoring their output. Your efforts will show results in the end, though in some cases, these may not be evident until several years after students have moved on.

Incorporating Students' Languages

Many learners of English continue to need access to their first language until their proficiency in English catches up to that of their English-speaking peers. This may take five years or more. Language learners can think at a higher level and deal with more complicated ideas in the language in which they are most proficient. For this reason, students' first language has a place in the classroom alongside English.

Even if you speak none of the languages of your students, you can help them use their languages to support or enhance their learning.

- *Encourage students to produce dual-language assignments.* This enables students who are proficient in languages other than English to make important contributions, emphasizes that all languages are valid means of communication, and encourages students to continue to develop their first language skills.

- *Provide opportunities for students to work with same-language partners* from time to time. This may enable students to complete challenging tasks more successfully than if they were required to work in English only. Provide time for them to switch languages and practice in English before they report to you or the class or before they hand in an assignment written in English. Students might, for example, discuss a mathematics problem with a partner in whatever language(s) they choose, but at the end of a specified period, they must be ready to give their solution in English. As students work, circulate and ask them to update you, in English, on what they have done so far.

- *Don't require English language learners to speak English in situations in which doing so is unnatural.* When students who share a first language are having a conversation that involves no English speakers, for example, they may find it frustrating and perhaps even pretentious to speak English to one another. Using their own language to enhance learning will not reduce their motivation to learn English; on the contrary, students who believe that their own language — and their ability to speak it — is respected are more likely to feel positive about learning English. And even though you don't understand what students are saying, you will not lose control of the lesson as long as learners are involved in meaningful and challenging activities and you have communicated clear expectations about the process and the product.

- *Establish class guidelines for using languages other than English.* Hold an open discussion and encourage students to establish guidelines about when it is — and is not — appropriate to use their first language. Encourage students to share their perspectives by asking questions like, "How does it feel to be shut out of a conversation?" and "How does it feel to try to express yourself in English when you are still learning the language?"

- *Create multilingual displays and signs.* Students might, for example, create a display comparing how things such as greetings, polite expressions, numbers, proverbs, animal sounds, and names are expressed in their first language(s). When they do this, encourage them to consult adult speakers of their first language. This will help expand their knowledge of their first language and provide parents with opportunities to become involved in their children's education. Keep in mind, too, that it may be necessary to show students how to transliterate from languages that do not use the Roman alphabet. Doing this helps reinforce common spelling conventions in English. Students whose first language is English can either be paired with a bilingual student or use a language they are learning at school.

This girl is writing in English after completing her first draft in Chinese.

- *Encourage students to write first drafts and outlines in their own language.* Many students are able to produce work of a much higher quality if they can do some of the preliminary thinking and planning in their own language.

- *Provide bilingual support for newcomers* by enlisting the help of classroom partners and cross-grade tutors. Train students to play these roles by highlighting key concepts you want taught or translated and by demonstrating instructional strategies you would like the tutors to use. Be sure to acknowledge publicly the value of the bilingual skills of these helpers.

- *Encourage beginners to write in their first language.* Students might, for example, write their first journal responses in their own language or insert words in their own language when they don't know the English word. If another student or a colleague can help by translating, you may be surprised by the quality of the students' writing in their own language compared with what they are able to produce in English.

Cooperative Learning

Many experts recommend organizing cooperative learning groups to provide opportunities for English language learners to practice using English and to receive feedback that promotes language acquisition. In addition, evidence suggests that students from some cultural backgrounds may be more comfortable in a classroom that balances collaboration with more traditional competitive activities and individual tasks. By focusing on the process as well as the product of group work, cooperative learning also enables students to work effectively with others from various cultural backgrounds, to develop friendships that might not happen otherwise, and to experience the satisfaction of helping others.

Cooperative learning is an essential strategy for supporting English language learners in ESL programs. It is also an ideal strategy for integrating English language learners into mainstream classrooms, where all students can benefit from opportunities to deepen their understanding and develop their problem-solving skills through purposeful talk.

The following sections offer brief suggestions for designing cooperative learning tasks, creating and managing groups, and developing the sociolinguistic skills students require to work effectively in groups in multilingual classrooms. For more detailed cooperative learning resources, see "To Learn More ..." at the end of this chapter.

Cooperative Learning Tasks

Cooperative learning tasks are carefully structured to promote purposeful talk and collaboration. Though there are many cooperative learning activities, those outlined in the following are especially effective with English language learners.

GROUP BRAINSTORMING

Use group brainstorming to generate ideas. Establish guidelines beforehand (e.g., all ideas are accepted without judgment; there is no commitment to a particular idea; and everyone has the right to pass). To encourage groups to work collaboratively, give each just one large sheet of chart paper and one marker.

Students might, for example, brainstorm to create a KWL (What We Know—What We Want to Know—What We Learned) chart to activate their previous knowledge in preparation for starting a new topic or reading or for generating ideas for projects. At the end of the unit or project, instruct group members to revisit their chart to check which statements in the Know column should be revised and which questions in the Want to Know column they can now answer. Then tell them to fill in the Learned column.

The chart following was created in preparation for a social studies unit on the Middle Ages.

Medieval Times		
What We **K**now	What We **W**ant to Know	What We **L**earned
Some people lived in castles. There were knights on horses. Some people were very poor. Robin Hood lived in medieval times.	Why did they live in castles? What did knights do? Why were some people so poor? What clothes did people wear? Did they have doctors and medicine in those days? Did kids have to work or go to school?	

These students are sharing their answers to a think-pair-share question.

THINK-PAIR-SHARE

Begin by posing a review or extension question to the class. Instruct students think about the question on their own, then turn to a partner to share their thoughts. Call on one or two students to share their ideas with the class.

GROUP REHEARSAL

Similar to think-pair-share, this activity is completed in a larger group and is an effective way of rehearsing vocabulary and expressing key ideas.

Begin by posing a question to the class (e.g., What does adjacent mean?). Give students time to confer briefly, then call on one or two to share their ideas.

THREE-STEP INTERVIEW

The three-step interview enables students to discuss ideas with a partner before speaking in a larger group or before the whole class.

- *Step 1*: Students form pairs, and one interviews the other, asking questions about a topic (e.g., Is it more important to spend money on building new roads for cars or on improving public transit?). Encourage the interviewers to ask follow-up questions and probe for details or explanations.

- *Step 2*: Students switch roles.

- *Step 3*: Students share what they discussed with a larger group or the whole class.

LEARNING TEAMS

Learning teams require students to work together to review or apply new concepts, ensuring that everyone on the team understands. This activity works well for rehearsing tests or assignments and prepares students to write a similar test or complete a similar assignment on their own. After presenting new material, for example, you might instruct the learning teams to discuss a review or extension question.

Learning teams also work well with problem-solving activities. Group problem solving in mathematics, for example, helps students practice using mathematical language and basic vocabulary.

- Assign a math problem to each learning team. The groups might work on the same problem or several different ones.
- Explain that everyone on the team is responsible for ensuring that all group members understand and are able to explain a solution. The goal is to be able to say, "We all understand it now."
- Tell team members to begin by making sure that everyone understands all the words in the problem. Then instruct students to discuss the problem and try out various solutions until they agree on one. Finally, tell them to help one another rehearse the explanation because you may call on any one of them to present the team's solution.
- When you check solutions, do not ask for volunteers; select students at random. Reduce stress by encouraging other group members to come to the aid of a student who gets stuck. This is learning opportunity, not a test. You might also try pairing a beginning language learner with a bilingual student to help explain the solution in English.

These students are supporting one another's learning by reviewing key concepts and vocabulary together.

Step 1: Base Groups

Teambuilding
Providing context
Pre-teaching key vocabulary

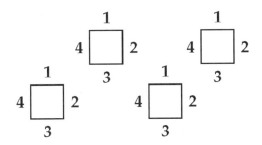

Step 2: Topic Groups

Reading/checking comprehension
Discussion/summarizing
Planning/rehearsing

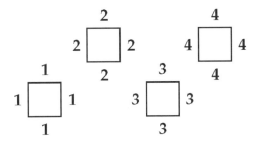

Step 3: Base Groups

Sharing information
Synthesis/application
Reporting to the class

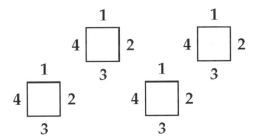

JIGSAW GROUPS

The jigsaw method is useful when students must handle a large amount of information or understand diverse points of view. The best jigsaw activities are open-ended and help develop higher-level cognitive skills such as evaluating and synthesizing facts and opinions, especially if the task involves problem solving as well as knowledge of facts.

- Assign a task and divide the class into base groups of three to five students.
- Assign a different subtopic to each student in the base group.
- Instruct students who have been assigned the same subtopic to join others assigned the same subtopic to work together on the assigned reading or research task.
- Provide guiding questions and instructions. Encourage students to help each other understand and rehearse the material. Circulate from group to group to offer help or guidance when needed. Depending on the task assigned and the organization of your time-table, students may spend more than one period working in their expert groups.
- Instruct students to return to their base groups to share and discuss what they have learned about their subtopic. They then work in their base group to complete the task, reach consensus, or solve a problem related to the information.

COOPERATIVE PROJECTS

Cooperative projects provide opportunities for students to become experts on different topics or subtopics and to make a unique contribution to the class. Though this method is especially suitable for end-of-course assignments and independent-study projects, students need plenty of experience with projects and teacher-directed group work before attempting a cooperative project.

- Identify a general topic or issue for investigation (e.g., Are our country's natural resources in danger?) and work with students to brainstorm a list of subtopics like those shown on the following page:
- Encourage students to make suggestions for refining and categorizing the questions. Use the questions to create a concept map showing the organization of the projects.
- Divide the class into groups to explore the subtopics. Rather than assigning students to specific groups, you might encourage them to join groups on the basis of their interest in the subtopic. If a group is too large, students can discuss how to subdivide it further to create smaller groups.
- Students meet in their groups to identify tasks for each group member. They may need to conduct preliminary research to find out what their subtopic involves.
- Organize a steering committee with a representative from each group. This group meets with you regularly to coordinate tasks and timelines.
- With your assistance as required, students conduct research, using the library, interviews and surveys, visual media, Internet resources, and so on. For suggestions on helping students with research projects, see Chapter 12.
- Students synthesize their information and prepare a group presentation.

A Sample Jigsaw Problem-Solving Task:

What should we do with the Toronto waterfront?

The Toronto waterfront is an unattractive area of the city with abandoned warehouses, polluted water, and empty land. People in Toronto have different ideas about how to bring the area back to life and make it an attractive area for people to live or visit.

These people are at a community meeting to discuss the future of the waterfront:

1. An environmentalist
2. A property developer
3. A local resident (a homeless person living in a tent city)
4. An expert from the city's planning department

These four people have different opinions on the question, "What should we do with the Toronto waterfront?" You will read the opinion of one of these people. Then you will play the role of this person in the meeting. Your job is to persuade the others to agree with your opinion.

Fish

Where are our fisheries?

What kinds of fish are caught?

How are fish caught?

What happens to the fish after they are caught?

How do the fish get to stores?

What environmental problems are associated with fishing?

Oil

What is oil?

Where does our oil come from?

How is oil pumped from the ground?

How is oil used?

How is oil delivered to homes and factories?

What environmental problems are associated with the use of oil?

Natural Resources

Forests

Where are our forests?

What kinds of forests does our country have?

How do we use trees?

How are trees cut?

What happens to the trees after they are cut?

What environmental problems are associated with the forestry industry?

Water

Where does our fresh water come from?

How do we use water?

How is hydro-electric power created?

How is water made safe to drink?

How is water delivered to homes?

What environmental problems are associated with water?

- Each group presents its information to the whole class. Ensure that the rest of the class takes notes on the presentation or instruct the groups to prepare a handout on their presentation.

Cooperative projects can also be used to investigate issues that have arisen within the school, such as whether the school should organize a Christmas concert or whether students should be required to wear uniforms. Teams of students can gather information on various aspects of the issue and make recommendations. One team might interview parents, for example, while another interviews students, another teachers, and another school administrators.

Creating and Managing Groups

To be effective, group work must be carefully structured and managed.

- *Assign students to heterogeneous groups.* Research indicates that heterogeneous groups are the most effective in promoting academic achievement and positive intercultural relationships. English language learners benefit from working in groups with more proficient English speakers who serve as language models and provide feedback. There may be times, however, when it is more beneficial to group English language learners together for a short time. One of these occasions might be during the expert group phase of a jigsaw activity.

  It is not usually a good idea to allow students to choose their own groups. Students naturally gravitate to those whom they perceive as similar to themselves and those with whom they have established a relationship. Because one of your goals is to provide all students with opportunities to expand their social world, explain this to students and then assign them to groups. You might start with random groupings that change daily until you know the students well enough to assign them to long-term groups that might work together throughout an entire unit of study.

Balance the groups as much as possible, taking into account factors such as gender, learning style, proficiency in English, expertise in the subject area, and so on. Whenever you change the groups, start with an icebreaker that helps students get to know one another. You might, for example, use a three-step interview on topics such as favorite sports, music, and so on.

- *Keep groups small* to maximize opportunities for every student to participate in activities and discussions. Most experts recommend groups of three to five students. Groups of four are flexible because they can easily be regrouped into pairs for some activities.

- *Emphasize collaboration* by establishing guidelines such as the following:
  - A task is not complete until everyone in the group has finished or understands the material.
  - The group's goal is not to finish first but to complete the task well.
  - The satisfaction of a job well done is its own reward.
  - People who learn how to work effectively with others will be more successful in the workplace and the community.
  - It feels good to help others.

- *Establish clear routines and expectations for group work.* Know what every group is doing at all times and establish a routine for getting students' attention quickly (e.g., a small bell, a tambourine, or three handclaps) so that you can give additional instructions or information, solicit feedback, and check on progress. In addition, establish routines to deal with matters such as student attendance or absence, distributing resources, collecting homework, and setting up the classroom. Every day, or every week if groups will be working together for some time, instruct each group to delegate a different member to fetch and distribute materials and equipment, collect and hand in homework, and so on. This person might also be responsible for checking that all group members have completed homework, have brought in required materials, and are prepared for class.

  Give instructions once only and say, "Now make sure everyone in your group knows what to do." This should result in a short, concentrated buzz of repetition and confirmation. Use the same technique at the end of class to review homework instructions. Provide clear timelines for completing tasks. If a task is expected to take five minutes, warn the class when one minute is left.

  Always place an extra chair at every table. You can use this when you visit the groups, or it can be used by other students when they are acting as consultants or interviewers.

Developing Sociolinguistic Skills

Cooperative learning emphasizes the social skills necessary for working effectively in groups. Some newcomers have had little experience with cooperative learning and may feel lost unless the work is highly structured, with strong support and monitoring from the teacher.

To implement cooperative learning successfully, it is important to develop students' social skills or sociolinguistic competence by providing instruction in the conversational strategies required to manage disagreement, take turns, offer help, and so on. For more information on conversational strategies, see Chapter 6.

Students involved in a problem-solving discussion involving differing perspectives on a controversial issue, for example, might disagree with one another. Unless they are skilled in managing disagreement, they may end up dismissing other students' opinions, ignoring others' contributions, or alienating others in various ways.

Managing disagreement requires work before the discussion begins. Say to the class, "You may have some differences of opinion as you work on this task. That's okay; this is a topic that people often disagree about, but you do need to hear what everybody thinks. You may learn something that will cause you to think again about your own opinion. You might think of a good argument to support your opinion, or you might want to change it after listening to someone else's. Let's talk about how you can express disagreement with someone without putting that person down. Brainstorm in your groups for a couple of minutes: Is it always necessary for everyone to agree? How can you express disagreement but keep the discussion going?"

Call on students from each group to contribute to a list of ways of expressing disagreement. You may need to expand the students' repertoire by adding some expressions, especially the more formal ones. Then, encourage students to categorize the language by creating a three-column chart like the one shown on this page.

What Can You Say When ... you disagree with someone's opinion?		
Formal or Polite	**Informal**	**Rude**
I have a different point of view.	We're not on the same wavelength.	No way!
I don't agree with you. Let me explain my position.	I don't go along with that.	That's a stupid idea.
I don't agree.	I don't really see it that way.	That's so dumb.
I disagree.	I don't see eye to eye with you on that.	Where did you get that idea?
I have another point of view.	Look at it this way.	You gotta be kidding!
I'm not sure about that.	My problem with what you're saying is ...	You're joking!
Let's take a vote.	Do you really think so?	Get outta here!
Let's agree to disagree.		Oh, come on!

It is important to explain that these distinctions are sometimes blurred. Close friends, for example, can sometimes be rude to each other without causing offense. In addition, whether an expression is interpreted as rude sometimes depends on tone of voice, gestures, and facial expression. In the classroom, however, encourage students to choose expressions from the first two columns, attempting consciously to expand their language repertoire.

Before the discussion begins, remind students to use the expressions discussed. Tell them: "Remember, I want to see you expressing your ideas and listening to one another. If you disagree, express your opinion in the constructive ways we just talked about."

As the groups work, circulate and observe how they handle disagreement. When you see students who are managing especially well, you may wish to ask them to model their discussion for the class. At the end of the session, discuss what you observed and encourage students to add to their list of ways of indicating disagreement.

Students' use of these conversational strategies may be a little forced at first. With practice and support, however, their use of this language will become more spontaneous. Post the chart and add new charts as the school year progresses. By the end of the year, several lists of conversational strategies may be displayed.

- What can you say when you want a turn?
- What can you say when you want to stop someone who is talking too much?
- What can you say when you want to bring the group back on topic?
- What can you say when it's time to finish?
- What can you say when you don't understand?
- What can you say to encourage someone who is too shy to speak?

Cooperative learning should be included in every teacher's repertoire, especially in classrooms where some or all of the students are learning the language of instruction. By participating in well-structured small-group activities, English language learners practice speaking English and receiving feedback in a supportive way. They also develop a variety of conversational strategies for use in real-life situations.

At the same time, working in heterogeneous groups helps students learn to work effectively in a mixed cultural setting and, perhaps, to expand their circle of friends. This is especially important for newcomers who might otherwise find it difficult to fit in and make friends. In addition, the academic benefits are clear: opportunities for purposeful talk improve understanding, help develop communication skills, and promote higher achievement among all students.

To Learn More …

Books and Articles

Abrami, P., B. Chambers, C. Poulsen, C. De Simone, S. d'Apollonia, and J. Howden. *Classroom Connections: Understanding and Using Cooperative Learning*. Toronto, Ont.: Harcourt Brace, 1995.

Introduction to cooperative learning provides theoretical background and summarizes methods.

Bartram, M., and R. Walton. *Correction: A Positive Approach to Language Mistakes*. Hove, U.K.: Language Teaching Publications, 1991.

Helpful advice on providing supportive feedback in response to students' oral and written language.

Bassano, S., and Christison, M.A. Community Spirit: A Practical Guide to Collaborative Language Learning. Burlingame, CA: ALTA Book Center, 1995.

Practical ideas for creating a supportive, collaborative classroom culture.

Clarke, J., R. Wideman, and S. Eadie. *Together We Learn: Co-operative Small Group Learning*. Scarborough, Ont.: Prentice-Hall (now Pearson Education), 1990.

A practical handbook for teachers at all levels.

Coelho, E. (1998) *Teaching and Learning in Multicultural Schools: An Integrated Approach*. Clevedon, U.K.: Multilingual Matters.

Examines schools and classrooms as cultural and linguistic environments and provides practical strategies for integrating diverse languages and cultures into mainstream programs.

Coelho, E. *Learning Together in the Multicultural Classroom*. Toronto, Ont.: Pippin Publishing, 1994.

Focuses on implementing cooperative learning in middle and secondary school classrooms where some or all of the learners are learning the language of instruction.

Coelho, E. *Jigsaw*. Toronto, Ont.: Pippin, 1991.

Content-based reading and discussion tasks and problem-solving activities for English language learners in middle and secondary school.

Coelho, E., and L. Winer. *Jigsaw Plus*. Toronto, Ont.: Pippin, 1991.

More content-based reading and discussion tasks and problem-solving activities for English language learners.

Cummins, J., et al. (2005) Affirming Identity in Multilingual Classrooms. *Educational Leadership* Vol. 63 No. 1, September 2005: 38-43.

This article explains the value of incorporating students' home languages and cultures into the classroom program, and describes some projects that use linguistic and cultural diversity as an asset.

Dörnyei, Z., and Murphey, T. *Group Dynamics in the Language Classroom*. Cambridge: Cambridge University Press, 2003.

Practical advice on how to manage group work. The focus is on the language classroom but the ideas are applicable in every classroom where some or all of the students are learning the language of instruction.

Edwards, V. (1996) *The Other Languages: a Guide to Multilingual Classrooms*. Reading: National Centre for Language and Literacy (U.K.): <www.ncll.org.uk>.

The language profiles in this booklet provide interesting and helpful information for teachers. The author also suggests ways of working with children to enhance the multilingual climate of the school, and provides models that teachers can use to conduct their own language surveys and develop new language profiles.

Edwards, V. (1998) *The Power of Babel: Teaching and Learning in Multilingual Classrooms*. Stoke-on Trent, England: Trentham Books.

This book recounts the experiences of teachers, parents and students working together on multilingual projects that allow all children to participate in a rich multilingual environment.

Erickson, T., R. Craig, and S. Noll. *Get It Together: Math Problems for Groups, Grades 4–12*. Berkeley, Calif.: Regents of the University of California, 1989.

Designed to promote the equitable participation of minorities and females in mathematics and science. Includes reproducibles. For more information about this and other materials that promote interactive problem-solving in math and science, visit the Lawrence Hall of Science site: </www.lawrencehallofscience.org/equals>.

Hadfield, J. *Classroom Dynamics*. Oxford, U.K.: Oxford University Press, 1992.

Activities for creating an environment that helps students interact comfortably when completing group tasks.

Hess, N. *Teaching Large Multilevel Classes*. Cambridge: Cambridge University Press, 2000.

Useful for teachers working with groups of students at various stages of English language proficiency.

Johnson, D., and R. Johnson. *Creative Controversy: Intellectual Challenge in the Classroom*. 3rd ed. Edina, Minn.: Interaction Book Company, 1995.

How to structure intellectual and academic conflicts within cooperative learning groups to promote critical thinking and problem solving.

Johnson, D., R. Johnson, and E. Holubec. *Circles of Learning*. 5th ed. Edina, Minn.: Interaction Book Company, 2002.

Introduction to cooperative learning.

Johnson, D.M. "Grouping Strategies for Second Language Learners." In F. Genesee, ed., *Educating Second-Language Children: The Whole Child, the Whole Curriculum, the Whole Community*. New York: Cambridge University Press, 1994.

Advice on grouping second language learners in ESL and mainstream classrooms and on promoting classroom interaction.

Keller, E., and S.T. Warner. *Conversation Gambits*. Hove, U.K.: Language Teaching Publications, 1988.

Originally developed for francophone civil servants in Canada, the activities in this book help students acquire a range of conversational strategies.

Samway, K.D., G. Whang, and M. Pippitt. *Buddy Reading: Cross-Age Tutoring in a Multicultural School.* Portsmouth, N.H.: Heinemann, 1995.

Authors share their experiences with cross-grade tutoring in an elementary setting. Suggestions for setting up the program and training tutors are helpful for teachers of all levels.

Scarcella, R. *Teaching Language Minority Students in the Multicultural Classroom.* Englewood Cliffs, N.J.: Prentice Hall (now Pearson Education), 1990.

Includes chapters on providing comprehensible lessons and incorporating students' languages and cultures.

Rigg, P., and V.D. Allen, eds. *When They Don't All Speak English: Integrating the ESL Student into the Regular Classroom.* Urbana, Ill.: National Council of Teachers of English, 1989.

Articles on topics such as program design, creating an effective language learning environment, language variation, language experience, and language through content.

Schecter, S., and J. Cummins, eds. *Multilingual Education in Practice: Using Diversity as a Resource.* Portsmouth, NH: Heinemann, 2003.

This book provides specific suggestions for incorporating students' linguistic and cultural knowledge into the school environment. Includes classroom stories with photographs and many examples of students' writing and artwork.

Sloan, S. *The Complete ESL/EFL Cooperative and Communicative Activity Book: Learner-Directed Activities for the Classroom.* Lincolnwood, Ill: National Textbook Company, 1991.

A variety of classroom activities for grades 6 to 12.

Thibault, N. *Using L1 to Support L2 Learning: Best Practices the OCDSB Way.* Canadian Association of Second Language Teachers, 2001. <www.caslt.org/research/l2_l1.htm>

Walker, S., Edwards, V., and Leonard, H. *Write Around the World.* Reading: National Centre for Language and Literacy (U.K.): 1998.

Practical ideas for producing bilingual resources in the classroom. <www.ncll.org.uk>.

Websites and Online Resources

Cooperative Learning Center. <www.clcrc.com>.

This organization develops and disseminates theory and research related to cooperative learning, as well as practical classroom strategies.

Family Pastimes < www.familypastimes.com >.

Cooperative games for large and small groups. Ideal for prompting problem-solving discussion and for helping students learn the value of cooperation.

International Association for the Study of Cooperation in Education. <www.iasce.net>.

International non-profit organization publishes a regular newsletter and hosts local and international conferences. Site includes annotated bibliography of resources on cooperative learning and second language instruction, as well as links to other resources and sites.

Jigsaw Classroom. <www.jigsaw.org>.

Background information on the development of the jigsaw technique, as well as its current application as a classroom strategy that serves many purposes.

Kagan Publishing and Professional Development. <www.kaganonline.com>.

Information on classroom resources and training workshops, including Spencer Kagan's source book, *Cooperative Learning.*

Tribes. <www.tribes.com>.

Information about the Tribes approach to creating a positive school or classroom environment, with an emphasis on collaborative groups, or tribes.

11 Supporting Beginning Language Learners

Newcomers of all ages arrive at schools with varying levels of proficiency in English. Many of them have had little or no previous exposure to English. These beginning language learners need special attention and support during their first months in the new school environment. They may spend part of the day in an ESL class, but there should also be times when they are integrated into the mainstream classroom alongside their English-speaking peers. The approaches and activities described in this chapter are appropriate for beginning language learners in both ESL and mainstream classrooms.

In ESL classes, the activities help beginners start developing basic communication skills. They emphasize a basic vocabulary, simple sentence patterns, and oral communication as the basis for completing subsequent reading and writing tasks.

In mainstream classes, the activities can be used when beginners cannot benefit from participating in the same activities as their English-speaking peers. Working alone on exercises is not an effective way to learn a language, however, so it is important to keep to a minimum the amount of individual work assigned to new learners of English. Remember that these students need opportunities to talk with more proficient English speakers who can serve as language models and peer tutors. For this reason, it is advisable to organize the class so that beginners can work on these activities with a partner, a volunteer, or a peer tutor. Though beginners may sometimes complete this work within the mainstream classroom, at other times they may benefit from working with a partner or a tutor in a separate location — for a short time.

Beginning language learners benefit from working with a partner.

Bilingual peer tutors and volunteers who speak the newcomer's language as well as English can help clarify instructions and orient students to school and classroom routines. Using beginners' first language will not hinder their acquisition of English; in fact, helping students feel relaxed and confident by explaining tasks in their own language encourages them to become more actively involved in classroom activities that support their learning English.

The following language-teaching techniques are especially helpful when working with beginners.

- functional language
- visual support
- copying and labeling
- physical activity
- choral work, song, and role plays
- a rich print environment
- experience-based learning
- language experience stories

- listening to stories on tape
- using games and puzzles

Functional Language

The goal of second language learners is to be able to use the language as richly and as flexibly as their English-speaking peers. To do this, however, they must start by learning the language of daily life: survival expressions, basic vocabulary, and simple script.

Survival Expressions

Newly arrived students must acquire some essential phrases to begin communicating in the classroom and finding their way around their new environment. At first, they may learn these survival expressions as chunks, with little or no understanding of the individual words.

Teach these expressions by modeling, using actions or pictures to support the meaning, and by involving students in repetition, choral practice, and simple role plays. With younger children, using puppets is effective. Focus on whole expressions and short exchanges that students can use immediately.

Basic Vocabulary

Teach the basic, functional vocabulary needed for daily use and classroom work. Because words that are not reinforced in the natural language environment will not be remembered, select words that students will hear others using and will use themselves. Beginners need to learn the names of classroom objects, places in the school, and the names and job titles of the people with whom they interact. They also need to learn simple words relating to food, body parts, clothing, animals, and physical actions.

As soon as learners can identify some of these words orally, they can learn to read them. Label classroom objects and pictures and point to the words as you say them, then ask students to repeat the words after you. You can also print the words on index cards and ask students to match them with objects and pictures.

You can also encourage students to make their own picture dictionaries, devoting a page or two to words relating to particular topics, such as classroom furniture, clothing, weather, sports, and so on, as well as specific curriculum areas, such as music and mathematics.

Simple Script

The first languages of many newcomers do not use the Roman alphabet. As a result, these students may not even be familiar with the direction of print in English and need to learn to recognize the letters, say their names, and use alphabetical order.

For most beginners, writing will consist mostly of copying familiar words and labeling pictures. Students who are new to the Roman alphabet will need explicit instruction on where to start and end a letter. Do not expect beginners to read or write cursive script, no matter how old

Some Essential Survival Expressions

May I go to the washroom? Yes, you may.

What's your name? My name is …

Where do you come from? I come from …

What language do you speak? I speak …

What time does school start? At …

What's this? It's a …

How old are you? I am …

I don't understand.

Please say it again.

Will you help me?

Please, thank you, you're welcome.

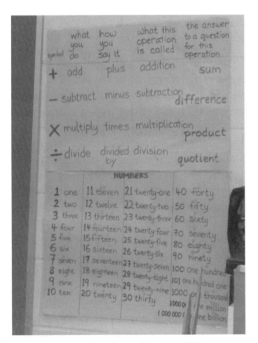

Beginners need to learn basic subject vocabulary right away.

they are. They need to start with hand printing or simple computer-generated text: 12-point type in a sans serif face such as Arial is best.

This kind of print is helpful to beginners of all ages.

Visual Support

Pictures, manipulatives, and physical objects are part of every language teacher's basic toolkit.

Pictures

Magazines, catalogues, supermarket flyers, and other advertising materials are good sources of photographs and drawings. Clip art packages are a useful source of visual material. Organize these pictures into categories, such as food, clothing, furniture, school, home, sports, and so on. Be sure your collection includes pictures of people of various ethnocultural backgrounds and both genders in various roles and contexts.

You might also take photographs of students as they take part in activities such as a field trip, a physical education class, or eating lunch in the cafeteria. These pictures can then be used to prompt oral retelling, as well as writing captions and speech balloons.

Picture dictionaries are especially useful for beginners because they present vocabulary through photographs or drawings that are organized by category or theme (e.g., school, home, and travel) rather than in alphabetical order. Give a page from the picture dictionary to the student and a volunteer, a classroom peer, or a cross-grade tutor, and instruct the helper to ensure that the language learner knows a specific set of words (i.e., can point to the pictures, say the words, read the words, and copy or write them) by the end of a specified period. Some picture dictionaries are available in bilingual versions.

Manipulatives and Physical Objects

As an aid to teaching basic vocabulary, collect real objects, such as items of clothing, fruits and vegetables, and household items, as well as replicas, such a teaching clock and toy animals.

Mathematics manipulatives are also very useful. You can use blocks in various shapes and sizes, colored rods, two-dimensional shapes, and so on to teach words relating to size, shape, and color as well as prepositions, such as *on*, *under*, *beside*, and *next to*.

Use manipulatives to teach words relating to size, shape, and colour as well as prepositions.

globe	car	teacher
student	bookshelf	wall map
book	desk	teachers
teacher and students	books	computer

Copying and Labeling

Copying and labeling activities are appropriate when students are either just starting to learn English or are in an early stage of literacy development. As soon as students have learned to recognize some words (i.e., when they can say the word and point to the correct object or picture when someone else says the word), give them a page of pictures and instruct them to draw from the list of words at the bottom to label each picture. Make this task a little more challenging by adding one or two extra words.

Physical Activity

The Total Physical Response approach helps beginning language learners feel comfortable as they begin to recognize and respond to their first English words, which relate to everyday physical actions. Students demonstrate their understanding by following oral instructions, but they are not required to speak until they are ready.

Engaging in physical activity helps students relate words to actions.

Later, students hear and repeat the words for physical actions as they watch and carry out actions. Repeating words and phrases at the same time as they carry out actions helps them acquire basic vocabulary as they learn a new dance, practice a specific movement, or participate in a game.

TPR works well in the context of games and physical education. Students learn words and phrases such as *run, jump, pass the ball, step back,* and *throw the ball.* They also learn adverbial expressions such as *not like that, like this, quickly,* and *smoothly,* as well as spatial expressions such as *on, over, to the right, clockwise,* and *through.* Physical activities also help the students learn the names of body parts as the teacher demonstrates expressions such as *bend your knees, on your toes,* and *from the shoulder.* Labeled drawings and written labels on the equipment help students learn to read and write the new English words.

Physical activity need not be restricted to the gym and playground, however. In the classroom, it can provide a change of pace that appeals to a variety of learning styles. Combined with chant or song, physical activity is very effective with young children, who enjoy songs that are accompanied by gestures. Older students can use the same technique when they must memorize facts and lists such as the multiplication tables or the periodic table of elements.

Choral Work, Songs, and Role Plays

Students develop confidence when they have opportunities to practice new expressions in a group, rather than individually. A variety of techniques can be used to do this.

- Use choral repetition to help students learn how to pronounce new words. When you introduce a word, articulate clearly and encourage students to repeat it in chorus. Say the word again — and encourage students to do the same — as you write it on the chalkboard or point to it on a chart.
- Provide a simple dialogue in which several students share one role. Lead the chorus yourself to provide support as students read.
- Read aloud often so that students become familiar with the rhythm and intonation patterns of English. Re-read phrases or short passages, encouraging students to chime in when they can.
- Introduce chants that set common expressions and sentence patterns to music. These help learners of all ages internalize stress and intonation patterns, as well as common expressions. See "To Learn More ..." at the end of this chapter for information on Carolyn Graham's *Jazz Chants.*
- Use songs to help students learn the rhythms of English, as well as simple vocabulary, through repetition. Choose songs that tell a story, feature a chorus or rhyme, can be accompanied by actions, or can be illustrated with pictures. Multicultural folk songs are a rich source of suitable material.
- Create cloze activities from songs by printing the lyrics and deleting individual words or short phrases that students must listen for.
- Provide opportunities for students to rehearse language in role-play situations. Because the point of the role play is to practice, not perform, it need not be presented to the class. Role-play situations may involve creating extensions to or alternative endings for stories or working out how to handle everyday problems and situations. A typical assignment might read as follows:

Work with a partner. One is the teacher and one is the student. The student did not finish the homework last night. Use the following words in your conversation:

I'm sorry …
I didn't …
Why didn't you …?
I will …
I won't …
Next time …

A Rich Print Environment

Surrounding students with print, in English and their own languages, encourages them to learn to recognize, read, and write words.

- Label classroom objects and places in the school in more than one language.
- Surround learners with environmental print such as street signs, brand names, labels, advertisements, and material written by students.
- Introduce students to computers and software. Some students from other countries have had limited access to computers, and many new immigrant families do not have a computer at home. Introduce simple word processing and graphic programs. Students can start by creating simple labels and captions for photos and classroom objects. They will learn more if they work with a partner, reading to each other, discussing choices, and taking turns at the keyboard.
- Provide plenty of reading material written at a level suitable for beginning language learners. Various publishers produce material that uses controlled vocabulary and sentence structure and is written specifically for beginning learners. See the list at the end of Chapter 5 for information on some of these materials.
- Create a word wall with charts of words and phrases related to specific concepts (e.g., words about size, words related to mathematics, or words related to a specific story). It's helpful to provide examples of some words in context. Picture cues are also helpful for beginners.

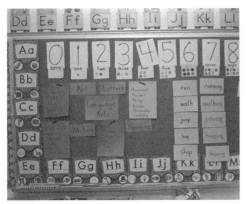

New words on this classroom's word wall are highlighted on different-colored cards.

Nouns	Verbs	Adjectives	Related Words	Examples
province		provincial		We live in the province of British Columbia. Our provincial government is in Victoria.
culture		cultural	multicultural	People from many cultures live in British Columbia.

Experience-Based Learning

Hands-on experiences inside and outside the classroom help language learners acquire basic vocabulary. The children in the photographs, for example, were making a kite. In the process, they used language about size, shape, and color; gave and followed instructions; and used polite forms such as, "May I have the scissors?" Then each talked about the kite before going outside to fly it. When they came inside again, the teacher instructed them to write or complete some patterned sentences about making and flying kites. Reading aloud a story about a kite is also a good idea.

To teach the names of fruits and vegetables and to provide practice in using the language of shopping, for example, you might escort a group to a nearby supermarket to see, touch, and buy fruits and vegetables, some of which may be new to the students. If there is no time for a trip to a store, bring some fruit and vegetables to the classroom. Students can handle the produce, cut it up and taste it, and learn related vocabulary. If English-speaking peers are involved, they can provide additional language models for the language learners.

Afterwards, write the words on flash cards and instruct students to match the cards to the fruits and vegetables. Later, they can copy the printed words. Children in the early primary grades and learners who are unfamiliar with the Roman alphabet can trace the words before they copy them.

Making a kite provides beginning language learners with opportunities to learn to use new vocabulary and practice language forms.

As students display the kite they made, each has an opportunity to talk about their creation and how they made it.

What better way to test a kite than to try flying it?

Language Experience Stories

Language experience stories, which are commonly used with primary children, can also be used effectively with beginning language learners of all ages. This approach involves teacher and students in working together to create a story based on a personal or a shared experience, such as a story, a field trip, photographs, a film, or a school event. At first, the "story" may amount to one-word labels for objects or pictures or captions for photos of a class activity.

How to Use the Language Experience Approach

Working with a group, ask each student to contribute one or two words or sentences for you to print in large letters on a sheet of chart paper.

- As students dictate, print their words verbatim. Control spelling and punctuation, but don't edit grammar.
- After writing each sentence, read it back to the student to check that you have written what the student intended. If others suggest changes, the student who dictated the sentence decides whether it should be changed.
- When the story is finished, read it aloud, running a finger under the words and speaking a little more slowly than normal but with normal phrasing and intonation. Do this several times, then encourage the students to read aloud with you.
- When the story is completely familiar, ask students to read it individually. At first, expect students to read only their own words or

These students are working with their teacher to create a

sentences. Then, ask each student to read the whole story aloud or suggest that they form pairs and read it to each other.

- Instruct students to copy the story into notebooks. Ruled primary notebooks work best with students who are just beginning to learn to write and those who are just starting to learn the Roman alphabet.
- Print new words on flash cards for students to read aloud. Ask them to match the cards to objects or pictures in the story.
- Print the story in sentence strips for students to arrange in the correct order. At first, they might do this in small groups, then individually. You can also cut the strips in half and instruct students to match the halves.
- Create cloze exercises based on the story by deleting some of the new words. To complete this exercise, some students may need a list of the missing words in random order.
- Analyze the form of words that follow particular patterns (e.g., all words that end in -ing, words that rhyme, words that follow a particular spelling pattern, or words that are related, such as big, bigger, and biggest; go and went). Expand students' understanding by encouraging them to volunteer other words that follow the pattern.

Listening to Stories on Tape

Listening to stories on tape while reading a print copy enables students to hear the language at the same time as they see it in print. They can re-read and hear sections again, paying attention to the pronunciation of specific words or listening to the phrasing and intonation. They can also stop the tape to look up new words or ask a question of the teacher. Unfortunately, most commercially produced books and stories on audiotape are read too quickly and feature language that is too difficult for beginning language learners.

The Carbo method of recording books, which is promoted by the National Reading Styles Institute, is more appropriate for both beginning language learners and students whose literacy experiences are limited. This method involves reading more slowly, with longer pauses between phrases and sentences, while maintaining natural phrasing and intonation. The idea is to provide time for the reader to see and hear every word. See "To Learn More ..." for information about the National Reading Styles Institute and the Carbo method.

You can also create your own recorded books using the Carbo method. Some of the graded readers listed at the end of Chapter 5 are suitable for this. Many children's picture books can also be used with beginning learners of English, including adolescents, especially if there is a repeated pattern and as long as the content and the illustrations are age appropriate. Look for material that includes people of varied ethnocultural backgrounds in differing social and geographic contexts.

When making your own tapes, add prompts such as, "Turn the page," and "Look at the picture." Use short tapes (10 minutes a side, if you can find them) so that readers can easily replay sections. You might also use a computer to make your recordings.

For beginners, avoid distractions such as sound effects. For students beyond the beginning stage, you might ask high school drama students

As students read along with a story on tape, they can repeat sections as necessary.

to create dramatic readings that include sound effects but maintain a slower pace. Encourage students to take the tapes home for repeat listening.

Games and Puzzles

Participating in games and solving puzzles help students internalize new words and sentence patterns. Because cooperative games stimulate talk and promote positive classroom relationships, try to make games cooperative rather than competitive. See "To Learn More ..." at the end of this chapter for sources of games and puzzles.

- *Simple language games*, such as I Spy and Simon Says, help students practice recognizing the names of objects, parts of the body, and simple actions.

- *Crossword and other puzzles* that use context-based clues are helpful, but word-search activities can confuse language learners; moreover, word-search activities are based on word recognition, not comprehension. Create simple crossword puzzles for students to work on in pairs, giving one student the across clues, and the other the down clues. Software programs are available to help create the puzzles.

- *Information-gap activities*, in which students must seek information in order to complete a puzzle or solve a problem, are very effective. The jigsaw approach is one kind of information-gap activity that helps stimulate the exchange of information. See Chapter 10 for more on the jigsaw approach.

- *Teacher-created board and card games* that require students to request or offer information or use specific words and phrases provide many opportunities to practice language.

- *Bingo games* are easy to create and help students develop a sight vocabulary of words that they immediately recognize in print. You might, for example, create a bingo game using a list of 20 classroom objects. Give each student a card with a different set of 12 words printed in three columns of four rows each. Acting as the caller, point to real objects or pictures or say the word as the students use counters to cover the word if they find it on their card. Alternatively, the card can show pictures, which students can cover as you say the word. Students can also take turns being the caller.

If You Want to Get Started...

This is a basic starter list for teachers who are setting up a new program that will include beginners. You will find suggestions for 'found materials,' teacher resource books and classroom materials, picture dictionaries, and websites or online resources. See also the list of graded readers on page 213.

Jigsaw Word Puzzles

Each student in a group of three or four has a different clue to a word, but all the clues are needed in order to identify the word. These clues are from activities based on some basic orientation information about North America:

Student A: It's a city.
Student B: It's in California.
Student C: It has two words.
Student D: It's not Los Angeles.
ALL: It's San Francisco!

Student A: It's a province.
Student B: It's in Atlantic Canada.
Student C: It has two words.
Student D: It's not Nova Scotia.
ALL: It's New Brunswick!

An example of Bingo games.

Found Materials

ESL teachers are inveterate collectors of visual materials, manipulatives, real objects, and authentic print materials that help introduce new vocabulary, illustrate concepts, and provide basic orientation information for newcomers. Many of these items are free or readily available in the school or community. Some can be borrowed from Kindergarten or primary classrooms, the art room, the school office, the health room, or various departments of the school.

- *Magazine pictures*: Collect pictures that feature people of diverse backgrounds in a variety of settings and situations. Many magazine advertisements depict interesting scenarios that can stimulate oral and written stories and role plays. Encourage students to imagine events before or after the scene shown in the picture.

- *Photographs*: Take photographs of students, as well as of scenes and locations around the school and in the community. Always take photos on field trips so that students can later create illustrated language experience stories or booklets. Bring your own family photographs to school and encourage students to bring theirs — and talk about them. Photographs can also be used to introduce and practice grammar structures (e.g., talking about an event shown in a photograph is a natural way to introduce the simple past tense).

- *Posters*: Public service organizations, government departments, and publishers often offer posters free of charge. Ensure that posters carry a simple message and that your selection depicts people of diverse backgrounds in a variety of settings and situations. Be cautious about posters using cartoon-like illustrations: caricatures of racial characteristics may be offensive. And use posters sparingly. Classroom walls and bulletin boards should always contain more student-produced material than professionally produced material.

- *Informational material from government departments and agencies*: Free materials, such as food guides, citizenship information and tourist brochures, are often available and may even be translated into various languages. Though the text of some of these resources may be too difficult for beginners to read, the illustrations are invaluable. An illustrated guide to balanced nutrition, for example, can be used to teach the names of various foods. Students might produce their own version of the guide by categorizing the foods they are accustomed to eating into the food groups.

- *Clocks*: Both a traditional and a digital clock are necessary to teach the two ways of expressing time (e.g., twenty to one and 12:40).

- *Puppets*: Hand puppets are useful for presenting dialogues, and students can use finger puppets to develop and present role plays. Students can also make their own puppets.

- *Art materials*: Keep a supply of construction paper, bristol board, markers, sticky colored paper, scraps of yarn and fabric, glue, tongue depressors, pipe cleaners, cotton wool, sparkles, wallpaper samples, cardboard boxes and rolls, packing materials, and other supplies for making books, posters, models, and so on.

These students are using puppets to present a role play.

- *Flyers, brochures, and advertisements*: Use announcements, supermarket flyers, and newspaper advertisements to help students learn basic vocabulary, read simple messages, and make comparisons (e.g., Which store has the cheapest tomatoes this week?).

- *Forms*: Help students complete school information cards, applications for a social insurance number, or a library card. Take students to the community library to hand in their application forms and borrow their first books. Some libraries allow teachers to borrow a boxful of books for classroom use. Invite parents to come along to check out adult materials for second language learners and new readers. Many public libraries also have multilingual collections.

- *Timetables and schedules*: Use school timetables, local transit schedules, garbage collection schedules, and so on to help students extract information from this kind of text.

- *Manipulatives*: Primary teachers and math departments may be able to lend you blocks, counters, interlocking two- and three-dimensional shapes, and so on. These can be used to teach prepositions, such as *on*, *beside*, and *in*, various mathematical terms and concepts, and the names of numbers, shapes, and colors.

- *Real objects*: Almost any interesting object can be used to stimulate discussion and develop descriptive language (e.g., interesting stones and leaves collected in the school yard or park, classroom and household objects, fruit and vegetables, clothing, sports equipment; tools and equipment for specialized subjects such as science or family studies; and interesting artifacts that students bring from home).

- *Money*: Use real money to teach students the names of coins and bills and to practice counting money and making change in English. Students can also use money in role-play situations.

- *Models*: Model cars, animals, and other toys make a change from pictures and may appeal to the kinesthetic learning style of many students. These models can be used to create scenes depicting what students are likely to see in the street, in the supermarket, and so on. When working with students in the upper elementary or secondary grades, use items that are not obviously childish.

- *Maps*: Students can learn prepositions and the words for directions at the same time as they become familiar with their new environment and learn about their new country. Begin with a map of the school and the neighborhood before moving on to maps of larger areas. Involve students in planning a field trip using local transit maps and schedules.

Resource Books and Classroom Materials

The following listings represent only a sampling of the materials available for beginning language learners and their teachers. Visit the publishers' websites to see more information and to request catalogues and sample copies.

Bailey, K., and L. Savage, eds. *New Ways in Teaching Speaking*. Alexandria, Va.: TESOL Publications, 1994.
  Collection of dialogues, role plays, games, and other activities that promote oral fluency.

Bassano, S. and Christison, M.A. *Drawing Out: Creative, Personalized, Whole Language Activities.* Burlingame, CA: ALTA Book Center, 1995.

Innovative activities using student-created images to promote communication.

Bassano, S. and Christison, M.A. *Look Who's Talking: Strategies for Developing Group Interaction* Burlingame, CA: ALTA Book Center, 1995.

A collection of engaging activities to promote communication in the language classroom.

Bassano, S. and Christison, M.A. *Purple Cows and Potato Chips: Multi-Sensory Language Acquisition Activities.* Burlingame, CA: ALTA Book Center, 1995.

Innovative activities to promote language acquisition through the exploration of the primary senses.

Bell, J., and B. Burnaby. *A Handbook for ESL Literacy.* Toronto, Ont.: Pippin Publishing, 1984.

Intended for teachers of adults learning English as a second language, this book suggests strategies that can be used to introduce literacy in English to adolescent immigrants with limited experience of schooling.

Boyd, J.R., and M.A. Boyd. *Before Book One: Listening Activities for Pre-Beginning Students of English.* 2nd ed. Englewood Cliffs, N.J.: Prentice Hall, 1991.

Activities help beginners become familiar with the sounds, simple sentence patterns, and basic vocabulary of English through topics such as numbers and letters, money and time, clothes, and the body.

Brookes, A., and Grundy, P. *Beginning to Write: Writing activities for elementary and intermediate learners.* Cambridge: Cambridge University Press, 1999.

Offers advice on how to teach many aspects of writing, including writing for beginning learners of English, teaching spelling and punctuation, using the writing process, and assessment of writing.

Commons, B., and E. Loffler. *Theme Booklets.* Toronto, Ont.: Toronto District School Board, 2001.

Activity booklets consist of illustrated pages and activities to introduce and practice basic vocabulary related to a specific theme such as My Family. Suitable for grades 1-6. For more information, contact <curriculumdocs@tdsb. on.ca>.

Einhorn, K. *Easy and Engaging ESL Activities and Mini-Books for Every Classroom.* Jefferson City, Mo.: Scholastic Inc, 2001.

Activities to welcome newcomers and help them begin learning English. Designed for children in grades 1-4.

English in My Pocket. Barrington, Ill.: Rigby Education, 2000.

A complete language development kit of eight thematic units for beginning learners of English in the primary grades. Kit includes books, charts, blackline masters, audiocassettes, manipulatives, and a teacher's manual. <www.rigby. harcourtachieve.com>.

Graham, C. *Jazz Chants: Rhythms of American English for Students of English as a Second Language.* New York: Oxford University Press, 1978.

A classic that is the first in a series of titles. Available in book and audiocassette format, the chants use jazz rhythms to help students improve pronunciation and intonation patterns and learn specific grammar patterns. Ideal for beginners.

Grundy, P. *Beginners.* Oxford, U.K.: Oxford University Press, 1994.

Useful activities and games that emphasize real communication.

Gunderson, L. *ESL Literacy Instruction: A Guidebook to Theory and Practice.* Englewood Cliffs, N.J.: Prentice Hall, 1991.

Useful for teachers planning and implementing literacy instruction for English language learners.

Hadfield, J. *Elementary Vocabulary Games: A Collection of Vocabulary Games and Activities for Elementary Students.* Harlow, England: Addison-Wesley Longman, 1998.

Activities for ESL students include matching, arranging, and board games, as well as role plays. Game materials may be photocopied.

Hutchinson, H.D. *ESL Teacher's Book of Instant Word Games for Grades 7-12*. West Nyack, N.Y.: Center for Applied Research in Education (now Jossey-Bass), 1997.

Includes an excellent article by Pat Rigg on the language experience approach.

Jordan, S. *Addition Unplugged*. Toronto, Ont.: Jordan Music Productions Inc. < www.sara-jordan.com>.

Uses music and chant to help students learn basic addition facts. Available in cassette-book and CD-book formats. Ideal for beginners learning number words and mathematical terms in English. Other titles in the series introduce subtraction, multiplication, etc.

Language games for students at all stages, including beginners.

Larimer, R.E., and L. Schleicher, eds. *New Ways in Using Authentic Materials in the Classroom*. Alexandria, Va.: TESOL Publications, 1999.

McCallum , G. *101 Word Games for Students of English As a Second or Foreign Language*. Oxford, U.K.: Oxford University Press, 1980.

Designed for adolescent and adult students, activities can be adapted for students of all ages.

Monaghan, F. (2004) *Practical Ways to Support New Arrivals in the Classroom*. Reading: National Centre for Language and Literacy (U.K.), 2004.

This book provides background information and practical advice on supporting newly-arrived students from other countries. More than 200 reproducible activities for learners in middle and secondary schools. Includes some activities for beginners.

Newcomer Communications. *Ontario Reader 2007*. Toronto, Ont.: Newcomer Communications, 2005. <www3.sympatico.ca/ontarioreader>.

Designed for adult ESL and literacy learners, this publication is also useful for younger learners. Stories are graded according to difficulty level. Includes language exercises and activities, a teacher's guide, and an answer key. *Ontario Reader* is published once every two years.

Palmer, A. *Back & Forth: Photocopiable Cooperative Pair Activities for Language Development*. Burlingame, CA: ALTA Book Center,1999.

32 activities to involve students in interchange that help to improve their listening and speaking skills.

Practical research-based suggestions for teachers of elementary school children.

Richards, I., and Gibson, C. *English Through Pictures*. Toronto, Ont.: Pippin Publishing, 2005.

This three-book set is an updated edition of a favourite among ESL teachers. The pictures illustrate the most widely useful English words and sentence patterns in English. Book 1 is based on 250 words. An additional 500 words are illustrated in developed in Book 2, and another 250 in Book 3, to build a basic vocabulary of 1000 key words which, by their defining power, enable learners to understand definitions and explanations of many thousands more.

Rinvolucri, M. *Grammar Games: Cognitive, Affective and Drama Activities for EFL Students*. Cambridge, U.K.: Cambridge University Press, 1985.

A classic that includes cooperative and competitive games to help students at all levels of English proficiency practice grammar structures.

Rinvolucri, M., and P. Davis. *More Grammar Games: Cognitive, Affective and Movement Activities for EFL Students*. Cambridge, U.K.: Cambridge University Press, 1996.

Includes physical activities and games that do not require beginners to produce language before they are ready.

Schinke-Llano, L., and R. Rauff, eds. *New Ways in Teaching Young Children*. Alexandria, Va.: TESOL Publications, 1996.

Activities that promote second language acquisition and social development among young children.

Short, D., ed. *New Ways in Teaching English at the Secondary Level*. Alexandria, Va.: TESOL Publications, 1999.

Ideas for adolescent language learners, including some activities for beginners.

Spangenberg-Urbschat, K., and R. Pritchard, eds. *Kids Come in All Languages: Reading Instruction for ESL Students*. Newark, Del.: International Reading Association, 1994.

Steinberg, J. *Games Language People Play*. 2nd ed. Toronto, Ont.: Pippin Publishing, 1991.

110 games promote specific language skills such as vocabulary. Many of the games are suitable for beginners.

Takahashi, N., and Frauman-Prickel, M. *Action English Pictures: Activities for Total Physical Response*. Burlingame, CA: ALTA Book Center,1999.

Provides hundreds of illustrations and activities for beginners on topics such as time, weather, and school.

Tom, A., and McKay, H. *The Card Book: Interactive Games and Activities for Language Learners*. Burlingame, CA: ALTA Book Center, 2000.

243 photocopiable cards and communication activities are arranged in nine sets under topics such as food, clothing, animals, and daily activities.

Toronto District School Board. *Co-operative Games and Activities (Grades K–8)*. Toronto, Ont.: Toronto District School Board, 2000.

Though not designed for ESL classes, this is a useful resource for teachers using the total physical response approach to language development. Strong focus on positive peer relationships and social skills. For ordering information, contact <curriculumdocs@tdsb.on.ca>.

Toronto District School Board. *Great Beginnings*. 2nd ed. Toronto, Ont.: Toronto District School Board, 2000.

Eight theme-based units for begnners (grades 3-6). For more information, contact <curriculumdocs@tdsb.on.ca>.

Yorkey, R. *Solo Duo Trio: Puzzles and Games for Building English Language Skills*. Brattleboro, Vt.: Pro Lingua Associates, 1997. More than 100 ready-to-use activities, many of which are suitable for beginners.

Picture Dictionaries

Various publishers produce picture dictionaries and support materials such as workbooks, audiocassettes, posters, and teacher's guides. The two listed below are staples in ESL classrooms.

Sagala, J. (ed) *Longman Photo Dictionary of American English*. Harlow: Pearson Longman, 2003.

More than 3,000 basic vocabulary items for beginning learners of English of all ages. Color photos are presented in plenty of detail and arranged in categories, such as school, home, and travel. British English version also available.

Shapiro, N., and J. Adelson-Goldstein. *Oxford Picture Dictionary*. New York, 1998.

Many versions of this ESL staple are available, including bilingual editions in several languages and a version that focuses on school vocabulary in various subject areas.

Graded Readers

These publishers offer graded or leveled readers suitable for English language learners.

Cambridge English Readers. <www.cambridge.org/elt/catalogue/readers/>.

For students in grade 7 and up. Six levels, from 400 to 3,800 headwords. The series consists of new fiction in various genres, including romance, mystery, adventure, and science fiction. Audiocassettes are available. There is also a series for younger readers.

Oxford Bookworms Library. <www.oup.com/elt/>.
  Six levels, from 400 to 2,500 headwords. Series includes adaptations of classics and contemporary adult fiction as well as original stories. Also available are Oxford Bookworms Starters and Oxford Bookworms Factfiles, a non-fiction series, and Oxford Progressive English Readers.
Penguin Readers. <www.penguinreaders.com/>.
  Six levels, from 200 headwords to 3,000. Series encompasses various genres, including biography and adaptations of classic and contemporary fiction. Also available are Penguin Young Readers, an illustrated series for children aged 5 to 11.
Porcupine Books. <www.curriculumplus.ca>.
  Leveled fiction and non-fiction for children in the primary grades. Though not designed specifically for English language learners, these illustrated books appeal to newcomers, and the non-fiction titles are also suitable for older beginners.

Websites and Online Resources

Family Pastimes < www.familypastimes.com >.
  Cooperative games for large and small groups. Some are especially suitable for beginners.
Dave's ESL Café. <www.eslcafe.com>.
  A site for language learners and teachers. Click on Ideas for activities and games.
Internet TESL Journal. <iteslj.org>.
  For teachers and learners. The section for students provides many online puzzles and other activities.
National Reading Styles Institute. <www.nrsi.com>.
  Resources and training for literacy. The Carbo recorded- book method is especially useful with students in the early stages of learning English or the early stages of literacy development.

IV Language Learning across the Curriculum

The chapters in this section describe how to support English language learners in all classrooms and all curriculum areas.

Chapter 12 suggests strategies for integrating content learning and language development, in various learning contexts, which may include

- mainstream classrooms in which English language learners study alongside English-speaking peers and in which teachers are usually subject specialists or grade-level teachers who may or may not possess expertise in teaching ESL.
- designated ESL subject classes, which are sometimes called sheltered or adjunct classes. These may include, for example, a secondary-level history class for ESL students and grade-level ESL core classes at the elementary level. All students in these classes are English language learners. Teachers may be subject specialists, grade-level teachers (preferably with some ESL training), or ESL specialists. Language instruction is integrated with subject matter adapted from the mainstream curriculum, and more or less equal emphasis is placed on learning language and content.
- ESL classes in which all students are English language learners and teachers are ESL specialists. The focus is on language instruction, using interesting and relevant content from various sources. These sources include, but are not limited to, topics from subjects in the mainstream curriculum.

Chapter 13 provides an overview of the developmental stages that language learners pass through on their way to achieving academic proficiency in English and offers guidelines for adapting instruction for students at various stages. The chapter also suggests alternative approaches to assessment that will help English language learners demonstrate what they have learned.

12 Integrating Language and Content Instruction

What is CALP?

CALP (Cognitive Academic Language Proficiency) consists of the ability to:

- understand and use many low-frequency Latin-based words. For example, students know "reside" as well as "live," and know when each is appropriate. They also know the various forms of words and how to use them, such as "reside," "resident," "residential," etc.;
- understand and use figurative expressions and imagery such as "run that by me again," "hard-hearted," or "as cold as steel;"
- read textbooks at the appropriate grade level, given the same level of teacher support and guidance as their English-speaking peers;
- write in a variety of forms and for various purposes and audiences, using **discourse features** such as transition words and paragraph structure at a level similar to that of their English speaking age peers;
- understand and use a wide variety of grammatical forms and sentence patterns, including various verb forms, passive verbs, and complex sentence patterns using reference words, embedding and subordination.

Most English language learners spend most of the school day in mainstream classrooms, attempting to keep up with their peers at the same time as they learn the language of instruction. In schools where there are small numbers of English language learners, ESL support may be limited, and even beginners may spend most of — or all — the school day in a mainstream classroom.

Whether you are teaching language learning in a mainstream classroom or an ESL class, it is important to ensure that the classroom environment supports language learning. This means that it is necessary to design special activities for beginners, as suggested in Chapter 10. It is also necessary to provide long-term support for English language learners, often for several years after they have "graduated" from an ESL program. This is because it typically takes at least five years for learners to develop the cognitive academic language proficiency (CALP) required to deal successfully with the mainstream curriculum.

The strategies described in this chapter are designed to help teachers at all grade levels and in all subject areas provide the support necessary for English language learners to participate successfully in the program at the same time as they develop their English skills. Many of the strategies also enhance the learning of English-speaking students. The strategies include

- key visuals
- guided reading
- integrated vocabulary instruction
- integrated grammar instruction
- writing scaffolds
- journals
- the writing process
- guided projects
- integrating the arts
- alternative resource material

Key Visuals

Key visuals are content-specific graphic organizers, such as concept maps, T-charts, Venn diagrams, flow charts, story maps, timelines, and decision trees. They are graphic representations of relationships among key ideas in a particular text, lesson, or unit of work.

Key Visuals ...

- were developed specifically to support English language learners
- are designed to match specific content
- enable English language learners to understand new concepts and information by reducing the language demands of the curriculum
- provide a visual representation of key ideas and relationships among ideas
- make visible the underlying organization of ideas such as classification and cause and effect
- support all 3 stages of the Guided Reading process (see page 220)
- illustrate and generate language patterns associated with specific kinds of thinking (e.g., organizing knowledge in a sequence may involve using various verb tenses and discourse markers, such as *first*, *next*, *then*, and *finally*)

Key visuals are extremely flexible and can be used to provide an introductory overview of a lesson or unit, preview a text, organize information during a lesson or unit, summarize information at the conclusion of a lesson or unit, or help with assessment and evaluation by allowing language learners to insert single words, short phrases, or even pictures that enable them to display their understanding more completely than they might otherwise be able to do.

Key visuals also

- help students gain a better understanding of how the parts of a lesson or text fit together
- help learners draw information from expository texts, videos, teacher presentations, or print resources that are beyond their independent reading level
- help students express the information that is displayed, using language patterns appropriate to the task (e.g., classification, description, and sequence)
- guide students as they write and help them organize their work on group and individual projects
- can be provided to the students blank, partially completed, or completed
- can be completed by the teacher and students together, by groups of students, or by students working alone
- may be supplemented by cloze, sentence-completion, and paragraph-frame activities to provide further support for written work (see "Writing Scaffolds" later in this chapter)

The following concept map is an example of a key visual that shows students how information in a chapter about about a country — in this case, Canada — is organized. It can be presented to students before they begin reading or conducting research. You might complete one component with the class, showing students how to use key words and phrases rather than copy word-for-word from the text. Then instruct students to read the rest of the chapter and work in groups to add two or three specific details or examples under each subheading. To provide additional support, supply a bank of words and phrases for students to choose from.

Texture Words	Antonyms
smooth	rough
	bumpy
	hairy
	coarse
	prickly
dry	

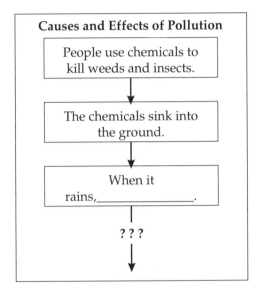

Causes and Effects of Pollution

People use chemicals to kill weeds and insects.

↓

The chemicals sink into the ground.

↓

When it rains,_____.

? ? ?

↓

T-charts like the one shown are simple organizers that help students view two aspects or attributes of a concept or problem. In a discussion of texture in a visual arts class, for example, students might feel various objects to develop the vocabulary. They might then complete the chart, choosing words from the chart to complete sentences such as, *The blue stones are* _____ *and* _____, or *The brown fabric is* _____ *and* _____.

The partially developed **flow chart** shows a sequence of events as well as the cause-and-effect relationships among the events. The students might examine the chart, then view a video or read a relevant passage to find the missing information. Using a transparency or wall chart, class members can work with the teacher to complete the organizer and express the information using words and phrases like *first, next, then,* and *as a result*. Each student or group might then be instructed to create a similar chart on a related topic. Students might also be asked to complete a similar chart for assessment purposes. They might, for example, insert single words or short phrases to demonstrate their understanding of key events and concepts.

The following **timeline** shows students the chronological sequence of events described in a chapter or unit on Canada and World War I. Each of the three topics listed together can stand alone and is therefore suitable for assigning as a jigsaw reading and discussion task.

Canada and World War I

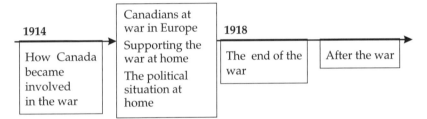

A **matrix** like the following organizes information into categories and may involve comparing or contrasting two or more items. In the following example, some information has been provided, and students are expected to gather the missing information from reference sources. They will then gather similar information about their country of origin or another country that interests them. Some of the information may be gathered from classmates with expert knowledge of a particular country.

Similar or Different? Comparing Canada with Another Country		
	Canada	
Climate	temperate colder in the north	
Oceans	Arctic, Pacific	
Lakes and rivers	Great Lakes	
Mountains		
Islands	Vancouver Island	
Resources and products		

A follow-up activity like the following helps students generate the language required to compare or contrast.

Comparing Canada and ...
Using information from your chart, write sentences that compare Canada and the other country. Use some of the following words and sentence patterns.

Similarities	
both	Canada and China are **both** large countries.
too	Poland produces steel, **and Canada does, too.**
so	Poland produces steel, **and so does** Canada.
neither	Poland doesn't produce bananas, **and neither does** Canada.
neither ... nor ...	**Neither Canada nor Poland** produces bananas.
Differences	
... than ...	Jamaica is much **smaller than** Canada.
not as ... as ...	The United States is **not as big as** Canada.
but	Canada has a lot of lakes and rivers, **but** Somalia doesn't.
whereas	India produces a lot of rice, **whereas** Canada produces a lot of wheat.

Guided reading enables students to draw meaning from text that is beyond their independent reading level.

Guided Reading

Most instructional text is beyond the independent reading level of English language learners — and of many English-speaking students as well. The support of a teacher is required to help them manage the text.

From Kindergarten through secondary school, it is important for all teachers to guide students through texts, demonstrating effective reading strategies and focusing on specific aspects of the text, such as organization, visual material, and vocabulary. This kind of teacher-directed intensive reading, often known as **guided reading**, helps all students develop strategies that they can use independently to read challenging texts. In the case of English language learners, the support provided by guided reading may make the difference between frustration and success.

The guided reading process consists of three stages: before reading, during reading, and after reading. This process also works well when students are using other media, such as documentary TV, instructional videos, and websites. To implement guided reading in your classroom, select appropriate strategies for each stage. You may choose to use one or more strategies at each stage, but do not skip any of the stages.

Before Reading

The following strategies help students activate their previous knowledge and develop background for a new topic.

- *Create a KWL chart* like the following by brainstorming with the class or groups.

What We **K**now about Whales	What We **W**ant to Know about Whales	What We **L**earned about Whales
Mammals Live in the sea Very large Killer whales	How do they breathe? We think they have a language. What do they eat? Are they dangerous?	To be completed at the end of the unit or project.

- *Develop students background knowledge.* Use pictures, photographs, films, speakers, field trips, concrete materials, and anecdotes to prepare the students conceptually for the material they are about to read. It is pointless to proceed if students do not have the background knowledge needed to make sense of the material.

- *Relate what students already know about the topic* to the information in the text. Some students, for example, have knowledge of government structures in other countries, and this knowledge helps them understand text that deals with government in their new country.

- *Guide the students in a survey of the text* so that they are familiar with the organization, content, and helpful features before they start reading. Direct their attention to features such as the table of contents, chapter introductions, chapter headings and subheadings, highlighted words, notes and supplementary information that may be included in text boxes or margins, end-of-chapter summaries and questions, the glossary and index, and visual material, such as maps, graphs, charts, diagrams, and photographs. Though proficient readers use these features to navigate text and get a sense of the content, many English language learners are so anxious about their comprehension that they bypass this step, plunging into a word-by-word reading, with little sense of the overall topic or purpose. After guiding students through this preview, encourage them to discuss with the class, a group, or a partner what they expect to find out by reading the assigned passage.

- *Use key visuals* to illustrate how ideas are related.

- *Teach some key words* that will help students understand the material. Don't teach *all* the new words, however, because during the reading, you will demonstrate how to use various strategies to understand unfamiliar words.

During Reading

Proficient readers read different material in different ways, according to their purpose for reading. They may, for example, skim a chapter to get the general idea, then return to read specific sections in more detail.

- *Chunk the text* into manageable sections. Numbering the paragraphs can be helpful for quick reference.

- *Provide a pre-reading question* related to the main idea of each chunk of text. As students become more proficient readers, encourage them to begin asking themselves questions as they read.

- *Instruct students to read silently,* skimming to find the main idea of the passage or section.

- *Read some sections aloud* to students. This will model pronunciation and help students develop a feel for the rhythm and intonation of English sentences.

- *Provide a key visual* for students to complete as they read.

- *Encourage students to continue reading* when they come to unfamiliar words. They can return to the passage afterwards to check vocabulary.

- *Stop after students have finished reading each section* to ensure that they have identified the main idea and to deal with their questions.

- *Think aloud* to demonstrate how to deal with new vocabulary. For more ideas for helping students develop strategies for handling new words, see "Integrating Vocabulary" later in this chapter.

After Reading

This stage of the process helps students review a passage, reinforce their understanding, and check their knowledge of new words. Many of these strategies can be rehearsed first in groups.

- *Encourage students to re-read specific sections* by asking questions that require them to return to the passage to find details that exemplify, support, or clarify the main idea, concept, or principle.

- *Invite students to read some passages aloud.* You might, for example, instruct them to find the most important sentence in each paragraph and be prepared to read it aloud and explain why it is important.

Should Students Read Aloud?

Reading unfamiliar material aloud is especially difficult for English language learners, who often concentrate more on pronunciation than on comprehension and may be so anxious about their performance that they are able to draw little or no meaning from a passage.

Asking students to read aloud is useful when students are familiar with the material and when the focus is not on comprehension but on some other aspect of performance, such as locating and identifying specific information, producing the stress and intonation patterns of English, or giving a dramatic interpretation.

It is best to invite students to read aloud during the after-reading stage of the guided reading process.

Thinking Aloud

Your modeling of the use of reading strategies by thinking aloud helps students develop competence in using these strategies. The following is an example of how to model a strategy.

Here's an interesting word: *nilometer*. What other words end in *meter*?

Yes, *thermometer* is a good example. What do you think *meter* means in these words?

Yes, something to do with measuring. Now, what about the *nil* part?

That's a good guess. It could mean zero, but I don't think it does here. Let's think about the context. We're reading about Egypt. What's the name of the great river?

Yes, so what did the Egyptians measure with a nilometer?

So it's something they used to measure how deep the Nile was, so that they knew when to plant their crops.

Do you think we need to add this word to our vocabulary list? Do you think you will ever need it again? Okay, we won't add it to our list, but we will remember how to break a word down and use context to figure out the meaning.

- *Encourage students to use context to infer the meaning of new words*. To help them figure out the meaning of *predominant*, for example, refer them to a specific paragraph and tell them to find a word that means the most important.

- *Refer students to a dictionary* as a last resort and only when a word is essential to comprehending the text (see "Integrated Vocabulary Instruction" later in this chapter).

- *Add new words to a word wall* or encourage students to record new words in their vocabulary notebooks (see "Integrated Vocabulary Instruction" later in this chapter).

- *Focus on connectives* and explain how these words are used. For more on connectives, see Chapter 6.
  Make a transparency of a text and highlight one specific kind of connective, as shown in the following passage, which uses various words and phrases indicating time and sequence. Create a chart of these expressions for display and add new expressions as they are encountered. As time goes by, develop and add to several charts showing different kinds of connectives.

  > Frogs live in or near water. <u>In early spring</u> they lay their eggs in shallow ponds, pools, and marshes, around lakes, and beside rivers and streams. <u>Later</u> they scatter on land to feed. <u>Sometimes</u> they wander quite far from the water, although they <u>always</u> stay in damp places. Frogs need to keep their skin moist in order to breathe properly. If a frog's skin becomes dry, the animal <u>soon</u> dies. Therefore, frogs cannot stay away from water <u>for long</u>.

- *Encourage students to make inferences* beyond the text or relate the information to their own knowledge or experience.

- *Encourage students to form opinions* about what they have read. They may engage in small group discussions or write a personal journal response (see "Journals" later in this chapter).

- *Show students how to paraphrase or summarize* what they have read. This is very difficult for English language learners, who are often so anxious about making grammar mistakes that they tend to copy whole chunks from the text.

- *Organize a role play*. Students might, for example, re-enact scenes from a novel or story, interview a character, or devise an alternative scene or ending. In history and social studies, they might interview a key historical figure or develop alternative outcomes. In other subjects, they could play the role of a famous musician, painter, scientist, or inventor. Encourage students to use new words in their role play by asking them to choose five new words and use each at least three times.

Integrated Vocabulary Instruction

As explained in Chapter 5, extensive reading helps students to expand their vocabulary. They also need focused instruction on key words, and on vocabulary acquisition skills.

Focused Instruction: Teaching New Words

Words that are important to understanding a specific concept or lesson are best taught in the academic context in which they occur. Focus on general-purpose academic words, such as *accurate*, *essential*, and *appropriate*, as well as subject-specific words, such as *photosynthesis*, *stanza*, and *longitude*. You can help students acquire new words for academic study by

- introducing new words in a meaningful context
- expanding students' word knowledge by studying common roots and affixes
- providing opportunities for students to practice using new words immediately and on several later occasions

FIRST ENCOUNTERS: INTRODUCING NEW WORDS

New words should be taught naturally as they arise in the context of a lesson or activity. Students need to see, hear, and say new words several times during the same lesson. Here are some guidelines for incorporating vocabulary instruction into daily lessons.

- Set realistic targets that will enable English language learners to catch up to their age peers in five years. For more information on the rates at which students must acquire new vocabulary, see Chapter 5.

   Go through the text or lesson and choose words that will be useful immediately and in the following days and weeks. Focus on important low-frequency words that students need to read, hear, write, or say several times during the lesson or unit and that will also be useful in other contexts. For example, words such as *elevated*, *sufficient*, *estimate*, *synthesis*, and *analysis* occur in many subjects. Limit the number of technical terms to those that are truly essential.

- Pre-teach some key words, especially if they are not explained or supported in the passage. You might also write five to 10 words on the chalkboard and ask students to discuss what the words mean and how they might relate to words in the passage.
- Don't pre-teach all the new words students are likely to encounter. They must also learn how to figure out meaning by using strategies such as inferring meaning from context, analyzing words, and referring to a dictionary. These strategies are explained in more detail in "Developing Vocabulary Acquisition Skills" on page 229.
- As you introduce each new word, print it clearly on the chalkboard or chart paper and say it, pointing to syllables while articulating clearly. It is especially important to emphasize the main stress in words of more than one syllable (e.g., **product** and *evolution*).
- Provide pronunciation practice so that students can recognize and use the new words orally as well as in print. Articulate the words clearly and invite students to repeat them, both chorally and individually. Every day, call on individual students to pronounce new

Pre-Teaching Key Words

Use pictures, gestures, analogies, and examples like the following to introduce new words that are essential to understanding a reading passage.

We are going to learn about bats. Here are some words that you will read.

radar	caves	legends
echolocation	nocturnal	species
vampire	insectivorous	mammals

Do you know what any of these words mean? Do you recognize any parts of these words?
Can you guess how these words relate to bats?

words learned the day before. In mainstream classrooms, it may be preferable to do this with small groups of English language learners before and after each lesson.

- Draw attention to the subject-specific meanings of common words, such as *product*.
- Explain figurative language. A student may understand every word in an expression like *Run that by me again* but have no idea what the idiom means!
- Don't forget connectives. These words link ideas, give clues about what is coming next, and are essential to understanding — and creating — text.

EXPANDING WORD KNOWLEDGE

Take advantage of every opportunity to make connections among words. For example, if you introduce the term *photosynthesis* in the science class, make the connection to the word *photograph* and explain the meaning of the root *photo*, which means light. Set up a word wall and post lists of new words and word families as they arise. Here are some suggestions for the word wall and related activities:

- Make lists of key words on chart paper, including sample sentences that provide a context for each word. Examples are more helpful than definitions: students can memorize a definition without understanding or being able to use the word.
- Limit the number of new words introduced in each lesson or unit, as students will also encounter new vocabulary in other lessons and subject areas. In a textbook for a Grade 4 unit on rocks and minerals, for example, the terms *igneous*, *sedimentary*, and *metamorphic* are introduced, but these terms are not included on the sample chart because only the 10 most useful and transferable words were chosen.
- Set up the lists as word families and introduce various forms of a word as appropriate, along with information about related words or useful roots. Students don't need to know the derivation of all words, but it does help to introduce roots found in many other words. It is also unnecessary to introduce all possible forms of a word at once: keep the load manageable and ignore some forms until they are needed at a later time. Some forms may never be needed. Help students with pronunciation by emphasizing the main stress in different forms of a word (e.g., **mineral** and *mineralogist*). Ask students to repeat the various forms of a word.
- Refer to lists regularly, removing each only when all the words are known.
- Draw students' attention to prefixes and suffixes and teach useful generalizations. On the list of top 10 words, for example, you might point out the suffix *-tion* in *formation* and encourage students to brainstorm to create a list of other words that include the same suffix (e.g., *location*, *description*, *information*, *question*, and *education*). Some words may be drawn from the lesson and others may be words they already know. Explain that the *-tion* ending nearly always signals that the word is an abstract noun.
- From the charts displayed on the word wall, select words with common affixes and add them to another list on a special section of the wall. Develop these lists gradually as new word families are added to the word wall. Draw attention to these lists when new words using the same affixes occur in a lesson, and ask students to contribute other words with the same affixes.

| | | | Top 10 Words | | |
| | | | Rocks and Minerals | | |

Verb	Noun	Adjective	Related Words	Word Roots	Examples
form	form formation	formal	inform reform deform	form = shape	This book has a lot of information about rock formations in various locations.
locate	location	local		loc = place	
describe	description	descriptive	scribe script prescription manuscript	scrib (scrip) = write	Use descriptive words to write about your sample rocks. Chinese script is different from English writing. If you need medicine, you must get a prescription from your doctor.
mine	mineral miner	mineral	mineralogy mineralogist		Mineralogists know all about oil, coal, diamonds, and other minerals.
classify	classification	classified	class		We classified our samples into rocks and minerals.
magnify	magnification	magnified magnifying	magnificent	magni = big, great	We used a magnifying glass to examine our rock and mineral samples.
examine	examination		school exam medical exam		After examining our samples, we recorded our observations on a chart. The chart is a record of our work.
record	record recorder	recorded			
observe	observation observer	observant			
	geology geologist	geological	geography geometry	geo = earth	Geologists know all about the earth and what's underneath.

The following is a chart of affixes encountered during a history unit.

Affixes					
Prefix	**Usual Meaning**	**Example**	**Suffix**	**Usual Meaning**	**Example**
a- (af-)	on	affix	-ant	noun: a person	immigrant
dis-	not	disagree	-or	noun: a person	governor
im-	not	impossible	-ence	abstract noun	independence
im-	in, into	immigrant	-ion	abstract noun	union
in-	not	independent	-ment	abstract noun	government
multi-	many	multicultural	-ry (-y)	abstract noun	slavery
pre-	before	prefix	-ate	verb	immigrate
sub-(suf-)	under, close to	suffix	-ize	verb	symbolize
un-	not	unhappy	-al	adjective	federal
			-ent	adjective	dependent
			-ful	adjective	resourceful
			-ed	past tense	depended
			-s	plural	resources

FOCUSED PRACTICE: BEGINNING TO USE NEW WORDS

Students must begin using new words right away in activities that enable them to focus on the new words without worrying about other aspects of language use. Two of the most useful activities are cloze passages and contextualized word puzzles.

Cloze Passages

A modified version of the cloze passage can be used to help students use new words and review content at the same time. Write a summary of key information from the lesson, deleting key words that you have taught. These may be content words (e.g., *immigration* and *photosynthesis*) or connectives (e.g., *however* and *as a result*). Provide a word bank for students to choose from. Always include two or three more words than needed.

The following passage is based on a chapter in a social studies textbook.

resources	products	service	produce
depend	population	manufacturing	transportation

Many jobs ___*depend*___ on natural _____, such as trees, fish, and oil. In cities, many people work in _____ industries, making _____ in factories. _____ industries such as finance, communications, and government are also important in urban areas.

The following sentences highlight common words in mathematics.

area   volume   cube   right   face   root

1a. The ___*volume*___ of the room was 24m³.
1b. Sanjay's mother asked him to turn down the ___*volume*___ of his stereo.
1c. Some books such as encyclopedias are so big that they come in more than one ___*volume*___.

2a. A 90° angle is a _____ angle.
2b. Do you have the _____ answer for this question?
2c. To find the library, go down the hall and turn _____.

The following example from a science lesson focuses on connectives.

if	and	as a result	because	because of
therefore	so	so that	in order to	although

I am a frog. I need to live in or near water ___*because*___ I must keep my skin moist. _____ I sometimes move away from the water, I don't go very far, and I always stay where it is damp. I must keep my skin moist _____ breathe properly. _____ I stay away from water too long, my skin will dry up. _____, I would probably die. _____, I always stay in or near wet places.

Word Puzzles

Crossword and other puzzles based on the content of lessons or units help students practice and internalize new words. Online software is available to help create the grid, which is otherwise time-consuming. Make crosswords interactive by providing the puzzle to students in pairs. Give one student only the across clues, and another only the down clues.

Jigsaw word puzzles, such as the simple one shown on this page, promote talk and collaboration at the same time as they provide opportunities to practice vocabulary as students work together to figure out the hidden word. This kind of puzzle is quick to prepare, and after completing one or two, pairs and small groups can create their own to share with others. The puzzle shown, which focuses on words about winter, was designed to be completed in pairs by young children and older students who are at the beginning stages of learning English. Each student in a pair has the same grid, but different clues. More complicated puzzles can be created by making up four different sets of clues for the words on the same grid.

Though both cloze activities and word puzzles are useful and interesting, they often involve words that are not yet part of students' active vocabulary. Once the words have been introduced, take advantage of

Student 1

1.							
2.							
3.							
4.							
5.							
6.							

1. Rhymes with go.
2. It's hard to walk on.
3. Don't forget to wear these!
4. Not shoes.
5. You can wear them on your feet.
6. Ends with f.

The hidden word is _____.

Student 2

1.							
2.							
3.							
4.							
5.							
6.							

1. It's white and cold!
2. Rhymes with rice.
3. Not gloves.
4. Wear them on your feet.
5. On the ice.
6. Don't forget to wear this!

The hidden word is _____.

every opportunity to encourage students to use them in less structured ways. You might, for example, write on the chalkboard some of the words you want students to use in a classroom discussion, then point to a specific word you want them to use when responding to a question. Or you might also list "words of the week" and instruct students to use some of the words in a journal entry.

Developing Vocabulary Acquisition Skills

Students need to learn to handle unfamiliar words that arise as they are reading or studying independently. To help them do this, show them how to use context, a problem-solving approach, and dictionaries to help figure out the meaning. Keeping a vocabulary notebook also helps.

CONTEXT

Use a think-aloud approach to demonstrate how to recognize help when it is provided in the text and how to decide whether it is really necessary to know the meaning of a specific word or group of words to understand the point of a sentence or paragraph.

In the following passage about birds, for example, the underlined words and phrases may pose challenges for language learners. If you read the passage with students, think aloud to demonstrate various reading strategies, as in the example below.

Text	Teacher's "think-aloud"
There are more than 8,500 <u>species, or kinds</u>, of birds. They live in deserts, tropical forests, along seashores, in gardens, woods, and big cities, and even in the icy polar regions. All the bird species look <u>different. Some, such as</u> vultures and eagles, are huge. <u>Others, such as</u> hummingbirds and sparrows, are only about as big as mice. <u>Some</u> birds have startling and beautiful colors. <u>A peacock's tail</u> <u>shimmers like a rainbow. Some other</u> birds are brown and drab.	I don't know the word *species*, but I'll keep on reading. Oh, I see. It says, "or kinds," so *species* must mean kinds. This section is about different kinds of birds. Hmmm. It says, "Some, such as vultures and eagles …" They must be birds, because *some* refers to *bird species* in the sentence before. "Others, such as hummingbirds and sparrows …" More birds. "A peacock's tail …" A peacock must be a kind of bird as well. These are all different kinds of birds. I guess that's good enough for now. "Shimmers like a rainbow …" I think this means that the tail is colorful and bright, like a rainbow. I think *drab* must mean the opposite of *startling and beautiful colors.* Not colorful or beautiful.
Gradually, over thousands of years, some bird species lost the power of flight. They had reached areas where there were few animals to compete with them for food and they no longer needed to fly. Their wings gradually became smaller and weaker. At the same time, they became better adapted for their lives in other ways. <u>Ostriches, rheas, and emus</u> all live on grasslands. Though they cannot fly to seek food or escape enemies, all are large birds and can run very fast. The ostrich is the largest living bird. It reaches a height of up to eight feet and has long legs for running. <u>Kiwis, cassowaries, and penguins</u> are other well-known flightless birds.	"Ostriches, rheas, and emus." I guess these are birds. They're all examples of birds that don't fly. "Kiwis, cassowaries, and penguins" are also birds that don't fly. I've heard of penguins. They live in the Antarctic. I wonder where kiwis and cassowaries live? I'll look at the picture to see these birds and find out where they live. That's interesting, but I don't need to know the names of all these birds right now. The main idea is that some birds do not fly.

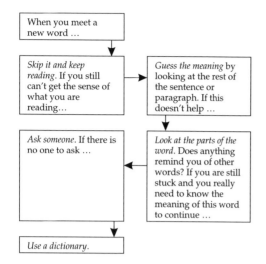

When you meet a new word …

Skip it and keep reading. If you still can't get the sense of what you are reading…

Guess the meaning by looking at the rest of the sentence or paragraph. If this doesn't help …

Ask someone. If there is no one to ask …

Look at the parts of the word. Does anything remind you of other words? If you are still stuck and you really need to know the meaning of this word to continue …

Use a dictionary.

A PROBLEM-SOLVING APPROACH

On the classroom wall, keep a chart like the one shown on this page. Refer to it before students read a passage or when discussing a passage they have just read.

DICTIONARIES

As illustrated by the chart in the previous section, consulting a dictionary is only one of several strategies for handling new words. For beginning language learners, bilingual dictionaries, including electronic dictionaries, are essential survival tools. In addition to providing bilingual dictionaries in the school library, encourage beginners to carry their own pocket dictionaries.

Many English language learners, however, cling to their bilingual dictionaries too long, referring to them every time they encounter a new word. This approach can slow down reading so much that comprehension suffers. In addition, many bilingual dictionaries do not list academic or technical words, such as *photosynthesis*. Even if words like these are listed, knowing the translation may not help if a student hasn't already studied the concept in his or her first language. Another drawback of bilingual dictionaries, especially pocket dictionaries, is that they do not provide all the possible meanings of words, such as *balance* and *product*, that mean specific things in specific subjects.

Once language learners are beyond the beginning stage, it is important to teach them to use English-only learner dictionaries. These dictionaries provide simple definitions, pronunciation guides, illustrations, and contextualized examples. Some also provide information about alternative forms of words, such as irregular past tense and plural noun forms. Learner dictionaries are more helpful to English language learners — and many native speakers as well — than standard reference dictionaries, which often provide explanations that are as difficult to understand as the word being looked up and require a sophisticated knowledge of language terms.

Because the system for identifying words, pronunciation, and so on varies from dictionary to dictionary, it is important to teach students how to use the information that is usually found at the beginning of a dictionary.

VOCABULARY NOTEBOOKS

Encourage students to keep vocabulary notebooks. To remember a word, students might copy the sentence in which the word occurred, write a translation (if they are familiar with the concept in their own language), or draw a diagram. A typical notebook page might look like the one shown on the following page.

Don't worry about teaching every unfamiliar word. Encourage students to skip words whose meaning they can guess at or understand in a general way. If a word is unlikely to recur, it doesn't matter if students have only a general understanding of its meaning. If a word is really important, it will recur, and students' understanding of its meaning will increase with each encounter.

Be careful. The common vocabulary-practice activities may not be as helpful as you might wish.

Date: September 8–12			Chapter or Topic: Ancient Civilizations
Nouns	Verbs	Adjectives Adverbs	Explanation, Example, and Translation
conclusion	conclude	conclusive conclusively	finish, end This book _concludes_ with chapters on Britain and Mexico. (p. 6) (ends) Explain how you arrived at your _conclusion._ (p. 17) (final opinion)
Idioms and Set Expressions			Explanation, Example, and Translation
walk the earth			. . . during the many thousands of years that humans have _walked the earth._ (p. 6)
the beaten track			You often want to leave _the beaten track_ and explore on your own. (p. 6)

- Looking up words and copying definitions: Students may copy and even memorize definitions but be unable to understand the words or use them independently. Concentrate instead on the real purposes of using dictionaries. Writers use dictionaries to check spelling and confirm meaning, and readers use dictionaries when they encounter a new word that is essential to understanding a passage. Second language learners also use dictionaries to check pronunciation and discover grammatical information, such as the past participle of an irregular verb. Students may also look up a word to figure out which of several meanings is most appropriate in a given context.
- Using new words in new sentences that show the meaning: If students could do this, they wouldn't need to. Most students need more supported practice, such as cloze activities, to help them use new words. For a more challenging assignment, provide a familiar context for the new words, and instruct students to choose five or six from a list of 10 that have been presented and practiced in class. This can be an oral or written group activity.
- Completing word-search activities: Many word searches depend on word recognition rather than comprehension. Choose only activities that include some context that supports comprehension, and be aware that word searches that arrange words diagonally, right to left, or from bottom to top can be confusing for second language learners, some of whom are still becoming familiar with the direction of English print.

Integrated Grammar Instruction

As noted in earlier chapters, grammar instruction is most effective when it is incorporated into daily lessons as specific patterns or problems occur in class. By drawing students' attention to recurring patterns, focusing on examples of the same structure in other contexts, and providing many opportunities for practice and feedback, you can integrate grammar and content instruction.

Recurring Patterns

Look for a recurring pattern in a text or a lesson. Some patterns, such as the following, occur over and over again in various academic contexts.

- Comparative and superlative forms of adjectives (e.g., *greater than*, *fewer than*, and *the highest*) occur regularly in mathematics and when interpreting graphs and charts.
- Past-tense verb forms appear in narrative fiction, history, and the retelling of personal experiences.
- The simple present tense and subject-verb agreement are required in many contexts, such as listing components (e.g., Each molecule of water *consists* of one atom of oxygen and two of hydrogen), describing (e.g., An isosceles triangle *has* two sides of equal length), and retelling stories (e.g., Romeo *falls* in love with Juliet at first sight).
- The passive voice is used to describe processes or results (e.g., science experiments: The water *was heated*; and agricultural or industrial processes: The logs *are transported*).

To focus students' attention on a specific pattern, make a transparency of a page that includes several occurrences of the feature. You might, for example, highlight the passive verbs in a model lab report or in a textbook description of a process, such as the formation of rocks. Explain that the passive voice is often used to describe how something is made, grown, and formed, and is especially important in science. Ask students to identify additional examples of this structure in the text.

Examples of the Same Structure in Other Contexts

Involve students in creating a chart that includes many examples of the target structure. To practice passive verbs, for example, invite students to contribute their responses to questions like these:

- Where (when) were you born?
- When was this school built?
- What is paper made of?
- What is grown on the Prairies?
- Why was the Great Wall of China built?
- How were the pyramids of Egypt built?

Opportunities for Practice and Feedback

Students need many opportunities to use new patterns in real communication. Cloze activities are especially useful for focusing students' attention on a language feature at the same time as they work with ideas from classroom lessons. The modified cloze passage shown on the following page is

Language Feature of the Week

No matter what subject or grade level you teach, you can help all students become more aware of how English works by focusing on a language feature of the week.

This focus need not be restricted to grammatical structures. You might also focus on other aspects of language, such as a specific word root or affix, or connectives. In all cases, the feature should be drawn from the context of the lessons you are teaching that week.

Sedimentary Rock

Use the passive form of the following verbs to complete this paragraph.

press	blow	wash
squeeze	form	break

How Sedimentary Rock Is Formed

Rocks and minerals <u>are broken</u> into smaller pieces when they <u>are washed</u> away by water or when they _____ _____ away by the wind. Many layers of these small pieces _____ _____ together until eventually they _____ _____ together into a solid mass.

This cloze passage provides practice in using passive verbs, which are commonly used to describe procedures and processes, especially in science:

To find the volume of a solid by using an overflow can and a graduated cylinder:

1. The spout of the can <u>was covered</u> with a finger.
2. The overflow can _____ above the level of the spout.
3. The can _____ on a level surface and the water above the spout _____ out.
4. The object _____ into the water, and the water that overflows _____ in the graduated cylinder.
5. The volume of water in the cylinder _____ by reading the graduated cylinder.

based on recent lessons. Students fill in the blanks to review or demonstrate their knowledge of key concepts from the lesson.

For more examples of cloze and other structured writing tasks that help students practice using specific language features as they summarize or paraphrase the content of a reading or lesson, see the following section, "Writing Scaffolds."

Students also need opportunities to use the structures in less supported situations, such as in journal responses. Provide a few sample sentences or a model journal entry, highlighting the use of the structure you want the students to use. For more suggestions for using journals of various kinds, see "Journals" later in this chapter.

When you respond to students' written work, pay specific attention to the pattern you have been highlighting — *but don't correct the students' work*. Instead, place an asterisk or another symbol in the margin to indicate that there is a problem with the language feature contained in that particular line. Students gain little from your corrections, but they learn a great deal from making their own corrections. Checking their corrections also helps you ensure that they have understood and can apply a particular feature. For more detailed suggestions on providing supportive feedback, see Chapter 10.

Writing Scaffolds

In teaching and learning, scaffolds are the supports that teachers and more proficient peers provide to help learners achieve a higher level of performance than they can manage on their own. Writing scaffolds are temporary frameworks that enable learners of English to use new words and phrases, practice specific grammar patterns, and produce sentences, paragraphs, and various forms of writing of a quality that they would be unable to produce without help. As language learners become more proficient, they need less and less support.

Cloze, sentence combining, sentence completion, paragraph frames, and composition templates are writing scaffolds that help students move from highly supported activities to activities that provide less support.

Cloze Activities

The cloze technique can be adapted to focus attention on and help students practice using specific language features. Create cloze passages that summarize or paraphrase the content of a reading or lesson, deleting the feature you want students to practice.

Cloze passages can appear deceptively simple. The example on the next page is from a science lesson. It is challenging for English language learners, because they must choose from among various forms of a word and because they may need to manipulate some grammatical endings.

Choose words from the list to complete the sentences that follow.

form	formation	formal
inform	information	informative
locate	location	local
describe	description	descriptive

This book is very _informative_. I learned a lot about rocks. For example, I learned that the Niagara Escarpment is a famous rock _____ in Ontario. There are many other interesting rock _____ in different _____ in Ontario, across Canada, and around the world.

The following passage from a social studies lesson provides practice using past-tense forms of verbs.

raise   stand   be   live   begin   eat   farm   use   start

The first people _lived_ in Africa more than three million years ago. Their brains _____ bigger than the brains of apes, and they _____ upright. They_____ fruits, roots, and berries for their food.
    During the next three million years, humans _____ to make tools and weapons. They _____ animals for their meat and their skins. They _____ to use fire. About 6,000 years ago, people _____ to live in settled communities. They _____ the land and _____ animals.

Sentence-Combining Activities

Sentence-combining activities help students begin working with longer sentences. The following example requires students to retell events in a story by choosing appropriate conjunctions to link parts of sentences. Similar activities can be created to focus on connectives that signal cause and effect, sequence, and so on.

Romeo and Juliet fall in love	and	she can think of a way out of it.
Romeo kills himself	so	
Romeo kills Tybalt	but	their families are involved in a feud.
Juliet will have to marry Paris	if	he helps her to make a plan.
Juliet begs Friar Lawrence for help	although	
	until	the Prince banishes him from the city.
	unless	
	because	he thinks Juliet is dead.

Sentence-Completion Activities

Sentence-completion activities provide a framework that helps students construct sentences of various types. The following example, based on the content of an elementary science lesson, focuses on cause and effect.

The plant on the window sill grew taller because …
The plant in the corner received less light. As a result, …
The plant in the closet received no light. Therefore, …
We conclude that … in order to grow.

Paragraph Frames

Paragraph frames help students organize their ideas into well-constructed paragraphs. Beginning with simple paragraphs, show students models of the kind of paragraph you want them to produce. Label the key components of the paragraphs, as shown in the model of basic English paragraph structure in the margin. This consists of a general topic sentence, supporting details, and a restatement of the main idea.

Modeled writing also helps students understand paragraph structure. On the chalkboard or chart paper, compose a paragraph to demonstrate the process. Think aloud as you write, showing how you make choices and revise. Use the terms you have discussed with the class (e.g., "I need to start with a topic sentence that tells what my paragraph is about").

Next, provide a paragraph frame like the following. It consists of a series of prompts that help students produce a well-constructed paragraph of their own.

A Model Paragraph	
topic sentence	Toronto is one of the most multicultural cities in the world.
supporting details or examples	Torontonians have roots in more than 120 countries and speak more than 80 languages. Whatever language you speak, you can probably find doctors, lawyers, hairstylists, grocery stores, car mechanics, and bank clerks who speak your language. Community newspapers are published in several languages, and public libraries contain multilingual material. Children from many language and cultural backgrounds study and play together in classrooms and schoolyards.
conclusion or restatement	Toronto's diversity makes the city an interesting and exciting place to live.

> San Francisco is one of the most beautiful cities in North America. To the west, … while to the east, … San Francisco has … There is … San Francisco residents also enjoy … People from across North America and around the world visit this beautiful city on the west coast.

The following paragraph frame, based on the content of a history lesson, is an explanation of cause and effect.

> There were four major causes of World War I. One was … Another reason war broke out was … A third reason was … The fourth major cause of the war was …

The following paragraph frame, based on the content of a class discussion, provides support for an opinion.

> Should we have a Christmas play this year?
> In my opinion, we should (should not) have a Christmas play this year. For one thing (First of all), … Another reason is … In addition (Furthermore), … Therefore, …

Composition Templates

Similar to paragraph frames, composition templates are used to help students write longer pieces of two or more connected paragraphs. Start by providing examples of the form of writing (see Chapter 7) you want students to produce (e.g., a recounting, an explanation, or an exposition). Then model the process on the chalkboard or chart paper, thinking aloud as students watch and listen. You may also invite them to contribute ideas. Then provide a template to guide students as they produce their own extended pieces of writing.

The following template might be used to create a journal entry in science.

Introduce the topic	Our group investigated …
Relate the topic to your own knowledge or experience	Before we started our investigation, I thought …
Retell (What happened?)	When we carried out our investigation we observed that …
Reflect (What did you learn?)	I learned that … I wonder …

A template like the following can be used for writing a simple exposition that argues a point of view.

Introduction (State your opinion)	In my … opinion … I have _ reasons for taking this point of view.
First argument	First, … For instance, …
Second argument	I would also like to point out that …
Third argument	Another problem (argument, consideration) is, … For example, …
Conclusion (restatement)	For these reasons, I believe …

Journals

Increasingly, teachers in all subject areas are encouraging students to keep journals. Journals encourage students to think aloud on paper, express their feelings and opinions, ask questions, and reflect on their learning in a personal way. Journal responses are usually more thoughtful if the students have first had an opportunity to discuss the information and ideas in small groups.

Journals may also help students prepare for other writing assignments. Journals are seldom marked or graded, although students may choose to revise and polish an entry for publication or evaluation (see "The Writing Process" later in this chapter). Teachers may also use the journals to note specific language difficulties that can become the focus of instruction at another time.

Various formats can be used for journal writing. Response journals, learning logs, and dialogue journals are especially useful and can be adapted for use in various subject areas.

Response Journals

Response journals encourage students to respond in writing to a reading passage, video, field trip, classroom speaker, or group discussion or activity, as well as to other sources of new information. These responses encourage students to make connections between their previous knowledge and new learning.

Be careful not to over-use response journals, however. Students can quickly become disenchanted with even the most exciting field trip or learning experience if they know they will be required to write a journal entry afterwards.

Most English language learners need help when they begin using response journals, and many teachers encourage journal writing by sharing some of their own entries. Providing models and templates encourages students to go beyond simply retelling what they have learned or discovered, prompting them to relate the new learning to their own lives or previous knowledge and reflect on its implications and applications.

Students in the early stages of learning English may benefit from writing in their first language. To encourage fluency, suggest that they substitute words from their first language when they don't know the English equivalents and look up the English words later.

The following template is based on a three-part model for Retelling, Relating, and Reflecting.

Title	Our Visit to the Science Center
Retell	What was the most important or interesting thing you learned during our visit to the Science Center?
Relate	How does this relate to what we have been studying in class?
Reflect	How might this be important? Do you have any opinions about what you learned? What questions do you still have?

Learning Logs

Learning logs are used to review a lesson or learning activity. For example, students might write their own explanations of a new concept or describe how they solved a problem. Students can also use learning logs to record their progress on major assignments, such as research projects or group presentations. Learning logs have become increasingly important even in subjects such as mathematics, in which writing has traditionally received little attention.

Learning logs help develop metacognitive skills by encouraging students to express their thoughts in writing and reflect on and make plans for their own learning. Teachers can use learning logs to gain insights into students' thinking about and understanding of new concepts, as well as their attitudes toward a subject and their individual learning styles. Learning logs can also provide teachers with valuable insights into their own teaching.

As with other kinds of writing, it is helpful to model the process and provide prompts or templates like those shown in the margin to help students get started.

Dialogue Journals

Students use dialogue journals to write directly and privately to a specific reader, who writes back. Students may use this kind of journal for a variety of real purposes, such as asking questions about an aspect of a lesson, sharing personal information, and offering opinions.

Because responding to dialogue journals is time-consuming, it's a good idea to enlist the help of others, whether this is a student in another grade or even someone who doesn't know the writer. Some teachers set up secret friend or secret correspondent partnerships. The partners may be introduced to each other at the end of the year.

A respondent who can write in a student's first language can be especially helpful to beginning learners of English. Responses should be thoughtful, personal, and non-evaluative, designed to stimulate thinking and provide models of language use. The respondent may notice specific errors in a student's writing and provide supportive feedback in the response by modeling and underlining the appropriate grammatical form or word choice. By using appropriate synonyms and antonyms, the responses may also help expand a student's vocabulary and repertoire of ways of saying the same thing. For resources on using dialogue journals with English language learners, see "To Learn More ..." at the end of this chapter.

Write about Today's Lesson

What did you learn?

What was the best part of the lesson?

What suggestions do you have for the teacher?

The Writing Process

The writing process involves students in purposeful writing for a real or imaginary audience and emphasizes the stages that "real writers" go through when creating a piece of writing. The process can be used in all subject areas and is especially helpful for second language learners.

Purposeful Writing

The writing process involves students in real writing tasks, or simulations, with a specific purpose and audience in mind. This means that, from the beginning, learners must think about how to communicate effectively.

Students need to be involved in a variety of writing tasks, from short, informal pieces to highly structured compositions completed with the careful guidance of the teacher. Students may, for example, write letters, personal and fictional narratives, poems, memos, notes, instructions, response journals, dialogue journals, and learning logs, as well as more traditional assignments such as lab reports, summaries, research projects, and essays. In every case, the quality of students' writing will be higher if they see examples of the required form before they start.

The following are examples of non-traditional writing assignments that involve students in writing for a variety of audiences and purposes.

Mathematics

In your textbook, look at some word problems about sports. Then work with a partner to write a word problem about a sport that you know well. Your problem should involve ratio, averages, or percentages. Include an explanation of the sport's rules that a person must know to solve the problem.
You can write your problem in two languages. Other students in the class will solve your problem.

History

You are a 19th-century Chinese worker building the railway. Write a letter home describing the work, the working conditions, and the way your co-workers and bosses treat you. Write about your wishes and dreams for the future, and ask about your family.

History

Look at the photographs of the Depression in the textbook. Write a descriptive piece based on one of the photographs, from the point of view of either an observer or one of the people in the picture. Include what you see and what you feel.

English or Language Arts

Imagine you are a character in one of the stories we have read this term. From your character's point of view, write a journal entry about the most dramatic or important event in the story.

Biology

Write and illustrate a children's book about one of the systems, such as the reproductive system or digestive system) that we have studied in human biology. Your book should help children become aware of their own bodies, without using difficult jargon. To get ideas about illustrations, language, and the use of humor, look at some of the children's books on display in the classroom. When your book is finished, you will present it to the children in Ms. Ahmed's class at Fairview Elementary School.

Note: Your book will be especially valuable if you produce a bilingual version in English and one of the languages spoken in our community.

Geography

Choose one of the regions we have studied this term and write an advertisement encouraging people to live there, to locate a new industry there, or to go on holiday there. Create an English version and a version for a community newspaper in another language.

Stages in the Writing Process

Proficient writers seldom sit down and write a piece, no matter how short, in one uninterrupted session. Instead, writers may make several starts before they know where they want to go with the piece. Even writing a simple memo or phone message may involve re-reading and correcting or making more than one attempt. Longer pieces may start with an outline, which may be revised several times before the writer starts to write. Most writers create several versions of a piece. Each version is more satisfying than the last, until they are confident that the piece is ready to be read. Teachers can model the writing process to demonstrate the planning, composing, and editing skills that are important to all writers.

The approach outlined in this section is especially helpful to students who are writing in a second language because it provides support and feedback at several stages of composition. Using a computer makes revising and editing much less tedious and often encourages students to produce more and take risks they might otherwise avoid.

The writing process consists of five stages.

- Pre-writing
- Writing the first draft
- Revising
- Editing
- Sharing the final product

PRE-WRITING

Help students explore ideas and get ready for writing. Group brainstorming is especially helpful in exploring a range of ideas. A key visual can help students organize their ideas into a logical pattern that involves classification, sequence, parallel ideas, or comparing and contrasting.

Show students models of the kind of writing you want them to produce and provide frameworks to help them do so. If you want a lab report in a specific format, for example, show students several models and discuss important elements, such as headings, labeled diagrams, and language features, such as the passive voice and connectives.

Provide some structure. You might, for example, provide starter sentences for students to choose among or questions they can respond to. A paragraph frame or composition template helps students organize their ideas. Give specific instructions about your expectations: specify the length and the number of supporting points that should be included, as well as specific words students should use.

Oh, No! Not the Writing Process Again!

Be flexible when using the writing process. If students spend a lot of time working through the entire process every time they write, writing will become a boring, time-consuming chore. It is not necessary for students to revise and polish all their work or to submit every piece for evaluation. Each term, you might, for example, specify only certain assignments for development through the writing process and require these to be submitted with all drafts.

WRITING THE FIRST DRAFT

Emphasize the exploratory nature of a first draft. If students want to cross out words or sections or reorganize their ideas, this is part of the process and does not mean that they have made mistakes. You might display copies of original manuscripts by famous writers to show students that even professional writers go through this stage. Today's students have a great advantage over writers of the past: they can use computers to explore ideas and make changes as they go.

Some students will produce better work if they write their first draft in their first language.

REVISING

This stage enables students to test their ideas on an audience, which may be a writing partner, a group of peers, or the teacher. Explain that the focus is on the overall meaning of the piece and the development of the ideas rather than details, such as spelling and grammar. These will be dealt with at the next stage.

Use questions like the following to create a checklist to help students respond to one another's work and analyze their own.

- Does the piece follow the model or template?
- Is the content relevant and interesting?
- Is the piece organized effectively in paragraphs or under appropriate headings?
- Do ideas need more development?
- Are more details or examples needed?
- Could more interesting or sophisticated vocabulary express the ideas more powerfully?
- Do appropriate connecting words link sentences and paragraphs?

After receiving this feedback, the writer considers the suggested changes and incorporates some of them into a second draft.

EDITING

The editing stage involves checking **surface features**, such as grammar, spelling, and punctuation. Teach students how to use the spellcheck feature of the word processing program they are using — but warn them that computer checkers are never perfect and that they must also use their own judgment. Students learn a great deal about English spelling patterns and idiosyncrasies when their spelling errors are flagged and alternatives are offered. Include peer-editing sessions and student-teacher conferences as part of this process.

Focus on specific kinds of language errors and demonstrate some of the rules and patterns of English to students who have not yet fully acquired them. Resist the temptation to point out every error, however. Focus instead on recurring patterns. Identify and explain the pattern or rule so that the student can make the corrections (see Chapter 10). Students then return to the second draft and edit to produce the final copy. At this stage, they may also work on the layout and illustrations.

SHARING THE FINAL PRODUCT

At this stage, which is sometimes called publishing, students' writing may be shared in many ways. It may be displayed in or outside the classroom, included in an anthology of class writing, presented to the teacher for formal evaluation, or sent to the appropriate audience, such as the school principal or a newspaper.

This girl is sharing a book she created.

A writing portfolio allows students to select several pieces of writing during the year, as a record of their best performance, for evaluation purposes. The portfolio can also be shared with parents at parent-teacher interviews.

Guided Projects

In North American classrooms, group or individual research projects are valuable learning activities. Students who have begun their education in other countries, however, may be very uncomfortable when the teacher does not direct and monitor every step of the learning process. Their parents, too, may feel less able to help their children than those who have the time, resources, and educational background to understand what is involved when their children are assigned projects. Those who are not comfortable speaking English may feel even less able to help.

When students do not understand the nature of the task or do not have the necessary resources, the quality of the product may be disappointing. Students may produce projects that are poorly organized and contain material that has been copied directly from a source, a practice that is valued in school systems where learning from the masters is emphasized.

To help all students produce successful projects, teachers need to provide guidance and support *in class*. It is important to introduce projects in a structured way and review the process every time you assign a project. Be ready to give direct, individual instruction to students who are less experienced in project work, and ensure that your expectations are realistic. If learning how to find information is an important outcome, for example, the volume of information is not tremendously important. To demonstrate that they have met this expectation at a level appropriate to their stage of proficiency in English, beginners might start by finding and reporting five relevant facts. More advanced students might be expected to write a longer and more detailed report.

The following approach helps increase students' confidence and improves their results.

- *Explain why projects are valuable.* Students and parents need to hear what the benefits are. Keep examples of projects on hand to show students — and their parents.

- *Provide a step-by-step checklist of the tasks involved*, and monitor each step. This enables you to give feedback at each step, redirect students who may be off track, offer extra help when needed, and help students plan their work and organize their time. Provide constructive feedback on the process as well as the product, basing your assessment on observation, as well as on students' notes, journals, and learning logs. A sample checklist is provided on the following page.

- *Help students choose a topic.* Faced with choosing a topic for the first time, many students will be unable to choose or may choose a safe topic that does not motivate them to learn anything new. Strategies such as brainstorming help students see the diversity of choices and how choices relate to one another. Remember that brainstorming in

Project Checklist

Use this checklist to plan and organize your group project. Check off each task as you go. Don't skip any steps.

Planning

- [ ] We have agreed on a topic.
- [ ] We have brainstormed some questions about the topic.
- [ ] We have predicted some possible answers to our questions.
- [ ] We have made a graphic organizer to organize topics and subtopics.
- [ ] We have given ourselves subtopics or tasks.
- [ ] We know what information we need.
- [ ] We have consulted the teacher about possible sources of information.
- [ ] Our teacher has seen and approved our work so far.
- [ ] We are ready to start our research.

Research

- [ ] We have planned research time in the school library or for interviews.
- [ ] We have helped one another by sharing resources.
- [ ] We have made point-form notes on the information we collected.
- [ ] We have discussed how our information answers our original questions.
- [ ] We have revised our graphic organizer and added notes under each subtopic.
- [ ] We have asked the teacher for help when necessary.
- [ ] Our teacher has seen and approved our work so far.
- [ ] We are ready to start preparing our final product.

Report Writing

- [ ] We have used the graphic organizer to plan an outline of our project.
- [ ] We have agreed on how we want to present our information.
- [ ] We have helped one another revise our first draft.
- [ ] We have met __ times to review progress and make sure everyone is on track.
- [ ] We have asked the teacher for help when necessary.
- [ ] We have read through our report or rehearsed our presentation together.
- [ ] We are ready to share our finished project.

small groups is less stressful for second language learners. Ask individual students to report the ideas brainstormed by each group.

- *Show learners a variety of models* of acceptable to outstanding performance. Show them projects completed by another class, perhaps on a different topic, so that they can see what a finished project looks like. The model projects should represent a wide range of performance. In addition, show students several ways of presenting information, such as posters, videotapes, comic books, interviews and role plays, as well as traditional written reports. Discuss the criteria used in assessing the models and encourage students to talk about the differences between satisfactory and excellent.

- *Emphasize the importance of content and organization*, rather than the technology used to present the material. Remember that students do not have equal access to computers, laser printers, color printers, spiral binding machines, and software.

- *Send home a short description of the project* and its pedagogical purpose. Remember that not all parents read English. If parental involvement is expected, this expectation should be realistic and specific, taking into account the language of the home, the time available, and parents' experience with this kind of activity.

- *Encourage students to explore topics relevant to their own lives and experiences* so that they can obtain information from parents and community sources. Encourage interviews as a method of collecting data, as these can be conducted in any language. You might also suggest that part of — or all — the project be presented in two languages.

- *Organize group projects.* This provides support for second language learners and enables students to draw on one another's skills, talents, and interests. It also helps students develop important social skills.

- *Help students organize existing knowledge and figure out where research is needed* by developing pre-writing charts or outlines. A KWL chart can help them get started, for example, and a concept map can help them categorize or sequence ideas.

- *Provide — or help students find — resource material.* Students who are unfamiliar with resource centers may not know how to use the school library. They may need help not only to find books and other materials, but also to use CD-ROMs and Internet resources. Work with the school librarian to design a program introducing the library. You might also take students to the public library, help them join if they are not already members, and ask the librarian to orient the class to its facilities and services. Many students, especially those who do not have study space or a computer at home, may find the public library an ideal place to do homework.

- *Teach students how to paraphrase.* Students who are accustomed to memorizing facts or passages from books need to practice selecting and paraphrasing information. If you want students to demonstrate their comprehension of material by paraphrasing it, show them how to do this. Write a sentence or a short paragraph from a reference book on the chalkboard and show the students several ways of wording it differently. Then provide several sentences for them to practice on. Remember that second language learners are bound to make mistakes in grammar and word choice. It is important not to penalize second language learners for these errors; if you do, they will revert to memorizing or copying from the text as a way of avoiding these errors.

- *Provide essential resources*, such as reference material, presentation folders, various kinds of paper, colored markers and crayons, glue and scissors, concrete materials for models, magazine pictures, and other materials that may not be available to students at home. If you don't have computers in your classroom, book time for students in the school's computer lab.

- *Review the process and the skills involved* in projects every time you assign one. Remember that newcomers arrive at every grade level and at all times of the year. You may need to provide individual instruction to newcomers.

Integrating the Arts

Arts education enriches the lives of all students. Involvement in the arts also promotes second language acquisition and social integration. Visual art, drama, music, and the games and activities in the physical education program provide opportunities for students in the early stages of second language acquisition to participate, to understand what is going on, and to demonstrate their special skills and talents. Students who are just beginning to learn English can respond emotionally to a piece of music or a painting and enjoy the physical exhilaration of an active game without knowing the rules in English.

Moreover, these fields are universal and highly valued in all cultures. Integrating arts activities into other subjects captures students' interest, supports comprehension, and encourages classroom interaction among English language learners and their English-speaking peers.

Visual Art

Many second language learners are able to communicate in pictures what they are not yet able to communicate in English. Creating artworks also provides meaningful opportunities for language learning as students talk to peers or the teacher about their drawing, painting, or sculpture. Students may be able to show their understanding of concepts, such as the water cycle, by producing an illustrated chart, and with the help of a peer tutor, may be able to add English labels or captions and learn key words.

Artwork can also help students express intensely personal feelings. Students who cannot describe in English their favorite place or person, for example, or their dreams for the future may be able to depict these ideas through art. Sometimes, students' artwork reflects traumatic or stressful experiences in their lives. The works of refugee children may

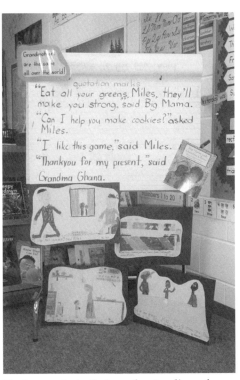

To demonstrate their understanding of concepts, students can draw pictures like these.

Reader's Theatre: These students are reading aloud a familiar story in role.

Drama and Role Play across the Curriculum

Mathematics

- Write a word problem and mime it for other students to put into words and solve.

Science

- Role play an important event in the life of a famous scientist.
- Role play a talk show in which the host interviews a scientist and a critic (e.g., the scientist might speak about the importance of nuclear energy, while a critic speaks about its dangers).
- Role play the right and wrong ways of conducting an experiment or using a piece of equipment.

History and Social Studies

- Role play a 19th-century scene in which a family is deciding whether to emigrate from their home country.
- Role play an interview with a 19th-century African American who fled to Canada to escape slavery in the United States.
- Make a newsreel about an aspect of World War II (e.g., women in the war).
- Make a television commercial to attract new residents or businesses to a city or region studied in class.

English and Language Arts

- Develop and act out scenes illustrating proverbs or idioms.
- Act out a scene from a story.
- Act out a scene from a story, changing a major element (e.g., setting or main character).
- Role play an alternative ending to the story, or a scene that might have taken place but was not included in the story.
- Write and rehearse an original play involving the same central theme or conflict depicted in a story.

show scenes of soldiers, tanks, airplanes, and bombs. Sharing difficult and painful experiences through visual expression can be therapeutic — but students should never be pushed to do so.

Some students are talented artists, and their talent does not depend on knowledge of English. As an alternative or supplement to written work, encourage students to produce storyboards, posters, comic strips, or models, as well as illustrated stories and reports. You might also organize author-and-illustrator partnerships, which enable students to work together to create classroom publishing projects, such as children's storybooks.

When working on group projects, beginning learners of English may be able to make a significant contribution with artwork. Instead of buying commercially produced charts and posters, you might involve these students in creating posters that illustrate, for example, specific activities in the gym or the safety rules in the science lab, the family studies kitchen or sewing room, or the industrial arts area. You can help students add captions by providing word lists. Students might also create logos for their groups or for the classroom.

Keep a file of pictures, including photographs, reproductions of classical and modern paintings, and photographs of sculptures, to illustrate events, concepts, and historical periods. Include art from many parts of the world in various cultural styles. Talk about the picture, pointing to objects and people, describing what is seen, and comparing composition, materials, and techniques.

Students who have recently arrived from other countries may have had few opportunities to use computers. Introduce the graphic arts capabilities of the computer, as well as word processing. Clip art collections, scanners, and digital photographs allow even unskilled artists to illustrate their work.

Drama and Role Play

Participating in drama provides opportunities for students to practice or rehearse language that they may use later in real-life situations. Even beginning language learners can learn a few simple lines. Repeating phrases and actions in rehearsal provides plenty of opportunity for students to figure out what the other participants are saying — and they are as capable as English speakers of participating in the nonverbal aspects of the performance.

It is also a good idea to incorporate dramatic techniques into your own instructional style. Think of teaching as a performance art: use gestures, mime, and facial expressions to illustrate words and concepts, and use your voice as a tool, modifying intonation, pace, and volume as an actor does to emphasize ideas and feelings.

Music

Students of all ages enjoy popular and traditional music of many kinds. Many English language learners know the words of popular songs in their new language long before they know what they mean. Choose songs that complement the themes being explored in class and play them for students. If you are studying rain forests, for example, you might play Bruce Cockburn's song, "If a Tree Falls."

Many traditional songs relate to themes and events in history. Songs that tell a story can be used to encourage students to write stories of their own, and orchestral pieces, such as Edvard Grieg's "Hall of the Mountain King," can inspire creative writing, especially poetry.

To help students develop their ear for English, provide them with a copy of the words to read as they listen to a song. You can also create a listening cloze activity by omitting a word from every line or by omitting words of a specific type, such as past-tense verbs.

Encourage students to bring in songs that relate to topics studied in class. If students bring songs in languages other than English, encourage them to provide translations so that everyone understands the lyrics. Establish some criteria for selecting music, however, as some of the songs that young people listen to include violent, sexist, or sexually explicit lyrics that have no place in a classroom.

Information that is set to music is easier to remember. Very young children memorize the alphabet this way. Familiar tunes can help students memorize number facts, spelling rules, the table of elements, names and events, and other factual information. If you provide the tune, some of the students may be able to make up a song to go with it.

Many people enjoy working to music, and some teachers play background music in the classroom to provide a relaxed environment as students work independently or in groups. This is an opportunity to introduce students to classical and traditional instrumental music from many cultures and periods. Students may enjoy taking turns helping you select the music, and they could also write a few sentences about the composers, performers, or instruments for display in the classroom.

Some students may have musical training or talent, and this is an area in which they can display skills without using English. Encourage these students to join music clubs, choirs, and orchestras. Most choir leaders welcome new recruits, though shy newcomers may need a student guide to escort them to the first session and introduce them to the teacher organizing the activity. Participating in these activities provides a wonderful opportunity for newcomers to make friends and learn English in a low-stress environment.

Joining the school orchestra helps language learners feel part of the school community — and is an opportunity to practice listening to and speaking English.

Alternative Resource Material

When planning lessons or units, it is important to assess the suitability of the existing resource material and, if necessary, to select or create alternative material for students who are learning the language of instruction. Many teachers develop their own materials for students in the early stages of second language acquisition.

Criteria for Choosing Learning Resources

Although the following criteria refer to content-area reading material, they can also be applied, with slight modifications, to the selection of non-print resources, such as videos, computer software, guided tours on field trips, and so on.

- *Format*: Does the format aid reading comprehension? Aids to comprehension include chapter overviews and graphic organizers, a clear hierarchy of headings and subheadings, chapter summaries, pre-reading questions, highlighting of key ideas or terms, and glossaries. A reader-friendly format also includes legible print;

Rewriting Text for Maximum Readability

- Focus on the key ideas or concepts that students must understand to progress in the subject.
- Address the reader directly (e.g., "In this chapter, you will find out about …").
- Keep technical and specialized terms to a minimum, and introduce this vocabulary after explaining the concept in simple terms. Refer to known concepts, provide examples, and use analogies to explain new ideas.
- Highlight or underline key words — but not too many!
- Avoid complex verb structures and keep sentences relatively short. Don't oversimplify, however. Eliminating all subordination may actually make the material harder to understand, because important transition signals, such as "because" and "although," may disappear. Include these expressions and explain them during the guided reading process.
- Build on previously learned vocabulary and concepts to ensure a steady progression of linguistic complexity from the beginning of the year or semester to the end. The material must match the students' gains in language acquisition and concept development and challenge them to learn even more.
- Provide titles, headings, and subheadings that students can use to understand how the text is organized. To focus readers' attention on the main ideas, provide an introduction or pre-reading question(s) as an advance organizer at the beginning of each chapter or section.
- Provide plenty of visual support. The textbooks rejected as too difficult may contain useful drawings, charts, and photographs that can be used as reference material.
- Devise pre-reading and follow-up activities to direct students' reading and focus on specific features of the text.

visual material, such as drawings, photographs, maps, charts and graphs; and plenty of white space.

- *Paragraph structure*: Do most paragraphs open with a topic sentence? Paragraphs are easier to read if they start with the main idea, and if there are enough examples to make it clear. Connectives help readers understand logical relationships, such as cause and effect, sequence, generalization and example, and comparison.

- *Sentence structure*: Does the text use straightforward syntax? Passive verbs, abstract nouns, difficult pronoun references, and complex subordination and embedding make text more difficult to read.

- *Vocabulary*: Is the vocabulary within the reach of most of the students? The more Latin-based words in a text, the more difficult it is to read. Other challenges include technical terms, words that have specific connotations in a given subject area, and figurative language. Do not automatically reject a text that includes challenging vocabulary, however; consider whether contextual support is provided for new or difficult words. Students can draw meaning from a text even if they don't fully comprehend every word. Focus on the essential content words for the topic: does the text explain them and provide examples that support comprehension?

- *Overall readability*: Can the students understand the text? Various readability formulae are available, but they tend to analyze text only in terms of word and sentence length and are usually based on the performance of native speakers of English. They do not take into account the reader's background knowledge or interest in a topic. It might be more helpful to assess a text's readability for a specific group of students by using the cloze procedure.

  You will find instructions for creating a cloze passage on page 28.

When You Can't Find Appropriate Materials

- *Supplement difficult text* with non-text material: pictures, postcards, slides, and videos. Slides and old-fashioned filmstrips are excellent, because you can pace the presentation to meet students' needs. Captioned filmstrips and printed scripts for slide or tape presentations are especially helpful because students can use the print version as a study aid. If the script of a slide-tape kit or video is too difficult, create your own simplified voice-over and give it to students, on audiotape or in print or both, so they can review it at home.

- *Supplement English-language material* with material in the students' own languages. Parents and other community members may be able to help you find materials.

- *Create alternative resources* by rewriting a text, or portions of it, for certain groups of students. This need not entail watering down the curriculum, as nearly any text can be linguistically simplified without abandoning key concepts.

To Learn More ...

Books and Articles

Brinton, D.M., and P. Master, eds. *New Ways in Content-Based Instruction*. Alexandria, Va.: Teachers of English to Speakers of Other Languages, 1997.

Activities for integrating language and content instruction in a variety of second language programs. Includes contributions from teachers working with learners in elementary, middle, and high schools.

Carasquillo, A., Kuker, S.B., and Abrams, R. (2004) *Beyond the Beginnings: Literacy Interventions for Upper Elementary English Language Learners*. Clevedon: UK: Multilingual Matters.

The authors offer detailed suggestions on literacy practices for English language learners who have acquired conversational fluency and basic literacy skills in English but need support in developing academic language skills.

Cary, S. *Working with Second Language Learners: Answers to Teachers' Top Ten Questions*. Portsmouth, N.H.: Heinemann, 2000.

Practical advice for new ESL teachers.

Chamot, A., and M. O'Malley. *The CALLA Handbook: Implementing the Cognitive Academic Language Learning Approach*. Reading, Mass.: Addison-Wesley, 1994.

Guide to integrating language and content instruction in grade-level and subject classrooms.

Echevarria, J., M.E. Vogt, and D. Short. *Making Content Comprehensible for English Language Learners: The SIOP Model*. Boston, Mass.: Allyn & Bacon, 2000.

Education Department of Western Australia. *First Steps*. Melbourne, Australia: Addison Wesley, 1994.

Distributed with training workshops through Pearson Education. Series provides strategies for assessing and teaching reading, writing, oral language, and spelling. Though suggested approaches and strategies are suitable for English language learners, developmental continua are inappropriate for beginners.

ESL history, policies, and practices in Australia, Canada, and England.

Freeman, Y.S., and D.E. Freeman. *Whole Language for Second Language Learners*. Portsmouth, N.H.: Heinemann, 1991.

Emphasizes the importance of involving students in meaningful language activities. Many practical examples.

Fried-Booth, D. *Project Work*. Second edition. Oxford: Oxford University Press, 2002.

A collection of 34 projects contributed by teachers around the world.

Genesee, F., ed. *Educating Second-Language Children: The Whole Child, the Whole Curriculum, the Whole Community*. New York: Cambridge University Press, 1994. Includes chapters on classroom practice for language, grade-level, and subject teachers.

Gibbons, P. *Scaffolding Language, Scaffolding Learning*. Portsmouth, N.H.: Heinemann, 2002.

Practical strategies for integrating English language learners into mainstream elementary classrooms.

Hill, J., Little, C., and Sims, J. (2004). *Integrating English Language Learners in the Science Classroom*. Markham, Ontario: Fitzhenry and Whiteside.

This book offers practical strategies for adapting the grade 6-8 science curriculum for English language learners. The approaches are equally useful at the secondary level.

Hyerle, D. *Visual Tools for Constructing Knowledge*. Alexandria, Va.: Association for Supervision and Curriculum Development, 1996.

How to use brainstorming, task-specific organizers, and thinking-process maps to help students use various kinds of thinking.

Includes chapters on language learning and literacy development for all teachers.

Introduces the concept of knowledge frameworks and key visuals to reduce language demands in various subject areas.

Kendall, J., and O. Khuon. *Making Sense: Small-Group Comprehension Lessons for English Language Learners*. Portland, Maine; Stenhouse Publishers, 2005.

In-depth treatment of reading strategy instruction, with lesson plans and samples of classroom dialogue and students' written responses. Each section of this book provides lessons for students at five different stages of proficiency in English. Although the examples focus on the elementary and middle school grades, the approach is adaptable for students in secondary school as well.

Lewis, M., and D. Wray. *Writing across the Curriculum: Frames to Support Learning*. Reading, U.K.: Reading and Language Information Centre, University of Reading, 1998.

Lewis, M., and D. Wray. *Writing Frames: Scaffolding Children's Writing in a Range of Genres*. Reading, U.K.: Reading and Language Information Centre, University of Reading, 1996.

Many examples of effective instructional strategies for teaching vocabulary, as well as learning strategies that students can use to acquire new words.

McWilliam, N. *What's in a Word? Vocabulary Development in Multilingual Classrooms*. Stoke-on-Trent, U.K.: Trentham Books, 1998.

Metropolitan Toronto School Board. *Building Literacy in the Classroom*. Toronto, Ont.: Metropolitan Toronto School Board (now Toronto District Board of Education), 1997.

Mohan, B. *Language and Content*. Reading, Mass.: Addison-Wesley, 1986.

Mohan, B., C. Lueng, and C. Davison, eds. *English as a Second Language in the Mainstream*. Harlow, U.K.: Longman, 2001.

More ideas for using writing frames to support students' writing in a variety of subject areas.

More than 100 activities for teaching vocabulary and developing vocabulary acquisition strategies.

Morgan, J., and M. Rinvolucri. *Vocabulary*. Oxford, U.K.: Oxford University Press, 1986.

Nagy, W.E. *Teaching Vocabulary to Improve Reading Comprehension*. Urbana, Ill.: National Council of Teachers of English, 1988.

Nation, I.S.P. *Teaching and Learning Vocabulary*. Boston, Mass.: Heinle & Heinle, 1990.

Nation, P., ed. *New Ways in Teaching Vocabulary*. Alexandria, Va.: Teachers of English to Speakers of Other Languages, 1994.

Ontario Ministry of Education. . *Think Literacy: Cross-Curicular Approaches, Grades 7-12.* . Toronto, Ont.: Queen's Printer for Ontario, 2003.

Examples of a variety of effective cross-curricular strategies that improve students' reading and writing skills.

Outlines the characteristics of six non-fiction writing genres and provides blank templates to scaffold children's writing.

Peregoy, S., and O. Boyle. *Reading, Writing, and Learning in ESL*. 2nd ed. Reading, Mass.: Addison-Wesley, 2000.

Classroom scenarios illustrate how to integrate English language learners into their new linguistic environment.

Peyton, J., ed. *Students and Teachers Writing Together: Perspectives on Journal Writing*. Alexandria, Va.: Teachers of English to Speakers of Other Languages, 1990.

Collection of articles on journal writing in various curriculum areas.

Peyton, J.K., and L. Reed. *Dialogue Journal Writing with Nonnative English Speakers: A Handbook for Teachers*. Alexandria, Va.: Teachers of English to Speakers of Other Languages, 1990.

Advice on using dialogue journals with students who are learning English.

Phillips, D., Burwood, S., and Dunford, H. *Projects with Young Learners*. Oxford: Oxford University Press, 1999.

Instructions for 50 activities that promote language learning for students aged 5-14.

Practical approaches to expanding children's vocabulary in all areas of the curriculum.

Real classroom situations and vignettes illustrate effective content-based instruction.

Research-based approach to teaching vocabulary.

Richard-Amato, P., and M. Snow, eds. *The Multicultural Classroom: Readings for Content-Area Teachers*. White Plains, N.Y.: Longman, 1992.

Collection of readings on theoretical background of and practical strategies for the integrated classroom.

Rigg, P., and V.D. Allen, eds. *When They Don't All Speak English: Integrating the ESL Student into the Regular Classroom*. Urbana, Ill.: National Council of Teachers of English, 1989.

Articles on topics such as program design, creating an effective language learning environment, language variation, language experience, and language through content.

Series of videos demonstrating exemplary literacy practices, including guided reading and writing. For information, contact <curriculumdocs@tdsb.on.ca>.

Short (42-page) booklet provides an overview of effective approaches to vocabulary instruction, with an emphasis on pre-reading activities.

Spangenberg-Urbschat, K., and R. Pritchard, eds. *Kids Come in all Languages: Reading Instruction for ESL Students*. Newark, Del.: International Reading Association, 1994.

Wisconsin Department of Public Instruction. *Strategic Learning in the Content Areas*. Madison, Wis.: Wisconsin Department of Public Instruction, 1991.

Analyzes the linguistic and conceptual demands of several subject areas and provides examples of graphic organizers and other strategies.

Websites and Online Resources

Crandall, J., A. Jaramillo, and L. Olsen. *Using Cognitive Strategies to Develop English Language and Literacy*. Washington, D.C.: Center for Applied Linguistics, ERIC Clearing House on Languages and Linguistics, 2002. <www.cal.org/ericcll>.

Digest article on how to develop students' English language and literacy skills and make academic content challenging, interesting, and accessible.

Hodge, T. Project Work. *English Language Teaching Journal*. 47, 3, July 1993.

This article develops a rationale for project work with English language learners, and provides guidelines for developing successful projects in the classroom. <www.oup.com/elt/teachersclub/articles/project_work?cc=ca>.

The Graphic Organizer. <www.graphic.org>.

Software for creating various kinds of graphic organizers, as well as free online resources.

Puzzlemaker. <www.puzzlemaker.com>.

Online software for creating word puzzles.

13 Planning Instruction and Assessment

As language learners acquire English, the instructional program must be planned to meet their needs at each stage of the developmental process. This chapter begins with an overview of the developmental process, with examples of what learners are able to do in English at each stage. This is followed by a framework for planning instruction, which includes a brief summary of key concepts from the work of Jim Cummins. These concepts are important in planning instruction and assessment for English language learners.

The next section suggests alternative ways of assessing and evaluating the language proficiency and academic achievement of English language learners and concludes with recommendations for the inclusion of language learners in large-scale assessments, such as mandated literacy tests. The chapter ends with a lesson-planning checklist that can be used to ensure that you are meeting the needs of the English language learners in your classroom.

Stages of Development in English as a Second Language

When learning English, language learners pass through a developmental sequence or continuum like the following:

0 Years	5+ years
No knowledge	Proficient to the level
of English	of a native speaker of the same age or grade

Most language learners immersed in an English-language environment take at least five years to achieve the same level of cognitive academic language proficiency as their native English-speaking age peers. They are most likely to achieve this goal by continuing to develop in their first language and with strong instructional support for development of the second. Many factors, such as interrupted education, emotional trauma, loss of self-esteem, attrition of the first language, and lack of high-quality bilingual or ESL support, may impede their progress, however.

To enable educators to track the progress of English language learners, the language acquisition continuum is often divided into stages.

Some ESL textbooks and graded readers, for example, are designed for three levels: beginner, intermediate, and advanced. Others are designed for four levels: beginner, low intermediate, intermediate, and advanced. And still others are based on a five-level system: beginner, high beginner, low intermediate, intermediate, and advanced. Furthermore, educational jurisdictions also describe the development of English language learners in varying ways.

Despite these differences, the basic features are the same. Each stage is described in terms of the oral and written language students are able to understand and produce. Two examples of developmental continua — one for oral language development and one for writing — are shown on the following pages. Similar versions are used in school districts throughout North America, as well as in the United Kingdom and Australia. Though the number of identified stages, the way each stage is analyzed in categories, and the indicators and examples vary, the central concept of a **developmental continuum** is consistent across jurisdictions.

When examining these or any other English-as-a-second-language continua, remember that students do not progress through the stages in a year-per-stage fashion. Most students progress very quickly through the early stages but continue to need considerable support to keep moving toward full proficiency in English.

It is also common for learners to display different levels of development in various aspects of language performance. The reading and writing skills of students who have studied English in their home country, for example, may outstrip their ability to speak the language because opportunities to use English in real interactions with fluent speakers were limited. Other students may arrive with limited literacy in their home language. They often have well-developed oral communication skills that enable them to acquire oral English much more quickly than reading and writing skills. As a result, it is important to assess newcomers' oral language proficiency, as well as their reading and writing skills, when they first arrive (see Chapter 1).

A Framework for Planning Instruction

Although the number of identified stages in the process of acquiring English varies from jurisdiction to jurisdiction, as does the way each stage is analyzed and described, the concept of a developmental continuum is consistent and provides a rationale for offering **differentiated instruction** to English language learners. Students at various stages perform differently in English and therefore require different levels of support to benefit from instruction. How can teachers determine how much support a student needs, and what kind? To answer that question we need first to return to a key concept about language acquisition that was briefly discussed in Chapters 8 and 12: the BICS and CALP distinction proposed by Jim Cummins. Then we can build on this concept to create an instructional framework.

BICS and CALP Revisited

Learning English is more than just a cumulative process. At different stages of the process, learners acquire different kinds of language.

Developmental Stages in Oral Communication in English

This six-stage model of oral language development is based on the work of educators in Fairfax, Virginia, and has been adapted for use in many school districts across Canada and the United States. According to this model, students at Stage 1 are new to English and have little or no ability to communicate in English, while students at Stage 6 have nearly caught up to their English-speaking age peers in oral communication. The indicators for each stage are general enough to be used for students at all grade levels. Some adapted versions identify students by age group and use indicators that reflect the context of learning and the demands of the curriculum for students in specific grades.

	1	2	3	4	5	6
Speaking	Begins to name concrete objects.	Begins to communicate personal and survival needs.	Begins to initiate conversation; retells a story or experience; asks and responds to simple questions.	Initiates and sustains a conversation with descriptors and details; exhibits self-confidence in social situations; begins to communicate in classroom settings.	Speaks in social and classroom settings with sustained and connected discourse; any errors do not interfere with meaning.	Communicates competently in social and classroom settings.
Fluency	Repeats words and phrases.	Speaks in single-word utterances and short patterns.	Speaks hesitantly because of rephrasing and searching for words.	Speaks with occasional hesitation.	Speaks with near-native fluency; any hesitations do not interfere with communication.	Speaks fluently.
Structure			Uses predominantly present tense verbs; demonstrates errors of omission (leaves words out, word endings off).	Uses some complex sentences; applies rules of grammar but lacks control of irregular forms (e.g., *runned, mans, not never, more higher*).	Uses a variety of structures with occasional grammatical errors.	Masters a variety of grammatical structures.
Vocabulary		Uses functional vocabulary.	Uses limited vocabulary.	Uses adequate vocabulary; some word-usage irregularities.	Uses varied vocabulary.	Uses extensive vocabulary but may lag behind native-speaking peers.
Listening	Understands little or no English.	Understands words and phrases, requires repetition.	Understands simple sentences in sustained conversation; requires repetition.	Understands classroom discussions with repetition, rephrasing, and clarification.	Understands most spoken language, including classroom discussion.	Understands classroom discussion without difficulty.

Common European Framework of Reference for Languages: self-assessment grid

The Common European Framework of Reference for Languages, developed by the Council of Europe, provides a model for a six-stage continuum of language proficiency. Designed for use with any language, this framework is widely used in Europe to standardize language curricula and assessment tools in many different languages. Many countries are also developing versions of a European Language Portfolio, which includes a self-assessment component based on this grid. The Framework and the associated materials provide invaluable guidance for the development of language assessment tools for use with students who are learning English as a second or additional language in English-language schools.

		A1	A2	B1
U N D E R S T A N D I N G	Listening	I can recognise familiar words and very basic phrases concerning myself, my family and immediate concrete surroundings when people speak slowly and clearly.	I can understand phrases and the highest frequency vocabulary related to areas of most immediate personal relevance (e.g. very basic personal and family information, shopping, local area, employment). I can catch the main point in short, clear, simple messages and announcements.	I can understand the main points of clear standard speech on familiar matters regularly encountered in work, school, leisure, etc. I can understand the main point of many radio or TV programmes on current affairs or topics of personal or professional interest when the delivery is relatively slow and clear.
	Reading	I can understand familiar names, words and very simple sentences, for example on notices and posters or in catalogues.	I can read very short, simple texts. I can find specific, predictable information in simple everyday material such as advertisements, prospectuses, menus and timetables and I can understand short simple personal letters.	I can understand texts that consist mainly of high frequency everyday or job-related language. I can understand the description of events, feelings and wishes in personal letters.
S P E A K I N G	Spoken Interaction	I can interact in a simple way provided the other person is prepared to repeat or rephrase things at a slower rate of speech and help me formulate what I'm trying to say. I can ask and answer simple questions in areas of immediate need or on very familiar topics.	I can communicate in simple and routine tasks requiring a simple and direct exchange of information on familiar topics and activities. I can handle very short social exchanges, even though I can't usually understand enough to keep the conversation going myself.	I can deal with most situations likely to arise whilst travelling in an area where the language is spoken. I can enter unprepared into conversation on topics that are familiar, of personal interest or pertinent to everyday life (e.g. family, hobbies, work, travel and current events).
	Spoken Production	I can use simple phrases and sentences to describe where I live and people I know.	I can use a series of phrases and sentences to describe in simple terms my family and other people, living conditions, my educational background and my present or most recent job.	I can connect phrases in a simple way in order to describe experiences and events, my dreams, hopes and ambitions. I can briefly give reasons and explanations for opinions and plans. I can narrate a story or relate the plot of a book or film and describe my reactions.
W R I T I N G	Writing	I can write a short, simple postcard, for example sending holiday greetings. I can fill in forms with personal details, for example entering my name, nationality and address on a hotel registration form.	I can write short, simple notes and messages relating to matters in areas of immediate need. I can write a very simple personal letter, for example thanking someone for something.	I can write simple connected text on topics which are familiar or of personal interest. I can write personal letters describing experiences and impressions.

B2	C1	C2
I can understand extended speech and lectures and follow even complex lines of argument provided the topic is reasonably familiar. I can understand most TV news and current affairs programmes. I can understand the majority of films in standard dialect.	I can understand extended speech even when it is not clearly structured and when relationships are only implied and not signalled explicitly. I can understand television programmes and films without too much effort.	I have no difficulty in understanding any kind of spoken language, whether live or broadcast, even when delivered at fast native speed, provided I have some time to get familiar with the accent.
I can read articles and reports concerned with contemporary problems in which the writers adopt particular attitudes or viewpoints. I can understand contemporary literary prose.	I can understand long and complex factual and literary texts, appreciating distinctions of style. I can understand specialised articles and longer technical instructions, even when they do not relate to my field.	I can read with ease virtually all forms of the written language, including abstract, structurally or linguistically complex texts such as manuals, specialised articles and literary works.
I can interact with a degree of fluency and spontaneity that makes regular interaction with native speakers quite possible. I can take an active part in discussion in familiar contexts, accounting for and sustaining my views.	I can express myself fluently and spontaneously without much obvious searching for expressions. I can use language flexibly and effectively for social and professional purposes. I can formulate ideas and opinions with precision and relate my contribution skilfully to those of other speakers.	I can take part effortlessly in any conversation or discussion and have a good familiarity with idiomatic expressions and colloquialisms. I can express myself fluently and convey finer shades of meaning precisely. If I do have a problem I can backtrack and restructure around the difficulty so smoothly that other people are hardly aware of it.
I can present clear, detailed descriptions on a wide range of subjects related to my field of interest. I can explain a viewpoint on a topical issue giving the advantages and disadvantages of various options.	I can present clear, detailed descriptions of complex subjects integrating sub-themes, developing particular points and rounding off with an appropriate conclusion.	I can present a clear, smoothly flowing description or argument in a style appropriate to the context and with an effective logical structure which helps the recipient to notice and remember significant points.
I can write clear, detailed text on a wide range of subjects related to my interests. I can write an essay or report, passing on information or giving reasons in support of or against a particular point of view. I can write letters highlighting the personal significance of events and experiences.	I can express myself in clear, well-structured text, expressing points of view at some length. I can write about complex subjects in a letter, an essay or a report, underlining what I consider to be the salient issues. I can select style appropriate to the reader in mind.	I can write clear, smoothly flowing text in an appropriate style. I can write complex letters, reports or articles which present a case with an effective logical structure which helps the recipient to notice and remember significant points. I can write summaries and reviews of professional or literary works.

According to Jim Cummins, whose work provides a foundation for understanding the needs of students who are learning English at and for school, most learners acquire basic interpersonal communication skills within about two years of immersion in the school environment. This means that they can use English confidently and competently in most day-to-day activities, and depending on their age, they may also have developed an accent that is indistinguishable from that of their English-speaking peers. They sound fluent and understand much of what is going on in their immediate language environment.

At this point, ESL instruction is often discontinued, especially for students in the elementary grades. Because these students appear to function well in the classroom, many teachers do not perceive them to be English language learners and may not provide continuing support for language acquisition. According to Cummins, however, these learners' fluency is misleading. They may have developed basic interpersonal communication skills, but they need at least five years of instruction to acquire the cognitive academic language proficiency necessary to use English for academic purposes.

Without continuing language instruction and support, English language learners may take much longer than five years to achieve CALP, and many never will. This may affect their long-term prospects. Researchers in Calgary, for example, have found that the overwhelming majority of adolescents who arrive as beginners do not complete high school.

The Cummins Model

Jim Cummins suggests a model for planning instruction and assessment for English language learners. The model consists of four quadrants created by the intersection of two continua, as shown in the chart in the margin.

The **context embedded-context reduced** continuum indicates the degree of contextual support or scaffolding that is provided. At the context-embedded end of the continuum, the language is embedded in a meaningful and familiar context and supported by face-to-face

Implications for Classroom and Subject Teachers

1. Despite the oral fluency and day-to-day proficiency demonstrated by many English language learners within a year or two, most need support and instruction for at least five years.
2. English language learners need more support than an ESL teacher alone can provide. Many English language learners receive direct support from an ESL teacher for the first year or two, the period when they are developing basic interpersonal communication skills.
3. Many students are "promoted" from the ESL program at just the time when they really need intensive support for accelerated development in CALP.
4. Classroom and subject teachers must provide support for English language learners — and continue to do so long after the time when learners appear to be fluent in using the language for non-academic purposes.

The Cummins Model

Cognitively Undemanding

Context Embedded   A   C   Context Reduced

B   D

Cognitively Demanding

Source: Jim Cummins

interaction, visual cues, hands-on experiences, simplified language, and other comprehension aids. At the opposite end of this continuum, the meaning is carried in the language alone.

The **cognitively undemanding-cognitively demanding** continuum represents the demands that are placed on the learner's thinking processes. At the cognitively-undemanding end of the continuum, the language is simple and the task is cognitively undemanding (e.g., understanding and providing factual information on a familiar topic). At the opposite end of this continuum, the language is complex and the learning tasks require students to learn new and challenging content and to use a variety of thinking processes to handle a larger volume of information (e.g., comparing, contrasting, and evaluating diverse sources or points of view).

Using the Cummins Framework to Plan Instruction

The Cummins model is the basis of the instructional framework represented in the margin. Figure 1 shows the instructional environment required to enable English language learners at various stages of development in English to catch up to the CALP of their English-speaking peers as quickly as possible.

For beginners, instruction must be designed in Quadrant A, with maximum contextual support for, or scaffolding of, tasks that are engaging but not academically challenging. Instruction focuses on developing basic interpersonal communication skills (BICS).

Before students have completely acquired BICS, instruction should begin moving into Quadrant B. Students continue to receive maximum support for comprehension and language production, but the tasks become more academically challenging, so that students begin to develop cognitive academic language proficiency at the same time as they continue to develop BICS.

Quadrant C activities are neither cognitively demanding nor embedded in a meaningful context. Activities like these are unlikely to enhance deep conceptual understanding or promote the development of CALP. English language learners should spend relatively little time engaged in Quadrant C activities. For this reason the white arrow shows a progression that moves from Quadrant B to Quadrant D, bypassing Quadrant C.

In Quadrant D, students continue to work on academically challenging tasks. Gradually, over a period of several years, less scaffolding is required, until by the end of this stage, students have caught up to the CALP of their English-speaking age peers.

Figure 2 shows a rough estimate of the time it takes students to progress through the quadrants toward CALP — as long as they continue to receive support through Quadrant D. Students who arrive with limited previous schooling, students whose first language does not continue to develop at least until they are able to express concepts adequately in English, and students who do not receive adequate support may take much longer. These students are at greater risk of school failure and early dropout.

The chart on the following pages is a planning guide that provides an overview of the kind of instruction required in each quadrant. It is important to continue providing support through Quadrant D, even though most students may be fully integrated into mainstream classrooms by this stage — and often much earlier. Mainstream classroom or

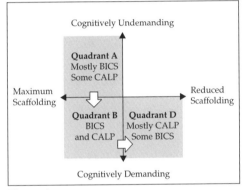

Figure 1

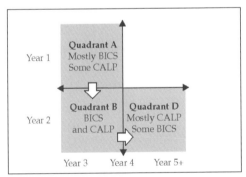

Figure 2

Teaching in the Quadrants

Cognitively Undemanding Tasks

Quadrant A — Beginner

— Students in the beginning stage of acquiring a second language start developing basic interpersonal communication skills through low-risk activities that are based on content related to their own lives and immediate needs. The following instructional strategies are essential for beginners (see Chapters 10 and 11):

— comprehensible instruction
— supportive feedback
— strategic use of students' languages
— cooperative learning
— functional language
— visual support
— copying and labeling
— physical activity
— choral work, songs, and role plays
— experience-based learning
— a rich print environment
— language experience stories
— stories on tape
— games and puzzles

Quadrant B — Intermediate

Students beyond the beginning stage can begin working on some tasks in Quadrant B even before they have completely acquired BICS. Many students who have studied English in their home country are ready to work on tasks in Quadrant B.

As learning tasks become increasingly demanding, the following strategies and approaches continue to be important (see Chapter 10):

— comprehensible instruction
— supportive feedback
— strategic use of students' languages
— cooperative learning

In addition, the following strategies (see Chapter 12) provide scaffolding that enables learners to begin developing CALP as well as learning strategies that will help them become effective language learners:

— key visuals
— guided reading
— integrated vocabulary instruction
— integrated grammar instruction
— writing scaffolds

— the writing process
— journal keeping
— guided projects
— arts generation
— alternative resource material

Cognitively Demanding Tasks

MAXIMUM SCAFFOLDING

Cognitively Undemanding Tasks

Quadrant C

Though tasks in Quadrant C are cognitively undemanding, they may be incomprehensible to many English language learners. Cognitively undemanding activities are unlikely to advance academic learning, and incomprehensible or decontextualized activities are unlikely to promote language acquisition.

Examples of Quadrant C activities include the "busy work" that is sometimes given to beginners. These activities may include coloring pictures that have little relevance to the academic program and copying notes and other material that students do not understand. Even activities that are intended to be academically challenging, such as research projects, can become Quadrant C tasks if students do not receive the necessary guidance and support.

English language learners and native speakers alike should spend relatively little time on Quadrant C activities!

Quadrant D — Advanced

Students who have achieved high-intermediate proficiency in English after several years of intensive ESL instruction in their home country or their new country are ready to be challenged by Quadrant D tasks, which are both cognitively and linguistically demanding. By this time, students' development in their first language may have fallen behind, and they must rely completely on English for further learning. Students in Quadrant D are able to work with the grade-level curriculum expectations and resources, as long as they continue to receive support, especially when culturally demanding material, such as a history textbook that assumes that students possess certain background knowledge, is involved. Students who need Quadrant B instruction in culturally difficult and linguistically demanding subjects, such as social studies, may benefit from Quadrant D instruction in other subjects, such as mathematics or music, in which they may have considerable background.

The following strategies continue to be important:

— comprehensible instruction
— supportive feedback
— cooperative learning
— key visuals
— guided reading

— integrated vocabulary instruction
— the writing process
— journals
— guided projects

The amount of scaffolding is gradually reduced over a period of two or more years, but should never be discontinued completely. *All* students benefit from scaffolded instruction.

Cognitively Demanding Tasks

REDUCED SCAFFOLDING

subject teachers, as well as ESL teachers, must integrate language instruction and support into all aspects of the curriculum, gradually reducing the amount of support as learners begin to match the performance of their English-speaking age peers.

It is important to note that the estimate of five years for students to progress through Quadrant D is an average. Students who arrive with strong academic background may progress more quickly, while students who arrive with limited schooling will need more support for a longer period of time.

Alternative Approaches to Assessment and Evaluation

In addition to adapting instruction and providing additional support for language acquisition, teachers may need to adapt learning outcomes or expectations to give English language learners a reasonable chance of success. Alternative assessment strategies and evaluation procedures may also be required to enable English language learners to demonstrate their learning. In addition, teachers and school administrators need guidelines for including English language learners in large-scale assessments such as state or provincial literacy tests.

Alternative Learning Outcomes

Curriculum outcomes and assessment tasks and criteria established with native speakers of English may be inappropriate for students who are learning the language, especially in the early stages. As a result, it may be necessary for learners to work toward alternative outcomes or expectations in some areas of the curriculum, at least until they have reached the stage at which the grade-level expectations are appropriate for them.

To be meaningful, learning outcomes must be attainable. Requiring an English language learner to perform at a level beyond his or her current stage of development in English is futile and leads to frustration and disappointment for teacher and student alike. In some programs, therefore, the learning expectations for English language learners may be different from the expectations for students who begin with a greater knowledge of English and greater background knowledge and experience. Modifications may include revising the expectations, reducing the number of expectations, and substituting alternative expectations that are more appropriate. As students move along the continuum of second language development — and through the instructional quadrants shown earlier in this chapter — they will require fewer modifications. The examples on the following pages show how curriculum outcomes or expectations can be modified to benefit English language learners at various stages of development.

In designing instruction for English language learners, opportunity to learn should be a guiding principle. It is neither equitable nor ethical to assess students' performance on the basis of knowledge or skills that they have had no opportunity to learn. Because language learners have not had the same opportunity as their peers to learn English, they cannot be expected to perform at the same level in English as their peers or to communicate their learning as effectively — until they have had enough time and enough appropriate instruction to catch up to their peers in English language proficiency. In addition, students who began their schooling in other countries have not had opportunities to develop the same knowledge and skills as their peers who have been immersed in the curriculum throughout their years of schooling.

Adaptations to instruction and assessment like those shown on the charts on the following pages enable English language learners to participate successfully in the classroom program as they gradually catch up to their age peers in using English for academic study.

Alternative Assessment Strategies

Language is the most important tool for learning — and for demonstrating learning. Most assessment tasks measure reading and writing skills in English as much as, or even more than, academic knowledge and skills.

Students who are learning the language of instruction are often unable to express what they have learned in the second language. They may have difficulty understanding what they are being asked to do, and they usually need more time than their English-speaking peers because they often think and work in two languages. When they write in En- glish, their teachers sometimes focus as much on students' incomplete knowledge of English as on the information they are trying to communicate. To compensate for these problems and to enable students to demonstrate learning in ways that do not depend completely on their proficiency in English, alternative assessment strategies are required.

The assessment strategies and adaptations suggested in the following sections enable students at higher levels of English proficiency to meet most program expectations without modification. Students in the earlier stages of English language development need the same kind of support to demonstrate their learning, but may work toward revised or alternative learning expectations or outcomes like those shown in the previous charts.

REDUCE THE LANGUAGE REQUIREMENT

You can give second language learners the best chance of demonstrating their learning by removing or lowering the language barrier.

- Encourage students who are literate in their first language to produce assignments and write tests in their first language if they are not yet able to do this in English, or to substitute words from their first language for English words they don't yet know. A bilingual teacher or trained tutor can help you assess their performance.
- Give an oral test. You could do this in two languages if you involve bilingual peers or members of staff.
- Invite beginning learners of English to show what they know by using concrete or visual representations. You might, for example, ask them to "point to ..., give me ..., show me ..., draw ..., or find the page (picture, the opposite, the word that says) ...." Students might also match captions to visual representations of information.
- Rather than expecting students to write complete sentences, paragraphs, or essays, provide support for their written responses. For example, create a cloze passage for students to complete. Charts and other visual organizers, such as the one shown in the margin,

The Fur Trade		
Complete this chart to show the benefits and negative consequences of the fur trade for the Aboriginal people of North America and for European traders and settlers.		
	Aboriginal People	European Traders and Settlers
Benefits (good things)		
Negative Consequences (bad things)		

Modifying Curriculum Expectations: Grade 5

Curriculum Area: Science and Technology (Ontario) — Earth and Space Systems: Weather
Expectation: Describe the water cycle in terms of evaporation, condensation, and precipitation.

	English Proficiency	Quadrant and Level of Support	Attainable Expectation
Year 1	**Beginner** Learners at this stage are beginning to develop BICS. Students acquire the first 2,000 words, including some basic subject terms.	Quadrant A Students need intensive ESL support. Instruction should provide maximum support for language comprehension and production.	The grade level expectation is not attainable for students who are just beginning to learn basic English vocabulary and sentence patterns. Beginning students can work toward an alternative expectation related to the topic (e.g., demonstrate understanding of basic weather vocabulary and sentence patterns by matching illustrations and captions, such as, "It's raining").
Year 2 **Year 3** **Year 4**	**Intermediate** Learners finish developing BICS as they begin to develop CALP. Students begin using English confidently in a wide variety of contexts. Vocabulary expands by 2,000+ words a year, including low frequency words.	Quadrant B Students continue to need intensive support for second language acquisition. Instruction should provide maximum scaffolding to enable students to meet higher cognitive demands. Students require intensive instruction in learning strategies such as inferring word meaning from context. Students need considerable support to demonstrate their learning in English (e.g., a student might select appropriate words from a list provided by the teacher).	Expectations can be more demanding as long as students continue to receive strong support. Students can work toward revised expectations with reduced language demands and strong scaffolding (e.g., demonstrate understanding of the water cycle by labeling a diagram using appropriate vocabulary, such as *evaporation, condensation,* and *precipitation,* and completing a series of sentences using vocabulary related to cause and effect and sequence to explain the cycle).
Year 5+	**Advanced** (level 5 in a 5-level continuum) By the end of this stage, students have caught up to their age peers in all aspects of language performance.	Quadrant D Students continue to need support for second language acquisition. Continued scaffolding enables students to meet high cognitive demands.	With this level of support, the grade-level curriculum expectation is attainable.

Modifying Curriculum Expectations: Grade 9

Curriculum Area: Canadian Geography (Ontario) — Understanding and Managing Change

Expectation: Use communication skills (e.g., letter writing, debating, consensus building) effectively to promote environmental awareness

	English Proficiency	Quadrant and Level of Support	Attainable Expectation
Year 1 / **Year 2**	**Beginner** Learners at this stage are beginning to develop BICS. Students acquire the first 2,000 words, including some basic subject terms.	Quadrant A Students need intensive ESL support. Instruction should provide maximum support for language comprehension and production.	The grade level expectation is not attainable for students who are just beginning to learn basic vocabulary and sentence patterns in English. Beginning level students can work toward alternative expectations related to the subject area and based on important background knowledge for newcomers (e.g., demonstrate understanding by matching captions with pictures showing various sources of environmental pollution; labeling a map to identify regions and resources).
Year 3 / **Year 4**	**Intermediate** Learners finish developing BICS at the same time as they begin to develop CALP. Students begin using English confidently in a wide variety of contexts. Vocabulary expands by 2,000+ words a year, including low-frequency words.	Quadrant B Students continue to need intensive support for second language acquisition. Instruction should provide continued scaffolding for language comprehension and production, as well as a strong focus on learning strategies such as inferring word meaning from context.	Expectations can be more demanding as long as students continue to receive strong support. Students can work toward revised expectations with reduced language demands and strong scaffolding (e.g., choosing from a bank of words and phrases provided by the teacher in order to complete a graphic organizer showing environmental problems, causes and solutions; creating a poster integrating graphics and text to promote environmental awareness).
Year 5+	**Advanced** Learners continue to need support to develop CALP. By the end of this stage, students have caught up to their English-speaking peers in all aspects of language performance.	Quadrant D Students continue to need support for second language acquisition. Continued scaffolding (e.g., modeled writing and writing templates) enables students to meet high cognitive demands.	With this level of support, the grade-level curriculum expectation is attainable for students.

help students display knowledge and demonstrate thinking without being required to produce large amounts of language.

- Phrase questions as simply as possible, avoiding vague terms such as *identify*, *describe*, and *discuss*. Traditional assignments such as "Discuss the economic effects of the war" provide insufficient guidance.
- Focus on content rather than language to assess what a student knows. Learn to read past the student's language mistakes and look for meaning.
- Assess performance by assigning tasks that involve several different aptitudes or talents. These may include demonstrations, oral and written reports, graphic displays, videotapes and audiotapes, concrete models, and bilingual submissions.
- Avoid multiple-choice and true-or-false questions that involve a lot of reading, as well as trick questions that depend on comprehending fine differences in meaning. Instead, use comprehsion tasks, such as matching captions to visual representations of information, filling in a partly completed organizer, or choosing from a list of words to complete a cloze passage. Scaffold longer written responses by providing sentence-completion tasks or a framework or model answer.

PROVIDE OPPORTUNITIES FOR PRACTICE AND FEEDBACK

Practice provides risk-free opportunities for students to rehearse using new knowledge and skills and receive constructive feedback. Practice should not "count" for marks.

- If students are required to complete two major projects in a year or course, they might receive extensive feedback on the first but receive marks only for the second attempt.
- Before a test, give students an opportunity to work in groups on practice tests, encouraging them to use their first language, if necessary, to clarify problem areas. The next day, administer an individual test that is the same or nearly the same as the practice test. In mathematics, for example, the problems may be the same, though the number values may be changed.
- Invite groups to design questions or problems for a test, following models provided in the textbook or on previous tests and assignments. This helps students understand the intent of various kinds of assessment and distinguish between main ideas or key concepts and examples or details. If each group prepares a question that focuses on a particular concept or skill, the questions can be distributed to all the groups to work on for practice. Some of the questions might be adapted and included on the final test or assignment.

CREATE PERFORMANCE-BASED ASSESSMENT TASKS

Performance-based assessment improves students' achievement by involving them in tasks that simulate real-life applications of the relevant skills and knowledge.

- Show learners a variety of models of acceptable to outstanding performance. These may include sample stories, lab reports, research projects, essays, and other written products; samples of practical work and artistic creations; videotapes of oral presentations and dramatic or musical performances; and demonstrations of practical skills and of physical performance in sports and fitness activities.

- Distribute the assessment criteria or rubric you plan to use and discuss the qualities that make the difference between various levels of achievement on a specific aspect of performance. Invite students to rank the models and encourage them to identify what distinguishes an excellent performance from an adequate one.

- Provide constructive feedback on the process as well as the product of students' learning. Base the assessment on your observations, as well as on students' notes or learning logs.

- Invite students to assess their own work and submit their best performance for summative assessment. If they complete three projects in a year, for example, they might choose one to submit for final evaluation.

USE PORTFOLIO ASSESSMENT

A portfolio is a file or box that contains evidence of a student's progress, such as samples of work, response-journal or learning-log entries, records of conferences, the teacher's observation comments or checklists, self- and peer-assessment forms and checklists, as well as more traditional test and quiz papers. Students add to the portfolio throughout the year or course, and teacher and students use the portfolio to assess performance and progress over time. This provides a more complete view of the learner's performance and capabilities than can be obtained from tests alone.

- Portfolios may include material in the first language. This acknowledges the student's proficiency and encourages continued development in that language.

- Over the course of a year or semester, samples in the portfolio usually show significant growth in English, in ways that may be more obvious than through traditional tests and exams.

- Portfolios provide opportunities for parents to be involved in selecting and assessing their children's work.

- Portfolios provide opportunities for students to assess and select the work they wish to include. If they write in their journals every week, for example, invite them to choose one or two pieces to polish for inclusion in the portfolio and submit for formal evaluation.

PROVIDE THINKING TIME

Second language learners often need to process ideas in two languages, especially when the task is complex or involves higher-level thinking. This means that they require more time than students who are thinking in one language only. When you administer written tests and examinations, give language learners more time to complete the test, or ask them to answer fewer questions in the time allotted.

PROVIDE DICTIONARIES

During tests and examinations, English language learners may need to consult dictionaries to understand questions and instructions. Beginning learners of English need bilingual dictionaries to help them translate even basic words in questions and instructions, and students beyond the beginning stage should be taught how to use learner dictionaries. A set of dictionaries can be kept in the school for use in tests and exams. If this is perceived as providing an unfair advantage to English language learners, why not provide dictionaries to all students?

Knowing how and when to use a dictionary is an essential academic skill. This book could not have been written without occasional recourse to a dictionary!

Standard Language and Literacy Assessment

Some school districts have adopted standard assessment procedures and criteria for classroom-based assessment of language and literacy skills. Though it is important to track the development of every student's English language skills, most commonly used procedures were developed with native speakers in mind and are unsuitable for assessing the development of students who are learning the language. To assess the reading and writing skills of these learners fairly, assessment tasks and procedures must be adapted.

READING ASSESSMENT

Many literacy assessment procedures use oral reading, running records, and miscue analysis to assess students' reading fluency, strategies, and comprehension. Other procedures rely on written answers to assess comprehension. Though these can be useful tools for assessing the reading of proficient English speakers, it may be inappropriate to use them with language learners until their language proficiency is close to that of their English-speaking peers. A number of factors, including the length of time spent in an English-language school environment, their previous educational experience, and their previous instruction in English may influence the effectiveness of these tools when used with language learners.

- Reading aloud for assessment purposes is inappropriate for English language learners, especially in the early stages. They cannot be expected to read fluently in a language they are still learning. They are often so anxious about pronouncing the words correctly that comprehension suffers.
- Miscue analysis and running records carried out in the second language may not provide reliable information about reading comprehension and reading strategies. Pronunciation errors and missed word endings, for example, may say more about a student's incomplete knowledge of the English sound system or English grammar than about reading comprehension or reading strategies.
- Assessment tools based on knowledge of print are usually based on knowledge of *English* print. Many students arrive in schools in their new country with knowledge of print in their own language. Chinese print, for example, is conceptual rather than phonetic and may be printed vertically rather than from right to left. As a result, Chinese students may have difficulty recognizing some features, of English print.
- Reading passages followed by multiple-choice questions, true-or-false questions, and questions requiring written answers should be used with caution, as newcomers may be unfamiliar with the format of multiple-choice and true-or-false questions. In addition, these questions often rely on comprehending and interpreting subtle nuances of language, which is unfair to English language learners. Questions that require extended written answers depend on writing skills at least as much as reading skills. Because the receptive competence of most language learners is greater than

their productive competence, their reading comprehension may be significantly higher than their writing proficiency. As a result, questions requiring extended written answers should be avoided when reading is the focus of the assessment.

- Comparing the reading performance of English language learners with that of native speakers (e.g., by assigning a grade-level score from a test designed for native speakers) is not helpful. The comparisons may reveal how far English language learners are lagging behind their English-speaking age peers but do not help teachers or administrators judge their performance as English language learners.

The preceding factors mean that reading assessment methods must be adapted for use with English language learners. This can be achieved in the following ways.

- Choose material that a student can reasonably be expected to be able to read, that reflect linguistic and cultural diversity, and that deal with topics and situations that are likely to be familiar to the students. This may include asking older students to read picture books normally used at the primary level, as long as the illustrations and situations depicted are not too obviously designed for young children. You might also use materials, such as graded ESL readers, that have been specifically designed for second language learners at various stages of development.
- Do not expect beginning learners of English to do more than recognize basic words and respond to very short, simple, illustrated reading passages. With more advanced students, you might use informal reading inventories, such as the Burns-Roe Informal Reading Inventory — but be cautious about interpreting grade-level scores.
- Ask the student to read the passage silently, then respond to oral questions about it. When students answer these questions, encourage them to refer to the passage to locate details, find specific words, and so on. For students in the early stages of learning English, the questions should be based on factual information, such as main idea, detail, and sequence. For students who are developing cognitive academic language proficiency, questions designed to elicit responses based on inference and opinion are also appropriate.
- If you are using graded material such as an informal reading inventory or leveled books, be very cautious about interpreting and sharing information about grade-level scores. An English language learner in Grade 6 who reads at the Grade 1 level in English, for example may read at or above grade level in his own language. Similarly, a 17-year-old who reads at a Grade 5 level in English may read at a level equivalent to Grade 12 in her first language.

    Rather than judging performance on the basis of grade-level scores normed using English-speaking students, use assessment criteria that compare learners of English with one another. The descriptors from the ESL standards or developmental continua in use in your jurisdiction can help determine whether a student is making appropriate progress. In some situations, however, informing a student and his or her parents about performance in relation to grade-level norms and expectations may be appropriate. This may occur, for example, when students — or parents — need a reality

Ask the students to read silently, and then respond to oral questions. Encourage students to refer back to the text if they need to check details or find a specific word.

check to help them plan a suitable educational path toward achieving these norms and expectations.

- You can collect information about reading in the first language by talking about reading and asking about the student's experiences and preferences. You may find that a beginning reader in English can already read signs and simple stories in Chinese or has learned to read the Qu'ran in Arabic. And an adolescent whose English reading comprehension is at the early elementary level may have read Tolstoy or Dostoevsky in Russian, may like to read about astronomy in Spanish, or may enjoy the poetry of Rabindranath Tagore in Bengali. With beginning learners of English, conduct interviews and conferences with the assistance of a bilingual volunteer or peer.

WRITING ASSESSMENT

Be cautious about using criteria developed for students who are native speakers of English and using exemplars gathered from those students. These may reveal how far the English language learners lag behind their English-speaking age peers — but English language learners cannot be expected to perform like native speakers. It may be more informative and more equitable to use assessment criteria that compare learners of English with one another, using the descriptors from the ESL standards or developmental continua in use in your jurisdiction.

Remember that the language skills of many students may be more highly developed in a language other than English. For this reason, it is important to gather information about each student's first language development. If you keep a portfolio that tracks each student's growth in reading and writing, for example, collect writing samples in each student's home language as well as in English. You may not be able to read the samples, but you can learn a lot by observing how the student tackles writing in the first language.

The following samples of a student's writing in her first and second languages demonstrate how informative gathering first-language writing samples can be. This student, a recent arrival from Iran, was unable — or unwilling — to do more than write out the alphabet in English. Her handwriting appears undeveloped for her age, and she mixes upper- and lower-case letters. On the basis of this sample, the only comment that can be made about this student's proficiency in English is that she cannot write to communicate in English, and her handwriting appears undeveloped for a child her age.

A B C D E f J H i j K L M N O P Q r s t u y w x y z.

The same student wrote in Farsi on the same day, producing the sample on the following page. This provides a much clearer picture of the student's literacy development. Even to teachers who do not read Farsi, it is obvious that her handwriting is well developed, that she is able to write continuous prose, and that she edits her own work, as shown by the insertion in the last line. According to the Farsi-speaking educator who assessed the sample, the student's literacy skills in Farsi are well developed and above the expected age or grade level. Though much can be learned by simply looking at a first-language sample, having it assessed by a trained volunteer or a trained student from the senior grades reveals a lot more.

بوج انٹ، سلام میں رنمت کو بس؛
بلای اولتن دحدم معی تخنتہ بیساں لعماس کریم سن جندے رچتی مو اونا سم حمسن مس بوژ.
کب بفر متر اشد بوند. من رین معتنوی علم جتہ علمماس لتنتی می کرم. عنو منا ادی چتا ھم اماس ژن
شل سجد جندفہ میطا ن بو کجبد لی مسد بتی مشت. عدولای دی رمی عملات کرم. اول آرم لنز
معی قم لہ کہ دوبرعی خانی لامعد کنت انجام مادستعمس. واریسا نا ھم کگگ دسس را رہ درباد
آن لو حمم یر مزلی وملا درتلغا ھند. لعلا صرعی خانریین بلای من سمعدی نداشت: بہ سادہ،
سیہ بزلک. سادیلگ؛ من عم ؟ اما صیعسلہ ؟ کہمسند. خن لجم عملس بلہ. ومد للماد حوی صی وصم
ترم بہ دشیح کرم. منو بینہ معی آدم سے علم کوکگی رمی سلا فلابنند و بمعی کرلش می خواھد دس مرد
کہت می لہ لسی لکسد لسی للکہ لد من نھلہ.

When you assign a writing task for assessment, be sure that the content is relevant to learners of English. Few newcomers can, for example, be expected to write about topics such as winter, specific regions or places such as the Rocky Mountains, or sports and leisure activities such as canoeing, hockey, and skiing.

It is also important to assign the task in a familiar form. If the piece is to be in the form of an exposition, for example, use modeled and guided writing, provide writing scaffolds and show the students models of performance at various levels. Even if English-speaking students are expected to be familiar with specific forms of writing at specific grade levels, the same assumption cannot be made about English language learners. In fact, many students educated in other countries have learned completely different conventions about how writing should be organized and how the writer should relate to the reader (see Chapter 7).

Evaluation and Reporting

At the end of each unit, term, and semester or year, teachers must review information gathered through various forms of assessment and evaluate or make summative statements about each student's achievement to that point. The following suggestions are designed to make this process as fair and accurate as possible for students who are learning the language of instruction.

- Use progress over time as the major criterion for evaluating the performance of English language learners: is the student on the right trajectory toward native-speaker competence?
- Give greater consideration to more recent evidence of achievement. The performance of English language learners often improves significantly as their English proficiency develops, and

more recent work provides a more accurate indication of their current performance.

- Continue using performance tasks and evaluation criteria that are appropriate to each student's stage of development in English. You may need to use alternative criteria or adjust the weighting of the various components of a task on which you base evaluations. If an evaluation rubric includes a communication or language component, for example, the criteria and weighting of this component should be adjusted for English language learners.

- Examine the grades that the English language learners have earned to ensure that your grading practices reflect the principles of equity and opportunity to learn. English language learners have not had the same opportunities as their English-speaking age peers to learn English and curriculum content. As a result, learning expectations or outcomes, instructional methods and resources, and the assessment tasks and criteria may need to be different from those that apply to English-speaking students.

  If the instructional program has been adapted appropriately, and if the assessment and evaluation tasks and criteria are based on the adapted program, English language learners should show the same kind of grade distribution as the class or grade as a whole. For example, if 25 percent of the English-speaking students achieve a mark of 85 percent or higher, then 25 percent of the English language learners, including beginners, should also receive marks of 85 percent or higher — when their performance is evaluated on the basis of a program that has been aligned with their stages of development in English. This is not a form of grade inflation, as the program, rather than the marks, has been adjusted. When the distribution of marks among English language learners is similar to that of English-speaking students, it suggests that the language learners are receiving appropriate support and are working to achieve attainable expectations. If English language learners are scoring lower marks as a group, however, the program may not have been appropriately adapted to meet their needs or the criteria used to judge their performance may not have been based on what can reasonably be expected of students at their present stage of development in English.

  Teachers should be as concerned about higher-than-average performance among some groups of learners as they are about lower-than-average performance among others. Students from some countries may have experienced a curriculum that places them ahead of their age peers in some curriculum areas, such as mathematics, science, and music, for example. In this case, the subject expectations may need to be adjusted to provide more of a challenge, as it would be when English-speaking students perform at a level higher than most of their peers. At the same time, familiar subject matter can be used as a vehicle for English language development.

- If you are using alternative curriculum outcomes or expectations for an English language learner, it is important to explain this to parents and students. In some jurisdictions, this can be indicated on computer-generated report cards. In others, it may be necessary to add a handwritten comment to this effect. Printed material in the languages of the community can help explain program adaptations and many other aspects of the program that may be mystifying to parents.

It is also a good idea to meet parents — with interpreters on hand to facilitate discussion. Emphasize that English language learners need fewer and fewer adaptations as they become more proficient in English, until eventually they will be working to achieve the same expectations as everyone else. Explain, however, that this process can take five or more years, depending on the student's starting point in English on arrival.

To report on students' development in English, use checklists and observation forms based on the ESL standards or developmental continua used in your jurisdiction. Use these regularly, tracking a certain number of students each week, noting the date(s) that each indicator is observed. Keep the form on file until the end of the course or assessment period. The form can be used in student-teacher conferences and parent-teacher interviews, and a copy can be attached to the report card to provide additional information about a student's development. The form can also be translated into the languages of the school so that it is meaningful to parents.

Large-Scale Assessment

The purpose of large-scale testing is to assess the effectiveness of an entire education system, such as that in a school district, province, or state. In general, English language learners should be included in these assessments, which can reveal the following information:

- how their performance as a group compares with that of their English-speaking age peers
- how their individual performance compares with that of other English language learners

The following conditions must be met in order for their participation to be meaningful, however.

- Students who are in the early stages of English language development should not be included. These students are not able to participate meaningfully in an assessment designed for English-speaking students.
- Students who have enough knowledge of English to understand what they are being asked to do and to participate meaningfully should be included as long as they have been in the jurisdiction long enough for their results to reflect the schooling they have received. In general, this means that they should have been in the jurisdiction no less than a full school year.
- Data, such as home language, country of birth, date of arrival in the country or years of attendance at an English-language school, and number of hours of ESL instruction provided by a specialist ESL teacher, should be gathered for each student participating in the assessment.
- The test results of English language learners who have been in the country fewer than 10 years should be disaggregated from those of the general population and reported separately. Within the group, the information should be further separated according to various criteria, such as length of time in the country, years of full-time schooling, country of origin, and number of hours of ESL instruction. This information can be helpful in determining how long it takes students to catch up to their age peers, how much and what kind of ESL or bilingual support is the most effective, whether

Planning Effective Lessons for English Language Learners	
Preparation	**Notes**
☐ Select, revise, or substitute subject outcomes (expectations), using the learners' stage(s) of development as a guide.	
☐ Add language outcomes appropriate to the stage(s) of development.	
☐ Plan assessment tasks that are appropriate to the students' stage(s) of development and that will enable you to assess achievement of the outcomes, using clear and attainable criteria for assessment or evaluation.	
☐ Select, adapt, or create resource materials to aid learning (e.g., alternative texts, visual material, multimedia resources, and manipulatives).	
☐ Plan meaningful activities that provide opportunities for reading, writing, vocabulary development, and oral language use.	
Instructional Strategies	**Notes**
Building Background	
☐ Link concepts to students' backgrounds and experiences.	
☐ Develop the necessary background knowledge, using stories, pictures, videos, and other media.	
☐ Introduce and illustrate key vocabulary (e.g., introduce, provide an example, write, repeat, add to word wall or vocabulary notebooks).	
Comprehensible Instruction	
☐ Adjust speech to students' proficiency level.	
☐ Explain academic tasks clearly (e.g., provide written and oral instructions, broken down into steps for complex tasks).	
☐ Use a variety of techniques to make language and concepts clear (e.g., modeling, visuals, manipulatives, hands-on activities, demonstrations, and gestures).	
☐ Ask clear questions and give enough wait time for students to respond.	
☐ Encourage students to work in pairs or groups, including the first language when appropriate, to clarify key concepts and vocabulary.	

Adapted from Short, D., and Echevarria, J. (1999). *The Sheltered Instruction Observation Protocol: A Tool for Teacher-Researcher*

Planning Effective Lessons for English Language Learners	
Instructional Strategies (cont'd)	**Notes**
Scaffolding ☐ Use scaffolding techniques to support reading and writing (e.g., key visuals, guided reading, patterned language use, modeled writing, writing scaffolds, the writing process, guided projects). ☐ Provide content-based activities for language development and practice (e.g., word puzzles, cloze passages, and sentence completion activities). ☐ Provide models of performance for all complex tasks.	
Interaction ☐ Use group activities to promote focused talk about the content of the lesson (e.g., think-pair-share, interviews, group brainstorming, and jigsaw). ☐ Focus on the process and language of group work (e.g., how to disagree, how to take turns, how to include everyone, and how to keep each other on task). ☐ Provide discussion questions and prompts that encourage various thinking and learning strategies (e.g., problem solving, predicting, summarizing, categorizing, analyzing, identifying patterns or inconsistencies, evaluating, and making inferences). ☐ Provide supportive feedback for students' language output. ☐ Provide prompts to elicit expanded or more elaborate responses. ☐ Monitor and encourage the participation of all students.	
Review and Assessment	**Notes**
☐ Assess students' comprehension and learning throughout the lesson (e.g., spot checking and group rehearsal and response). ☐ At the end of the lesson, provide a comprehensive review of key vocabulary and concepts. ☐ Involve students in self-assessment (e.g., "Today I learned …" or "In our group today, we ….").	

Collaboration and Professional Development. Center for Research on Education, Diversity & Excellence.

some groups of students need more — or different kinds of — support (e.g., students from refugee-producing countries may have had limited educational opportunities before emigrating). This information is essential to help school jurisdictions become accountable for the education of English language learners and to ensure that all groups are adequately served.

Putting It All Together: Planning Effective Lessons for English Language Learners

The chart on the previous pages is a lesson-planning checklist that incorporates many of the instructional approaches and strategies recommended in this book. This checklist can be used to plan stimulating, supportive, and academically challenging lessons for English language learners. All the items do not necessarily apply to all lessons, however. Use only those that are relevant to the lesson you are planning.

If you are teaching an ESL class, be sure that the content that forms the basis of language instruction is relevant and interesting and provides students with opportunities to develop the language and thinking skills required in the mainstream classroom. If you are teaching a mainstream class, you may find that lesson components included for the benefit of English language learners also benefit their English-speaking peers.

The chart includes space for you to write notes, list the textbooks and other resources you plan to use, list the key vocabulary you plan to teach, indicate group activities that students will be involved in, list handouts or prompts you will provide for scaffolded language production, list the prompts and questions you will use for guided reading, and so on. If you are involved in a peer-coaching or mentoring partnership with another teacher, you could visit each other's classrooms with this checklist as a guide for observation.

To Learn More …

Books and Articles

Agor, B., ed. *Integrating the ESL Standards into Classroom Practice: Grades 9–12.* Alexandria, Va.: Teachers of English to Speakers of Other Languages, 2001.

Model units showing how to use D. Short et al.'s *ESL Standards for Pre-K–12 Students* to guide instruction and assessment.

Baker, C., and N.H. Hornberger, eds. *An Introductory Reader to the Writings of Jim Cummins.* Clevedon, U.K.: Multilingual Matters, 2001.

Readings selected from three decades of Cummins' work include articles introducing the concept of BICS and CALP and the four-quadrant framework.

Brown, J.D., ed. *New Ways of Classroom Assessment.* Alexandria, Va.: Teachers of English to Speakers of Other Languages, 1998.

Alternative assessment activities for language teachers.

Burns, P., and B. Roe. *Burns/Roe Informal Reading Inventory.* 6th ed. Boston, Mass.: Houghton Mifflin, 2002.

Graded reading passages that are useful for assessing and tracking reading comprehension. With English language learners, the reading passages are best used for silent reading comprehension rather than reading aloud.

Cline, T., and N. Frederickson, eds. *Curriculum Related Assessment, Cummins and Bilingual Children.* Clevedon, U.K.: Multilingual Matters, 1996.

Articles showing how to apply Cummins' conceptual framework to curriculum-related assessment.

Council of Europe. *Common European Framework of Reference for Languages: Learning, Teaching, Assessment.* Cambridge: Cambridge University Press, 2001.

Valuable reference tool for the development of language assessment tools and criteria. Also available online at <www.coe.int/t/dg4/linguistic/CADRE_EN.asp>.

Cummins, J. *Language, Power and Pedagogy: Bilingual Children Caught in the Crossfire.* Clevedon, U.K.: Multilingual Matters, 2000.

Detailed and updated explanations of BICS, CALP, and the four-quadrant framework. Includes a discussion of bilingual education.

Farr, B. P., and E. Trumbull. *Assessment Alternatives for Diverse Classrooms.* Norwood, Mass.: Christopher-Gordon Publishers, 1996.

Provides a framework for equitable assessment in linguistically diverse schools and suggests alternative assessment strategies.

Genesee, F., and Upsur, J.A. *Classroom-based Evaluation in Second Language Education.* Cambridge: Cambridge University Press, 1996.

Advice on planning and implementing effective assessment and evaluation of second language learning in order to make instruction more effective.

Irujo, S., ed. *Integrating the ESL Standards into Classroom Practice: Grades 6–8.* Alexandria, Va.: Teachers of English to Speakers of Other Languages, 2001.

Model units show how to use D. Short et al.'s *ESL Standards for Pre-K–12 Students* to guide instruction and assessment.

O'Malley, J.M., and L.V. Pierce. *Authentic Assessment for English Language Learners: Practical Approaches for Teachers.* Reading, Mass.: Addison-Wesley (now Pearson Education), 1996.

Very helpful book showing how to develop and use various types of assessment for different purposes.

Roessingh, H., Kover, P., and Watt, D. Developing Cognitive Academic Language Proficiency: The Journey. *TESL Canada Journal*, 23, 1, 2005.

The study documented in this article has significant implications for policy development and program planning for English language learners, confirming that these students, including those who arrive

Samway, K., ed. *Integrating the ESL Standards into Classroom Practice: Grades 3–5.* Alexandria, Va.: Teachers of English to Speakers of Other Languages, 2001.

Short, D., et al. *ESL Standards for Pre-K–12 Students.* Alexandria, Va.: Teachers of English to Speakers of Other Languages, 1997.

Describes appropriate goals in second language acquisition, provides sample progress indicators, and uses classroom vignettes to illustrate instructional approaches that enable English language learners to reach the goals.

Smallwood, B., ed. *Integrating the ESL Standards into Classroom Practice: Grades Pre-K–2.* Alexandria, Va.: Teachers of English to Speakers of Other Languages, 2001.

Watt, D.L.E., and H. Roessingh. "Some You Win, Most You Lose: Tracking ESL Student Dropout in High School (1988–1993)." *Canadian Modern Language Review.* Vol. 26, no. 3: 1994.

Alberta study showing that the overwhelming majority of newcomers who arrived as beginning learners of English did not graduate from high school.

Watt, D.L.E., and H. Roessingh. "The Dynamics of ESL Drop-Out: Plus Ça Change…" *Canadian Modern Language Review.* Vol. 58, no. 2: 2001.

Examines high school completion rates among ESL learners and the effects of recent cuts in levels of ESL support.

Websites and Online Resources

Coltrane, B. "English Language Learners and High-Stakes Tests: An Overview of the Issues." Washington, D.C.: Center for Applied Linguistics, 2002. <www.cal.org/ericcll>.
This digest discusses how English language learners can be included equitably in high-stakes tests. Addresses adaptation of test procedures and accurate interpretation of test results.

Menken, K. "What Are the Critical Issues in Wide-Scale Assessment of English Language Learners?" (Issue Brief No. 6). Washington, D.C.: National Clearinghouse for Bilingual Education, 2000. <www.ncela.gwu.edu/pubs/issuebriefs>.
Discusses the inclusion of English language learners in large-scale assessments.

Short, D., and J. Echevarria. "The Sheltered Instruction Observation Protocol: A Tool for Teacher-Researcher Collaboration and Professional Development." Washington, D.C.; Center for Research on Education, Diversity and Excellence, 1999. <www.cal.org/crede/pubs/edpractice/EPR3.htm>.
Includes an observation tool and checklist for planning lessons for English language learners. Teacher's manual and video are also available.

Afterword: A Great Adventure

If you are a new ESL teacher or a classroom teacher just beginning to explore some of the options and dilemmas in multilingual education, you are embarking on a great adventure. Though this book may help you get started, your students will be your greatest source of new knowledge. Watch, listen, and learn from them. Your own linguistic and cultural knowledge will be immeasurably enriched through your work with students and families from linguistic and cultural backgrounds different from your own. At the same time, you will develop a stronger awareness and appreciation of your own linguistic and cultural identity. Through your contacts with students whose roots are in countries around the world, you will also enhance your global awareness and understanding of current world events.

I originally wrote this book in 2003, after many years spent working with both teachers and students in multilingual classrooms. This revised printing is an updated version that includes more recent references and resources to help teachers get started on an incredible adventure of linguistic and cultural discovery and self-discovery. Bon voyage!

Elizabeth Coelho
Toronto, August 2007

Glossary

active vocabulary

The words a person can understand and use independently

affective filter

Emotional factors that may inhibit learning.

alphabetic writing system

A writing system in which each symbol represents a phoneme of the language.

anti-racist education

Educational practices designed to reduce prejudice and discrimination, promote equitable educational outcomes among all ethnocultural groups, and enable learners to recognize and challenge instances of cultural bias and racial discrimination

assessment portfolio

A collection of a student's work showing progress over time.

audiolingual approach

A part-to-whole approach to language instruction. The emphasis is on listening and speaking as learners are presented with many examples of a particular grammatical structure, which they then practice to fix the pattern as an automatic response.

authentic communication

Use of language in real-life situations.

basic interpersonal communication skills (BICS)

The language necessary to achieve fluency in participating in day-to-day conversation.

biculturalism

The ability to function equally well in two different cultural environments.

bilingual

Able to function equally well in two languages.

bilingual dictionary

A translation dictionary (e.g., English–French) in which the learner can look up a word in the first language and find its equivalent in English, and vice versa.

bilingual education

A educational program that uses both English and a student's first language as the languages of instruction.

bound morpheme

A morpheme that cannot stand alone as an individual word, but can be used only in combination with other morphemes.

case

A grammatical form that, in English, changes to show the relationship of nouns and pronouns to other words.

cognitive academic language proficiency (CALP)

The language skills required to achieve academic success.

cognitive strategy instruction

Teaching students how to use certain learning strategies for specific purposes (e.g., creating a graphic organizer to express key ideas).

communication strategy

A way of compensating for incomplete knowledge of the language.

communicative approach

A whole-to-part approach to language instruction. Real communication is emphasized, and grammar is learned inductively from examples that occur naturally in the context.

communicative competence

The ability to communicate effectively in real situations.

communicative function

A specific purpose for using language (e.g., apologizing, taking a turn, or disagreeing).

comprehensible input

Language that is made comprehensible through the use of visual aids, familiar content, modified input, and so on.

connective

A word or phrase that links ideas.

contact assignment

An assignment that requires language learners to use English with native speakers outside the classroom.

content-based language instruction

A communicative approach to language instruction. It integrates language and content instruction so that students learn important curriculum-based knowledge and skills at the same time as they learn language.

consonant cluster

A group of two or more consonant sounds that occur together (e.g., /sks/ in *desks*).

content words

Words, such as nouns, verbs, and adverbs, that convey the meaning of a sentence.

contextual support

The presentation of language that is strongly linked to the context.

conversational strategy

A way of initiating, steering, and concluding a conversation.

cultural capital

Vocabulary and background knowledge that helps children learn.

culturally biased

Based on cultural knowledge that cannot be assumed to be common to all students.

derivational morpheme

A prefix or suffix that is added to a word to form a new word.

developmental continuum

A sequence of stages in the development of language or literacy.

developmental errors

Language errors that most learners make as part of the learning process.

dialect

A variety of a language marked by differences in accents, grammar, and vocabulary. A dialect may be related to a geographic region (e.g., Newfoundland English) or to characteristics, such as social class and education (e.g., standard English).

differentiated instruction

Choosing learning outcomes, instructional strategies, resources, and assessment tools and criteria that are appropriate for students with differing needs.

discourse competence

The ability to link ideas effectively, using appropriate linking words and phrases and organizing ideas into recognizable forms or genres of language.

dominant language

The language in which an individual is most proficient. This term may also refer to the language of the dominant community and its institutions, such as education, government, and the legal system.

embedding

The inclusion of a linguistic unit, such as a phrase or clause, in another linguistic unit.

English as a foreign language (EFL)

A subject taught in situations where English is not the language of the community, region, or country.

English as a second language (ESL)

A subject taught to speakers of other languages in a situation in which English is the main language of the community, region, or country.

ESL core program

An instructional program for English language learners in which the content of core subjects, such as language arts, social studies, mathematics, and science, is used as a vehicle for language instruction.

ESL integration program

An ESL program that includes English language learners in mainstream classrooms and adapts instruction to meet their needs.

ESL resource support program

An ESL program that provides language learning support to individuals or small groups of language learners for part of each school day.

fossilization

An interlanguage pattern that becomes permanent.

free morpheme

A morpheme that can stand alone as an individual word.

function word

Words, such as prepositions, articles, and conjunctions, that help connect content words into meaningful sentences.

gender

A way of grouping words into formal classes, using labels such as masculine, feminine, and neuter.

general academic vocabulary

Words that occur frequently in many areas of the curriculum (e.g., *indicate* occurs in many subject areas and is more academic than the common word *show*).

graded readers

Books that are graded by vocabulary level and sentence structure (e.g., a graded reader at the 1,000 -word level would include only the 1,000 most common words in English).

grammar

The language patterns that indicate relationships among words in sentences.

grammar-translation approach

A deductive approach to language instruction. It focuses on learning vocabulary and grammar patterns, with an emphasis on reading and writing.

guided reading

A teacher-directed, intensive approach to reading. The teacher helps students develop reading strategies by demonstrating effective strategies and focusing on specific aspects of the text.

heritage language program (international language program)

An instructional program intended to help learners maintain their first or heritage language.

high-frequency word

A word that is used frequently in many different contexts.

holistic approach (to assessment)

Considering the overall competence of the student rather than focusing only on discrete skills such as spelling, punctuation, or using correct verb forms.

ideographic writing system

A writing system that uses symbols or combinations of symbols to represent a word or concept rather than a sound.

inflectional morpheme

Usually a suffix that provides grammatical information about gender, number, person, case, degree, and verb form.

innatist

A theory of language learning. It suggests that children learn language because they have an innate predisposition that enables them to discover patterns on the basis of the language used in their environment.

instructional text

Textbooks and other text-based learning resources designed for use in an instructional setting.

instrumental motivation

A desire to learn the language to achieve a specific goal, such as becoming an engineer.

integrative motivation

A desire to learn a language to become fully competent in many situations and to become part of the mainstream society.

interactionist

A theory of learning that stresses the importance of interaction between the learners and an older or more proficient peer, adult, or family member.

interference

A language learner's transferring of features of the sound system of her or his first language to the new language.

interlanguage

Intermediate forms of language produced by learners.

intonation

The characteristic patterns of rise and fall in pitch.

key visuals

Content-specific graphic organizers, such as concept maps, T-charts, Venn diagrams, flow charts, and timelines.

language style (register)

Ways of using language that may vary according to purpose, situation, audience, and the social characteristics of the speaker.

learning strategy

A mental or cognitive activity that students use when learning (e.g., associating a word with a mental image).

logogram

A visual symbol representing a word or concept. Logograms may be understood in many languages.

low-frequency word

A word that occurs relatively infrequently.

meaningful output

The production of language that others can understand.

metacognition

The analysis and planning of one's own learning processes.

minimal pair

Two words that are identical except for one specific vowel or consonant sound (e.g. *bet* and *bed*).

modeled writing

Demonstrating the writing process by composing and thinking aloud in front of students.

modified input

Language that is simplified for young children and other language learners.

morpheme

The smallest contrastive unit of grammar.

morphology

The study of word structure.

multicultural education

Educational practices that acknowledge the contributions and perspectives of diverse ethnocultural groups.

needs assessment

An assessment carried out to assess a student's level of English proficiency and needs so that an instructional program can be designed to meet those needs

number

The grammatical distinction between singular and plural, or one and more than one.

overgeneralization

Applying a language pattern generally, without awareness of exceptions or variations.

part-to-whole instruction

An analytical approach to instruction. It focuses on the components of the language (e.g., grammar patterns) that will then be applied in communication.

person

A grammatical form that, in English, applies to pronouns and affects the form of verbs.

phoneme

The smallest unit of sound that can affect meaning in a language.

phonemic awareness

The ability to perceive sounds and subtle differences among sounds.

phonics

The teaching of specific sound-symbol correspondences so that children can sound out words.

phonological system

The sounds of a language and the patterns used to combine them into words and sentences.

phonological writing system

A writing system in which the written symbols represent the sounds of the language.

phonology

The study of the sound systems of a language.

pictograph

A pictorial symbol representing a concrete object. Pictographs were used in the earliest writing systems.

productive competence

The ability to produce language.

receptive (passive) vocabulary

The words a person can recognize or understand in print or when other speakers use them.

receptive competence

The ability to understand oral language and written text.

rhythm

The pacing of the stressed syllables in a sentence.

scaffolding

Providing temporary supports that enable learners to perform at a higher level than they would be able to achieve without support.

self-contained ESL program

A program in which learners of English are taught in a separate class or program, with little or no integration into mainstream classrooms.

sheltered instruction

An alternative term for content-based language instruction.

sight word

One of the most common words in a language (e.g., *the*).

sociolect

A variety of language related to a specific social class.

sociolinguistic competence

The ability to recognize and produce language that is appropriate in various social contexts and relationships.

standard English

The variety of English that is used in textbooks and by most educated English speakers, though they may speak another variety of English with members of their own family or community.

strategic competence

The ability to use various verbal and nonverbal strategies to participate effectively in a conversation.

stress

The degree of force with which a syllable is uttered.

structural competence

The ability to use the grammatical structures of a language.

subject-specific word

A word likely to occur only within a specific field of work or study.

subordination

The joining of a subordinate clause to a clause of higher value, often by using connectors.

syllabic writing system

A writing system in which each symbol represents a spoken syllable.

syntax

The study of word combinations or sentence structure.

tone language

A language that uses tone or pitch to distinguish between words that otherwise sound exactly the same.

Total Physical Response (TPR)

A meaning-based, whole-to-part approach to language instruction. It relies on physical cues and actions to teach new vocabulary and grammar structures.

whole-to-part instruction

A holistic approach to instruction. It focuses on meaning and activities designed to promote real communication. Instruction in "parts," such as grammar patterns, is provided as these features occur or are required to communicate.

word class

A grammatical category, often called a part of speech, that identifies how a word is used in a sentence (e.g., as a noun, verb, etc.).

word family

A set of related words (e.g., *grammar, grammatical, grammarian*).

zone of proximal development

A level slightly beyond the learner's current level of development, but within reach if appropriate support is provided.

Index

bilingualism, 18, 32, 42, 141, 168

biology curriculum, 239

Black English, 116. *See also* Caribbean languages; Jamaican Creole

book circles, 104. *See also* multicultural literature circles

books on tape. *See* audiotapes

bound morphemes, 99

brainstorming. *See* group brainstorming

Burns-Roe Informal Reading Inventory, 267

C

CALP. *See* cognitive academic language proficiency (CALP)

Cantonese. *See* Chinese

capitalization, 131

Carbo method, 207

Caribbean languages, 116, 118, 164. *See also* Black English

Caribbean students, 28

case (in grammar), 71–72

chants. *See* songs

Chinese, 58, 62, 76, 94, 100, 126, 128, 131, 132, 135, 266, 268

Chomsky, Noam, 143

choral work, 65, 201, 204, 224

classroom behavior, 22, 32, 187, 190, 195, 196–197. *See also* code of conduct

classroom displays, 33, 34, 37, 38, 39, 40–41, 42, 114, 190, 223, 241, 247

clauses, 84–85, 87

cloze passages
    as learning activities, 104, 207, 218, 227–228, 231, 232–234, 247
    assessment use, 27, 28, 248, 261, 264

code of conduct, 22, 32. *See also* classroom behavior

cognitive academic language proficiency (CALP), 152–153, 156, 217, 251, 252, 256–260, 262, 263, 267

cognitive strategy instruction, 163

Collier, Virginia, 153

comics, 103, 242, 246

Common European Framework, 254, 255

communication strategies, 118, 119

communicative approach, 178–179

communicative competence
    assessment of, 23

components of, 106–122
    defined, 106
    development of, teaching strategies for, 108, 110, 114, 117–118, 119, 120, 122, 147
    See also discourse competence; productive competence; receptive competence; sociolinguistic competence; strategic competence; structural competence

communicative functions, 179

community and school, 20, 21, 32, 33

composition. *See* writing

composition templates, 235–236, 240

comprehensible input, 147, 183–186

comprehensible instruction, 147, 183–186

computer speech, 64

computers, 133, 205, 208, 240, 241, 244, 245, 246, 270. *See also* computer speech; word processing programs

condensed syntax, 86

conditional sentences, 85–86

confidence, 18, 19, 91, 161, 162–163, 172, 186, 200, 204, 242, 256

connectives
    in discourse competence, 106, 107
    in instructional text, 133
    teaching the concept of, 94, 223, 225, 228, 234

conjunctions, 234

consonant clusters, 58, 61

contact assignment, 179

content words, 28, 60, 228

content-based instruction, 118, 171, 173, 179–180, 217–248

contextual support, 17, 148, 180, 257
    in learning resources, 248

contractions, 60–61, 185

conversational strategies, 118, 120–122, 196, 197

cooperative games. *See* games

cooperative learning, 190–191
    and development of social skills, 147, 160, 161, 183, 196–197
    management strategies for, 120, 122, 195–197
    teaching strategies for, 191–195
    See also cooperative projects; games; group activities; group brainstorming; group rehearsal; jigsaw groups; learning teams; think-pair-share; three-step interview

cooperative projects, 193–195

core curriculum, 171

first language
    as component of identity, 154
    assessment, 25, 26, 29, 31, 160, 268

first language acquisition
    in young children, 58, 68, 141, 148–149
    theories of, 141–142, 143–144, 145–146, 147–148

first language development
    in bilingual education, 167–169
    parent participation in, 22, 32, 154
    supporting, teaching strategies for, 17, 154–155, 189
    See also heritage language programs

first language use
    in assessment, 261
    in the writing process, 240
    supporting, teaching strategies for, 17, 183, 189–190

fluency. *See* language proficiency

forms of address, 109–111, 114

fossilization, 145, 151

fourth-grade slump, 157

free morphemes, 98–99

French
    as origin of English spelling, 129
    capitalization in, 131
    cultural norms in, 112
    English vocabulary derived from, 90
    gender, 69
    negative statements in, 80
    pronunciation, 53, 142
    stress patterns in, 59
    students, 16
    vocabulary, 91

French immersion, 179–180

French language instruction, 169, 174–175, 176

function words, 28, 60

functional language, 201–202

G

games, 208. *See also* puzzles

gender (in grammar), 69

general academic vocabulary, 95, 104, 224

Genesee, Fred, 181

genitive case. *See* case (in grammar)

genre
    of language, 108
    of writing, 133, 135–136
    See also non-fiction genre

geography curriculum, 109, 180, 240, 263

German, 69, 74, 81, 91, 131

gerunds, 81–82

grade-level scores, 267

graded readers
    levels of, 252
    assessment use, 27, 267
    creating recorded books with, 207
    vocabulary development with, 95, 103

graded reading, 27, 28, 103

grading practices. *See* evaluation

grammar
    acquisition of, 142, 148, 155–156, 253, 255
    defined, 68
    elements of, 69–86
    in other languages, 16, 116
    instruction, teaching strategies for, 86–88, 155–156, 175–176, 179, 180, 232–233
    learner errors with, 70, 71, 72, 73, 74, 75, 76, 77, 79, 80, 81, 82, 83, 84, 85, 86
    rules, 67–68

grammar-translation approach, 175–176

Greek, 130, 131

group activities
    assessment use, 185, 196–197, 264
    development of social skills in, 122, 147, 160, 161, 196–197, 244
    examples of, 46, 47, 178, 191–195, 204–205, 206–207, 218, 221, 224, 231
    management strategies for, 160, 185, 195–197
    See also cooperative projects; games; group brainstorming; group rehearsal; jigsaw groups; learning teams; think-pair-share; three-step interview

group brainstorming
    as cooperative learning task, 191, 196
    in guided projects, 242
    in guided reading, 221
    in multicultural literature circles, 46
    in vocabulary instruction, 227
    in the writing process, 240

group rehearsal, 192

guidance counselors, 20, 30

guided projects, 241–246

guided reading
    and instructional text, 108
    and vocabulary acquisition, 104
    as a learning strategy, 163, 274
    defined, 221
    introducing quality literature through, 103
    stages of, 221–224

guided writing, 108, 136, 269

modal verbs, 75, 77

modeled writing, 235, 240, 269

models (concrete), 210, 245, 264

modified input, 145

morphemes, 69, 98–100, 126. *See also* bound morphemes; derivational morphemes; free morphemes; inflectional morphemes

morphology, 69–74. *See also* case; degree; gender; number; person; verbs

motivation. *See* learner motivation

multicultural education, 43–45

multicultural literature circles, 45–47

multilingual classroom, 42–43, 190

multilingual resources, 33, 43, 210, 248

multiple-choice questions, 264, 266

music, 246–247. *See also* songs

music curriculum, 30, 270

N

National Reading Styles Institute, 207

needs assessment, 179

negatives, 79–80, 87

newcomer
adjustment, 15, 16, 17–19, 25, 169
adults, 179
assessment and placement, 22–30
statistics, 16
support, 16, 17, 18, 19, 25, 30, 41, 42, 174, 175, 180, 186, 190, 196
welcoming procedures, 20–33, 36–39
See also beginning language learners

non-count nouns, 70

non-fiction genre, 135–136

nonverbal language, 113–114, 185

nouns, 70, 71, 74. *See also* long noun groups; non-count nouns

number (in grammar), 70, 155, 158

O

objective case. *See* case (in grammar)

Ontario Education Act, 169

oral language
compared to written language, 125–126, 127
difficulties with, 16, 58, 60, 62
in approaches to second language instruction, 176–177, 178–179, 180

proficiency, age, as factor in, 151–152
proficiency, assessment of, 23, 24, 26–27, 252
proficiency, development of, 152–154, 252, 253, 256
providing feedback on, 186–187
teacher's use of, 185
See also basic interpersonal communication skills; communicative competence; pronunciation

oral literacy. *See* oral language proficiency

oral participation, 18, 159, 160–161

oral presentations, 46–47, 111, 162, 194, 264

oral tests, 263

orientation, 20–22, 25, 170, 200, 208

overgeneralization (in language acquisition), 73, 82, 144–158, 188

P

paragraph frames, 235, 240

paraphrasing, 244

parent information, 21–22, 31, 270

parent networks, 30

parent participation
in assessment, 265, 267–268
in creating multilingual classrooms, 31–33, 42
in homework, 43, 242, 244

parent-teacher meetings, 22, 32, 241, 270, 271

part-to-whole instruction, 175, 176, 177, 178, 179, 180

participles, 76, 78, 81

parts of speech. *See* word classes

passive vocabulary. *See* receptive vocabulary

passive voice, 78, 86, 232

peer tutors
benefits of, 41
instructional support from, 17, 30, 65, 103, 170, 186, 200, 202, 206, 274
orientation role, 30
See also bilingual partners; mentors; student ambassadors

performance-based assessment, 264–265, 269, 270

person (in grammar), 70–71, 87

phonemes, 54, 55, 126

phonemic awareness, 64–65

phonetic symbols, 55, 56, 57

phonics, 156–157

phonological writing system, 53, 54, 126

phonology, 53

photographs, 36, 37–38, 202, 209, 246

speech. *See* oral language

spelling
   difficulties with, 58, 73, 129
   improvement through reading, 100
   in the writing process, 241
   irregularities, 129–131, 157

standard English, 114–116, 118, 125, 164

standardized tests, 27, 95, 104, 266

strategic competence
   communication strategies, 118, 119
   conversational strategies, 118, 120–122
   defined, 106
   teaching, 119

strategies. *See* assessment strategies; learning strategies;
   teaching strategies

stress (in speech), 58–60, 64, 65, 225

stress (psychological). *See* anxiety

stress pattern. *See* rhythm (in speech)

structural approach. *See* part-to-whole instruction

structural competence, 106. *See also* grammar;
   pronunciation; vocabulary

student ambassadors, 22

student placement. *See* placement

student questionnaires, 38

student-teacher conferences, 22, 188, 241, 271

subject-specific words, 91, 94, 96, 98, 224

subjective case. *See* case (in grammar)

subordination, 84–85, 131

suffixes. *See* affixes

support staff, 20

surface features, 241

survival expressions, 201

Swain, Merrill, 147

syllabic writing system, 126, 128

syntax
   activities, 234
   defined, 69
   features of, 74–86
   in graded readers, 103
   in instructional text, 133–135
   in other languages, 74
   learner errors with, 74, 75, 76, 77, 78, 79, 80, 81, 82, 83,
     84, 85, 86
   See also condensed syntax; conditional sentences

T

tag questions, 80–81

Tamil, 128

teaching resources. *See* resource material

teaching strategies
   for cooperative learning, 191–195
   for developing communicative competence, 108, 110,
     114, 117–118, 119, 120, 122, 147
   for grammar instruction, 86–88, 155–156, 175–176,
     179, 180, 232–233
   for phonics instruction, 156–158
   for providing comprehensible instruction, 183–186
   for reading instruction, 100, 103, 136–137, 205,
     206–207, 221–224, 244, 247
   for supporting first language development, 154–155,
     189
   for supporting first language use, 17, 183, 189–190
   for vocabulary instruction, 100, 103–104, 183–184,
     201, 203, 207, 217, 223, 224–231
   for writing instruction, 136–137, 187–189, 201–202,
     205, 206–207, 218, 233–241
   See also instruction planning; lesson planning

tense. *See* verbs

Test of English as a Foreign Language, 104, 162

testing. *See* evaluation

Thai language, 131

think-pair-share, 192

Thomas, Wayne, 153

three-step interview, 192, 195

TOEFL. *See* Test of English as a Foreign Language

tone languages, 62, 65. *See also* Chinese; Vietnamese

total physical response approach (TPR), 160, 177–178,
   203–204

TPR. *See* total physical response approach

transfer errors, 160. *See also* interference (from first
   language)

true-or-false questions, 27, 264, 266

V

verbs
   and person, 70–71
   and tense, 73–74, 75–77, 82, 144, 180, 232
   and voice, 78–79, 87, 180, 232
   and word order, 74
   classified, 75–77, 81–82
   in other languages, 76, 81
   learner errors with, 73, 74, 76, 77, 79, 80, 81
   teaching concept of, 87, 88
   use in forming questions, 79–81, 83
   See also auxiliary verbs; lexical verbs; linking verbs;
     modal verbs; phrasal verbs

Credits

Photo Credits

20 Welcome poster: Printed with permission of the Toronto District School Board, Communications and Public Affairs. **24, 29** Assessment pictures: Reprinted with permission of ESL/ESD Resource Group of Ontario. **32** Announcements: Reprinted by permission of Pineway School, Toronto, Ontario. **174** Poster: Printed by permission of Toronto District School Board, Continuing Education Department.

Text Credits

97 Graded Word List: Burns/Roe, *Informal Reading Inventory*, Fifth Edition. Copyright © 1999 by Houghton Mifflin Company. Used with permission. **128, 129, 131, 132** Text samples: Printed with permission of Toronto District School Board, Continuing Education Department. **154** Excerpt from *Maclean's*: Reprinted by permission of *Maclean's*. **218** Concept map: Coelho, E., and M. Wong. *My Country, Our History*: Teacher's Resource Book. Copyright © Pippin Publishing Corporation, 2006. Reprinted by permission. **253** Developmental Stages in Oral Communication in English: O'Malley, J.M., and L.V. Pierce. *Authentic Assessment for English Language Learners: Practical Approaches for Teachers*. Copyright © Addison Wesley, 1996. Reprinted by permission. **254** Secondary Written Language Matrix: Printed by permission of British Columbia Ministry of Education, Special Programs Branch. **257** Framework for Instruction: Reprinted by permission of Jim Cummins/Multilingual Matters. **272, 273** Adapted from Short, D., and Echevarria, J. (1999). *The Sheltered Instruction Observation Protocol: A Tool for Teacher-Researcher Collaboration and Professional Development*. Center for Research on Education, Diversity & Excellence: http//www.cal.org/crede/pubs.